CAST OF CHARACTERS

BODACIOUS SPACE PIRATES
THE MOVIE ABYSS OF HYPERSPACE

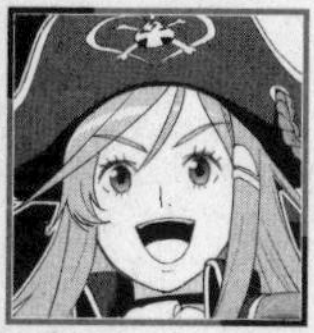

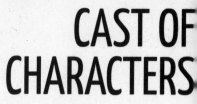

Marika Kato
A high school girl attending Sea of the Morning Star's Hakuoh Academy and Captain of the space pirate ship Bentenmaru. She leads a very busy life between her work as a space pirate, her position as President of the Yacht Club, and her part-time job as a café waitress.

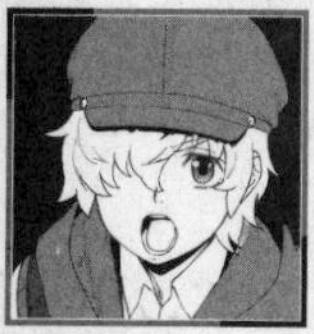

Kanata Mugen
A mysterious boy in possession of a Galaxy Pass, an item owned only by VIPs. He has been on the run along with Flint, a robot parrot sent to him by his father, Professor Mugen. While traveling on a luxury cruise, Kanata crossed paths with Marika when she was working as a space pirate. As a result, he started traveling on the Bentenmaru.

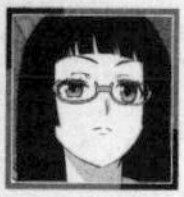

Chiaki Kurihara
The only daughter of the captain of the space pirate ship Barbaroosa.

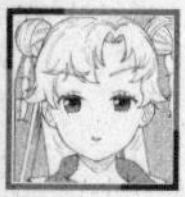

Grunhilde Serenity
Gruier's younger sister and the eighth princess of the Serenity Royal Family.

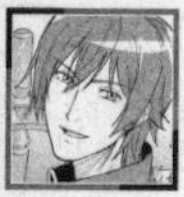

Kane McDougal
The skilled and handsome helmsman of the Bentenmaru.

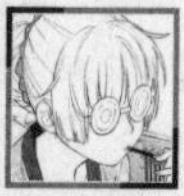

Coorie
Bentenmaru's Electronic Warfare and Communications Specialist. Her trademarks are her spiraling glasses and her dotera kimono.

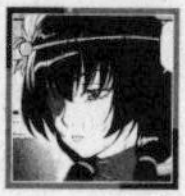

Luca
Bentenmaru's Navigator. She carries an air of mystery about her, with an eye-patch over one eye. She is always garbed in a frilly dress.

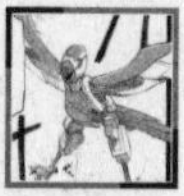

Flint
A robot parrot, traveling with Kanata. He can transform into the shape of a book.

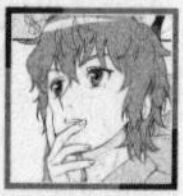

Ly
La

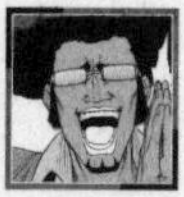

S
Th
the Bentenmaru.

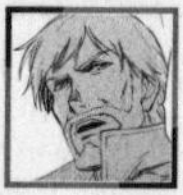

Professor Mugen
A specialist in the field of hyperspace travel technology, the basis on which FTL travel operates. He was also Kanata's father.

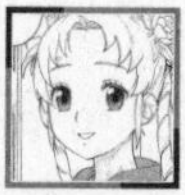

Gruier Serenity
The seventh princess of the Serenity Royal Family.

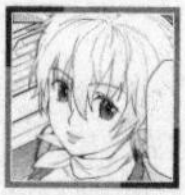

Misa Grandwood
The doctor on the Bentenmaru. She is also known as Bloody Misa.

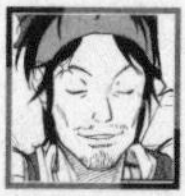

Hyakume
Bentenmaru's Communications, Intelligence and Analysis Specialist. He has both abundant knowledge and experience.

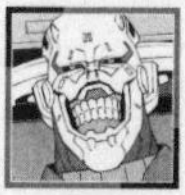

Schnitzer
A space cyborg who serves as the Bentenmaru's Tactical Officer and Firearms Control Officer.

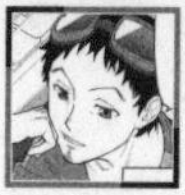

San-Daime
Bentenmaru's Engineer and Damage Control Specialist. He is the youngest member of the crew.

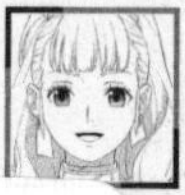

Jenny Dolittle
Former President of the Yacht Club from two years ago. Currently she runs a space travel agency.

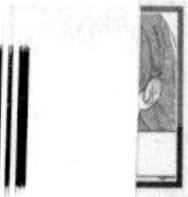

Ririka Kato
Marika's mother. She is also known as as the legendary pirate "Blaster Ririka."

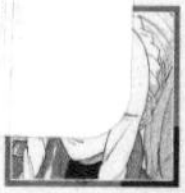

Scarlett Cypher
A mysterious beauty riding within the Hughroque chasing after Kanata.

Bodacious Space Pirates
ABYSS OF HYPERSPACE

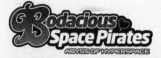

THE STORY SO FAR

BODACIOUS SPACE PIRATES
THE MOVIE ABYSS OF HYPERSPACE

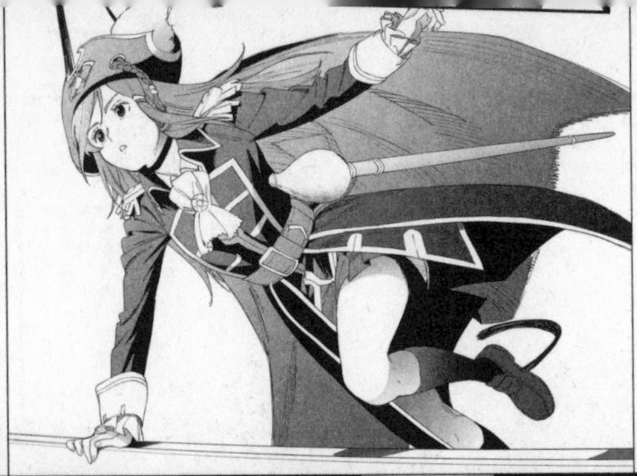

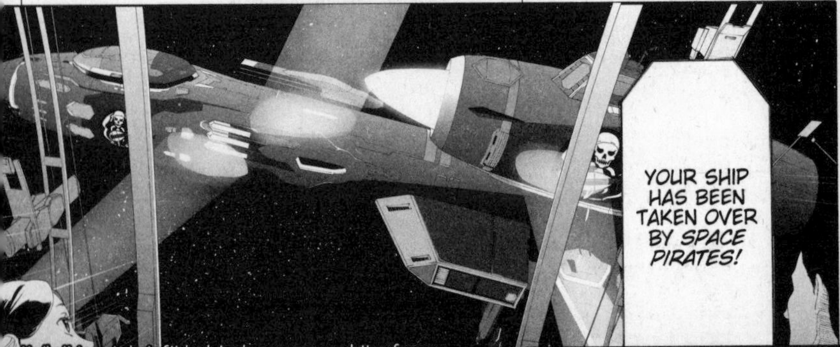
YOUR SHIP HAS BEEN TAKEN OVER BY *SPACE PIRATES!*

Marika Kato, a student of Hakuoh Academy, possesses a letter of marque issued by the government that makes her a legalized pirate. She leads an extremely busy life between schoolwork, her position as President of the Yacht Club, her part-time job at the café Lamp House, and her work as Captain of the space pirate ship Bentenmaru.

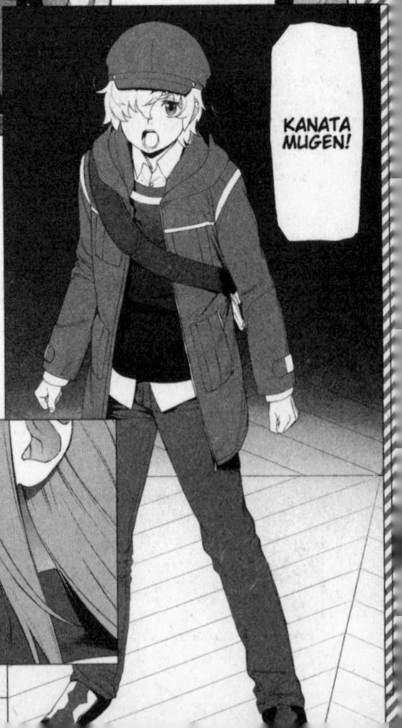
KANATA MUGEN!

One day during spring break, before her final year of high school, Marika and the crew of the Bentenmaru are engaged in a space pirate gig on a luxury cruiser when she discovers the name of Kanata Mugen, a holder of a Galaxy Pass, on the passenger list. In order to fulfill a promise made with Kanata's father, the famous Professor Mugen--known around the universe as the Hyperspace Diver--Marika reaches out to Kanata during her space pirate show.

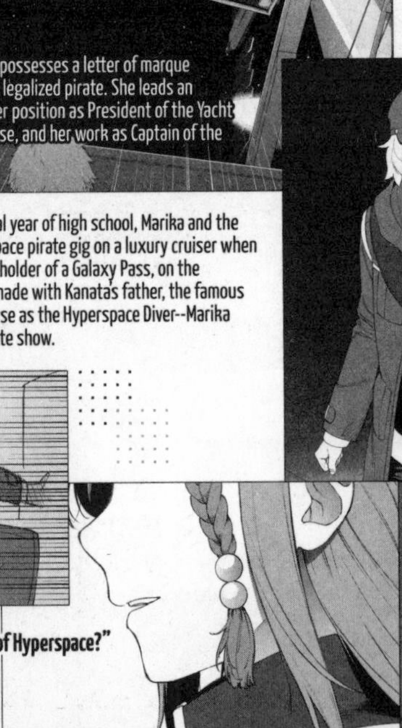

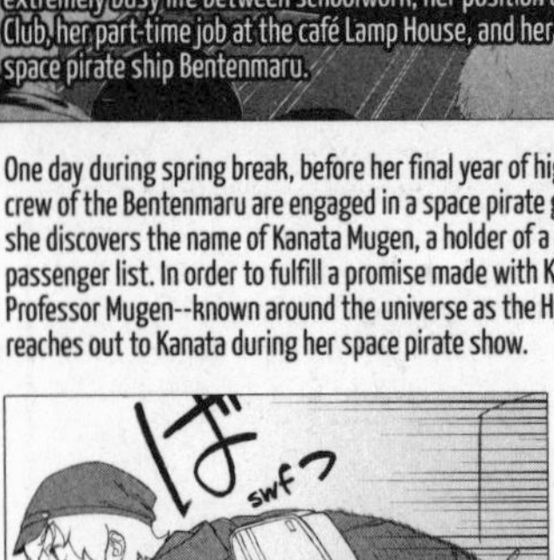
swf

"What color lies at the end of the flow of Hyperspace?"

Thus began a hyperspace-spanning adventure between the pirates and the boy!

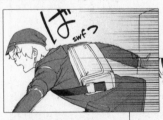

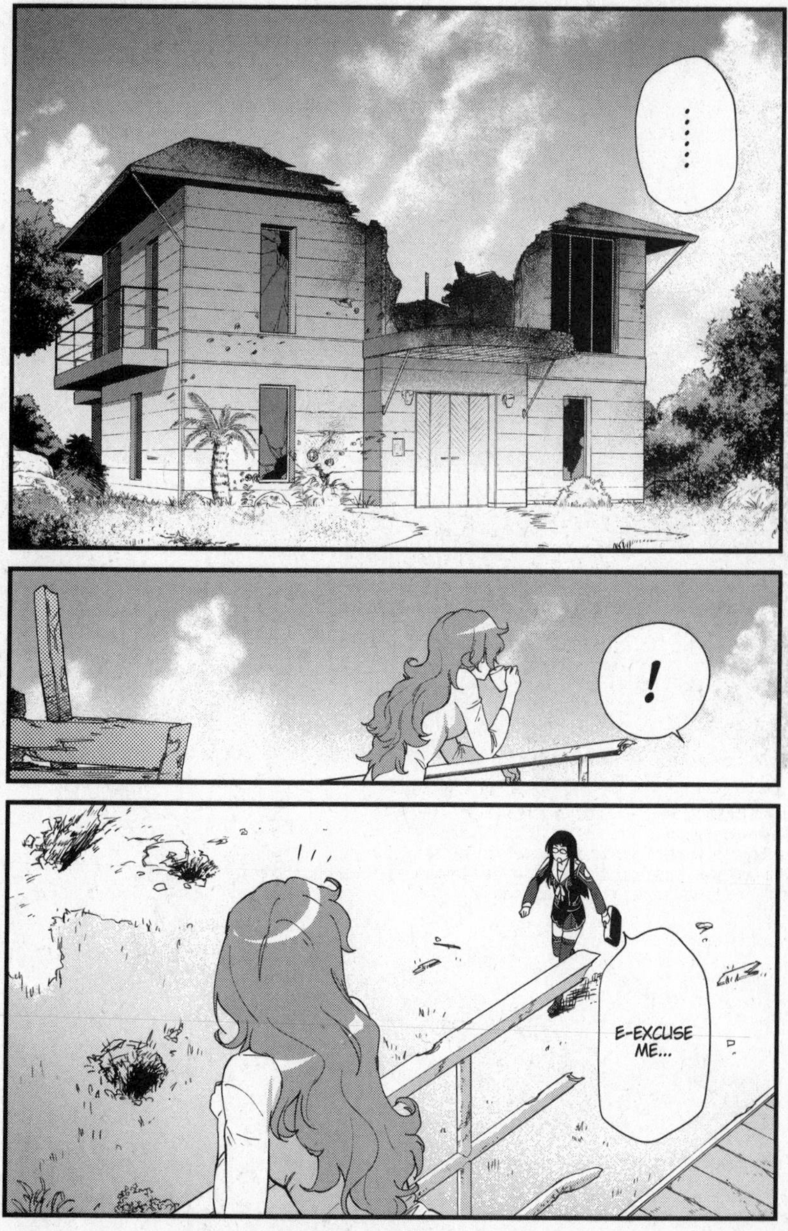
......
!
E-EXCUSE ME...

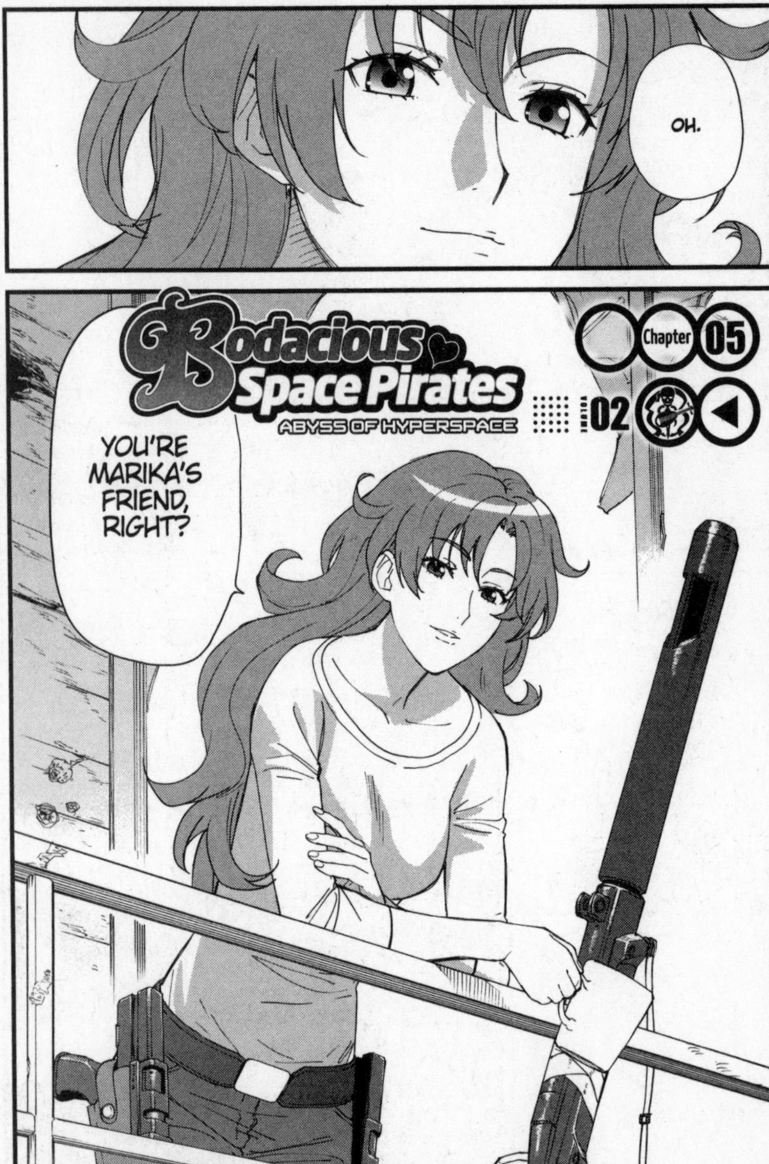
OH.
Bodacious Space Pirates
ABYSS OF HYPERSPACE
VOLUME 02
Chapter 05
YOU'RE MARIKA'S FRIEND, RIGHT?

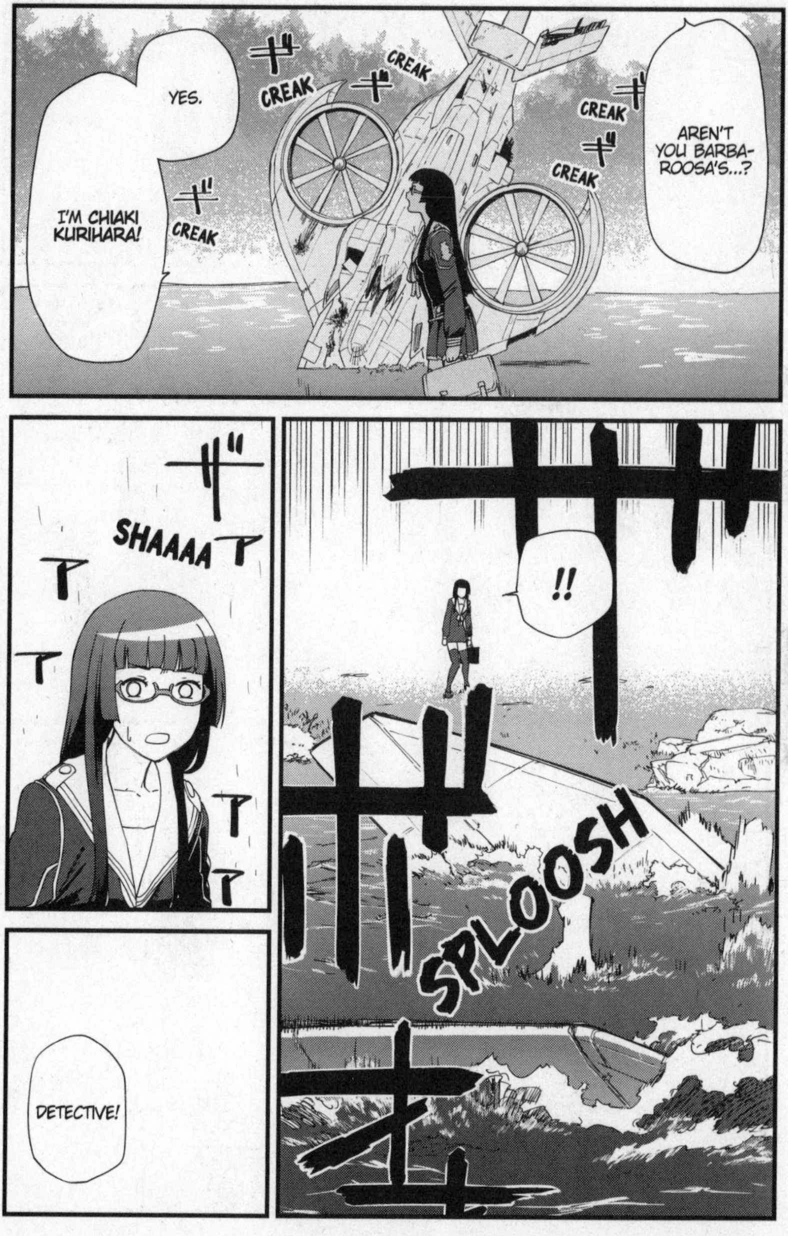
AREN'T YOU BARBA-ROOSA'S...?
CREAK
CREAK
CREAK
CREAK
YES.
I'M CHIAKI KURIHARA!
CREAK
!!
SPLOOSH
SHAAAA
DETECTIVE!

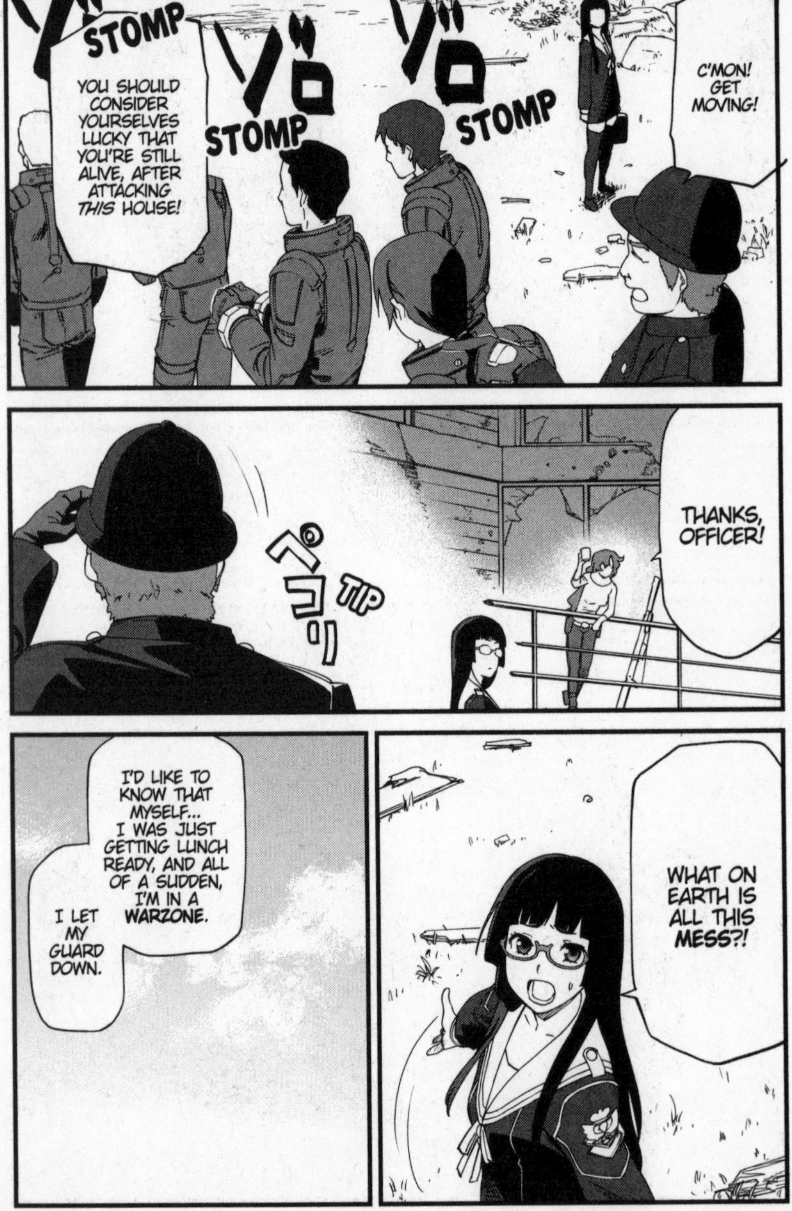
C'MON! GET MOVING!
STOMP
ゾロ
STOMP
ゾロ
STOMP
STOMP
YOU SHOULD CONSIDER YOURSELVES LUCKY THAT YOU'RE STILL ALIVE, AFTER ATTACKING *THIS* HOUSE!
THANKS, OFFICER!
ペコリ
TIP
WHAT ON EARTH IS ALL THIS MESS?!
I'D LIKE TO KNOW THAT MYSELF... I WAS JUST GETTING LUNCH READY, AND ALL OF A SUDDEN, I'M IN A WARZONE.
I LET MY GUARD DOWN.

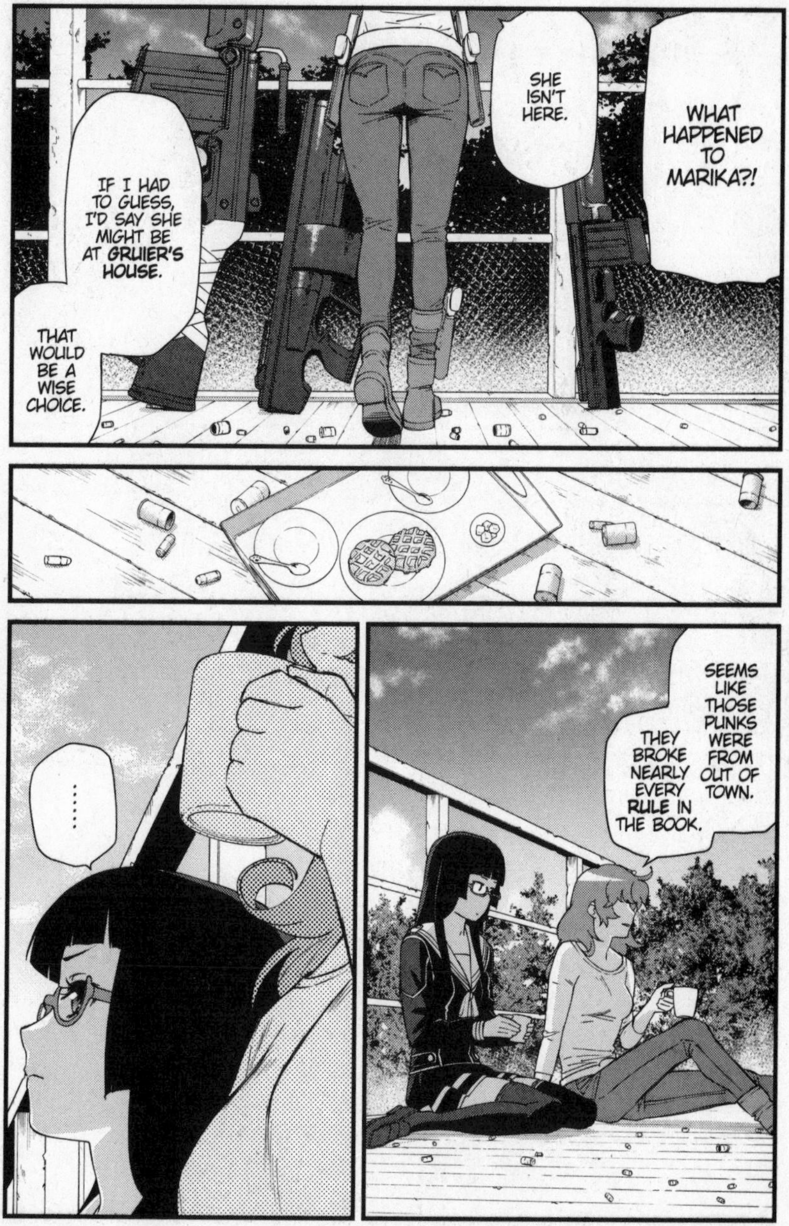
WHAT HAPPENED TO MARIKA?!
SHE ISN'T HERE.
IF I HAD TO GUESS, I'D SAY SHE MIGHT BE AT GRUIER'S HOUSE.
THAT WOULD BE A WISE CHOICE.
SEEMS LIKE THOSE PUNKS WERE FROM OUT OF TOWN.
THEY BROKE NEARLY EVERY RULE IN THE BOOK.
......

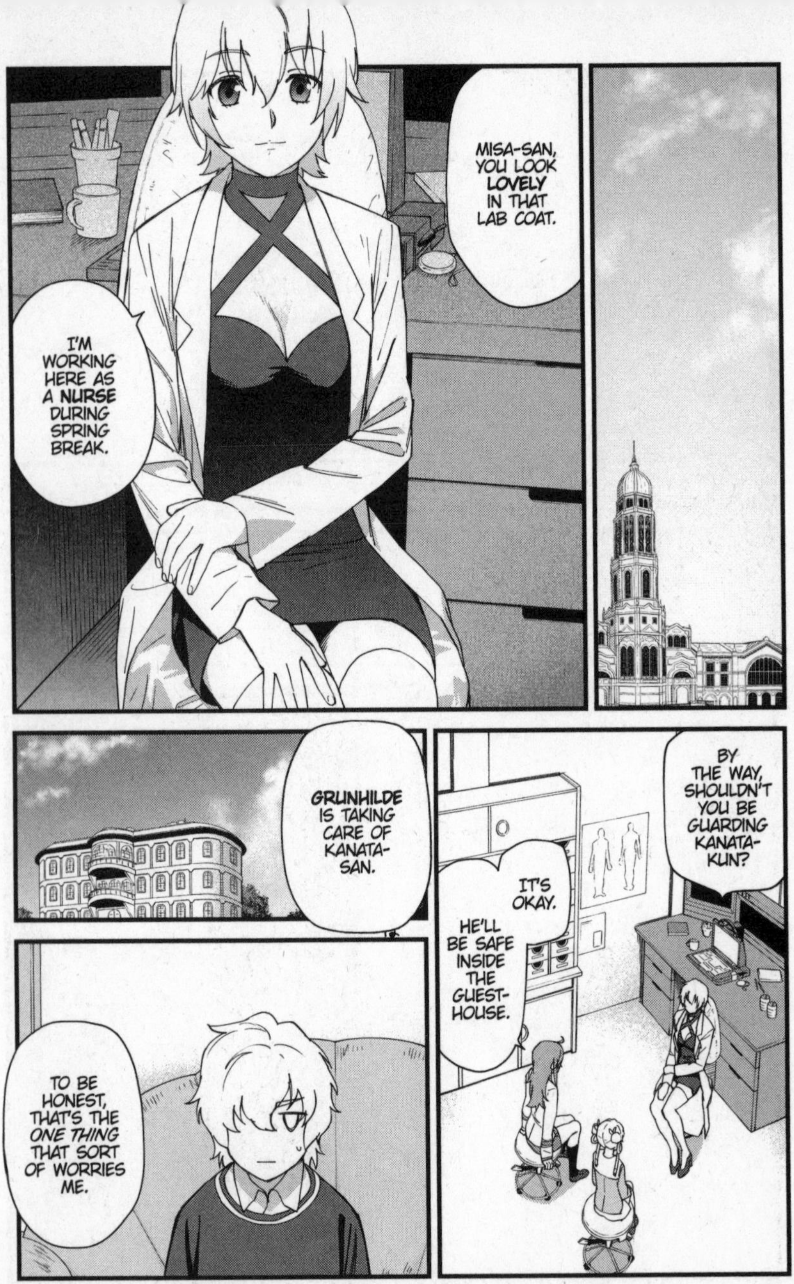
MISA-SAN, YOU LOOK **LOVELY** IN THAT LAB COAT.
I'M WORKING HERE AS A **NURSE** DURING SPRING BREAK.
BY THE WAY, SHOULDN'T YOU BE GUARDING KANATA-KUN?
IT'S OKAY.
HE'LL BE SAFE INSIDE THE GUEST-HOUSE.
GRUNHILDE IS TAKING CARE OF KANATA-SAN.
TO BE HONEST, THAT'S THE *ONE THING* THAT SORT OF WORRIES ME.

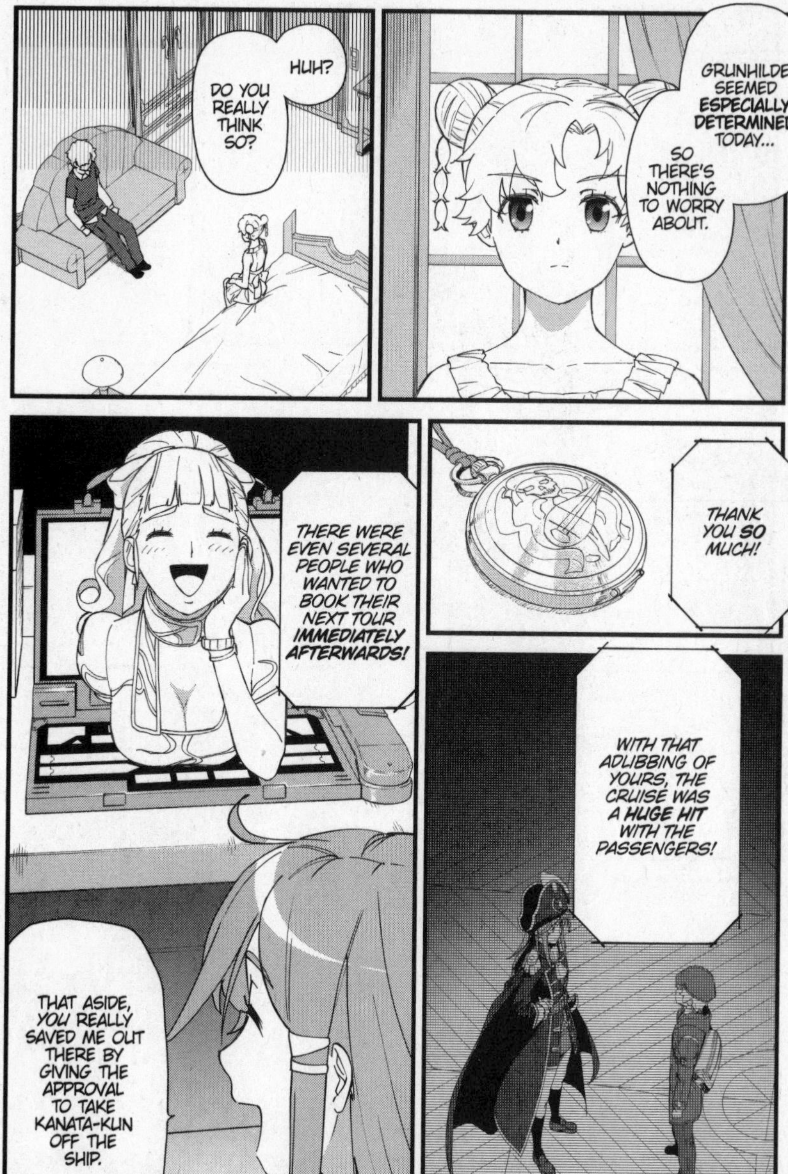
GRUNHILDE SEEMED ESPECIALLY DETERMINED TODAY...
SO THERE'S NOTHING TO WORRY ABOUT.
HUH?
DO YOU REALLY THINK SO?
THANK YOU SO MUCH!
WITH THAT ADLIBBING OF YOURS, THE CRUISE WAS A HUGE HIT WITH THE PASSENGERS!
THERE WERE EVEN SEVERAL PEOPLE WHO WANTED TO BOOK THEIR NEXT TOUR IMMEDIATELY AFTERWARDS!
THAT ASIDE, YOU REALLY SAVED ME OUT THERE BY GIVING THE APPROVAL TO TAKE KANATA-KUN OFF THE SHIP.

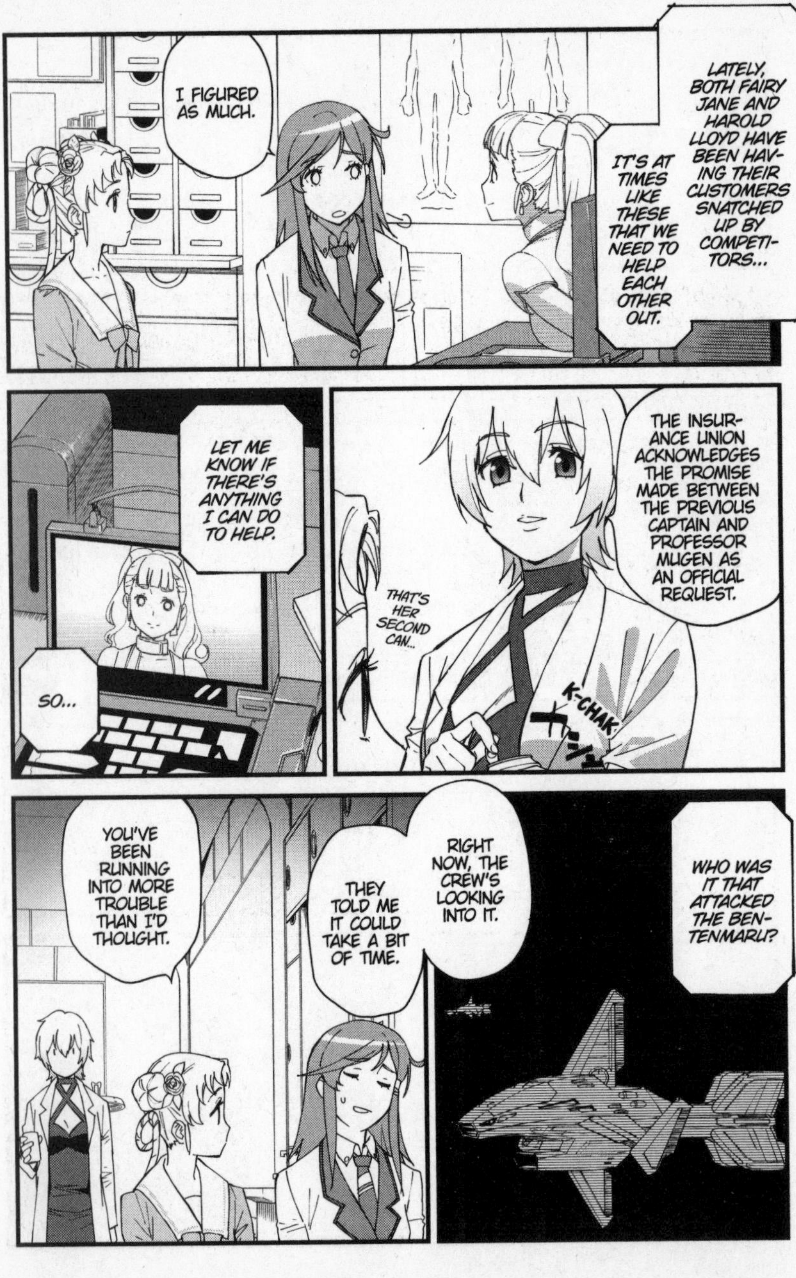
LATELY, BOTH FAIRY JANE AND HAROLD LLOYD HAVE BEEN HAVING THEIR CUSTOMERS SNATCHED UP BY COMPETITORS...
IT'S AT TIMES LIKE THESE THAT WE NEED TO HELP EACH OTHER OUT.
I FIGURED AS MUCH.
THE INSURANCE UNION ACKNOWLEDGES THE PROMISE MADE BETWEEN THE PREVIOUS CAPTAIN AND PROFESSOR MUGEN AS AN OFFICIAL REQUEST.
THAT'S HER SECOND CAN...
K-CHAK
LET ME KNOW IF THERE'S ANYTHING I CAN DO TO HELP.
SO...
WHO WAS IT THAT ATTACKED THE BENTENMARU?
RIGHT NOW, THE CREW'S LOOKING INTO IT.
THEY TOLD ME IT COULD TAKE A BIT OF TIME.
YOU'VE BEEN RUNNING INTO MORE TROUBLE THAN I'D THOUGHT.

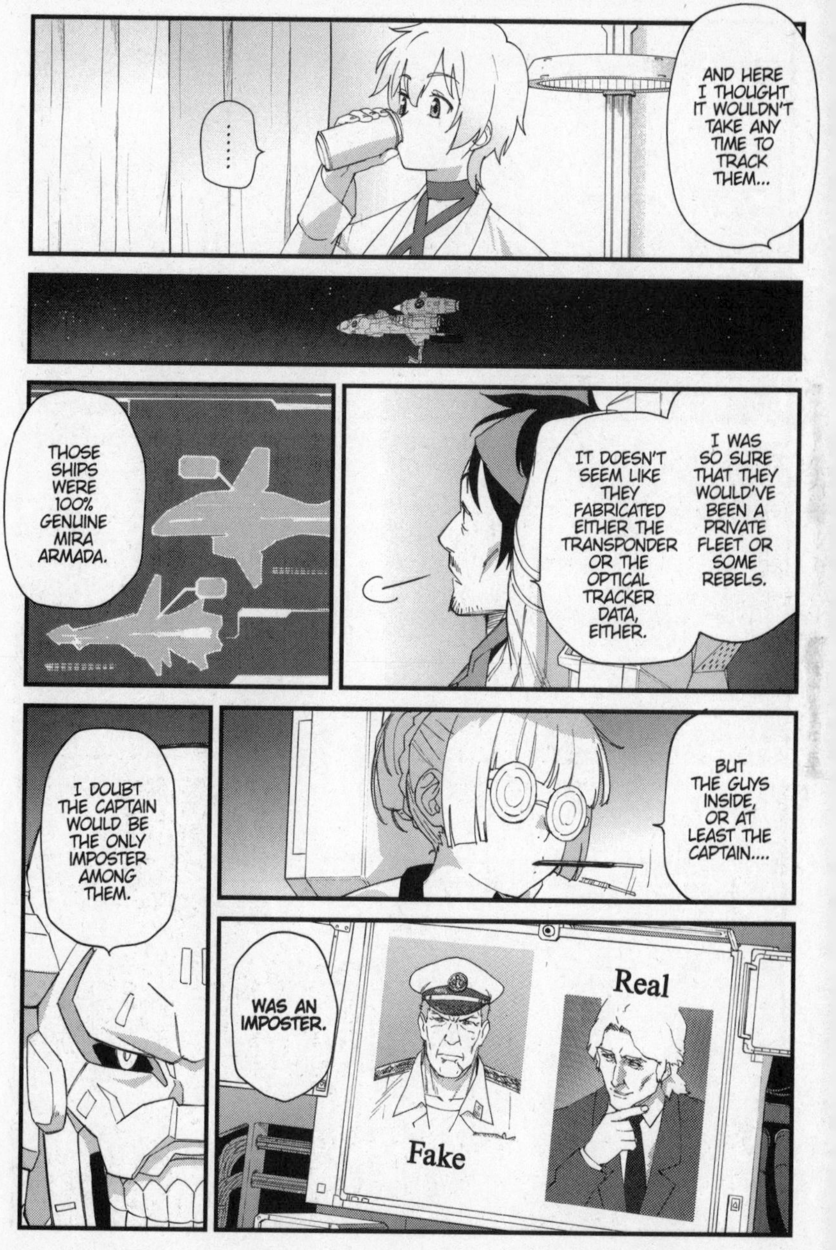
AND HERE I THOUGHT IT WOULDN'T TAKE ANY TIME TO TRACK THEM...
......
I WAS SO SURE THAT THEY WOULD'VE BEEN A PRIVATE FLEET OR SOME REBELS.
IT DOESN'T SEEM LIKE THEY FABRICATED EITHER THE TRANSPONDER OR THE OPTICAL TRACKER DATA, EITHER.
THOSE SHIPS WERE 100% GENUINE MIRA ARMADA.
BUT THE GUYS INSIDE, OR AT LEAST THE CAPTAIN....
WAS AN IMPOSTER.
Real
Fake
I DOUBT THE CAPTAIN WOULD BE THE ONLY IMPOSTER AMONG THEM.

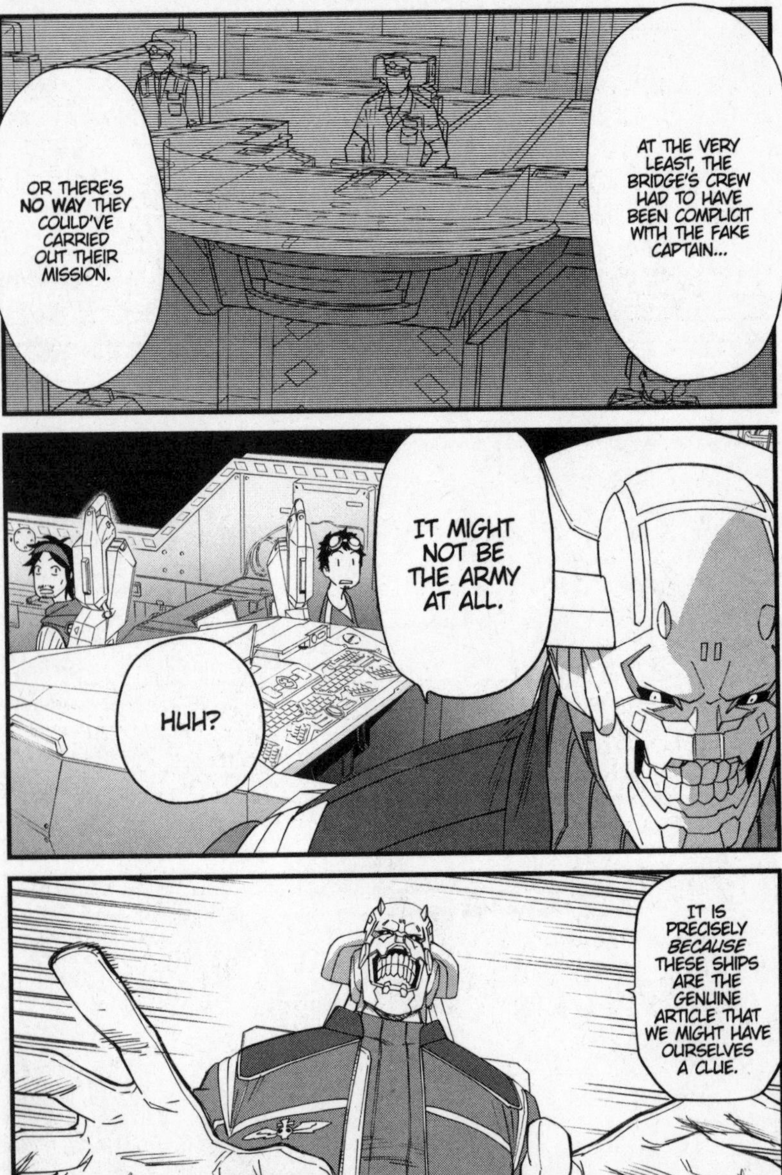
AT THE VERY LEAST, THE BRIDGE'S CREW HAD TO HAVE BEEN COMPLICIT WITH THE FAKE CAPTAIN...
OR THERE'S NO WAY THEY COULD'VE CARRIED OUT THEIR MISSION.
IT MIGHT NOT BE THE ARMY AT ALL.
HUH?
IT IS PRECISELY *BECAUSE* THESE SHIPS ARE THE GENUINE ARTICLE THAT WE MIGHT HAVE OURSELVES A CLUE.

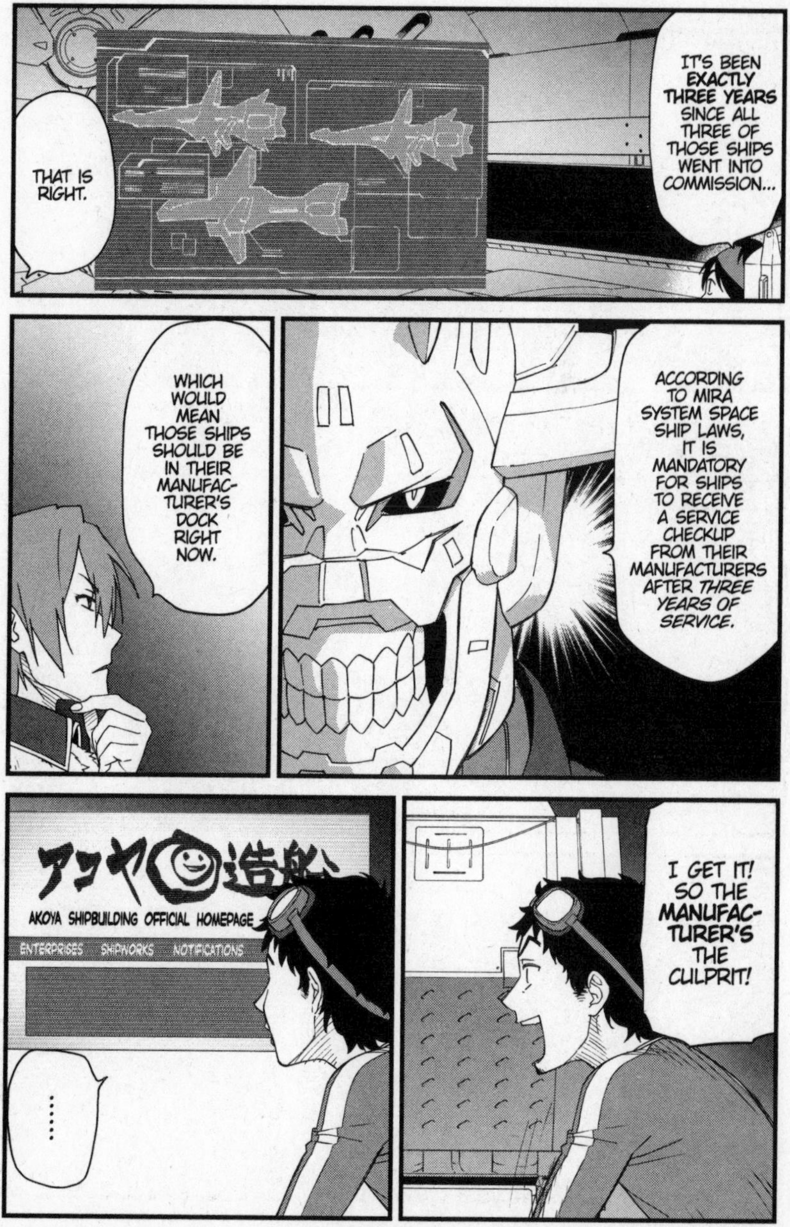
IT'S BEEN EXACTLY THREE YEARS SINCE ALL THREE OF THOSE SHIPS WENT INTO COMMISSION...
THAT IS RIGHT.
ACCORDING TO MIRA SYSTEM SPACE SHIP LAWS, IT IS MANDATORY FOR SHIPS TO RECEIVE A SERVICE CHECKUP FROM THEIR MANUFACTURERS AFTER THREE YEARS OF SERVICE.
WHICH WOULD MEAN THOSE SHIPS SHOULD BE IN THEIR MANUFACTURER'S DOCK RIGHT NOW.
I GET IT! SO THE MANUFACTURER'S THE CULPRIT!
アコヤ造船
AKOYA SHIPBUILDING OFFICIAL HOMEPAGE
ENTERPRISES SHIPWORKS NOTIFICATIONS
……

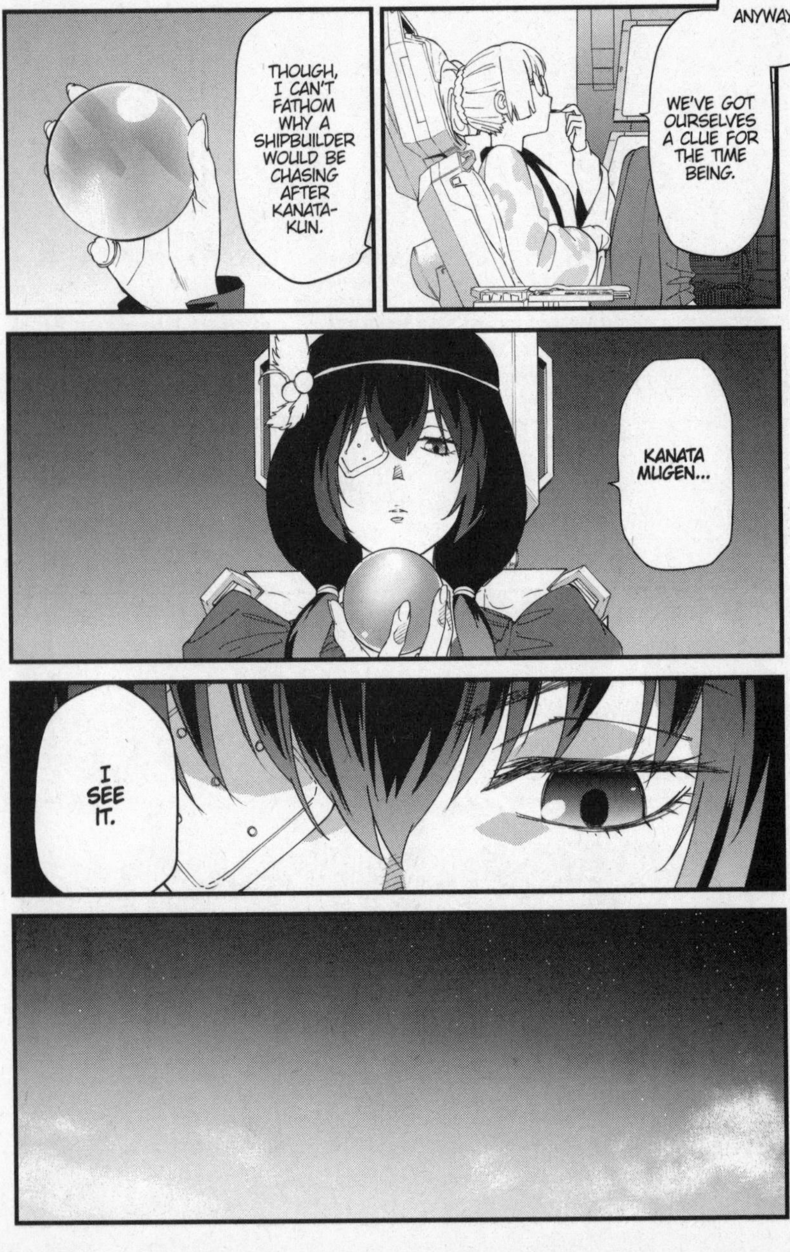
ANYWAY...
WE'VE GOT OURSELVES A CLUE FOR THE TIME BEING.
THOUGH, I CAN'T FATHOM WHY A SHIPBUILDER WOULD BE CHASING AFTER KANATA-KUN.
KANATA MUGEN...
I SEE IT.

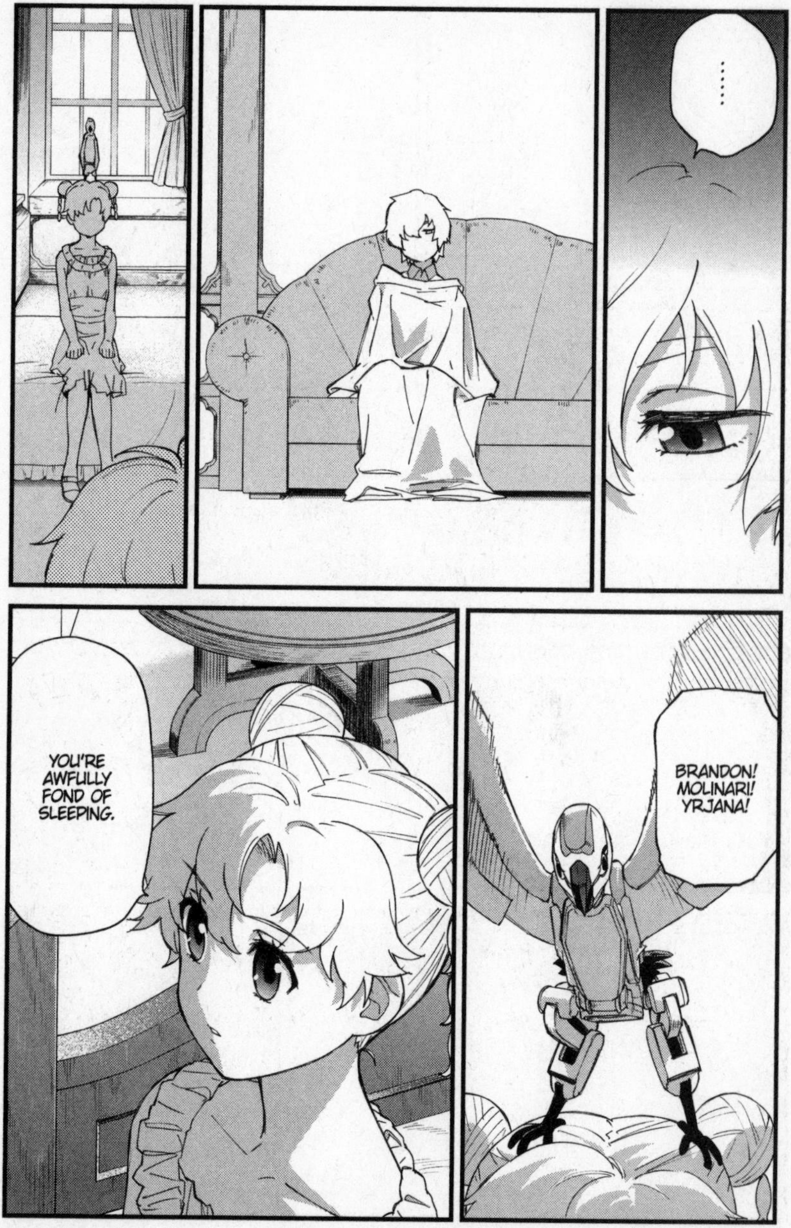
......
BRANDON! MOLINARI! YRJANA!
YOU'RE AWFULLY FOND OF SLEEPING.

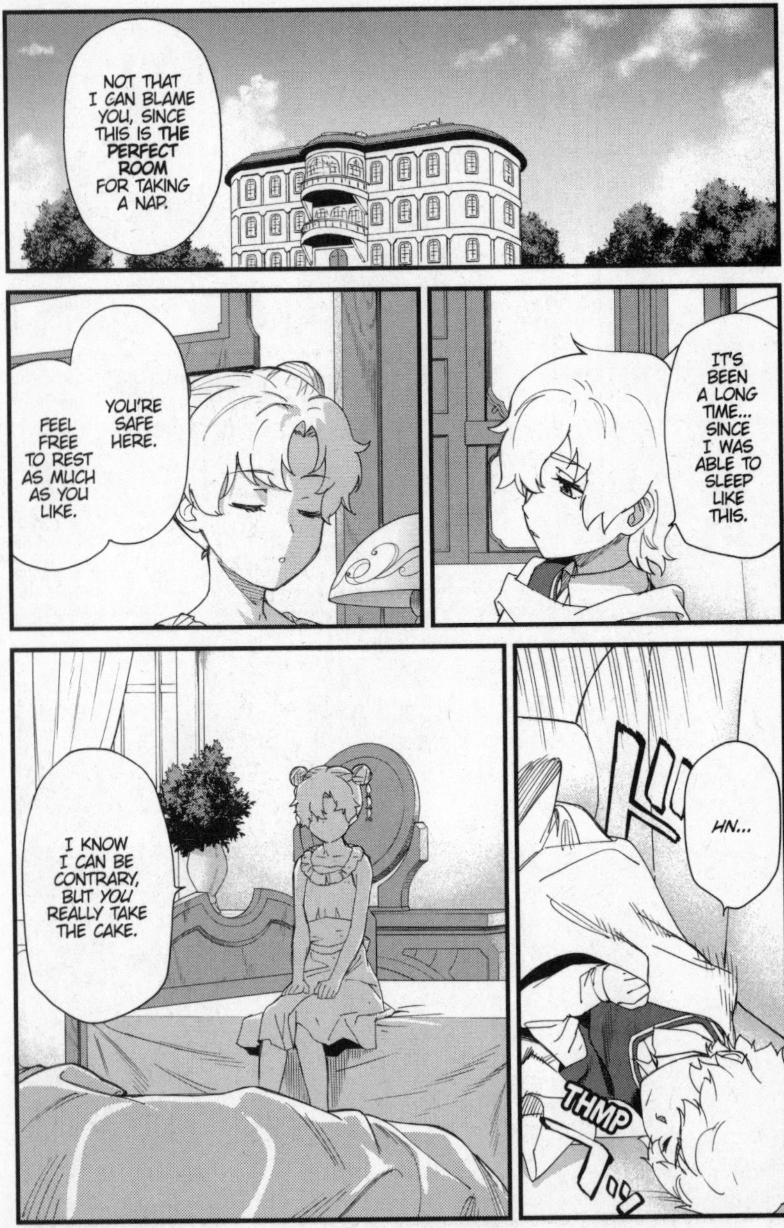
NOT THAT I CAN BLAME YOU, SINCE THIS IS THE PERFECT ROOM FOR TAKING A NAP.
IT'S BEEN A LONG TIME... SINCE I WAS ABLE TO SLEEP LIKE THIS.
YOU'RE SAFE HERE.
FEEL FREE TO REST AS MUCH AS YOU LIKE.
HN...
THMP
I KNOW I CAN BE CONTRARY, BUT *YOU* REALLY TAKE THE CAKE.

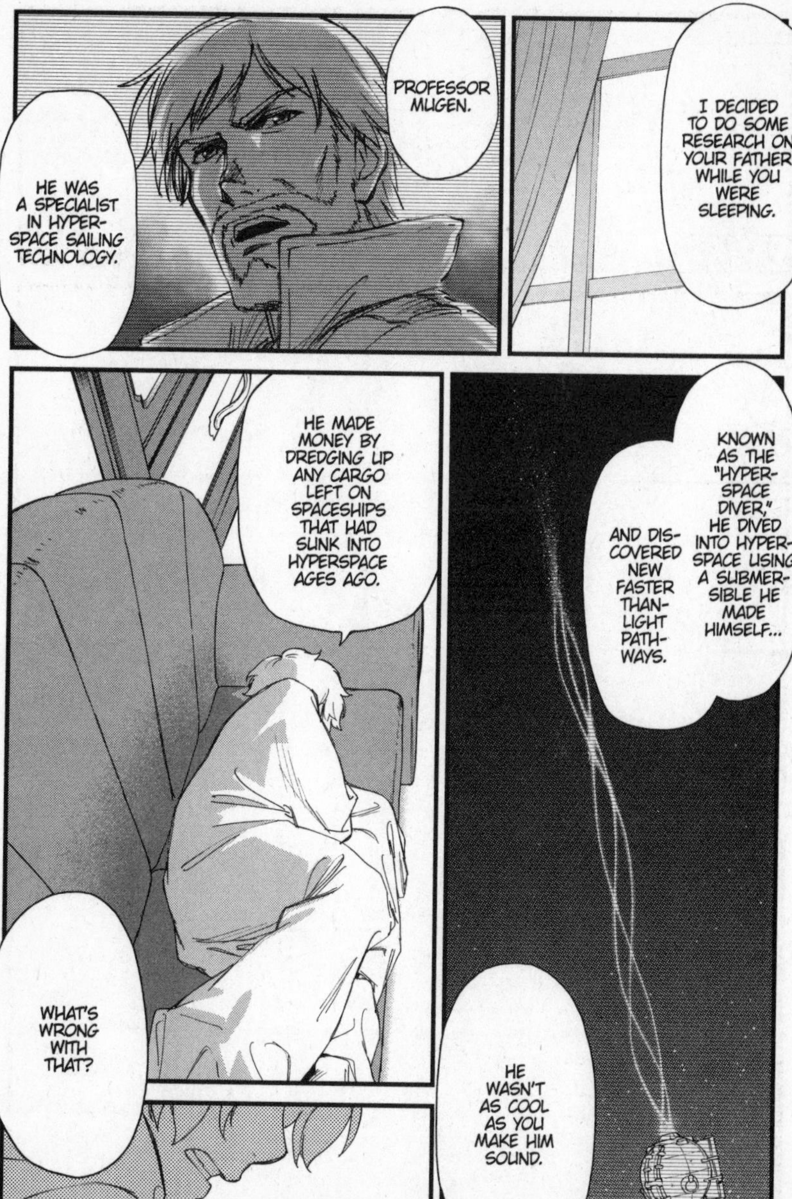
I DECIDED TO DO SOME RESEARCH ON YOUR FATHER WHILE YOU WERE SLEEPING.
PROFESSOR MUGEN.
HE WAS A SPECIALIST IN HYPER-SPACE SAILING TECHNOLOGY.
KNOWN AS THE "HYPER-SPACE DIVER," HE DIVED INTO HYPER-SPACE USING A SUBMER-SIBLE HE MADE HIMSELF...
AND DIS-COVERED NEW FASTER THAN-LIGHT PATH-WAYS.
HE MADE MONEY BY DREDGING UP ANY CARGO LEFT ON SPACESHIPS THAT HAD SUNK INTO HYPERSPACE AGES AGO.
HE WASN'T AS COOL AS YOU MAKE HIM SOUND.
WHAT'S WRONG WITH THAT?

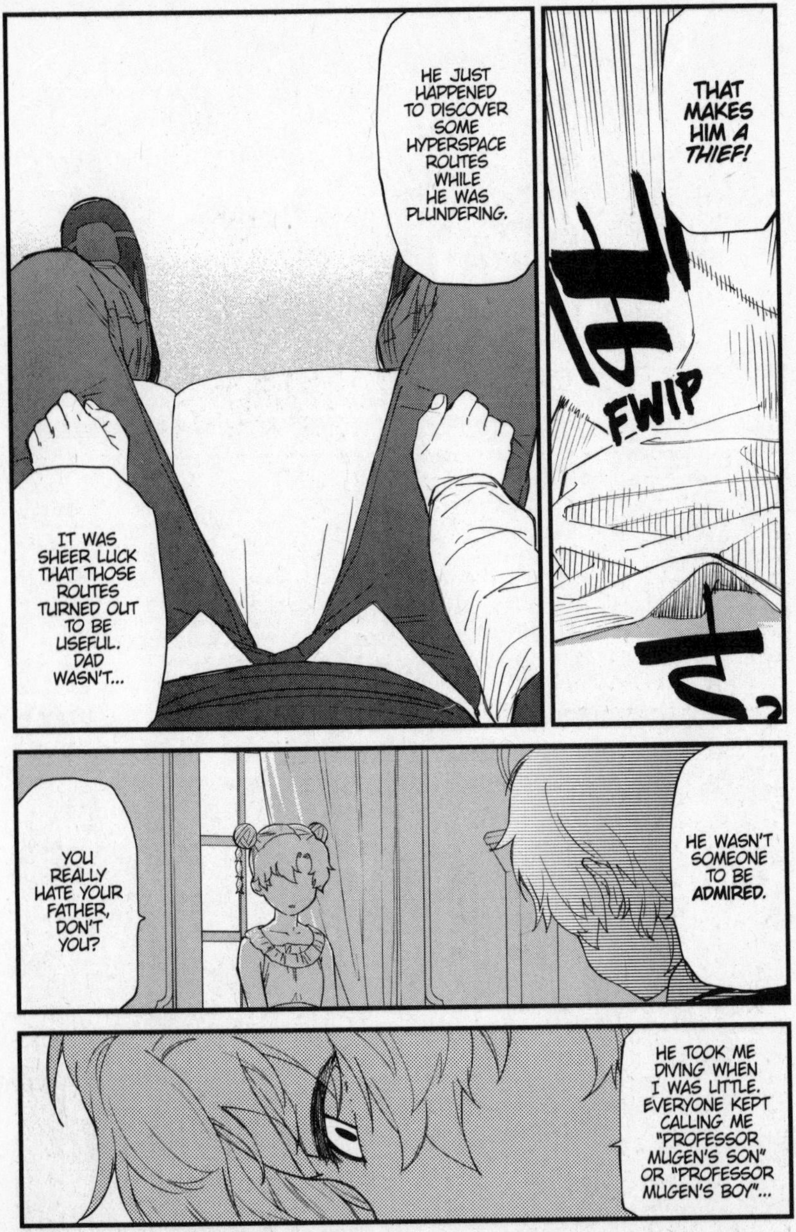
THAT MAKES HIM A *THIEF!*
FWIP
HE JUST HAPPENED TO DISCOVER SOME HYPERSPACE ROUTES WHILE HE WAS PLUNDERING.
IT WAS SHEER LUCK THAT THOSE ROUTES TURNED OUT TO BE USEFUL. DAD WASN'T...
HE WASN'T SOMEONE TO BE ADMIRED.
YOU REALLY HATE YOUR FATHER, DON'T YOU?
HE TOOK ME DIVING WHEN I WAS LITTLE. EVERYONE KEPT CALLING ME "PROFESSOR MUGEN'S SON" OR "PROFESSOR MUGEN'S BOY"...

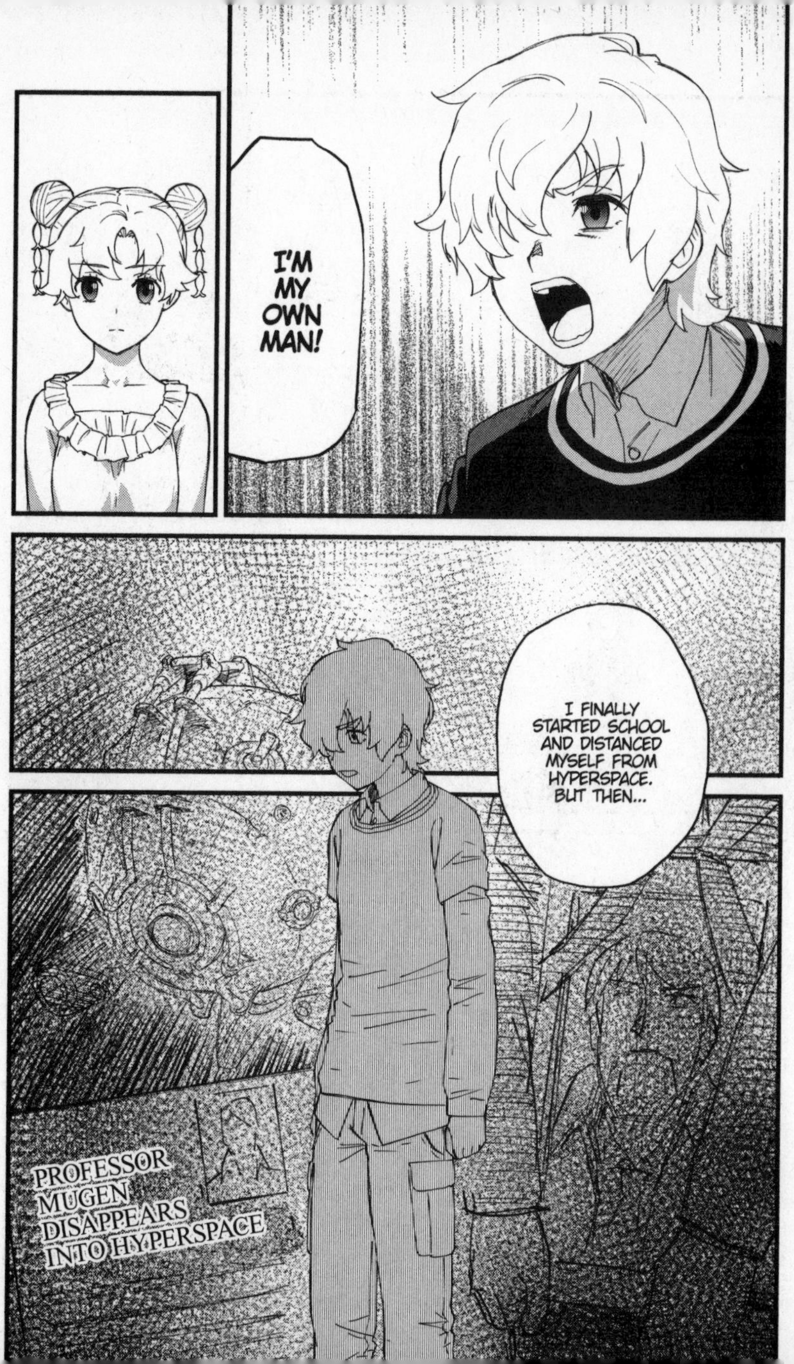
I'M MY OWN MAN!
I FINALLY STARTED SCHOOL AND DISTANCED MYSELF FROM HYPERSPACE. BUT THEN...
PROFESSOR MUGEN DISAPPEARS INTO HYPERSPACE

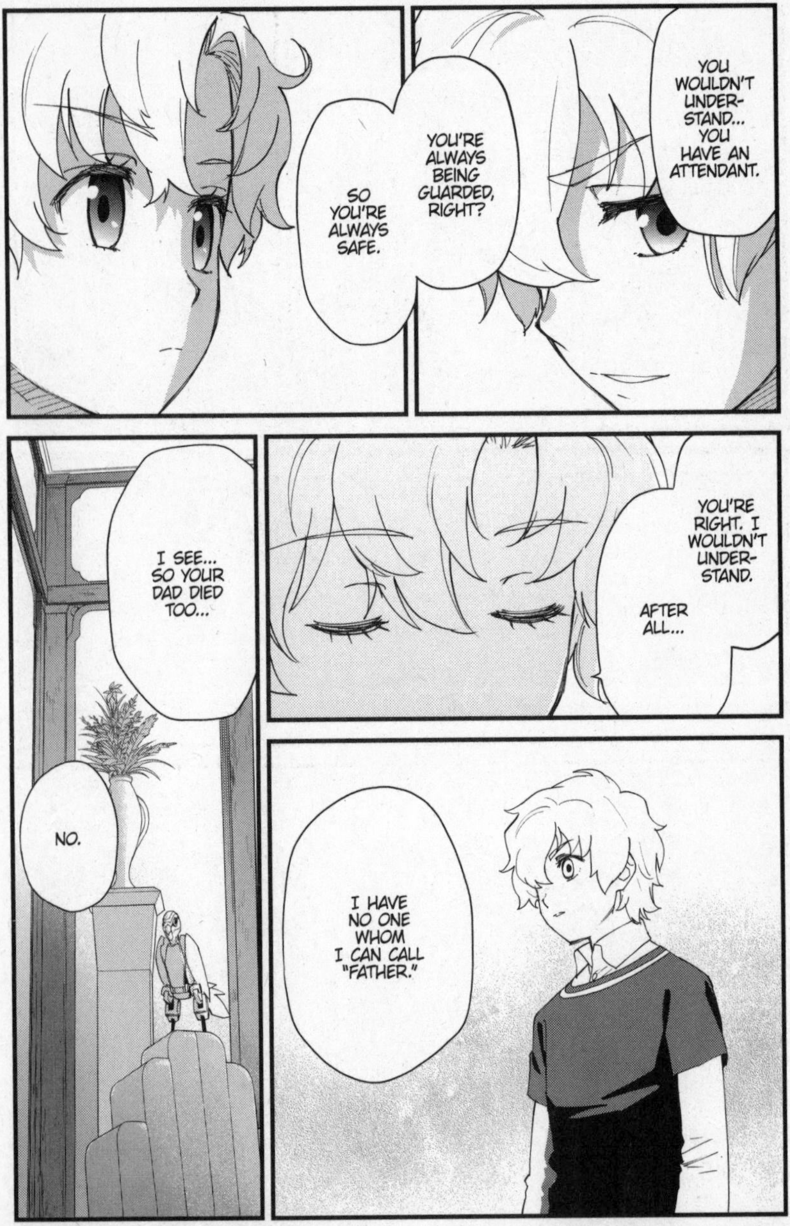
YOU WOULDN'T UNDER-STAND... YOU HAVE AN ATTENDANT.
YOU'RE ALWAYS BEING GUARDED, RIGHT?
SO YOU'RE ALWAYS SAFE.
YOU'RE RIGHT. I WOULDN'T UNDER-STAND.
AFTER ALL...
I HAVE NO ONE WHOM I CAN CALL "FATHER."
I SEE... SO YOUR DAD DIED TOO...
NO.

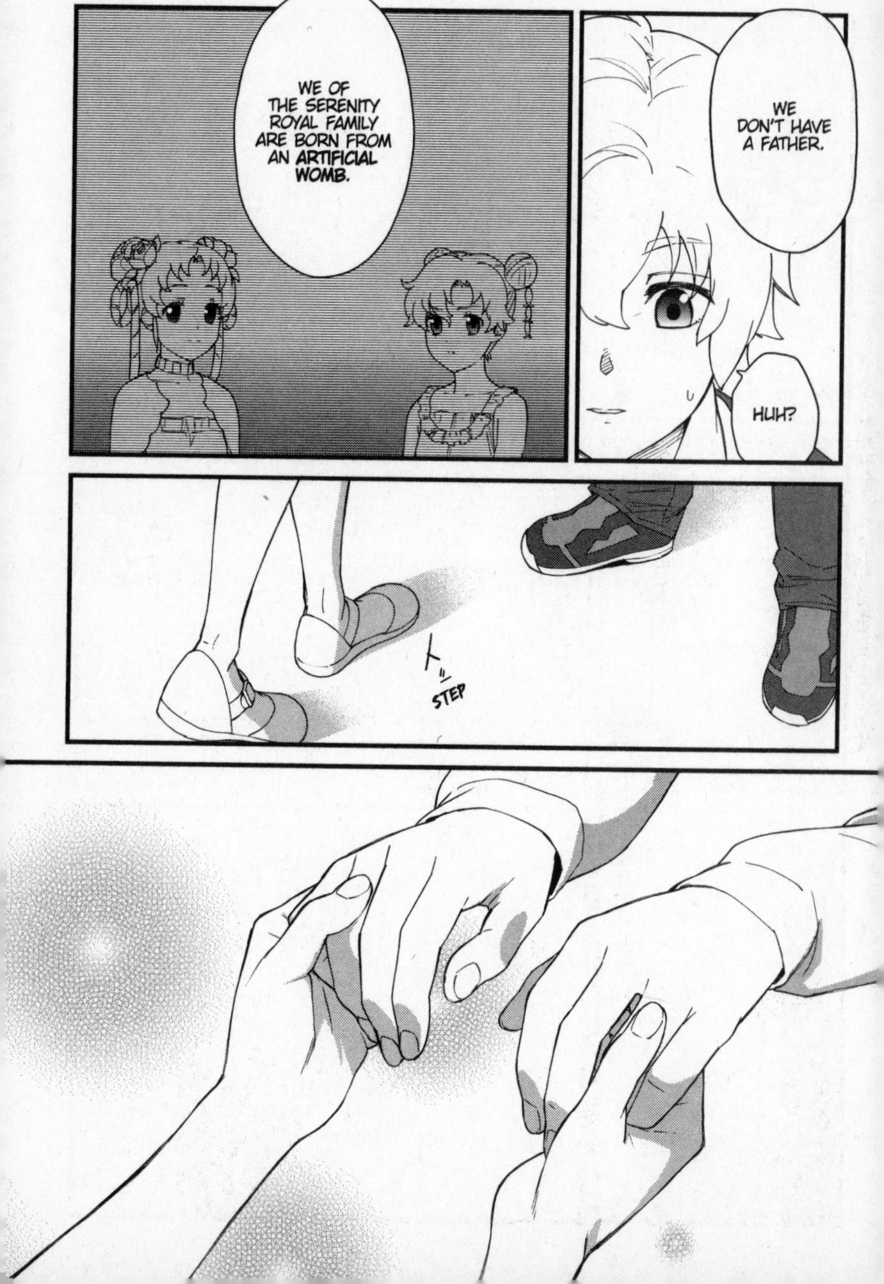
WE DON'T HAVE A FATHER.
HUH?
WE OF THE SERENITY ROYAL FAMILY ARE BORN FROM AN ARTIFICIAL WOMB.
STEP

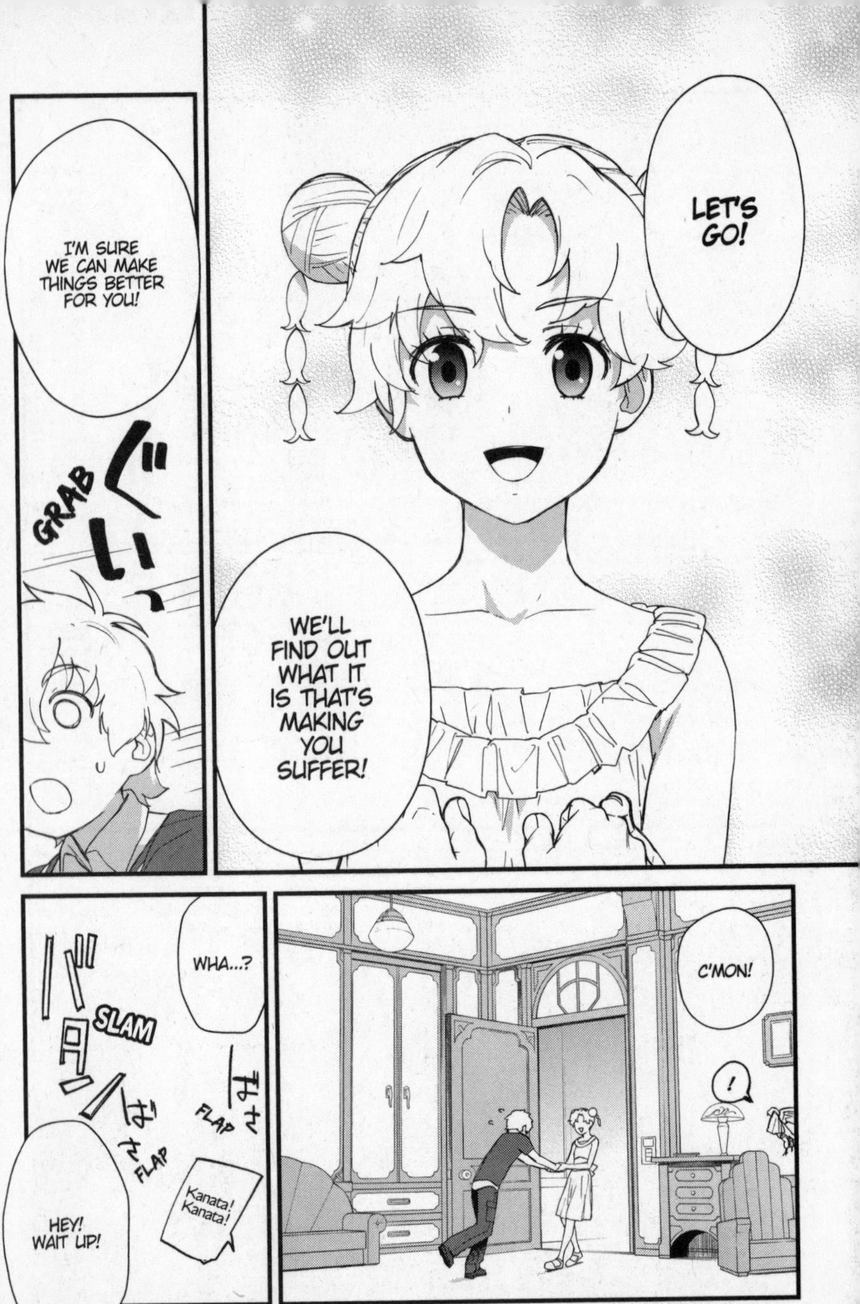
LET'S GO!
WE'LL FIND OUT WHAT IT IS THAT'S MAKING YOU SUFFER!
I'M SURE WE CAN MAKE THINGS BETTER FOR YOU!
GRAB
C'MON!
!
WHA...?
FLAP
FLAP
SLAM
Kanata! Kanata!
HEY! WAIT UP!

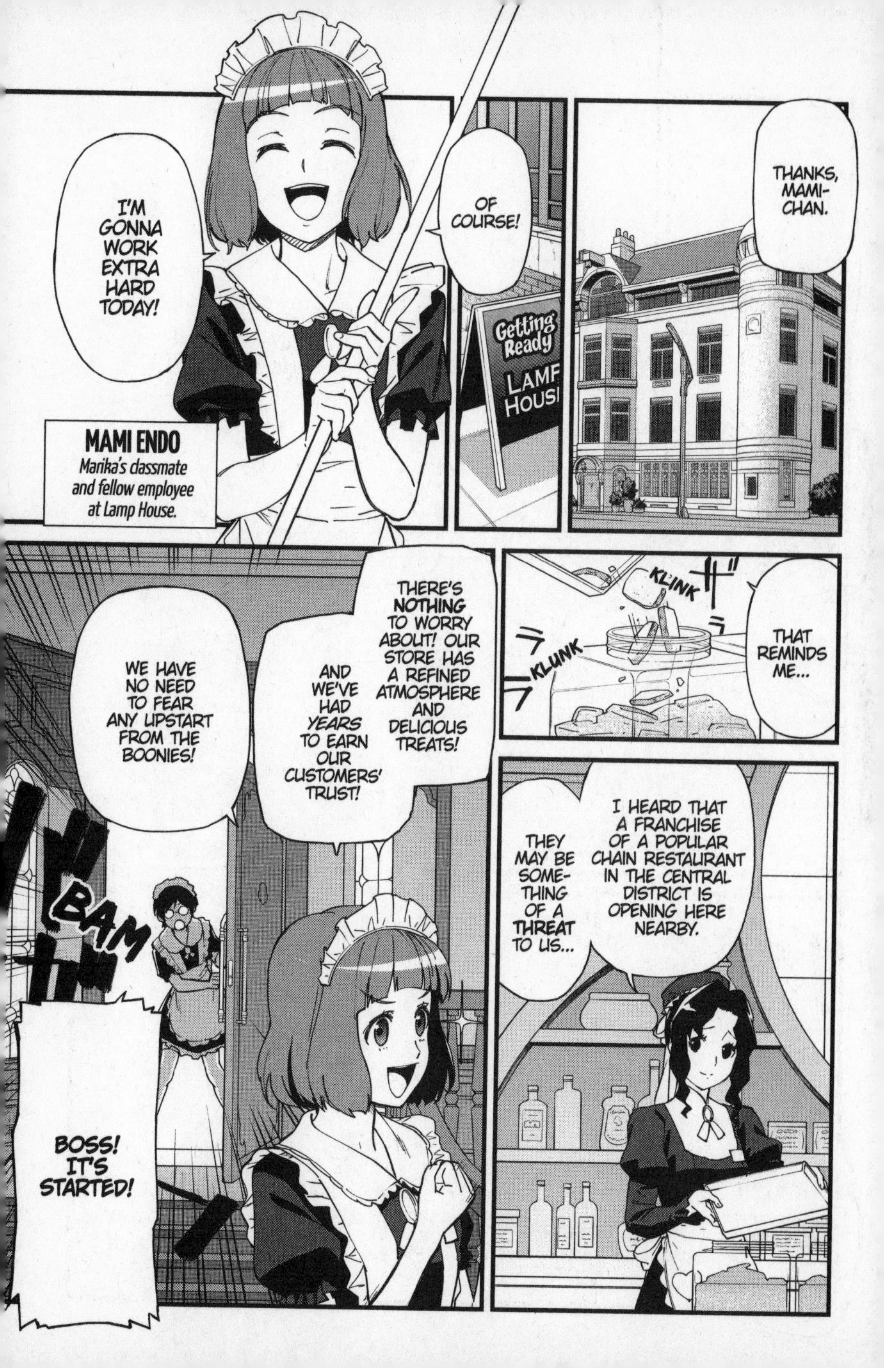
THANKS, MAMI-CHAN.
Getting Ready
OF COURSE!
I'M GONNA WORK EXTRA HARD TODAY!
MAMI ENDO
Marika's classmate and fellow employee at Lamp House.
KLINK
KLUNK
THAT REMINDS ME...
I HEARD THAT A FRANCHISE OF A POPULAR CHAIN RESTAURANT IN THE CENTRAL DISTRICT IS OPENING HERE NEARBY.
THEY MAY BE SOME-THING OF A THREAT TO US...
THERE'S NOTHING TO WORRY ABOUT! OUR STORE HAS A REFINED ATMOSPHERE AND DELICIOUS TREATS!
AND WE'VE HAD YEARS TO EARN OUR CUSTOMERS' TRUST!
WE HAVE NO NEED TO FEAR ANY UPSTART FROM THE BOONIES!
BAM
BOSS! IT'S STARTED!

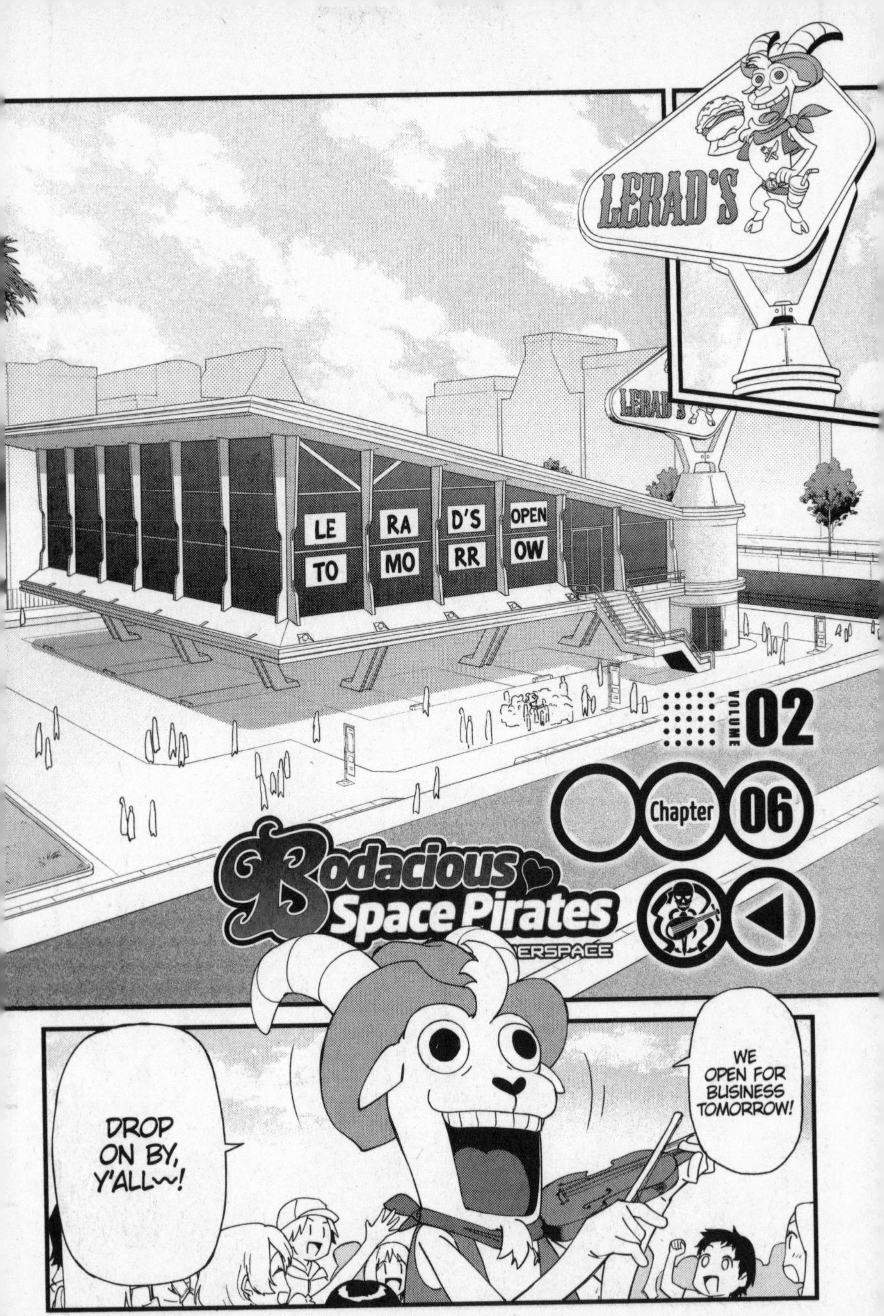
LERAD'S
LERAD'S
LE RA D'S OPEN
TO MO RR OW
VOLUME 02
Chapter 06
Bodacious Space Pirates
WE OPEN FOR BUSINESS TOMORROW!
DROP ON BY, Y'ALL~!

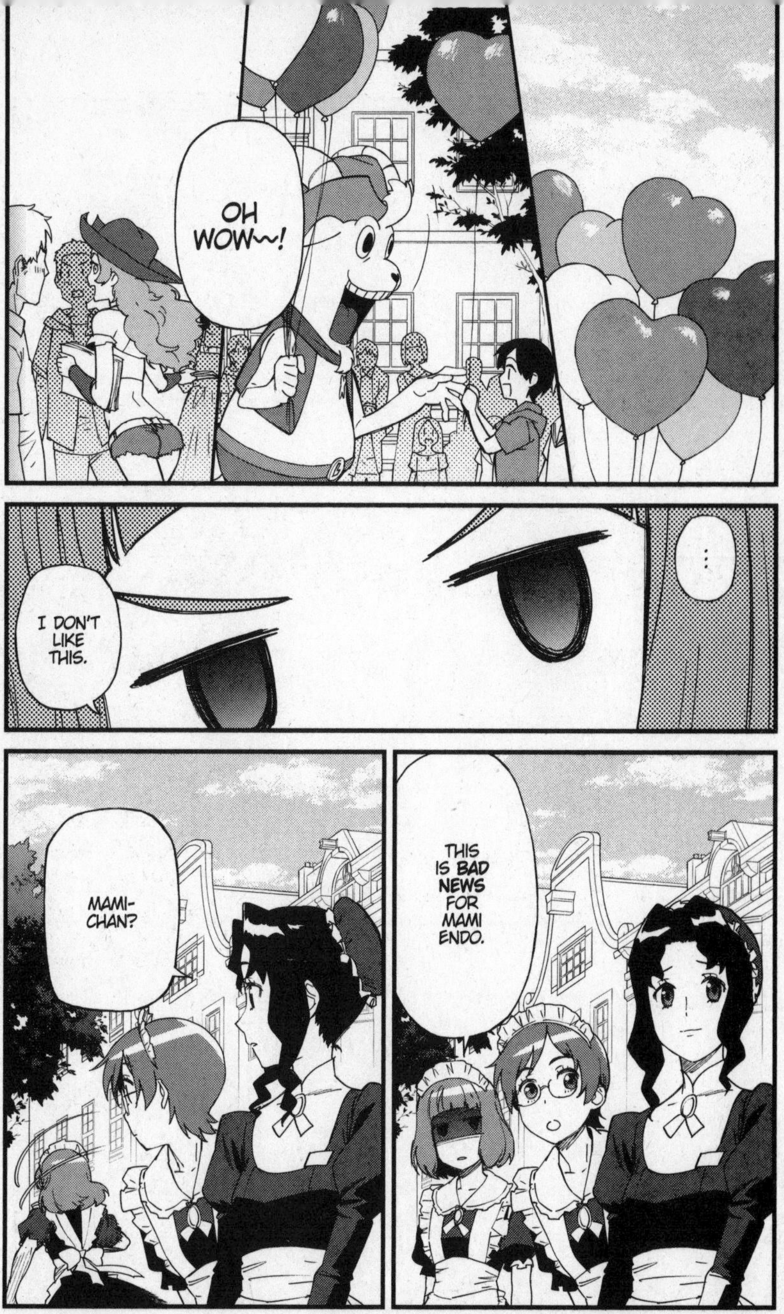
OH WOW~~!
...
I DON'T LIKE THIS.
THIS IS BAD NEWS FOR MAMI ENDO.
MAMI-CHAN?

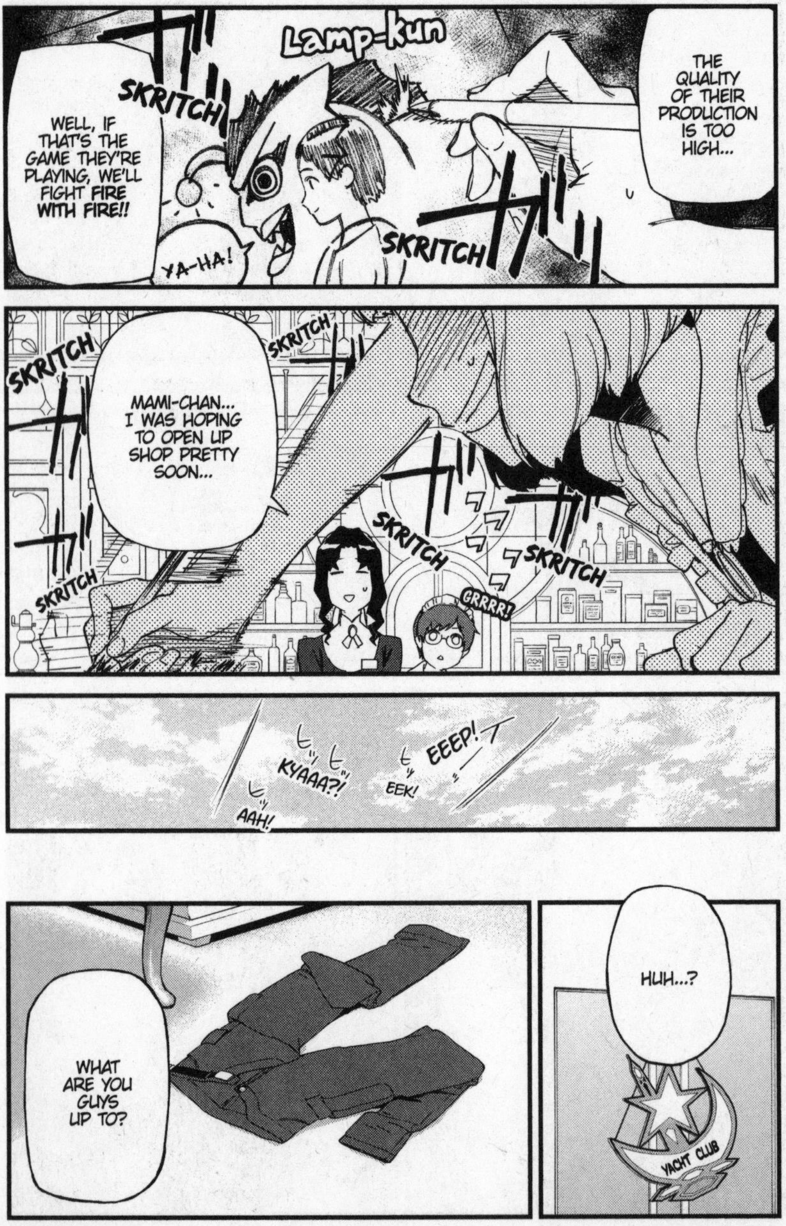
Lamp-kun
THE QUALITY OF THEIR PRODUCTION IS TOO HIGH...
SKRITCH
WELL, IF THAT'S THE GAME THEY'RE PLAYING, WE'LL FIGHT FIRE WITH FIRE!!
SKRITCH
YA-HA!
SKRITCH
SKRITCH
MAMI-CHAN... I WAS HOPING TO OPEN UP SHOP PRETTY SOON...
SKRITCH
SKRITCH
GRRRR!
SKRITCH
EEEP!
EEK!
KYAAA?!
AAH!
HUH...?
YACHT CLUB
WHAT ARE YOU GUYS UP TO?

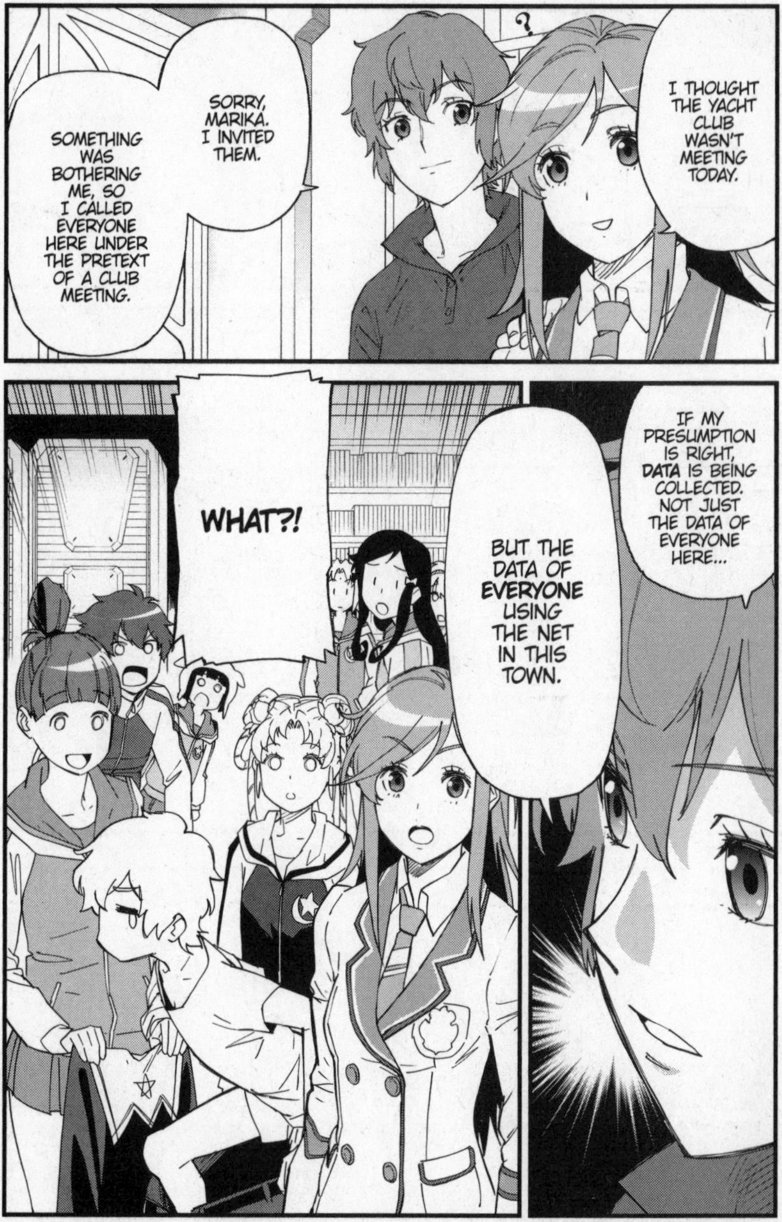
I THOUGHT THE YACHT CLUB WASN'T MEETING TODAY.
SORRY, MARIKA. I INVITED THEM.
SOMETHING WAS BOTHERING ME, SO I CALLED EVERYONE HERE UNDER THE PRETEXT OF A CLUB MEETING.
IF MY PRESUMPTION IS RIGHT, DATA IS BEING COLLECTED. NOT JUST THE DATA OF EVERYONE HERE...
BUT THE DATA OF EVERYONE USING THE NET IN THIS TOWN.
WHAT?!

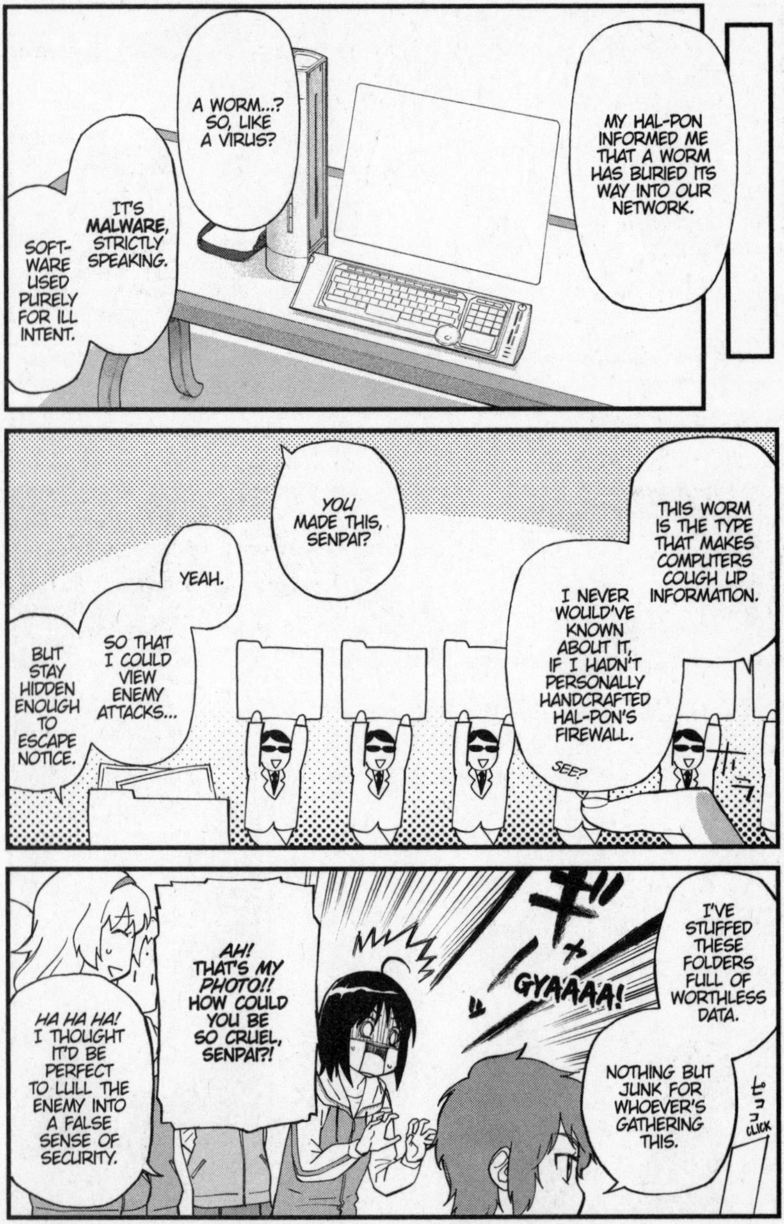
MY HAL-PON INFORMED ME THAT A WORM HAS BURIED ITS WAY INTO OUR NETWORK.
A WORM...? SO, LIKE A VIRUS?
IT'S MALWARE, STRICTLY SPEAKING.
SOFT-WARE USED PURELY FOR ILL INTENT.
THIS WORM IS THE TYPE THAT MAKES COMPUTERS COUGH UP INFORMATION.
I NEVER WOULD'VE KNOWN ABOUT IT, IF I HADN'T PERSONALLY HANDCRAFTED HAL-PON'S FIREWALL.
SEE?
YOU MADE THIS, SENPAI?
YEAH.
SO THAT I COULD VIEW ENEMY ATTACKS...
BUT STAY HIDDEN ENOUGH TO ESCAPE NOTICE.
I'VE STUFFED THESE FOLDERS FULL OF WORTHLESS DATA.
NOTHING BUT JUNK FOR WHOEVER'S GATHERING THIS.
ピコッ CLICK
GYAAAA!
AH! THAT'S MY PHOTO!! HOW COULD YOU BE SO CRUEL, SENPAI?!
HA HA HA! I THOUGHT IT'D BE PERFECT TO LULL THE ENEMY INTO A FALSE SENSE OF SECURITY.

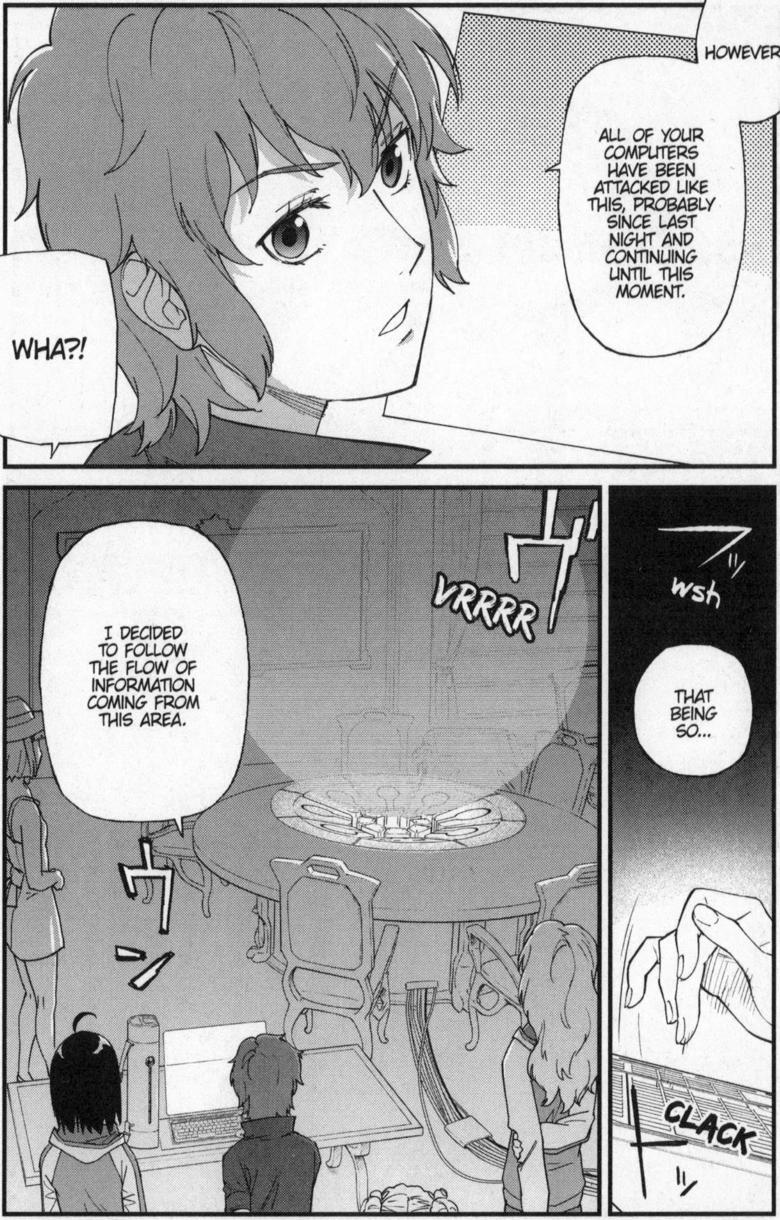
HOWEVER...
ALL OF YOUR COMPUTERS HAVE BEEN ATTACKED LIKE THIS, PROBABLY SINCE LAST NIGHT AND CONTINUING UNTIL THIS MOMENT.
WHA?!
wsh
THAT BEING SO...
CLACK
VRRRR
I DECIDED TO FOLLOW THE FLOW OF INFORMATION COMING FROM THIS AREA.

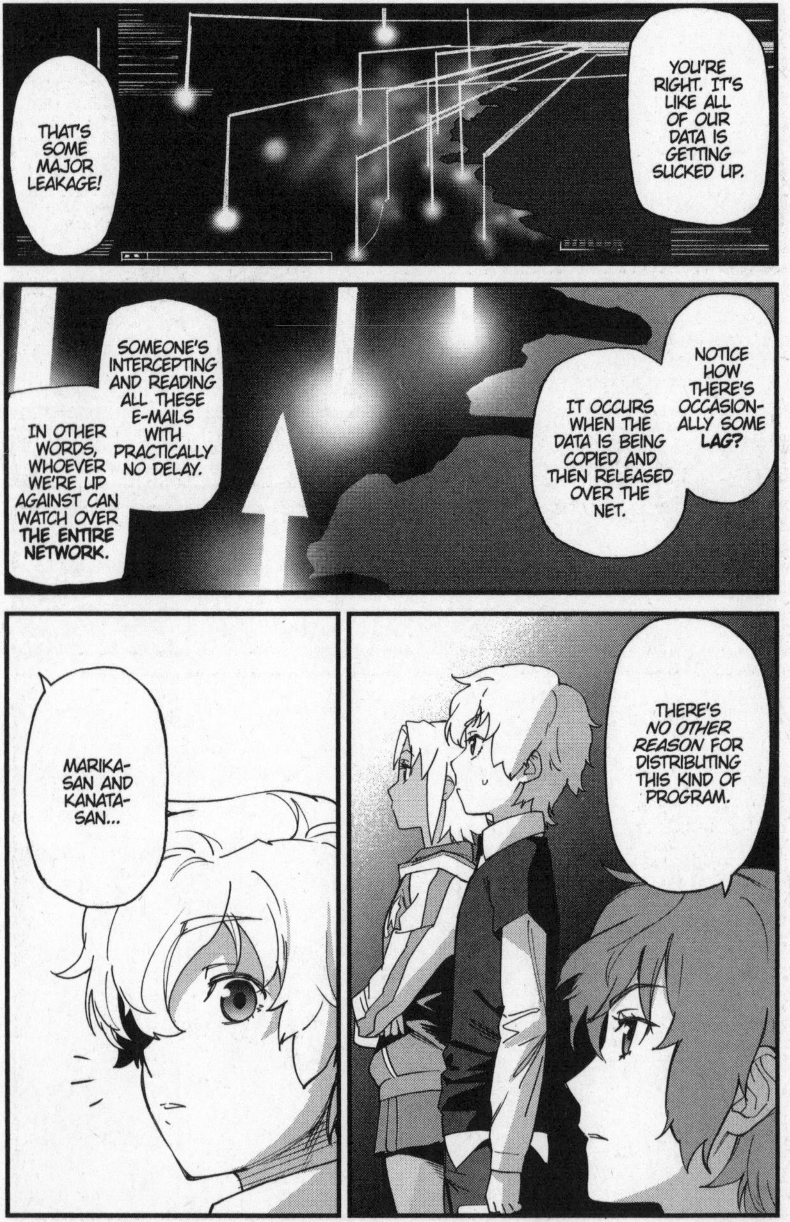
YOU'RE RIGHT. IT'S LIKE ALL OF OUR DATA IS GETTING SUCKED UP.
THAT'S SOME MAJOR LEAKAGE!
NOTICE HOW THERE'S OCCASION-ALLY SOME **LAG?**
IT OCCURS WHEN THE DATA IS BEING COPIED AND THEN RELEASED OVER THE NET.
SOMEONE'S INTERCEPTING AND READING ALL THESE E-MAILS WITH PRACTICALLY NO DELAY.
IN OTHER WORDS, WHOEVER WE'RE UP AGAINST CAN WATCH OVER THE ENTIRE **NETWORK.**
THERE'S *NO OTHER REASON* FOR DISTRIBUTING THIS KIND OF PROGRAM.
MARIKA-SAN AND KANATA-SAN...

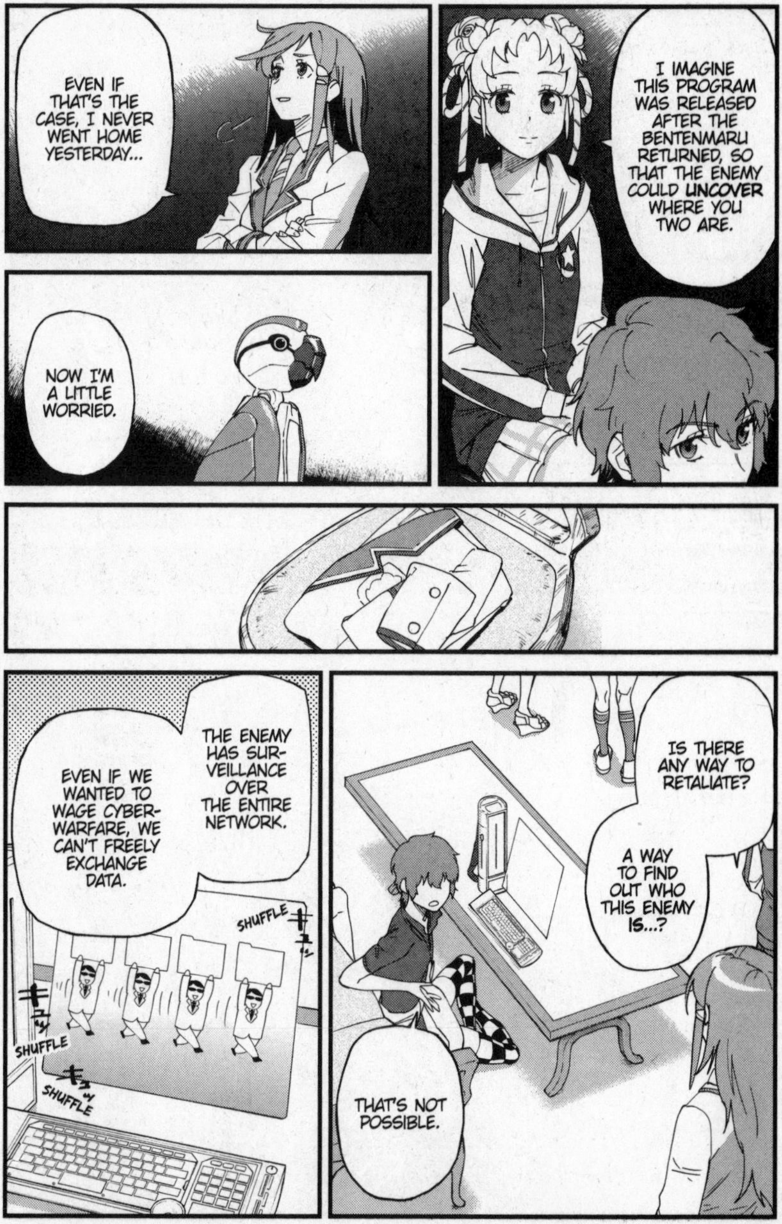
I IMAGINE THIS PROGRAM WAS RELEASED AFTER THE BENTENMARU RETURNED, SO THAT THE ENEMY COULD **UNCOVER** WHERE YOU TWO ARE.
EVEN IF THAT'S THE CASE, I NEVER WENT HOME YESTERDAY...
NOW I'M A LITTLE WORRIED.
IS THERE ANY WAY TO RETALIATE?
A WAY TO FIND OUT WHO THIS ENEMY IS...?
THAT'S NOT POSSIBLE.
THE ENEMY HAS SUR-VEILLANCE OVER THE ENTIRE NETWORK.
EVEN IF WE WANTED TO WAGE CYBER-WARFARE, WE CAN'T FREELY EXCHANGE DATA.
SHUFFLE
SHUFFLE
SHUFFLE

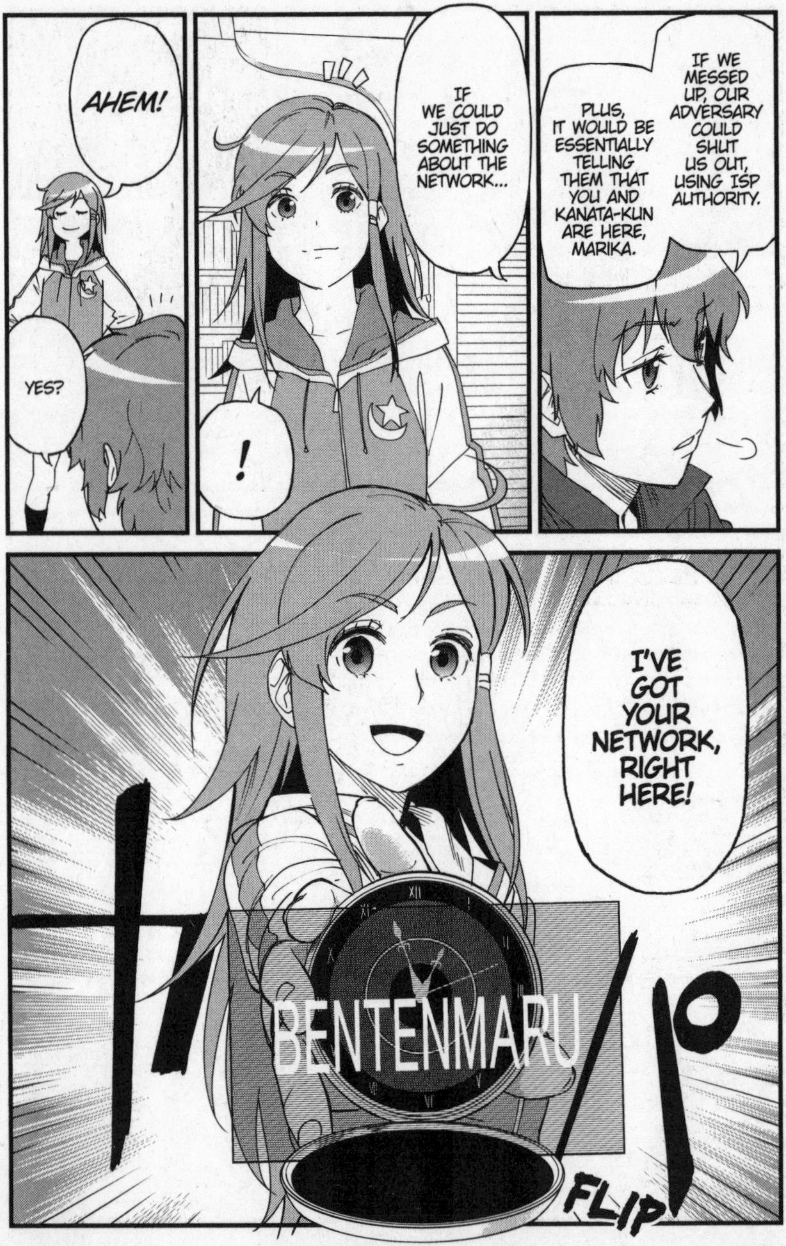
IF WE MESSED UP, OUR ADVERSARY COULD SHUT US OUT, USING ISP AUTHORITY.
PLUS, IT WOULD BE ESSENTIALLY TELLING THEM THAT YOU AND KANATA-KUN ARE HERE, MARIKA.
IF WE COULD JUST DO SOMETHING ABOUT THE NETWORK...
!
AHEM!
YES?
I'VE GOT YOUR NETWORK, RIGHT HERE!
BENTENMARU
FLIP

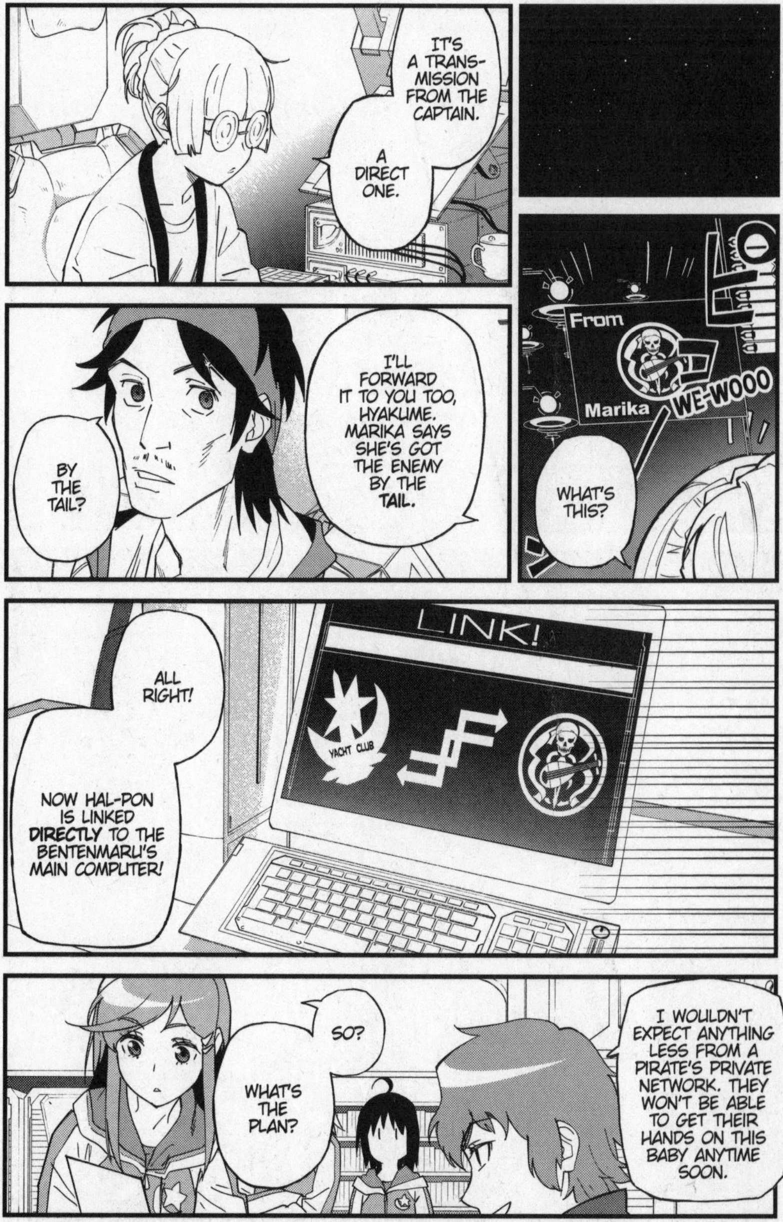
IT'S A TRANSMISSION FROM THE CAPTAIN.
A DIRECT ONE.
From
Marika
WE-WOOO
WHAT'S THIS?
I'LL FORWARD IT TO YOU TOO, HYAKUME. MARIKA SAYS SHE'S GOT THE ENEMY BY THE **TAIL.**
BY THE TAIL?
LINK!
YACHT CLUB
ALL RIGHT!
NOW HAL-PON IS LINKED **DIRECTLY** TO THE BENTENMARU'S MAIN COMPUTER!
I WOULDN'T EXPECT ANYTHING LESS FROM A PIRATE'S PRIVATE NETWORK. THEY WON'T BE ABLE TO GET THEIR HANDS ON THIS BABY ANYTIME SOON.
SO?
WHAT'S THE PLAN?

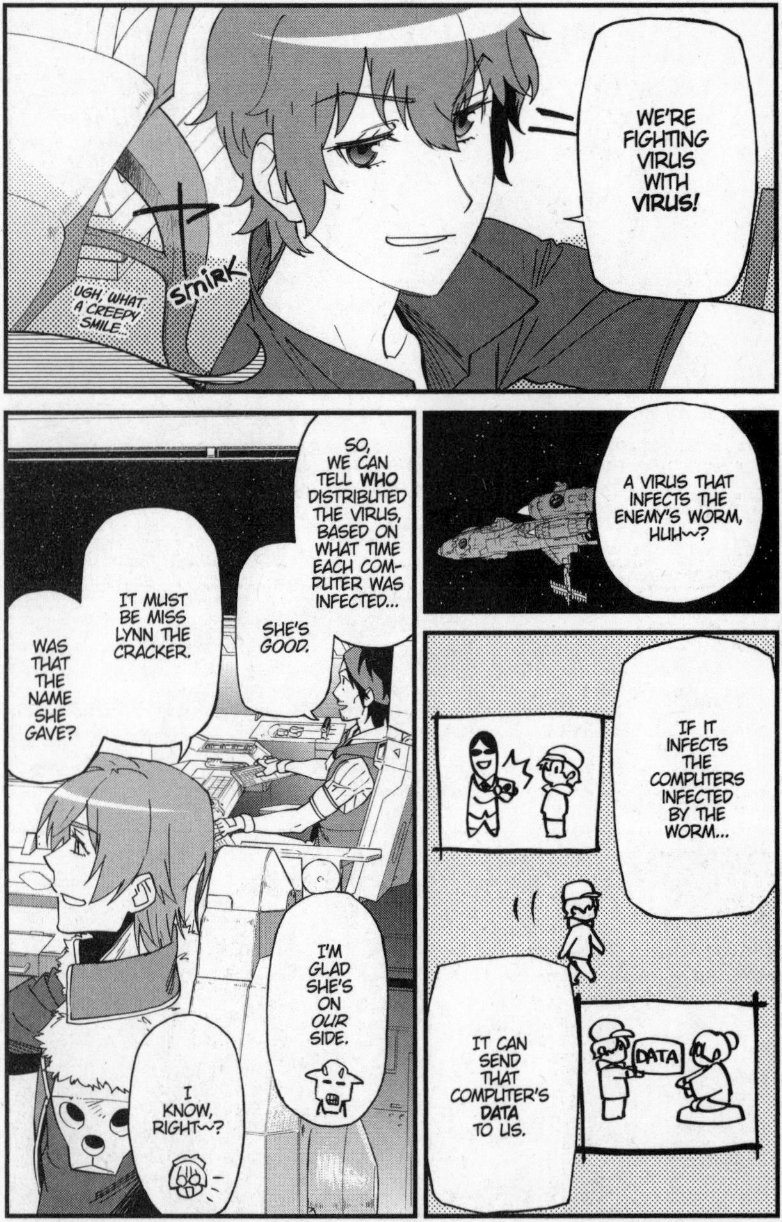
WE'RE FIGHTING VIRUS WITH VIRUS!
SMIRK
UGH, WHAT A CREEPY SMILE...
A VIRUS THAT INFECTS THE ENEMY'S WORM, HUH~?
IF IT INFECTS THE COMPUTERS INFECTED BY THE WORM...
DATA
IT CAN SEND THAT COMPUTER'S DATA TO US.
SO, WE CAN TELL WHO DISTRIBUTED THE VIRUS, BASED ON WHAT TIME EACH COMPUTER WAS INFECTED...
SHE'S GOOD.
IT MUST BE MISS LYNN THE CRACKER.
WAS THAT THE NAME SHE GAVE?
I'M GLAD SHE'S ON *OUR* SIDE.
I KNOW, RIGHT~?

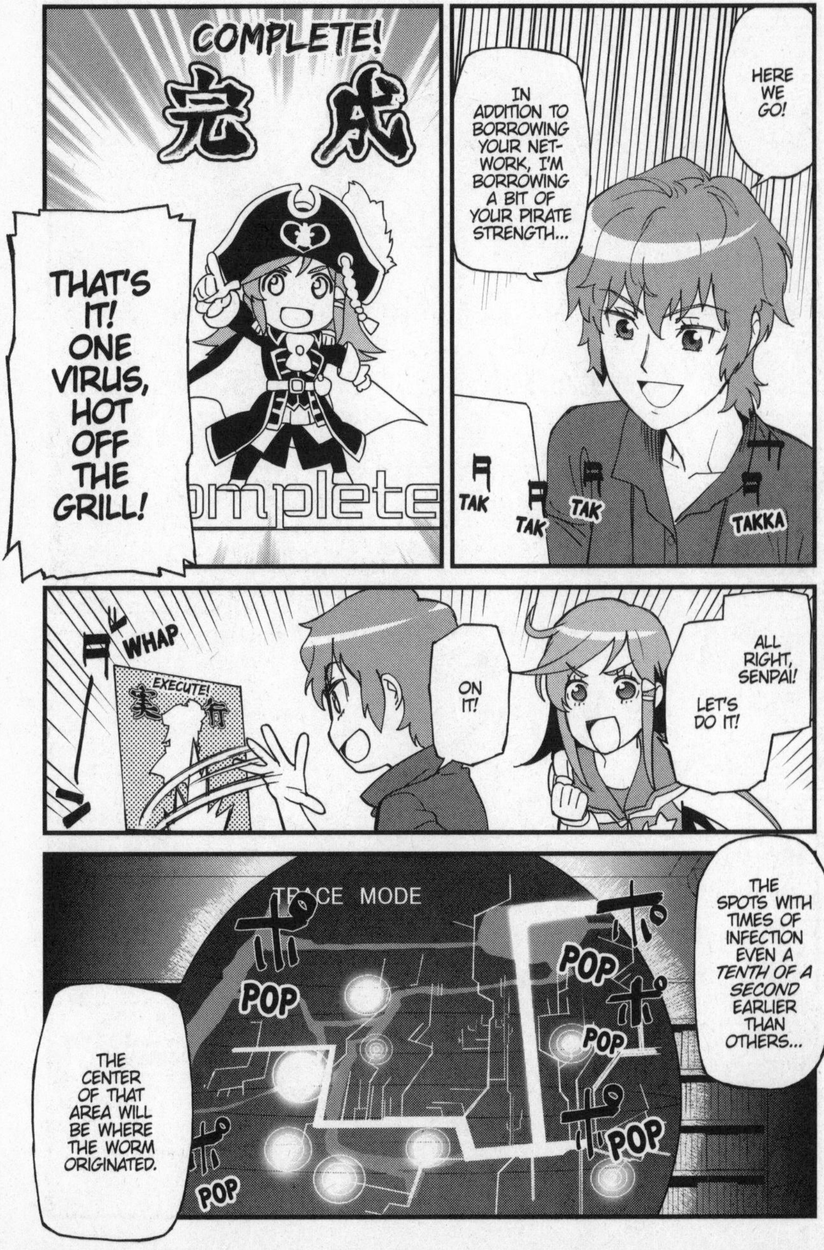
HERE WE GO!
IN ADDITION TO BORROWING YOUR NET-WORK, I'M BORROWING A BIT OF YOUR PIRATE STRENGTH...
TAKKA
TAK
TAK
TAK
COMPLETE!
完成
THAT'S IT! ONE VIRUS, HOT OFF THE GRILL!
ALL RIGHT, SENPAI!
LET'S DO IT!
ON IT!
WHAP
EXECUTE!
実行
TRACE MODE
THE SPOTS WITH TIMES OF INFECTION EVEN A *TENTH OF A SECOND* EARLIER THAN OTHERS...
POP
POP
POP
POP
POP
THE CENTER OF THAT AREA WILL BE WHERE THE WORM ORIGINATED.
POP

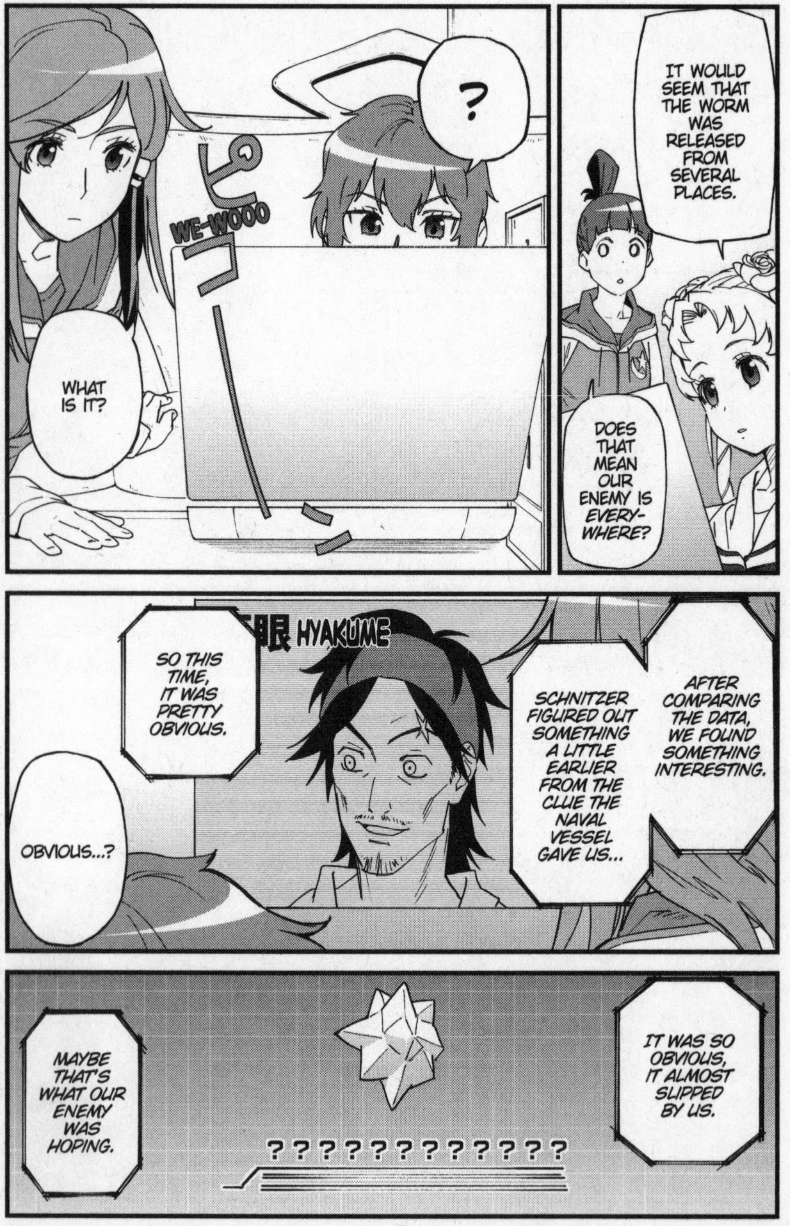
IT WOULD SEEM THAT THE WORM WAS RELEASED FROM SEVERAL PLACES.
DOES THAT MEAN OUR ENEMY IS EVERY-WHERE?
?
WE-WOOO
WHAT IS IT?
AFTER COMPARING THE DATA, WE FOUND SOMETHING INTERESTING.
SCHNITZER FIGURED OUT SOMETHING A LITTLE EARLIER FROM THE CLUE THE NAVAL VESSEL GAVE US...
HYAKUME
SO THIS TIME, IT WAS PRETTY OBVIOUS.
OBVIOUS...?
IT WAS SO OBVIOUS, IT ALMOST SLIPPED BY US.
? ? ? ? ? ? ? ? ? ? ? ? ?
MAYBE THAT'S WHAT OUR ENEMY WAS HOPING.

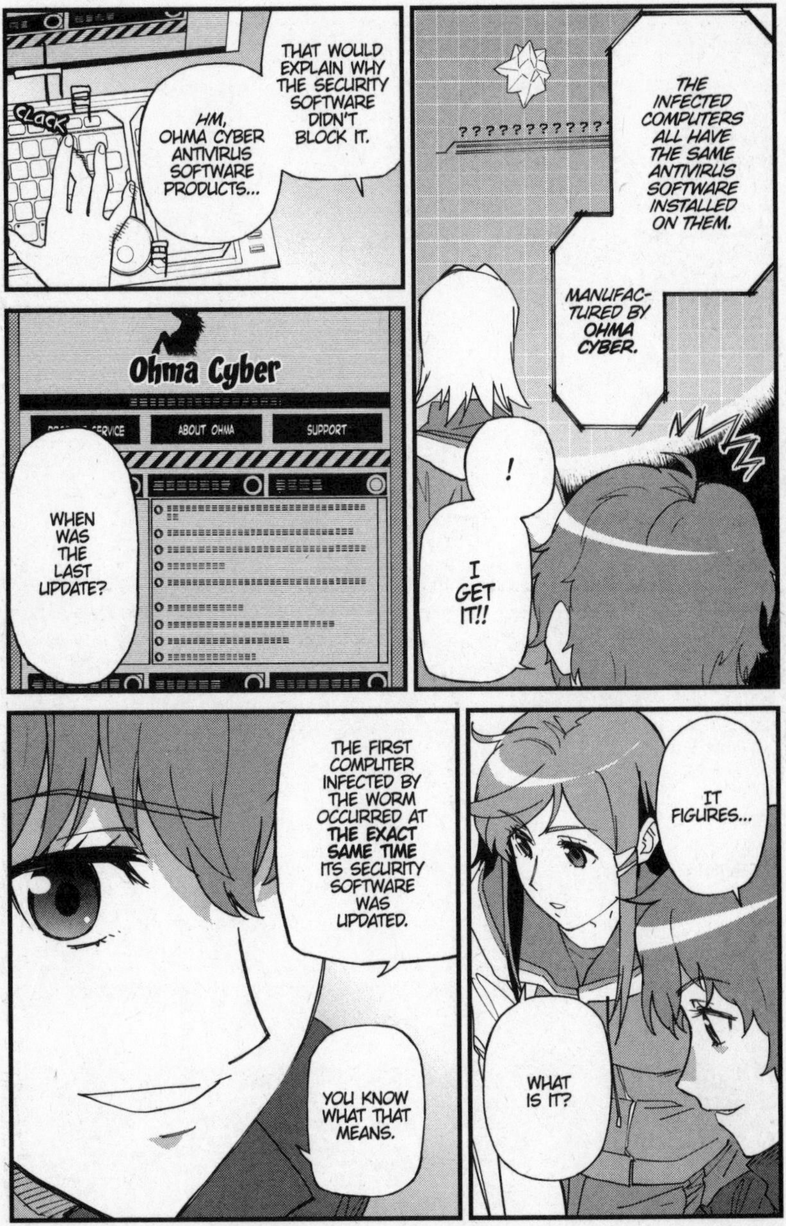
???????????
THE INFECTED COMPUTERS ALL HAVE THE SAME ANTIVIRUS SOFTWARE INSTALLED ON THEM.
MANUFACTURED BY OHMA CYBER.
!
I GET IT!!
THAT WOULD EXPLAIN WHY THE SECURITY SOFTWARE DIDN'T BLOCK IT.
HM, OHMA CYBER ANTIVIRUS SOFTWARE PRODUCTS...
CLACK
Ohma Cyber
ABOUT OHMA
SUPPORT
WHEN WAS THE LAST UPDATE?
IT FIGURES...
WHAT IS IT?
THE FIRST COMPUTER INFECTED BY THE WORM OCCURRED AT THE EXACT SAME TIME ITS SECURITY SOFTWARE WAS UPDATED.
YOU KNOW WHAT THAT MEANS.

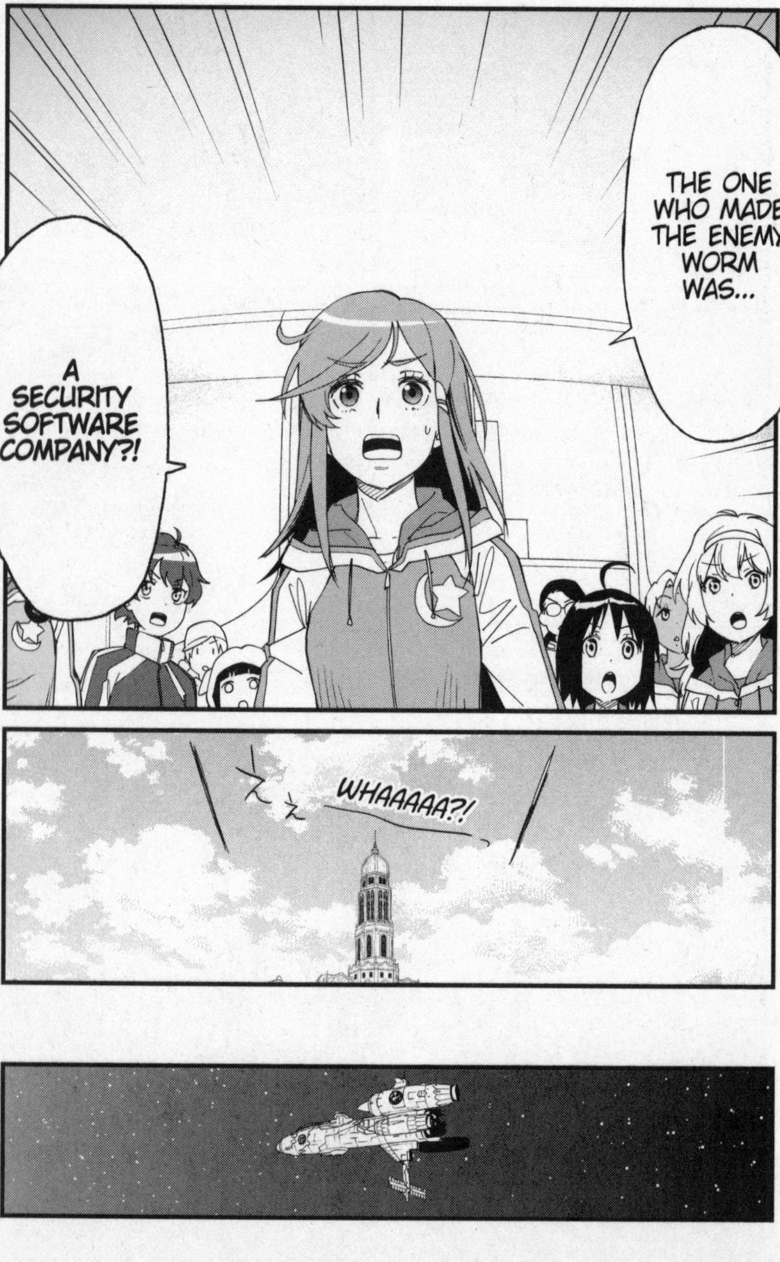
THE ONE WHO MADE THE ENEMY WORM WAS...
A SECURITY SOFTWARE COMPANY?!
WHAAAAAA?!

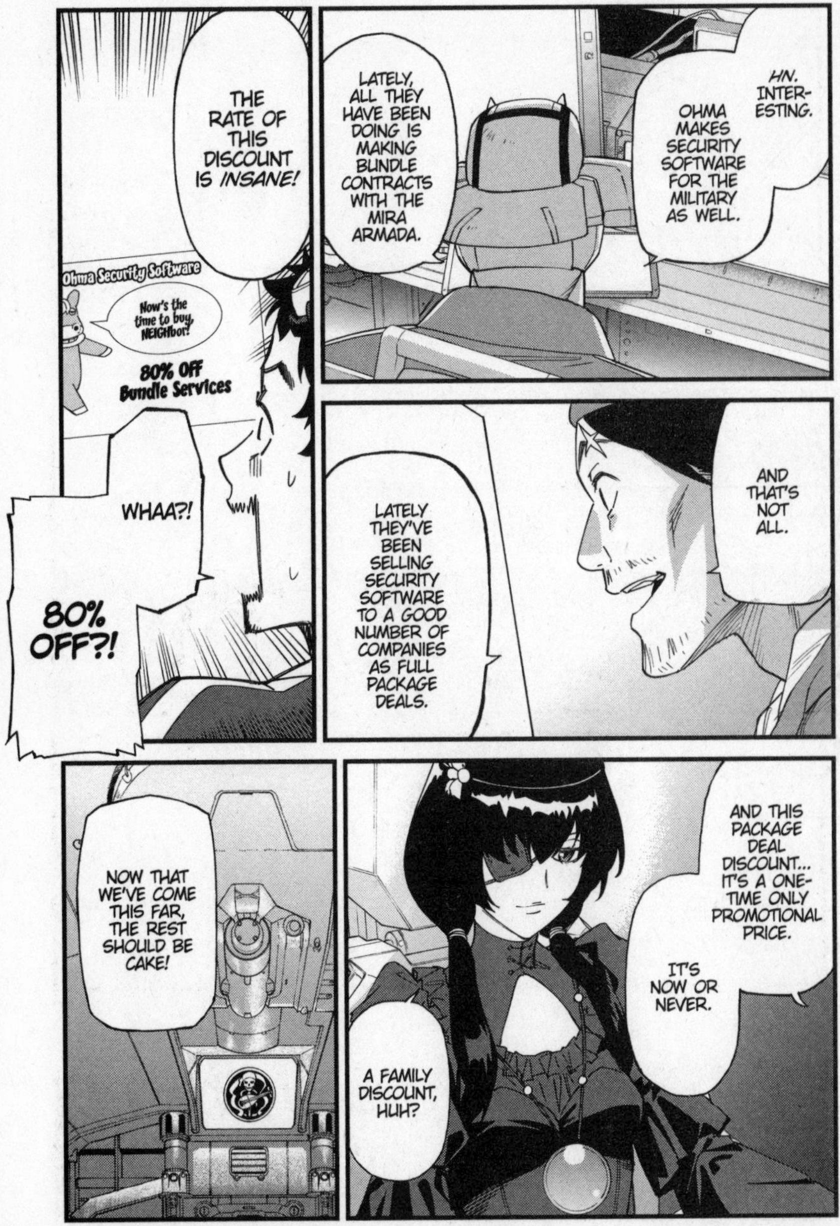
HN. INTERESTING.
OHMA MAKES SECURITY SOFTWARE FOR THE MILITARY AS WELL.
LATELY, ALL THEY HAVE BEEN DOING IS MAKING BUNDLE CONTRACTS WITH THE MIRA ARMADA.
AND THAT'S NOT ALL.
LATELY THEY'VE BEEN SELLING SECURITY SOFTWARE TO A GOOD NUMBER OF COMPANIES AS FULL PACKAGE DEALS.
THE RATE OF THIS DISCOUNT IS *INSANE!*
Ohma Security Software
Now's the time to buy, NEIGHbor!
80% Off Bundle Services
WHAA?!
80% OFF?!
AND THIS PACKAGE DEAL DISCOUNT... IT'S A ONE-TIME ONLY PROMOTIONAL PRICE.
IT'S NOW OR NEVER.
A FAMILY DISCOUNT, HUH?
NOW THAT WE'VE COME THIS FAR, THE REST SHOULD BE CAKE!

IT'S TIME TO *ROOT OUT* THE COMPANIES THAT WENT THROUGH WITH THE BUNDLE PURCHASES!

LET'S GO!!

WSH

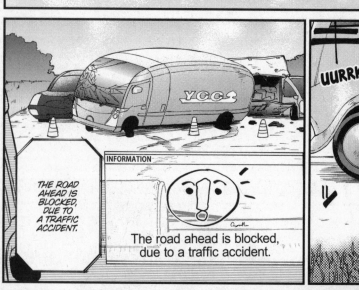

UURRK

THE ROAD AHEAD IS BLOCKED, DUE TO A TRAFFIC ACCIDENT.

INFORMATION

The road ahead is blocked, due to a traffic accident.

YCC
Drink Provide Service

......

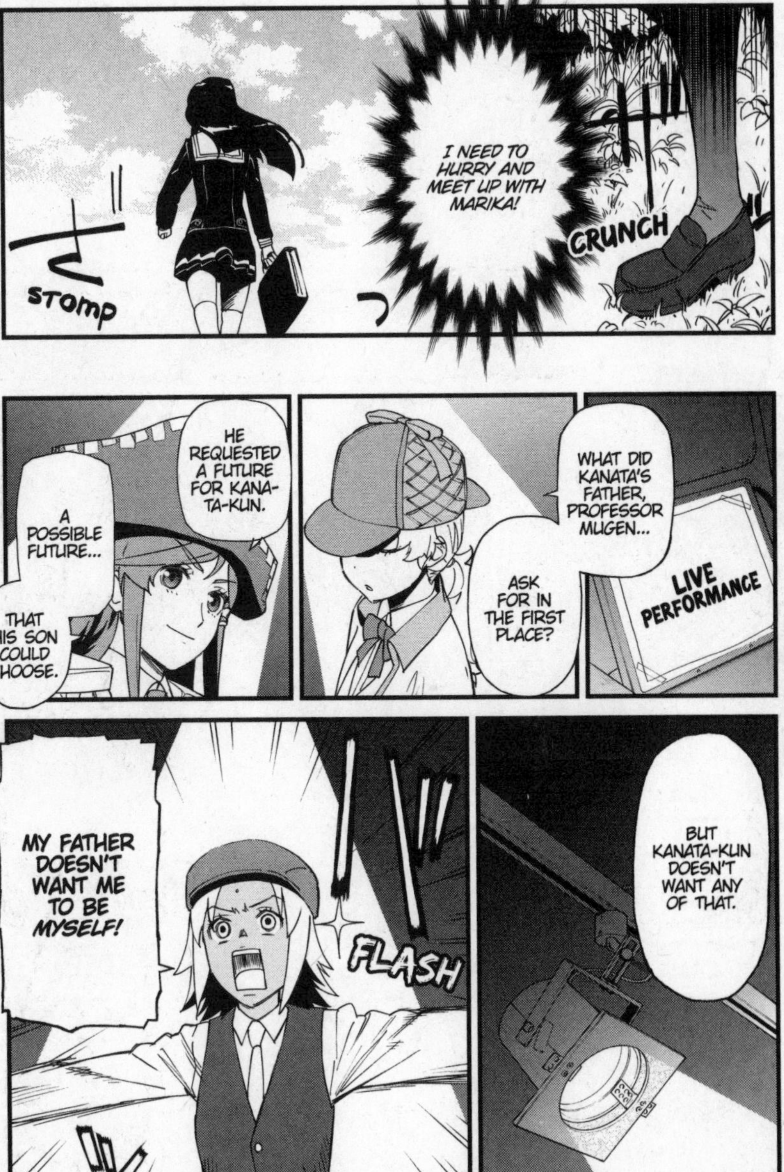
I NEED TO HURRY AND MEET UP WITH MARIKA!
CRUNCH
STOMP
LIVE PERFORMANCE
WHAT DID KANATA'S FATHER, PROFESSOR MUGEN...
ASK FOR IN THE FIRST PLACE?
HE REQUESTED A FUTURE FOR KANA-TA-KUN.
A POSSIBLE FUTURE...
THAT HIS SON COULD CHOOSE.
BUT KANATA-KUN DOESN'T WANT ANY OF THAT.
FLASH
MY FATHER DOESN'T WANT ME TO BE MYSELF!

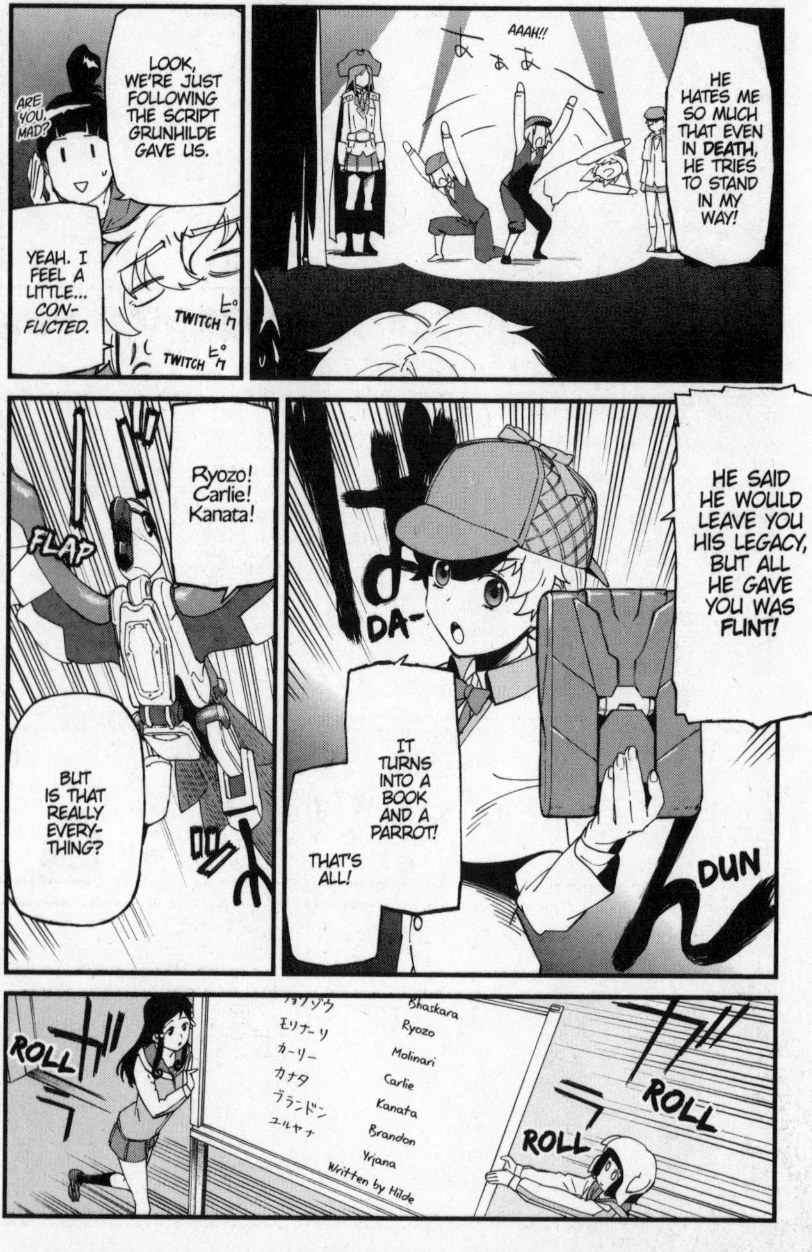
AAAH!!
あぁあ〜
HE HATES ME SO MUCH THAT EVEN IN DEATH, HE TRIES TO STAND IN MY WAY!
LOOK, WE'RE JUST FOLLOWING THE SCRIPT GRUNHILDE GAVE US.
ARE YOU, MAD?
YEAH. I FEEL A LITTLE... CON-FLICTED.
TWITCH
TWITCH
HE SAID HE WOULD LEAVE YOU HIS LEGACY, BUT ALL HE GAVE YOU WAS FLINT!
DA-
DUN
IT TURNS INTO A BOOK AND A PARROT!
THAT'S ALL!
Ryozo! Carlie! Kanata!
FLAP
BUT IS THAT REALLY EVERYTHING?
ROLL
ROLL
モリナーリ
カーリー
カナタ
ブランドン
ユルヤナ
Bhaskara
Ryozo
Molinari
Carlie
Kanata
Brandon
Yrjana
Written by Hilde
ROLL

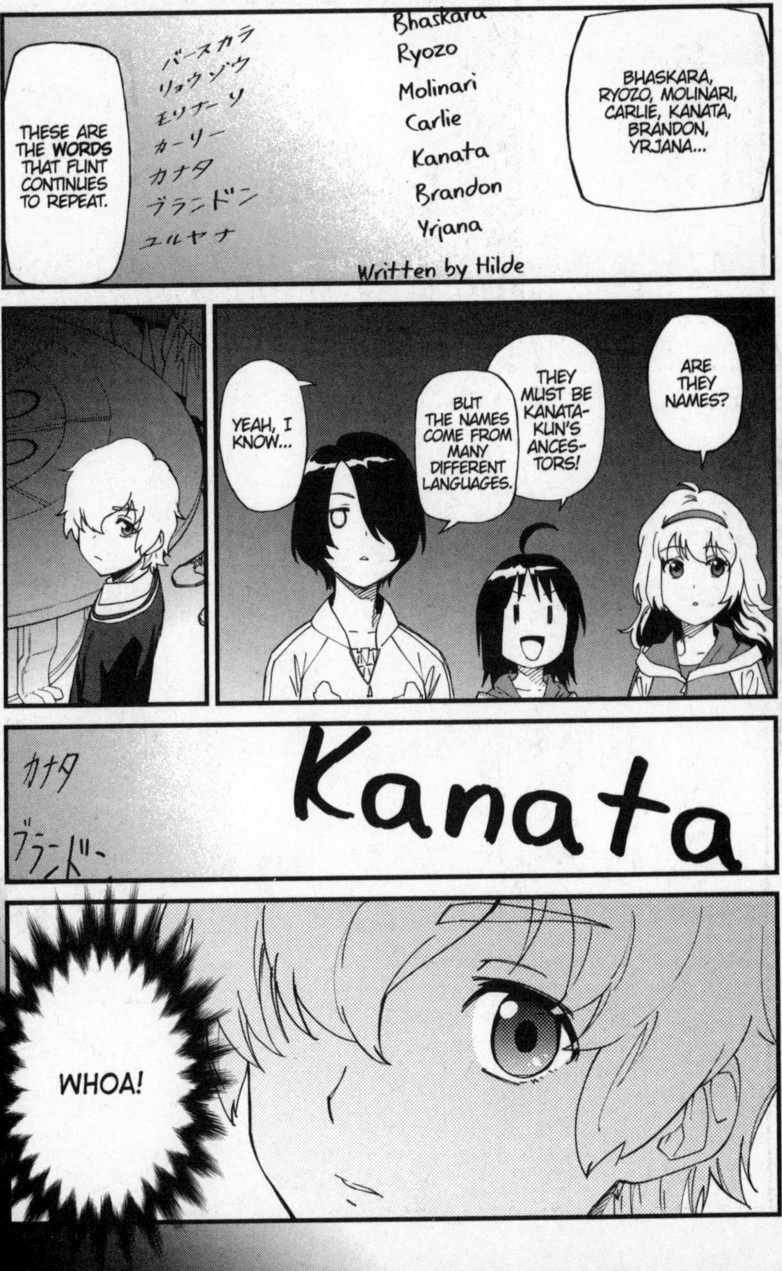
BHASKARA, RYOZO, MOLINARI, CARLIE, KANATA, BRANDON, YRJANA...
Bhaskara
Ryozo
Molinari
Carlie
Kanata
Brandon
Yrjana
Written by Hilde
バースカラ
リョウゾウ
モリナーリ
カーリー
カナタ
ブランドン
ユルヤナ
THESE ARE THE **WORDS** THAT FLINT CONTINUES TO REPEAT.
ARE THEY NAMES?
THEY MUST BE KANATA-KUN'S ANCESTORS!
BUT THE NAMES COME FROM MANY DIFFERENT LANGUAGES.
YEAH, I KNOW...
Kanata
カナタ
ブランドン
WHOA!

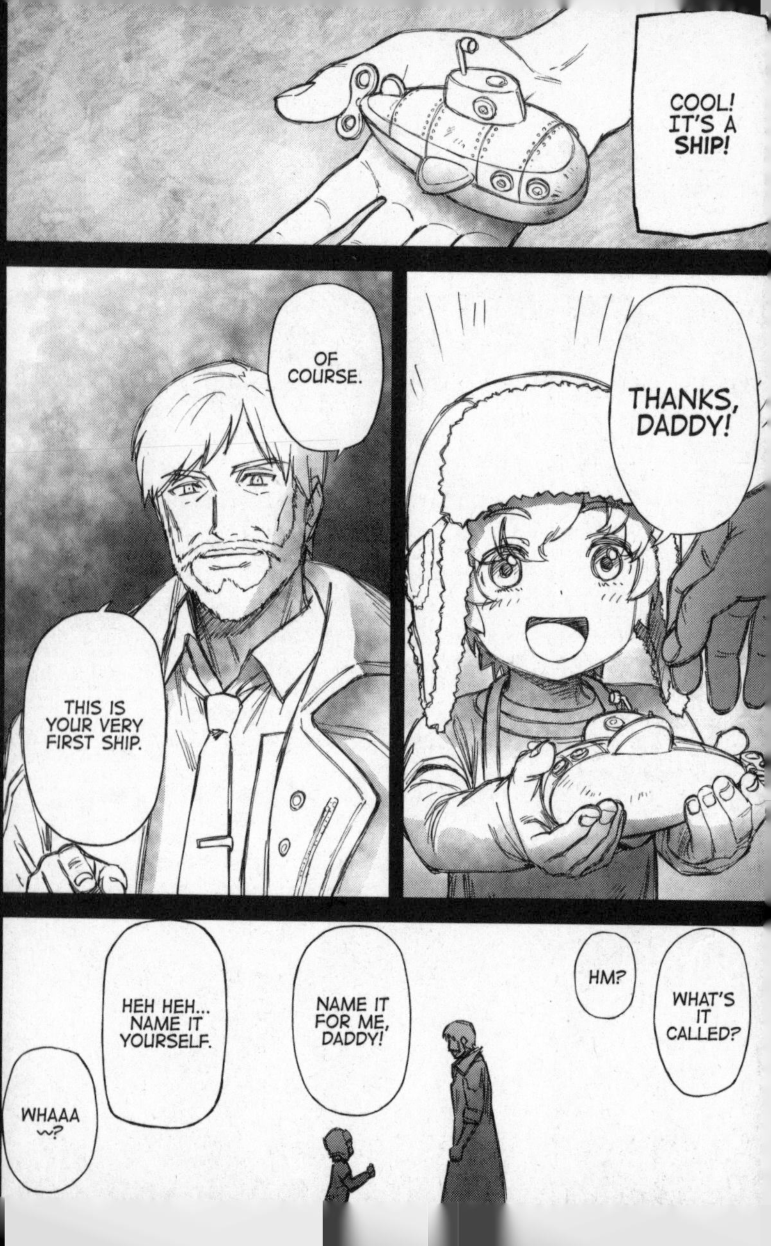
COOL! IT'S A SHIP!
THANKS, DADDY!
OF COURSE.
THIS IS YOUR VERY FIRST SHIP.
WHAT'S IT CALLED?
HM?
NAME IT FOR ME, DADDY!
HEH HEH... NAME IT YOURSELF.
WHAAAw?

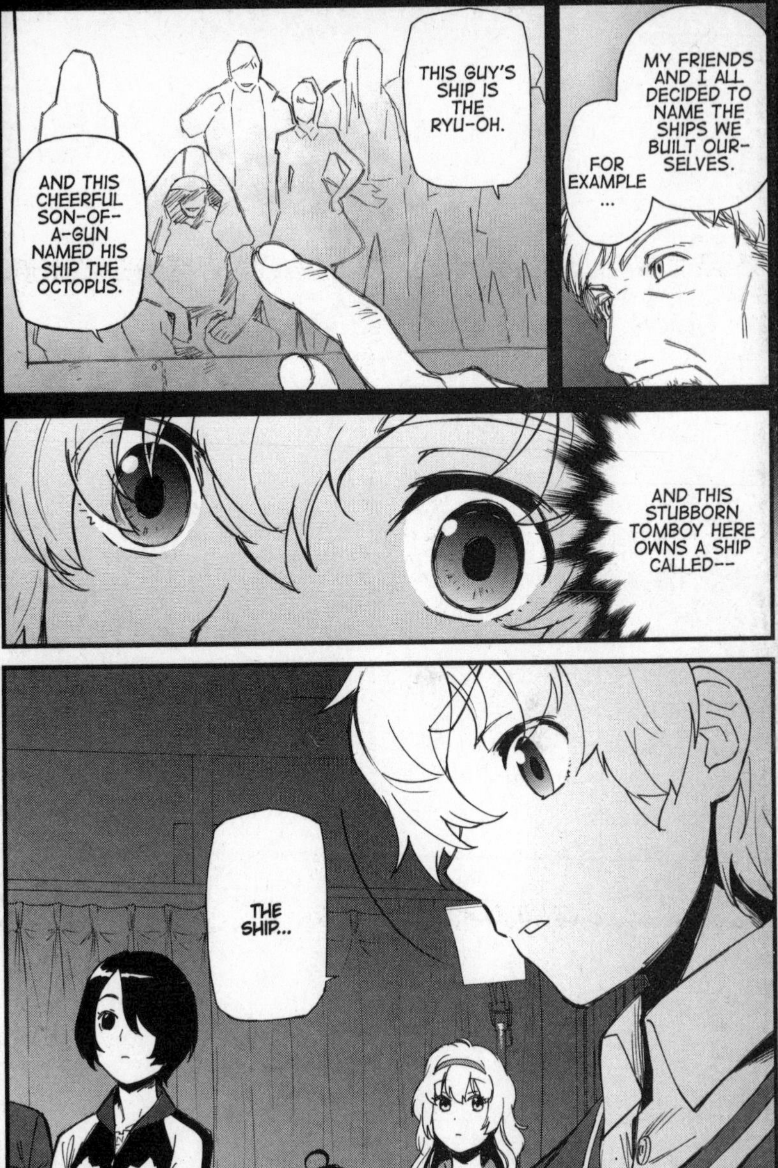
MY FRIENDS AND I ALL DECIDED TO NAME THE SHIPS WE BUILT OUR-SELVES.
FOR EXAMPLE ...
THIS GUY'S SHIP IS THE RYU-OH.
AND THIS CHEERFUL SON-OF-A-GUN NAMED HIS SHIP THE OCTOPUS.
AND THIS STUBBORN TOMBOY HERE OWNS A SHIP CALLED--
THE SHIP...

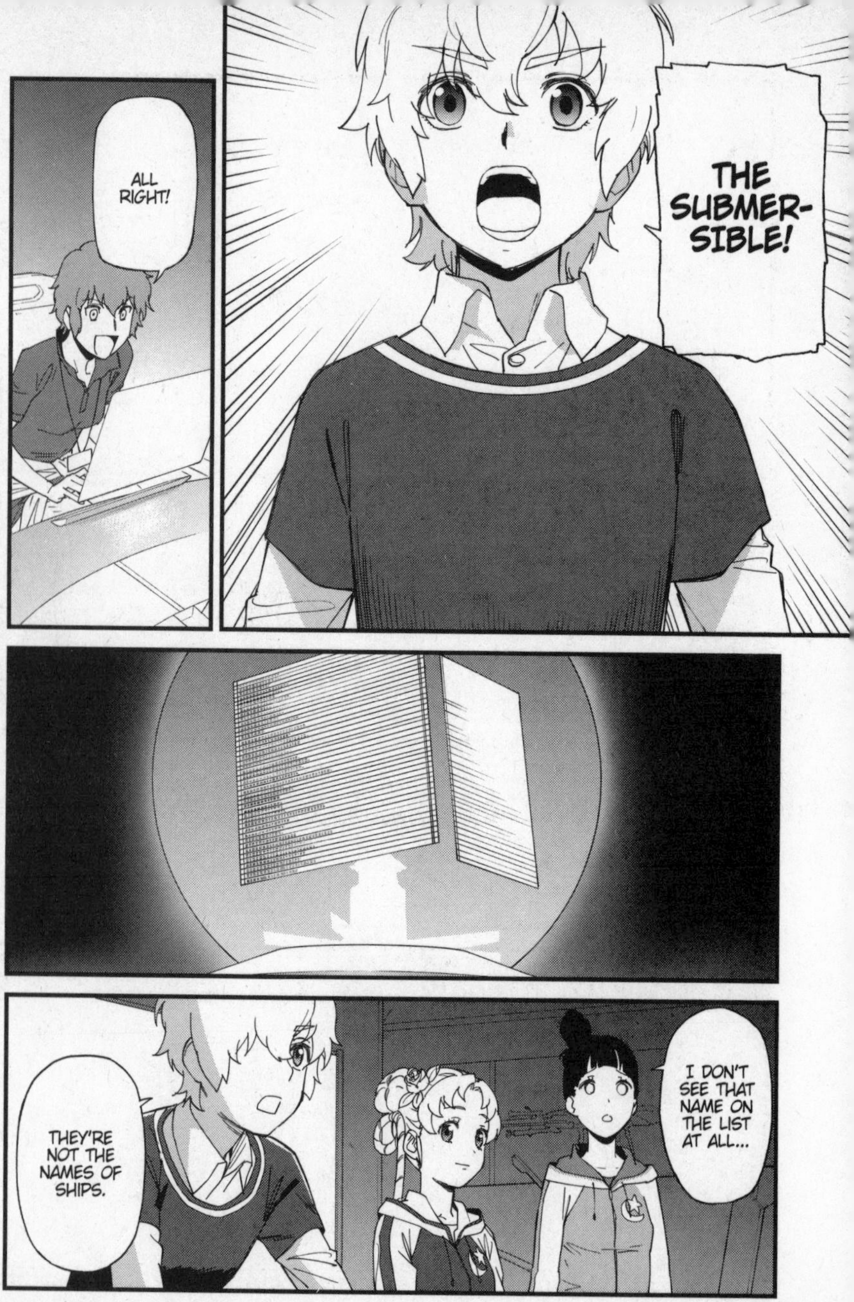
THE SUBMER-SIBLE!
ALL RIGHT!
I DON'T SEE THAT NAME ON THE LIST AT ALL...
THEY'RE NOT THE NAMES OF SHIPS.

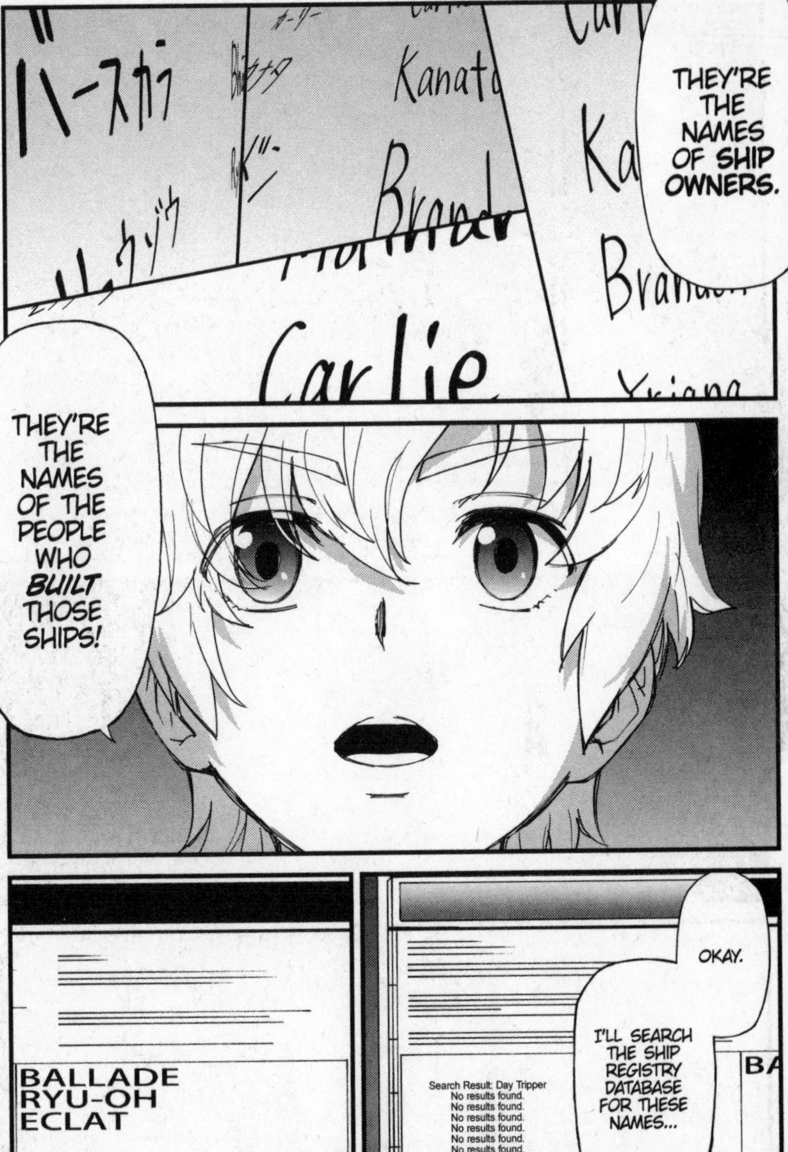
THEY'RE THE NAMES OF SHIP OWNERS.
Kanato
Carlie
THEY'RE THE NAMES OF THE PEOPLE WHO *BUILT* THOSE SHIPS!
OKAY.
I'LL SEARCH THE SHIP REGISTRY DATABASE FOR THESE NAMES...
Search Result: Day Tripper
No results found.
No results found.
No results found.
No results found.
No results found.
No results found.
No results found.
No results found.
BALLADE
RYU-OH
ECLAT
Search Results

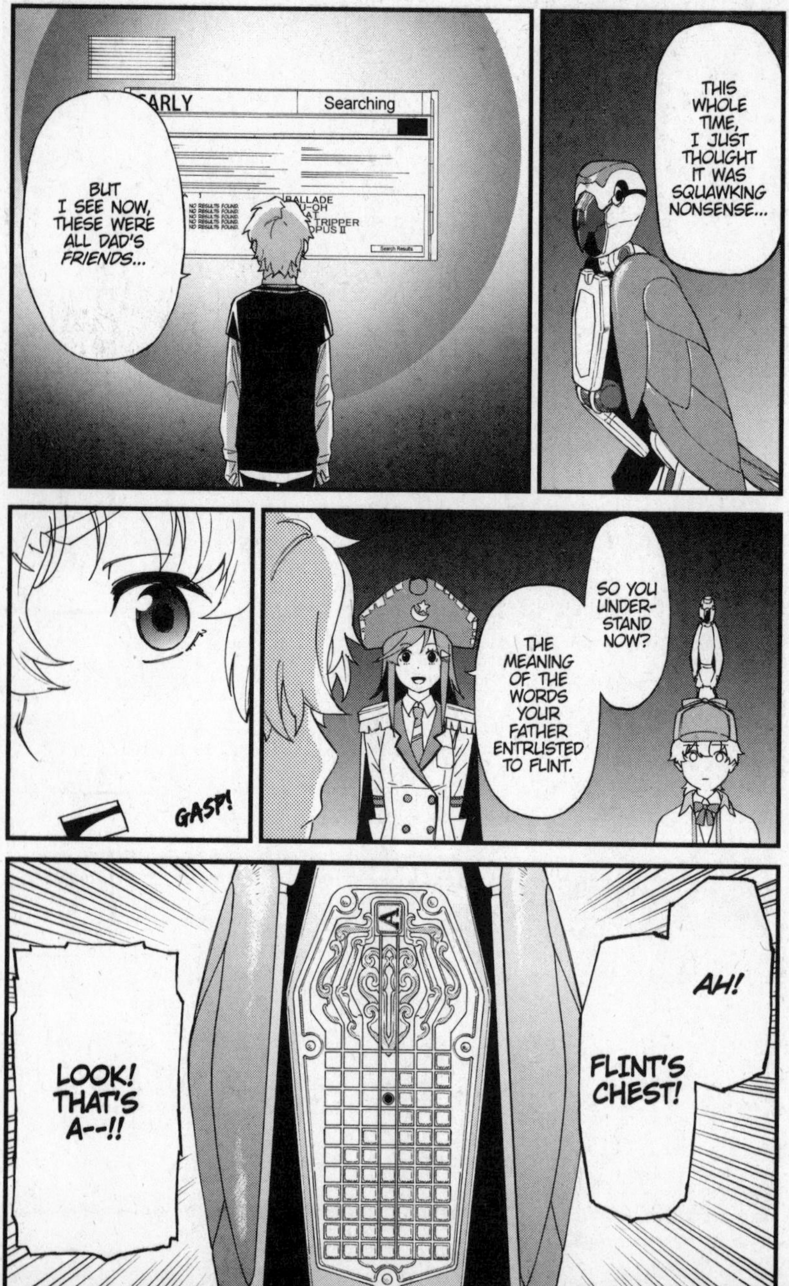
THIS WHOLE TIME, I JUST THOUGHT IT WAS SQUAWKING NONSENSE...
Searching
BALLADE
BUT I SEE NOW, THESE WERE ALL DAD'S FRIENDS...
SO YOU UNDER-STAND NOW?
THE MEANING OF THE WORDS YOUR FATHER ENTRUSTED TO FLINT.
GASP!
AH!
FLINT'S CHEST!
LOOK! THAT'S A--!!

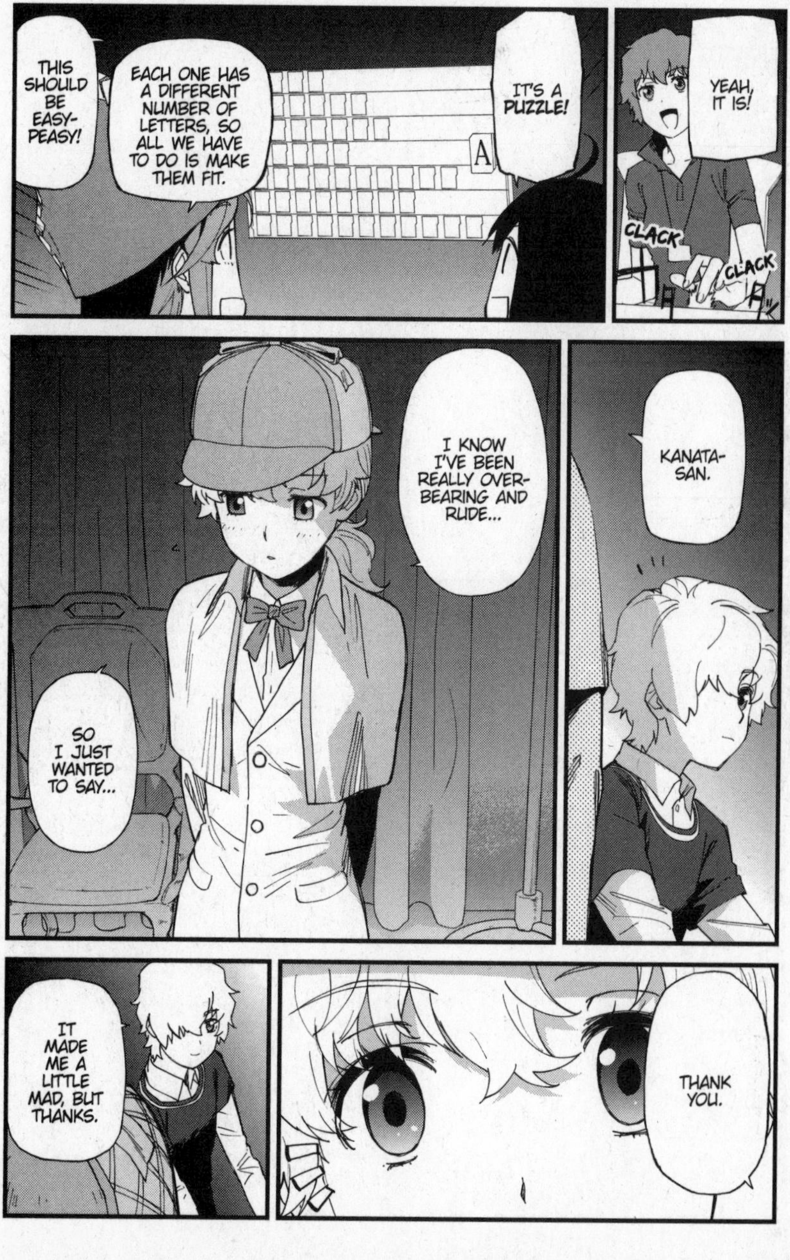
YEAH, IT IS!
CLACK
CLACK
IT'S A PUZZLE!
EACH ONE HAS A DIFFERENT NUMBER OF LETTERS, SO ALL WE HAVE TO DO IS MAKE THEM FIT.
THIS SHOULD BE EASY-PEASY!
KANATA-SAN.
I KNOW I'VE BEEN REALLY OVER-BEARING AND RUDE...
SO I JUST WANTED TO SAY...
THANK YOU.
IT MADE ME A LITTLE MAD, BUT THANKS.

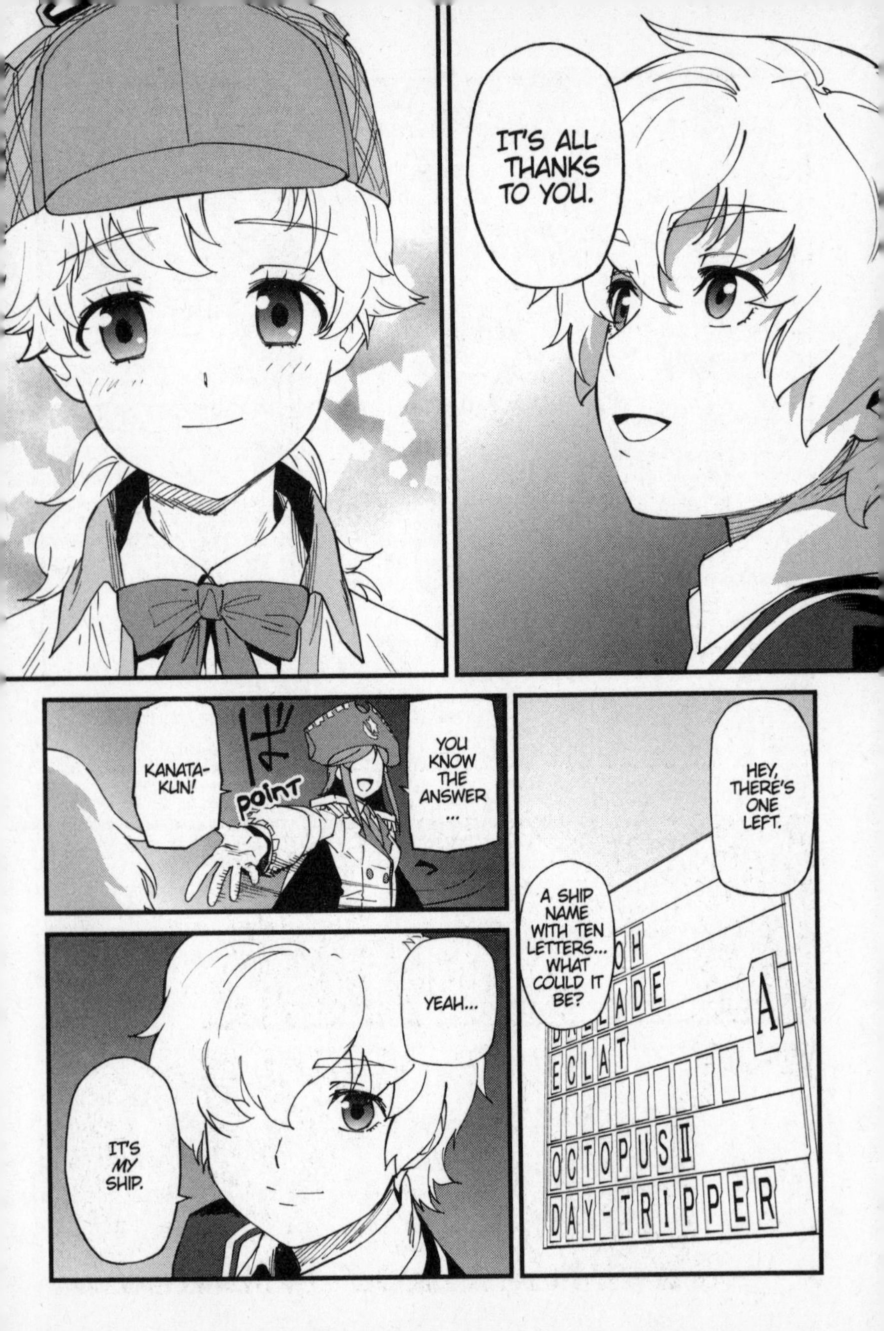
IT'S ALL THANKS TO YOU.
HEY, THERE'S ONE LEFT.
A SHIP NAME WITH TEN LETTERS... WHAT COULD IT BE?
A
ECLAT
OCTOPUS II
DAY-TRIPPER
YOU KNOW THE ANSWER ...
point
KANATA-KUN!
YEAH...
IT'S MY SHIP.

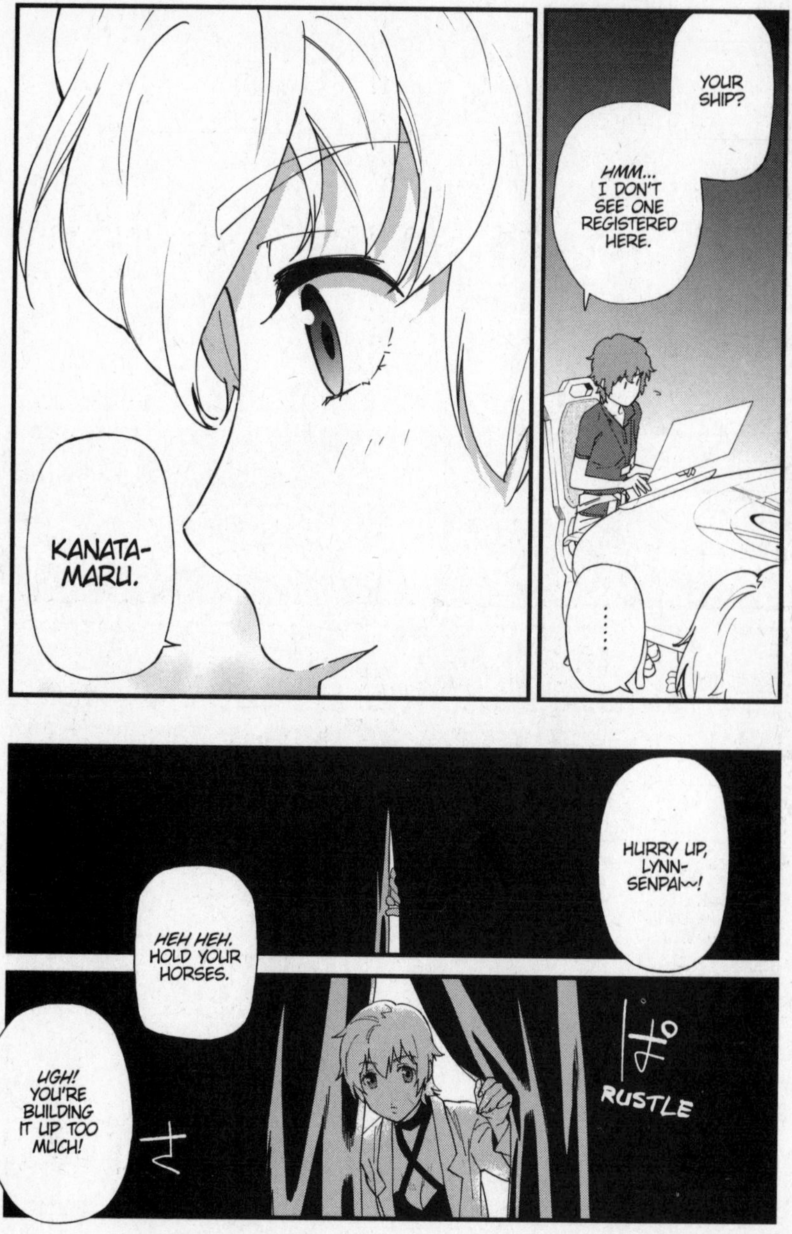
YOUR SHIP?
HMM... I DON'T SEE ONE REGISTERED HERE.
......
KANATA-MARU.
HURRY UP, LYNN-SENPAI~!
HEH HEH. HOLD YOUR HORSES.
RUSTLE
UGH! YOU'RE BUILDING IT UP TOO MUCH!

NOW SEARCH FOR ANY WORDS THAT POP UP WHEN YOU READ THE LINES VERTICALLY, HORIZONTALLY, OR DIAGONALLY!

IT'S COMPLETE!

H	O	R	A						
R	Y	U	-	O	H				
B	A	L	L	A	D	E			
E	C	L	A	T					
K	A	N	A	T	A	M	A	R	U
O	C	T	O	P	U	S	II		
D	A	Y	-	T	R	I	P	P	E	R

A

ROGER!

THE HRBEK ODA!

A SHORT-PERIOD COMET IN THE HAWKINGS SYSTEM...

OKAY!

WE'VE GOT A HIT!

I THINK IT WAS PROBABLY A QUESTION FROM THE PROFESSOR TO KANATA-KUN.

SO IT WASN'T A PUZZLE AFTER ALL.

I'VE HEARD RUMORS OF A SAILOR LIKE THAT.

A HYPER-SPACE DIVER LIVING ON A COMET...

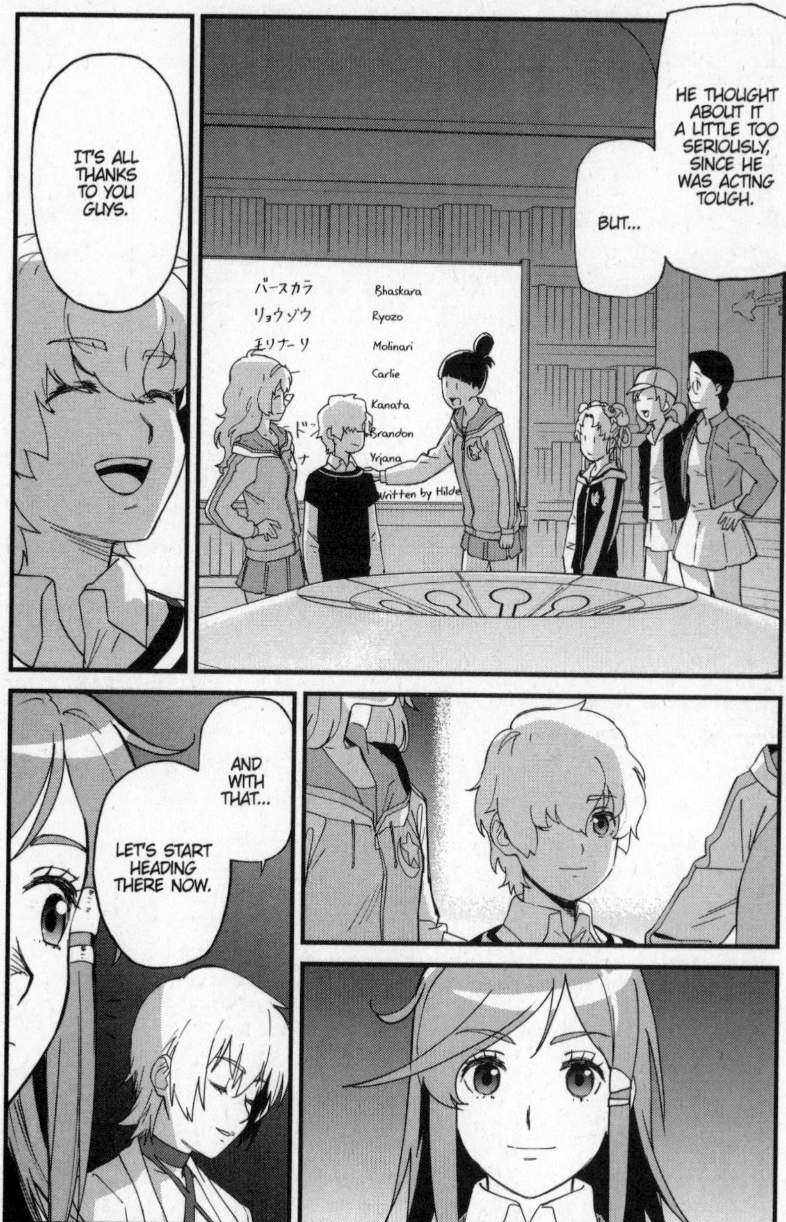
HE THOUGHT ABOUT IT A LITTLE TOO SERIOUSLY, SINCE HE WAS ACTING TOUGH.
BUT...
バースカラ
リョウゾウ
モリナーリ
Bhaskara
Ryozo
Molinari
Carlie
Kanata
Brandon
Yrjana
Written by Hilde
IT'S ALL THANKS TO YOU GUYS.
AND WITH THAT...
LET'S START HEADING THERE NOW.

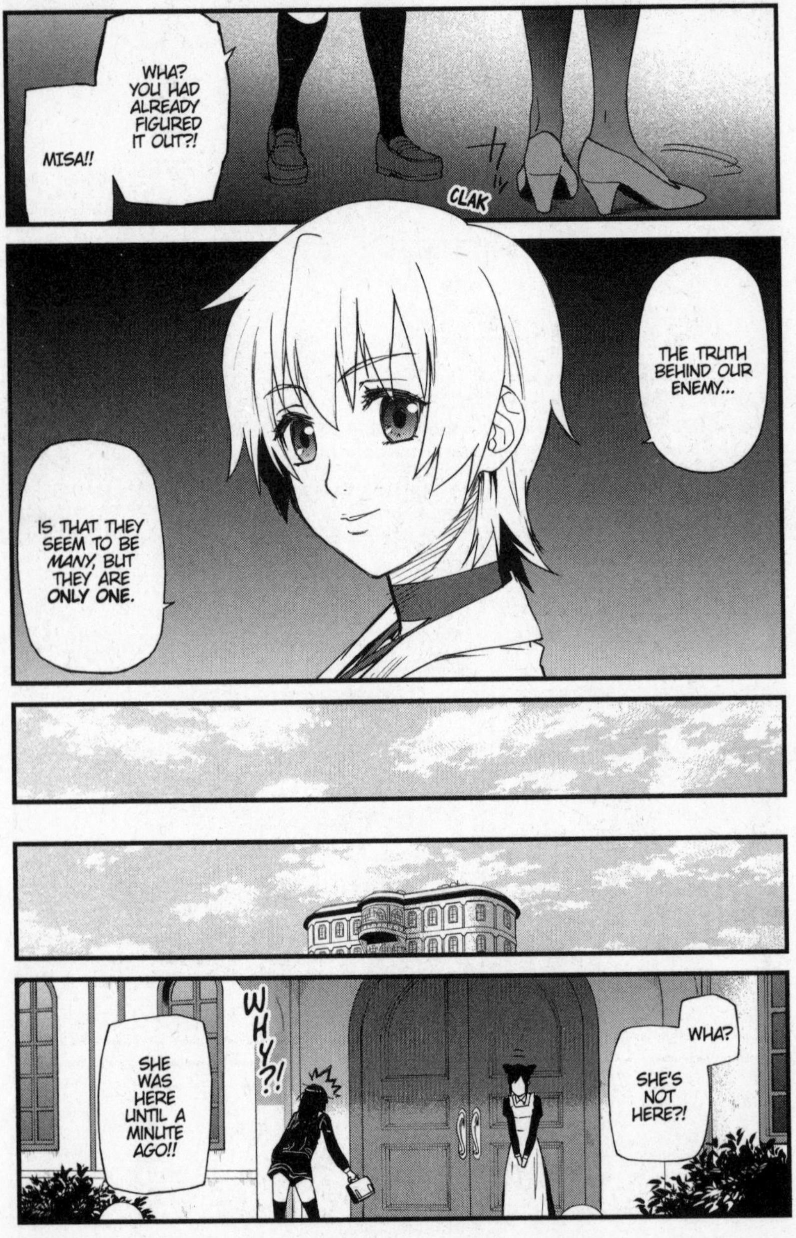
CLAK
WHA? YOU HAD ALREADY FIGURED IT OUT?! MISA!!
THE TRUTH BEHIND OUR ENEMY...
IS THAT THEY SEEM TO BE MANY, BUT THEY ARE ONLY ONE.
WHA?
SHE'S NOT HERE?!
WHY?!
SHE WAS HERE UNTIL A MINUTE AGO!!

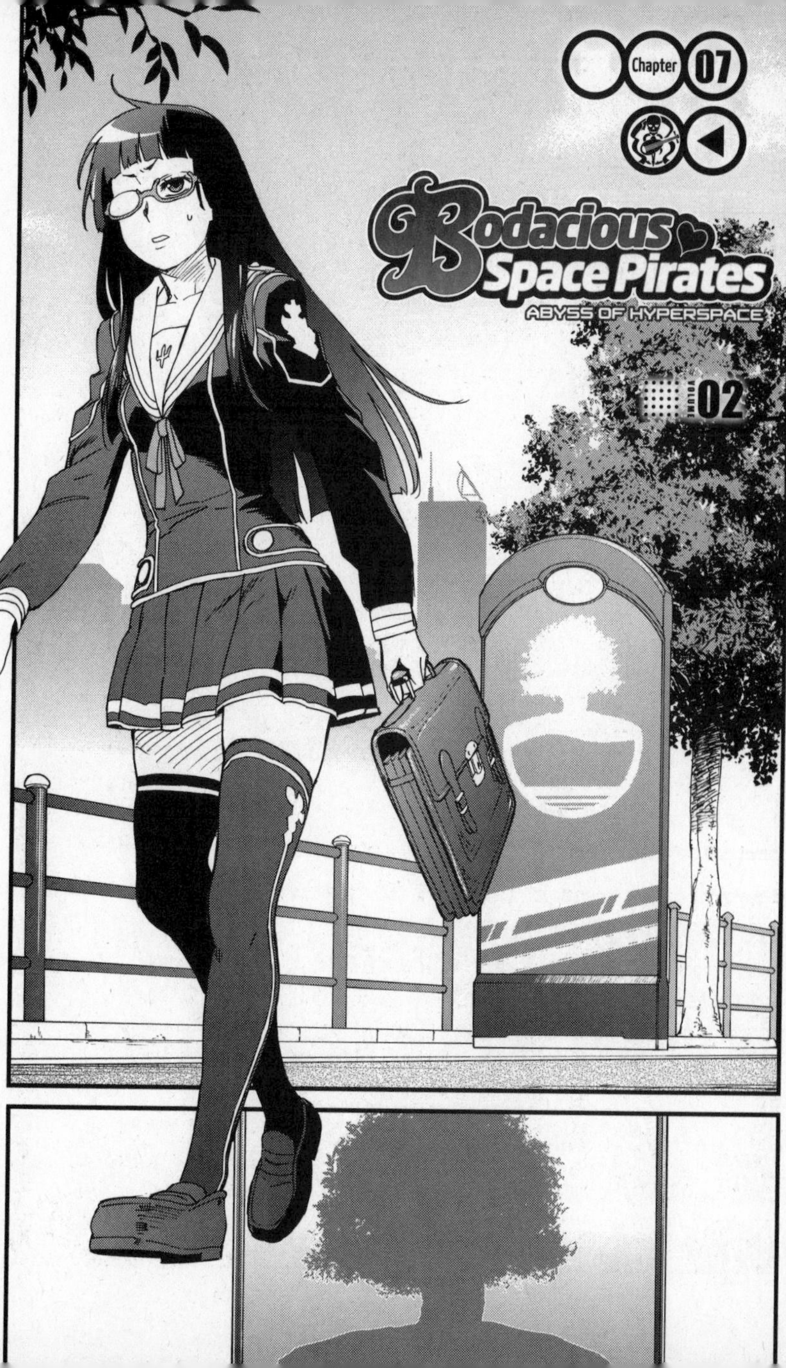
Chapter 07
Bodacious Space Pirates
ABYSS OF HYPERSPACE
VOLUME 02

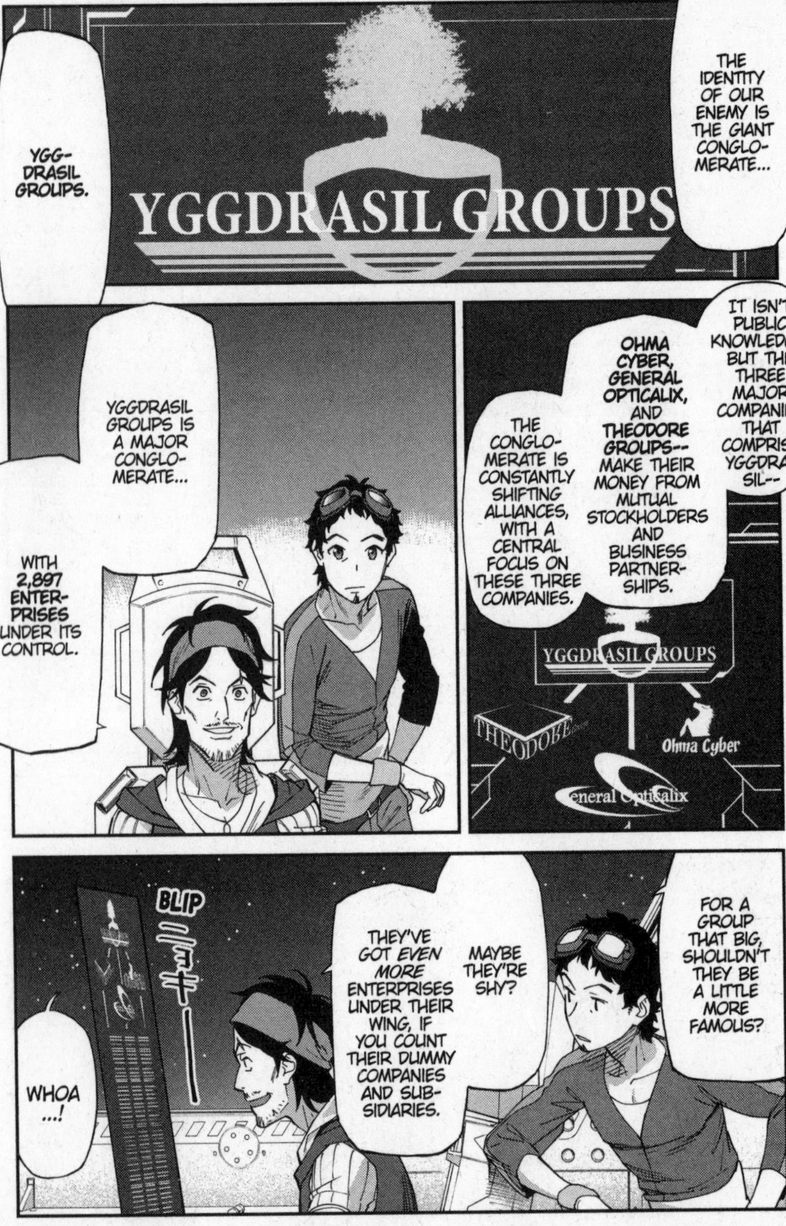
THE IDENTITY OF OUR ENEMY IS THE GIANT CONGLOMERATE...
YGGDRASIL GROUPS
YGG-DRASIL GROUPS.
IT ISN'T PUBLIC KNOWLEDGE, BUT THE THREE MAJOR COMPANIES THAT COMPRISE YGGDRA-SIL--
OHMA CYBER, GENERAL OPTICALIX, AND THEODORE GROUPS-- MAKE THEIR MONEY FROM MUTUAL STOCKHOLDERS AND BUSINESS PARTNER-SHIPS.
THE CONGLO-MERATE IS CONSTANTLY SHIFTING ALLIANCES, WITH A CENTRAL FOCUS ON THESE THREE COMPANIES.
YGGDRASIL GROUPS
THEODORE
Ohma Cyber
eneral Opticalix
YGGDRASIL GROUPS IS A MAJOR CONGLO-MERATE...
WITH 2,897 ENTER-PRISES UNDER ITS CONTROL.
FOR A GROUP THAT BIG, SHOULDN'T THEY BE A LITTLE MORE FAMOUS?
MAYBE THEY'RE SHY?
THEY'VE GOT *EVEN MORE* ENTERPRISES UNDER THEIR WING, IF YOU COUNT THEIR DUMMY COMPANIES AND SUB-SIDIARIES.
BLIP
WHOA ...!

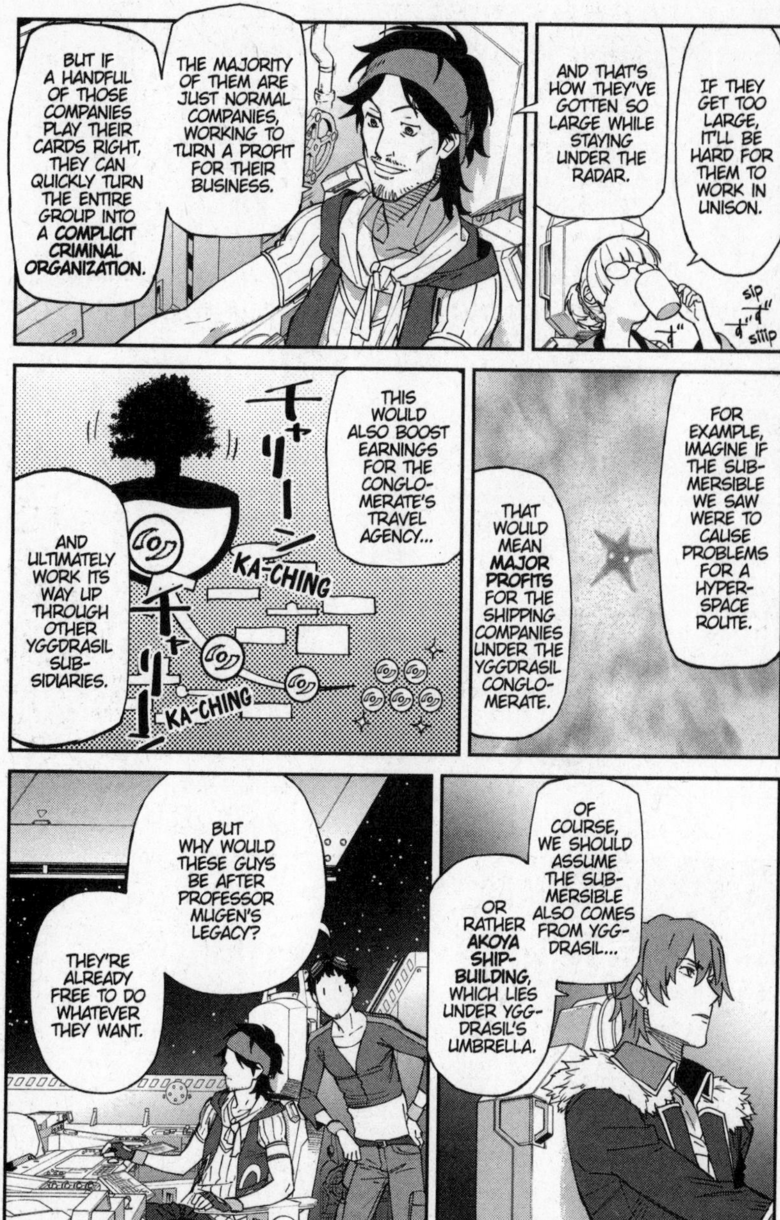
IF THEY GET TOO LARGE, IT'LL BE HARD FOR THEM TO WORK IN UNISON.
AND THAT'S HOW THEY'VE GOTTEN SO LARGE WHILE STAYING UNDER THE RADAR.
sip
siiip
THE MAJORITY OF THEM ARE JUST NORMAL COMPANIES, WORKING TO TURN A PROFIT FOR THEIR BUSINESS.
BUT IF A HANDFUL OF THOSE COMPANIES PLAY THEIR CARDS RIGHT, THEY CAN QUICKLY TURN THE ENTIRE GROUP INTO A **COMPLICIT CRIMINAL ORGANIZATION.**
FOR EXAMPLE, IMAGINE IF THE SUBMERSIBLE WE SAW WERE TO CAUSE PROBLEMS FOR A HYPERSPACE ROUTE.
THAT WOULD MEAN **MAJOR PROFITS** FOR THE SHIPPING COMPANIES UNDER THE YGGDRASIL CONGLOMERATE.
THIS WOULD ALSO BOOST EARNINGS FOR THE CONGLOMERATE'S TRAVEL AGENCY...
チャリーン
KA-CHING
AND ULTIMATELY WORK ITS WAY UP THROUGH OTHER YGGDRASIL SUBSIDIARIES.
KA-CHING
OF COURSE, WE SHOULD ASSUME THE SUBMERSIBLE ALSO COMES FROM YGGDRASIL...
OR RATHER **AKOYA SHIPBUILDING,** WHICH LIES UNDER YGGDRASIL'S UMBRELLA.
BUT WHY WOULD THESE GUYS BE AFTER PROFESSOR MUGEN'S LEGACY?
THEY'RE ALREADY FREE TO DO WHATEVER THEY WANT.

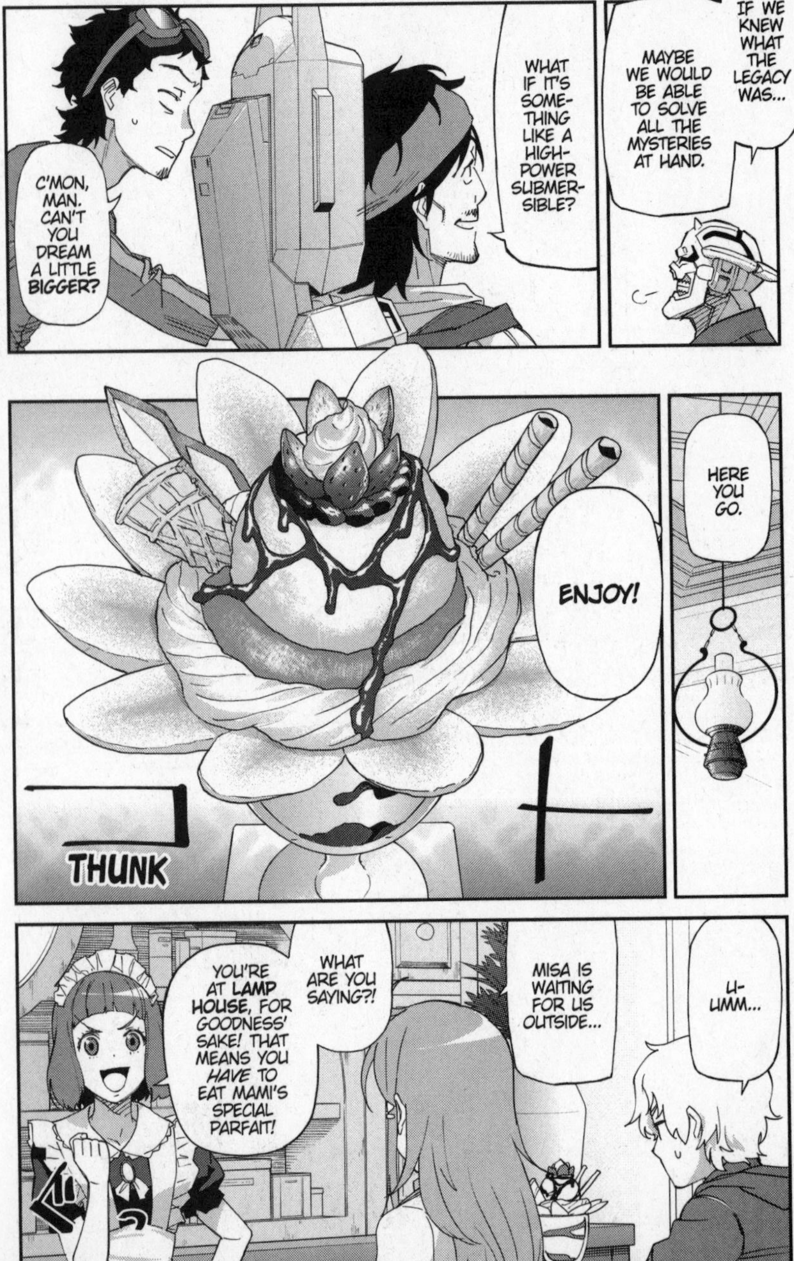
IF WE KNEW WHAT THE LEGACY WAS...
MAYBE WE WOULD BE ABLE TO SOLVE ALL THE MYSTERIES AT HAND.
WHAT IF IT'S SOMETHING LIKE A HIGH-POWER SUBMERSIBLE?
C'MON, MAN. CAN'T YOU DREAM A LITTLE BIGGER?
HERE YOU GO.
ENJOY!
THUNK
U-UMM...
MISA IS WAITING FOR US OUTSIDE...
WHAT ARE YOU SAYING?!
YOU'RE AT **LAMP HOUSE**, FOR GOODNESS' SAKE! THAT MEANS YOU *HAVE* TO EAT MAMI'S SPECIAL PARFAIT!

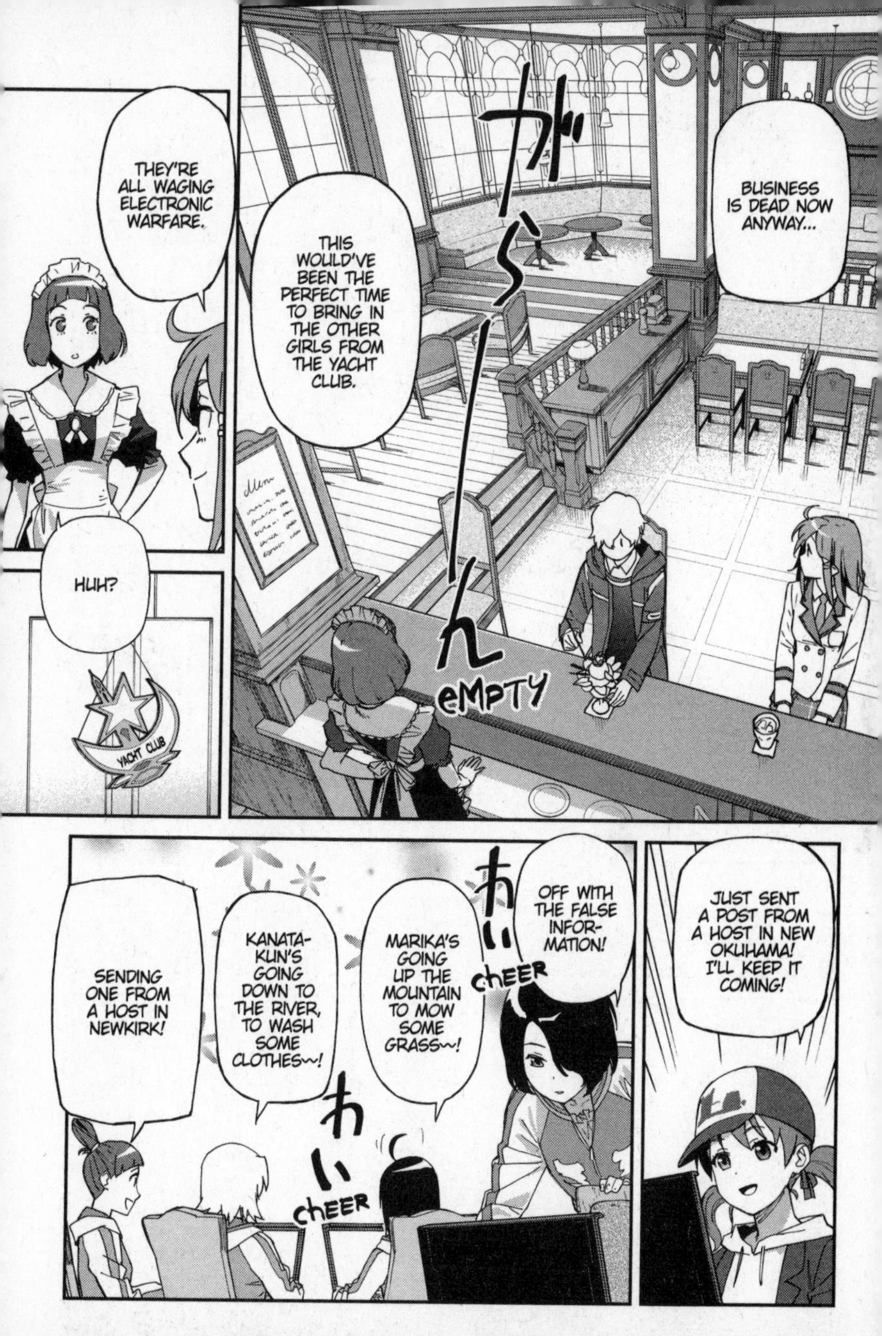
BUSINESS IS DEAD NOW ANYWAY...
EMPTY
THIS WOULD'VE BEEN THE PERFECT TIME TO BRING IN THE OTHER GIRLS FROM THE YACHT CLUB.
THEY'RE ALL WAGING ELECTRONIC WARFARE.
HUH?
YACHT CLUB
JUST SENT A POST FROM A HOST IN NEW OKUHAMA! I'LL KEEP IT COMING!
OFF WITH THE FALSE INFORMATION!
CHEER
MARIKA'S GOING UP THE MOUNTAIN TO MOW SOME GRASS~!
KANATA-KUN'S GOING DOWN TO THE RIVER, TO WASH SOME CLOTHES~!
CHEER
SENDING ONE FROM A HOST IN NEWKIRK!

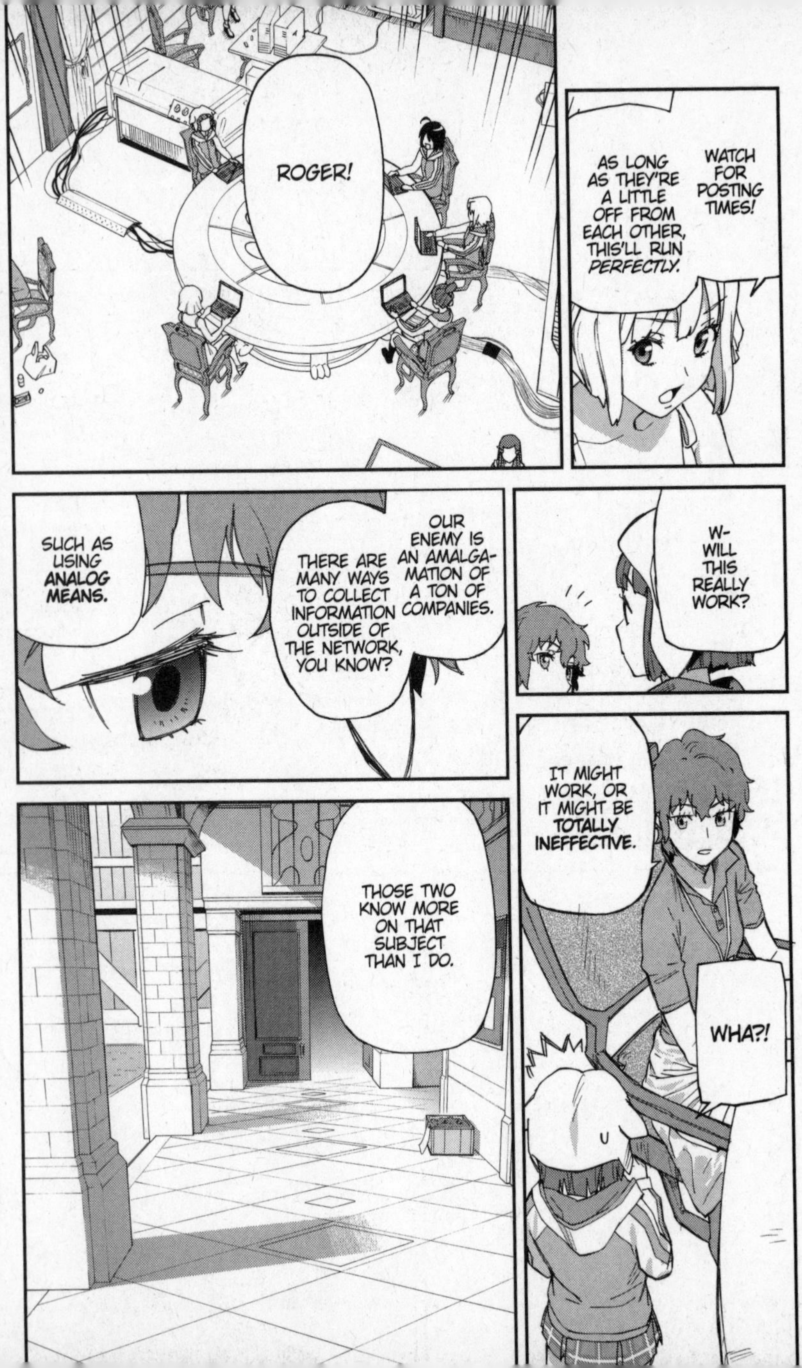
WATCH FOR POSTING TIMES!
AS LONG AS THEY'RE A LITTLE OFF FROM EACH OTHER, THIS'LL RUN *PERFECTLY.*
ROGER!
W-WILL THIS REALLY WORK?
OUR ENEMY IS AN AMALGAMATION OF A TON OF COMPANIES.
THERE ARE MANY WAYS TO COLLECT INFORMATION OUTSIDE OF THE NETWORK, YOU KNOW?
SUCH AS USING **ANALOG MEANS.**
IT MIGHT WORK, OR IT MIGHT BE **TOTALLY INEFFECTIVE.**
WHA?!
THOSE TWO KNOW MORE ON THAT SUBJECT THAN I DO.

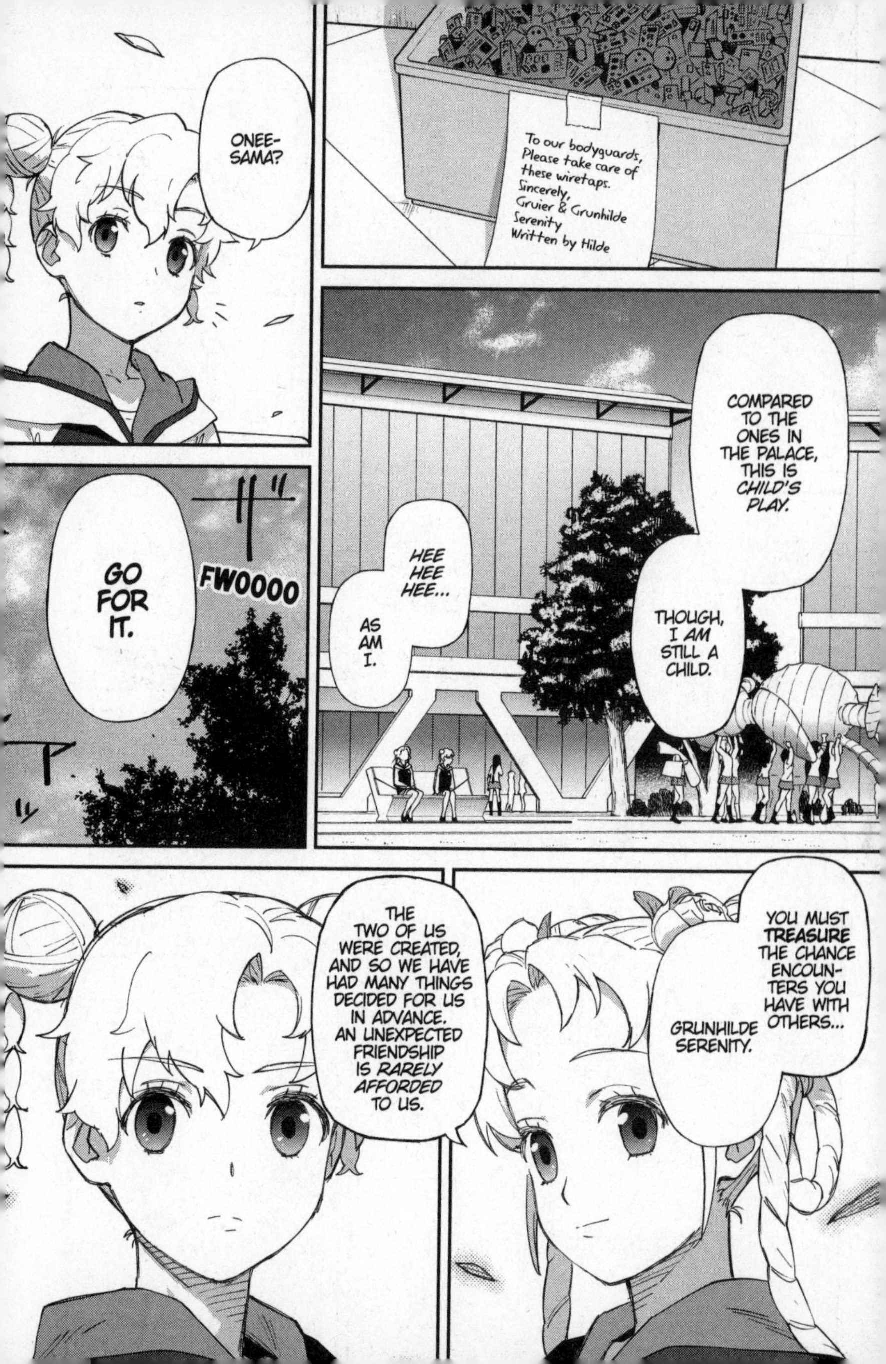
To our bodyguards,
Please take care of
these wiretaps.
Sincerely,
Gruier & Grunhilde
Serenity
Written by Hilde
ONEE-SAMA?
COMPARED TO THE ONES IN THE PALACE, THIS IS CHILD'S PLAY.
THOUGH, I AM STILL A CHILD.
HEE HEE HEE...
AS AM I.
GO FOR IT.
FWOOOO
YOU MUST TREASURE THE CHANCE ENCOUNTERS YOU HAVE WITH OTHERS...
GRUNHILDE SERENITY.
THE TWO OF US WERE CREATED, AND SO WE HAVE HAD MANY THINGS DECIDED FOR US IN ADVANCE. AN UNEXPECTED FRIENDSHIP IS RARELY AFFORDED TO US.

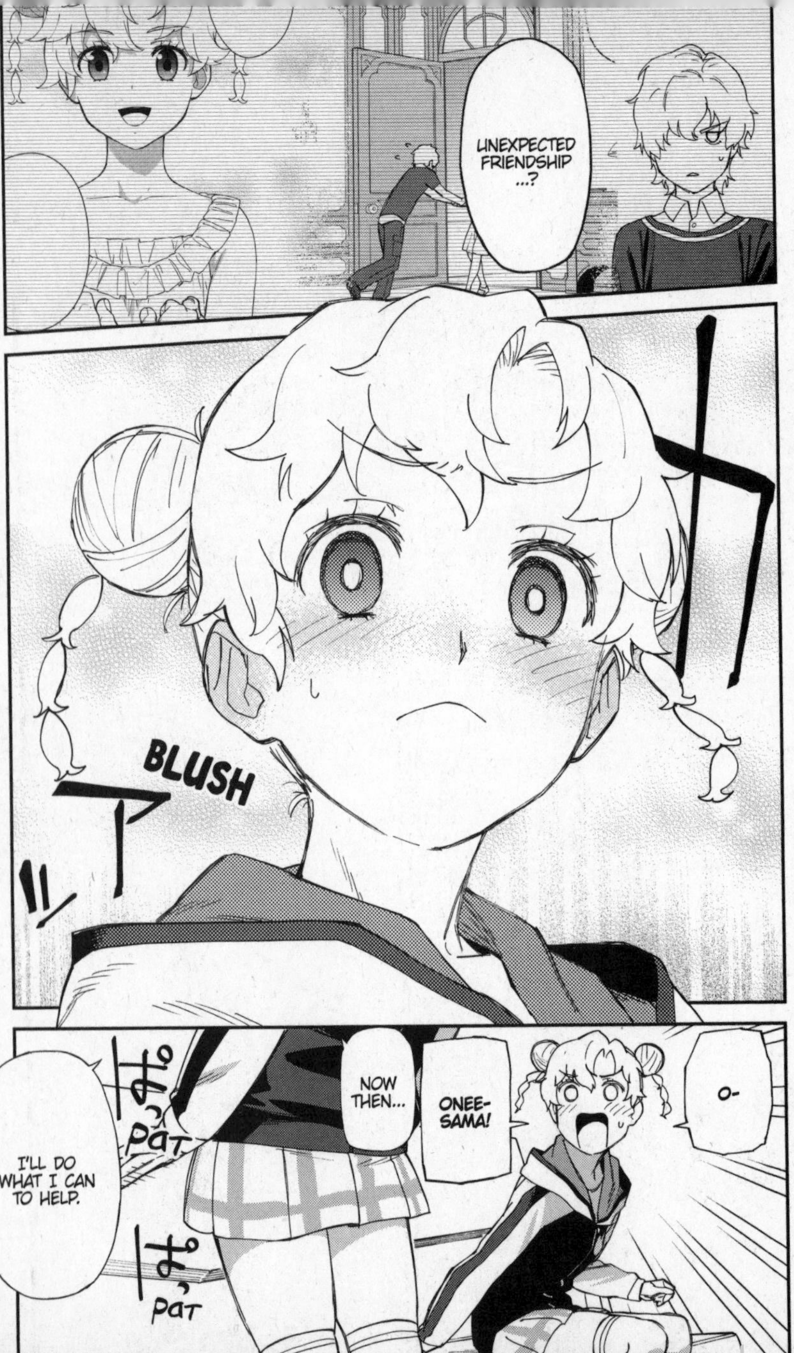
UNEXPECTED FRIENDSHIP ...?
BLUSH
O-
ONEE-SAMA!
NOW THEN...
ぱっ PAT
I'LL DO WHAT I CAN TO HELP.
ぱっ PAT

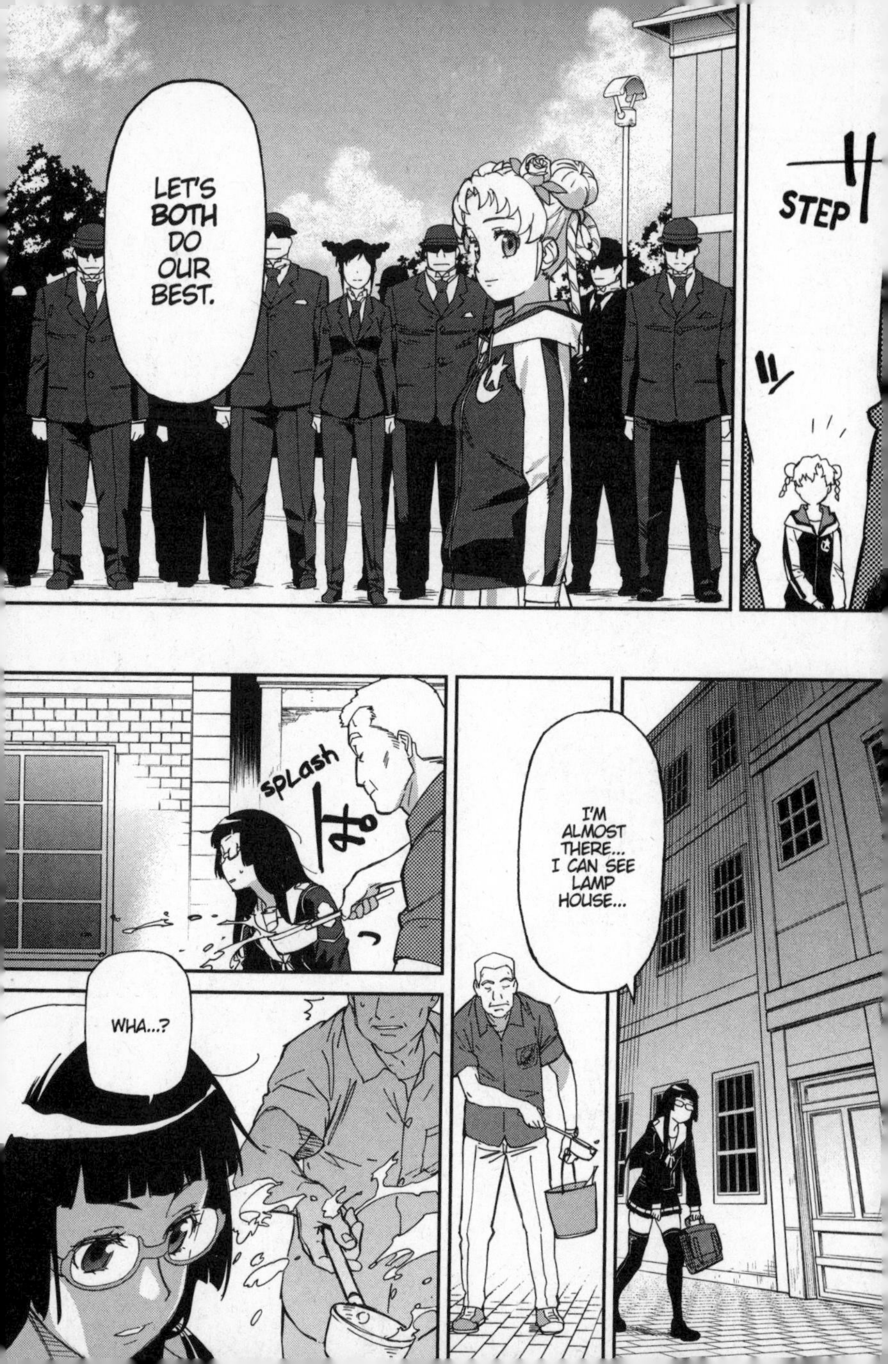
STEP
LET'S BOTH DO OUR BEST.
I'M ALMOST THERE... I CAN SEE LAMP HOUSE...
splash
WHA...?

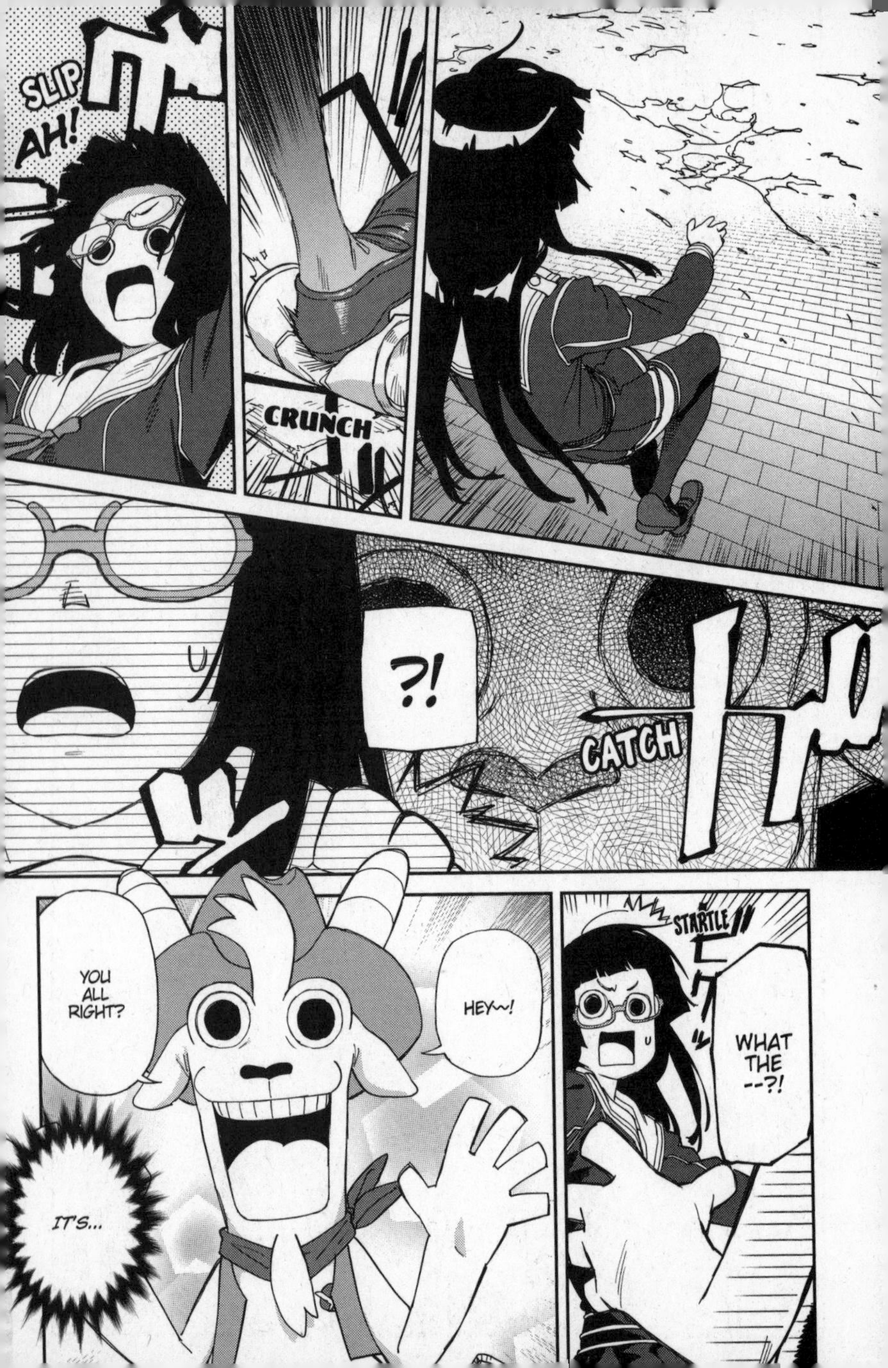
CRUNCH
SLIP
AH!
?!
CATCH
STARTLE
WHAT THE --?!
HEY~~!
YOU ALL RIGHT?
IT'S...

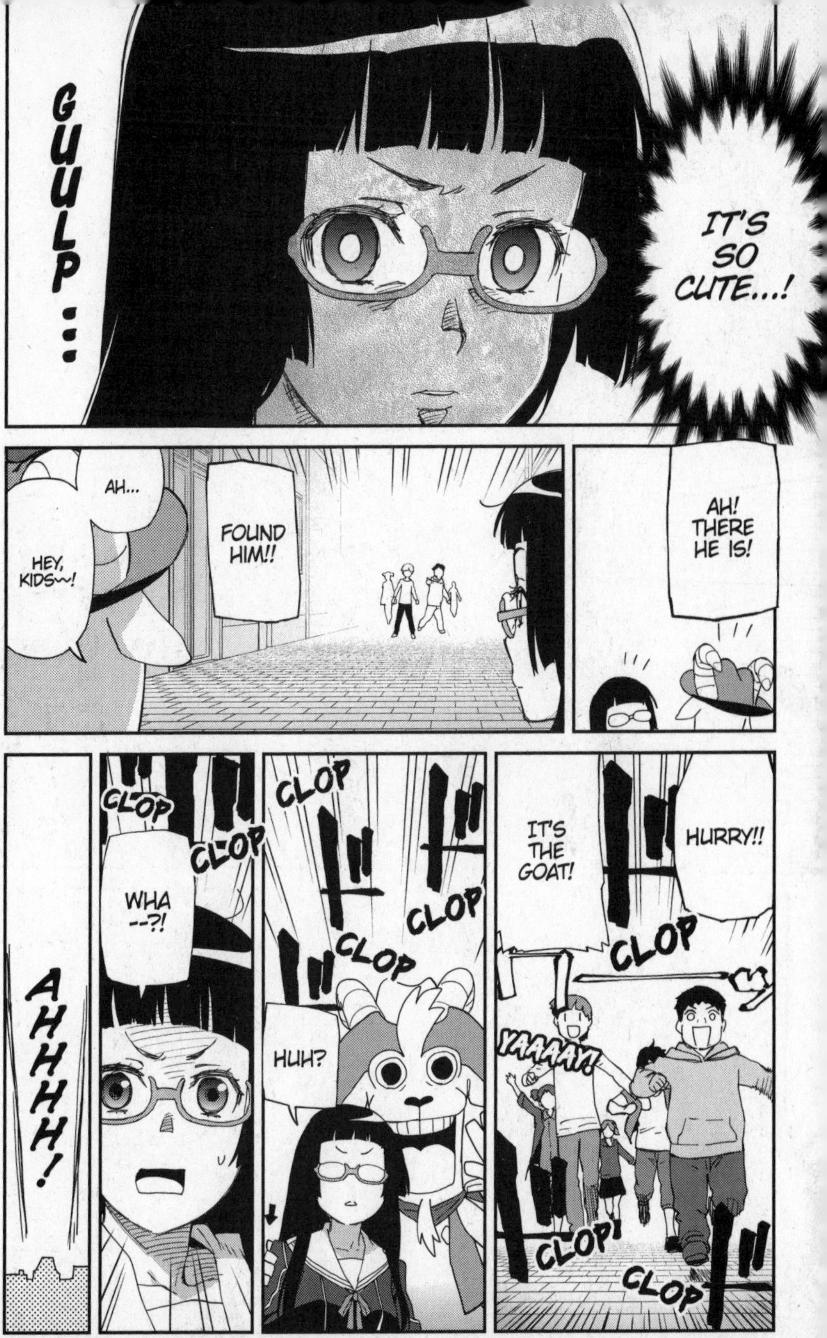

IT'S SO CUTE...!
GUULP...
AH! THERE HE IS!
FOUND HIM!!
AH...
HEY, KIDS~!
HURRY!!
IT'S THE GOAT!
CLOP
YAAAAY!
CLOP
CLOP
CLOP
CLOP
CLOP
HUH?
CLOP
CLOP
WHA--?!
AHHHH!

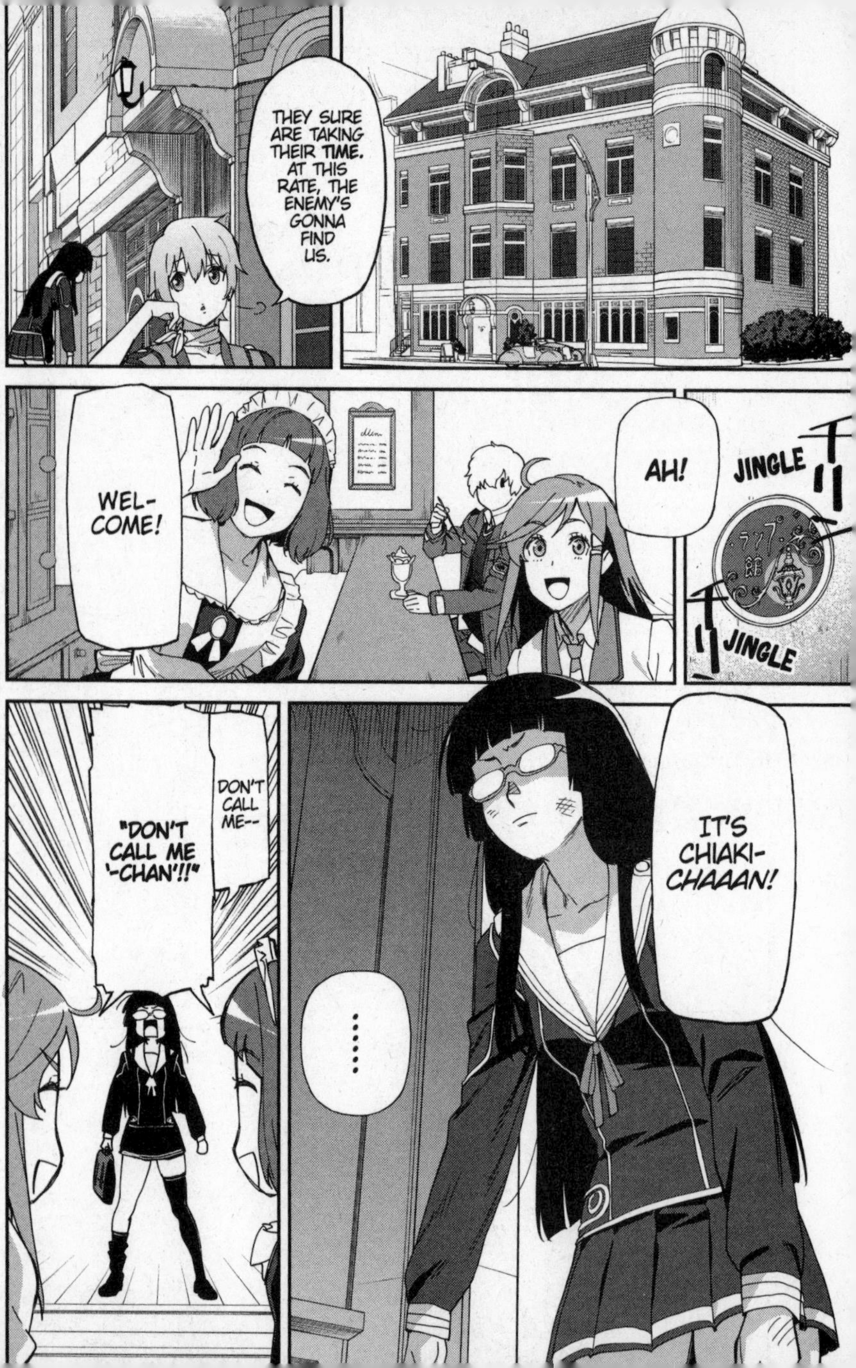
THEY SURE ARE TAKING THEIR TIME. AT THIS RATE, THE ENEMY'S GONNA FIND US.
JINGLE
JINGLE
AH!
WEL-COME!
IT'S CHIAKI-CHAAAN!
......
DON'T CALL ME--
"DON'T CALL ME '-CHAN'!!"

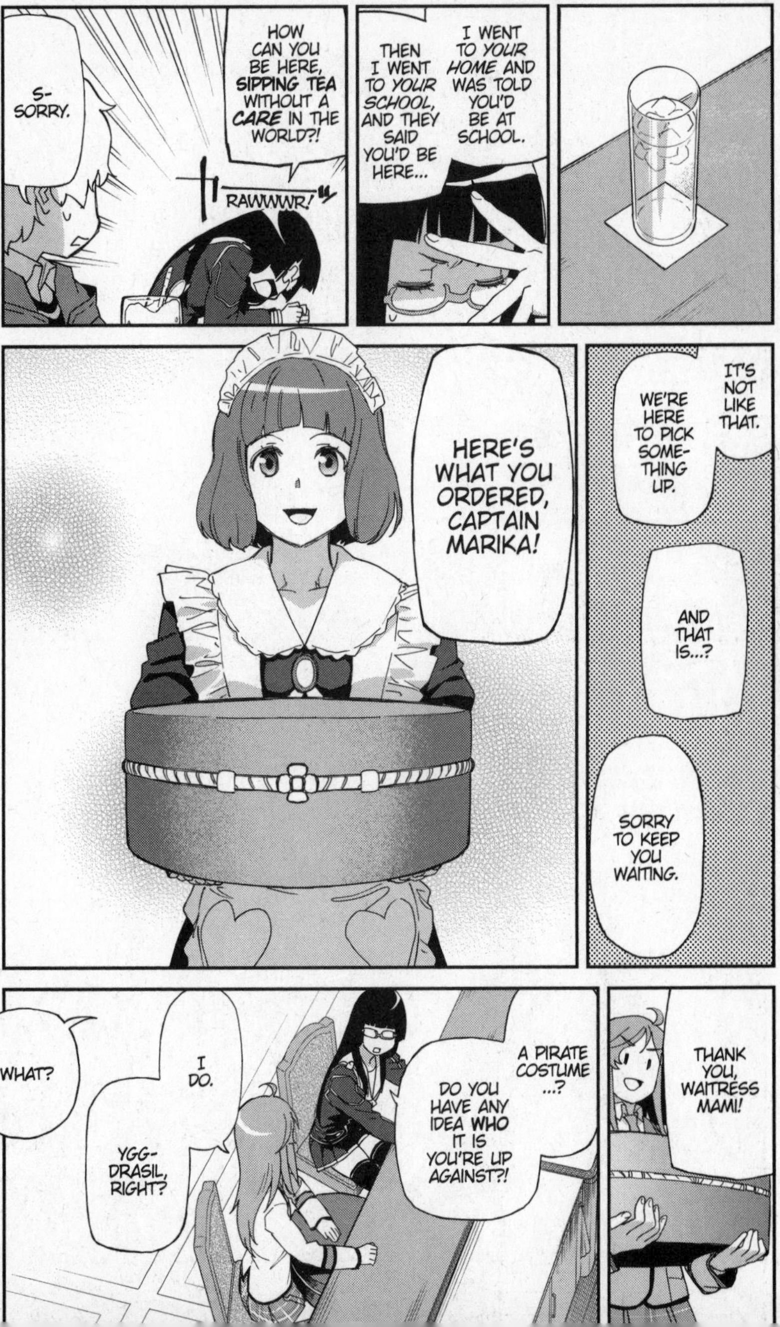
I WENT TO YOUR HOME AND WAS TOLD YOU'D BE AT SCHOOL.
THEN I WENT TO YOUR SCHOOL, AND THEY SAID YOU'D BE HERE...
HOW CAN YOU BE HERE, SIPPING TEA WITHOUT A CARE IN THE WORLD?!
RAWWWR!
S-SORRY.
IT'S NOT LIKE THAT.
WE'RE HERE TO PICK SOME-THING UP.
AND THAT IS...?
SORRY TO KEEP YOU WAITING.
HERE'S WHAT YOU ORDERED, CAPTAIN MARIKA!
THANK YOU, WAITRESS MAMI!
A PIRATE COSTUME ...?
DO YOU HAVE ANY IDEA WHO IT IS YOU'RE UP AGAINST?!
I DO.
YGG-DRASIL, RIGHT?
WHAT?

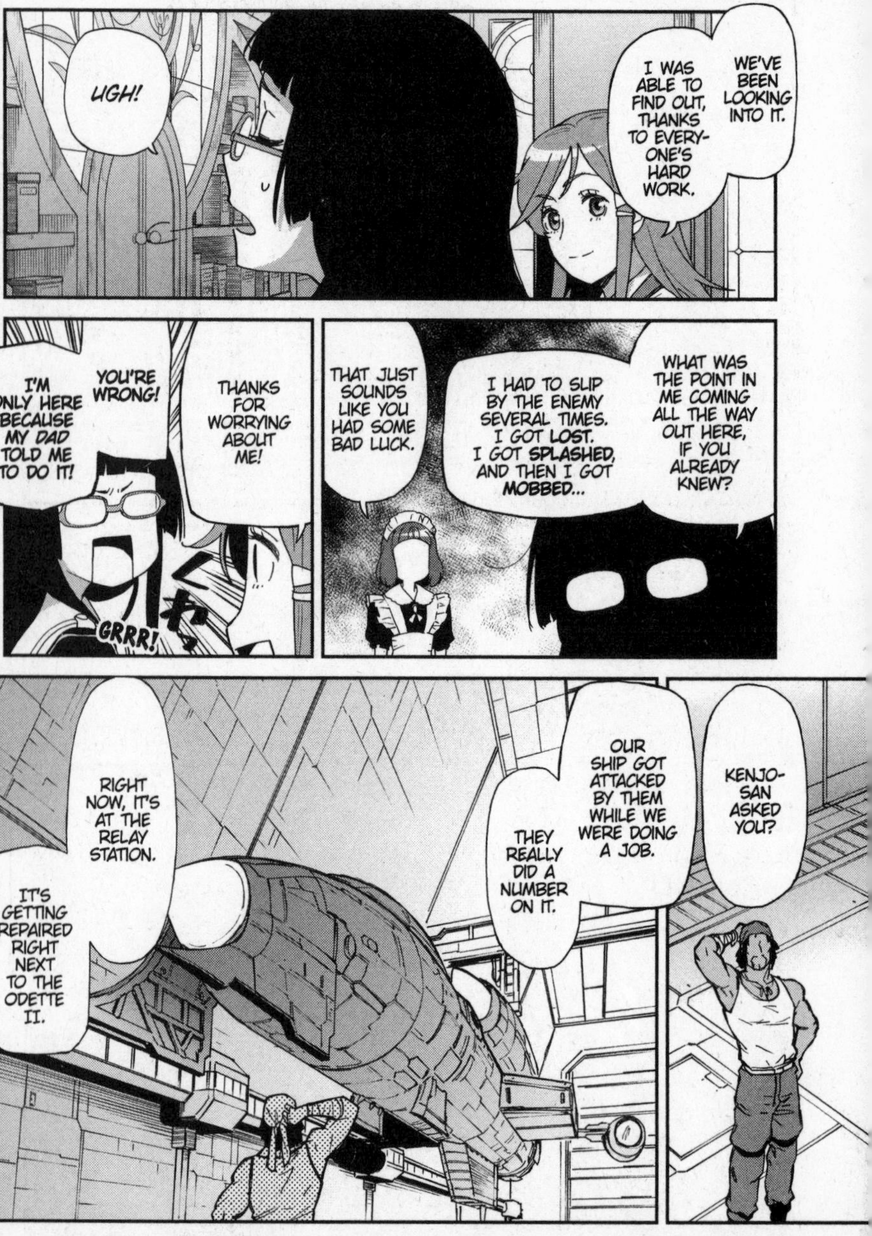
WE'VE BEEN LOOKING INTO IT.
I WAS ABLE TO FIND OUT, THANKS TO EVERYONE'S HARD WORK.
UGH!
WHAT WAS THE POINT IN ME COMING ALL THE WAY OUT HERE, IF YOU ALREADY KNEW?
I HAD TO SLIP BY THE ENEMY SEVERAL TIMES. I GOT LOST. I GOT SPLASHED, AND THEN I GOT MOBBED...
THAT JUST SOUNDS LIKE YOU HAD SOME BAD LUCK.
THANKS FOR WORRYING ABOUT ME!
YOU'RE WRONG!
I'M ONLY HERE BECAUSE MY DAD TOLD ME TO DO IT!
GRRR!
KENJO-SAN ASKED YOU?
OUR SHIP GOT ATTACKED BY THEM WHILE WE WERE DOING A JOB.
THEY REALLY DID A NUMBER ON IT.
RIGHT NOW, IT'S AT THE RELAY STATION.
IT'S GETTING REPAIRED RIGHT NEXT TO THE ODETTE II.

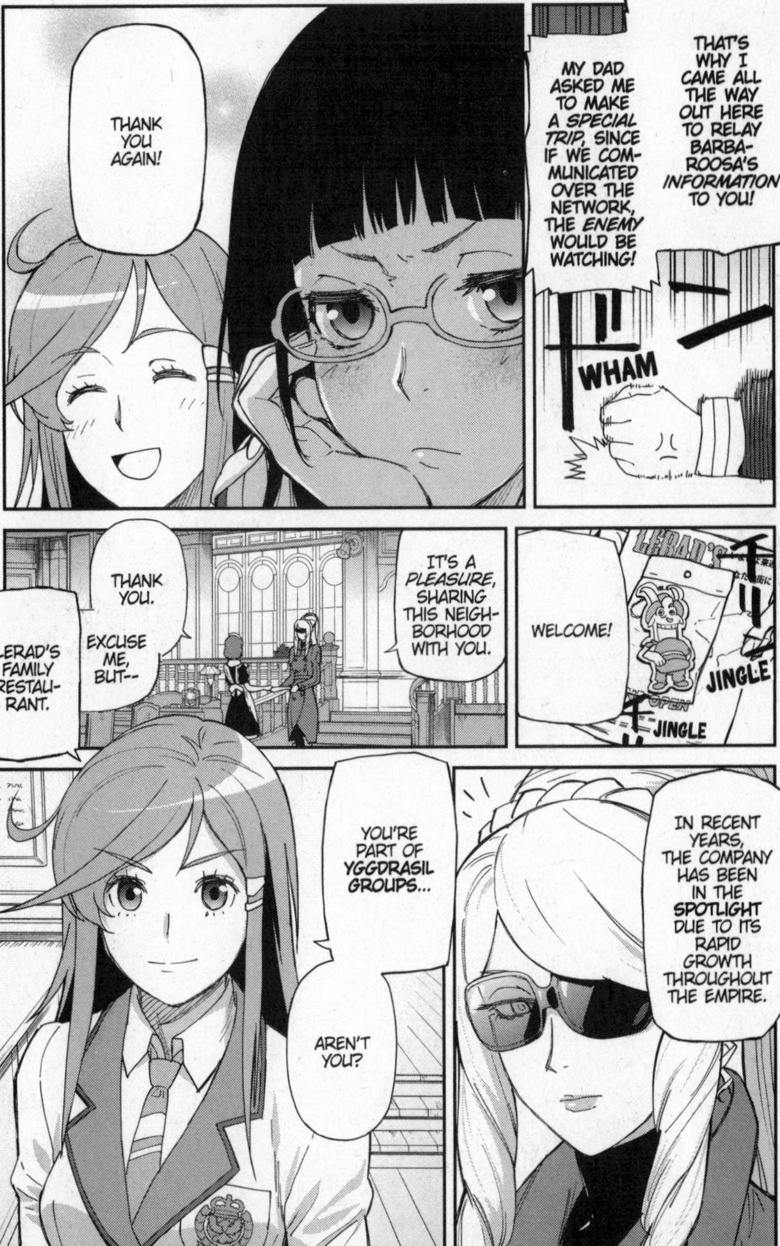
THAT'S WHY I CAME ALL THE WAY OUT HERE TO RELAY BARBAROOSA'S INFORMATION TO YOU!
MY DAD ASKED ME TO MAKE A SPECIAL TRIP, SINCE IF WE COMMUNICATED OVER THE NETWORK, THE ENEMY WOULD BE WATCHING!
WHAM
THANK YOU AGAIN!
LERAD'S
JINGLE
JINGLE
OPEN
WELCOME!
IT'S A PLEASURE, SHARING THIS NEIGHBORHOOD WITH YOU.
THANK YOU.
EXCUSE ME, BUT--
LERAD'S FAMILY RESTAURANT.
IN RECENT YEARS, THE COMPANY HAS BEEN IN THE SPOTLIGHT DUE TO ITS RAPID GROWTH THROUGHOUT THE EMPIRE.
YOU'RE PART OF YGGDRASIL GROUPS...
AREN'T YOU?

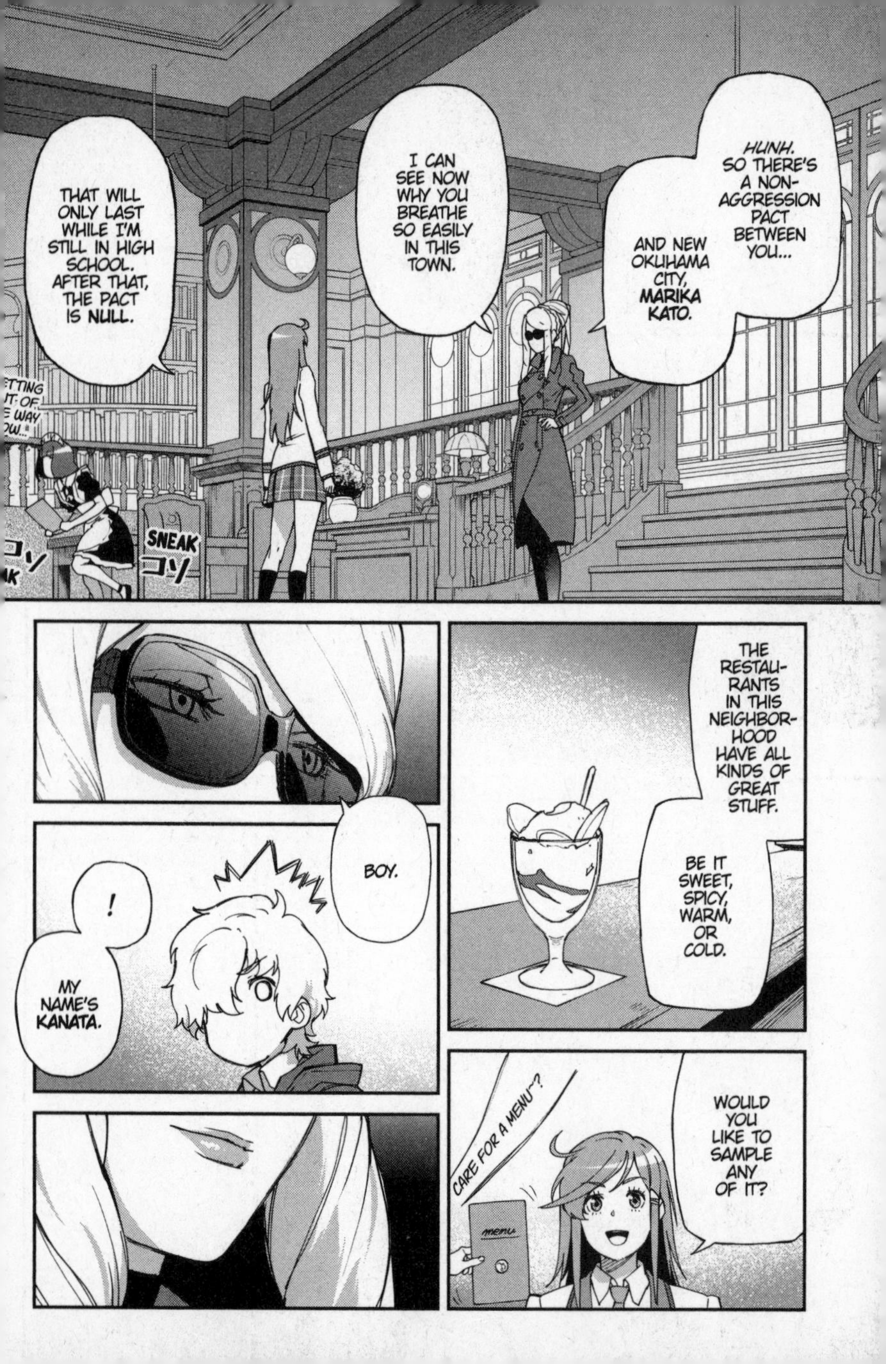
HUNH. SO THERE'S A NON-AGGRESSION PACT BETWEEN YOU...
AND NEW OKUHAMA CITY, MARIKA KATO.
I CAN SEE NOW WHY YOU BREATHE SO EASILY IN THIS TOWN.
THAT WILL ONLY LAST WHILE I'M STILL IN HIGH SCHOOL. AFTER THAT, THE PACT IS NULL.
SNEAK
コソ
コソ
THE RESTAURANTS IN THIS NEIGHBORHOOD HAVE ALL KINDS OF GREAT STUFF.
BE IT SWEET, SPICY, WARM, OR COLD.
BOY.
!
MY NAME'S KANATA.
WOULD YOU LIKE TO SAMPLE ANY OF IT?
CARE FOR A MENU~?
menu

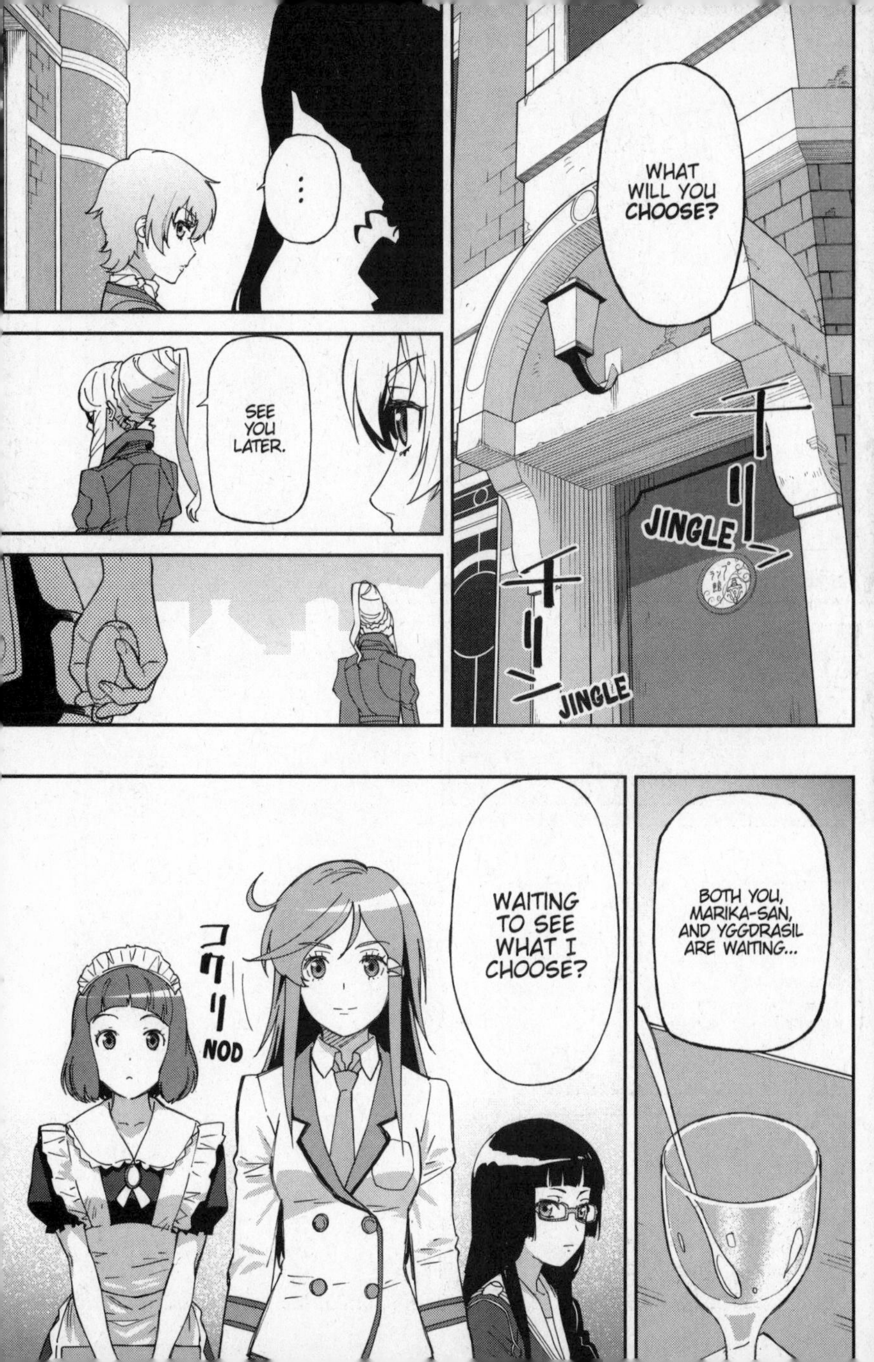
WHAT WILL YOU CHOOSE?
JINGLE
JINGLE
...
SEE YOU LATER.
BOTH YOU, MARIKA-SAN, AND YGGDRASIL ARE WAITING...
WAITING TO SEE WHAT I CHOOSE?
NOD

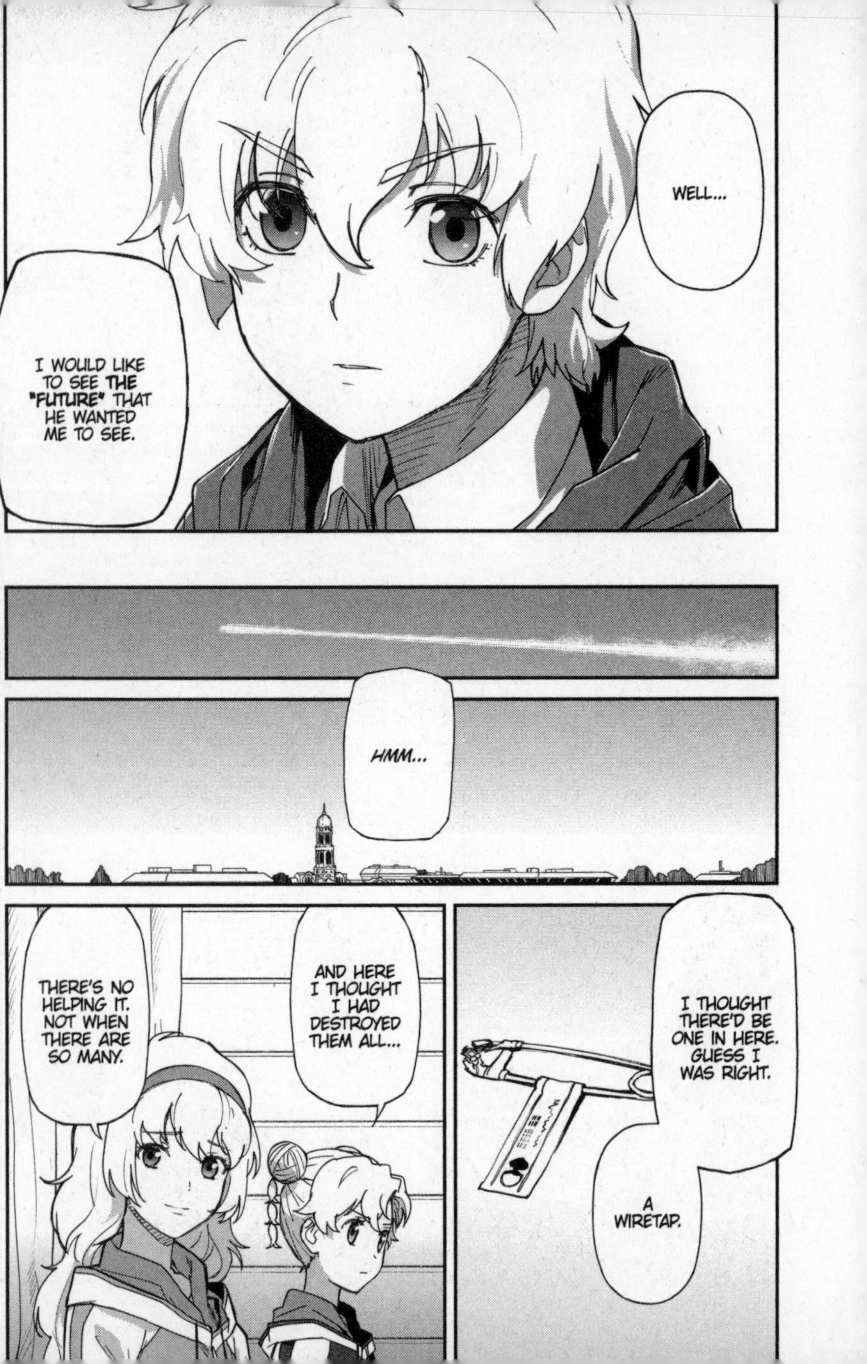
WELL...
I WOULD LIKE TO SEE THE "FUTURE" THAT HE WANTED ME TO SEE.
HMM...
I THOUGHT THERE'D BE ONE IN HERE. GUESS I WAS RIGHT.
A WIRETAP.
AND HERE I THOUGHT I HAD DESTROYED THEM ALL...
THERE'S NO HELPING IT. NOT WHEN THERE ARE SO MANY.

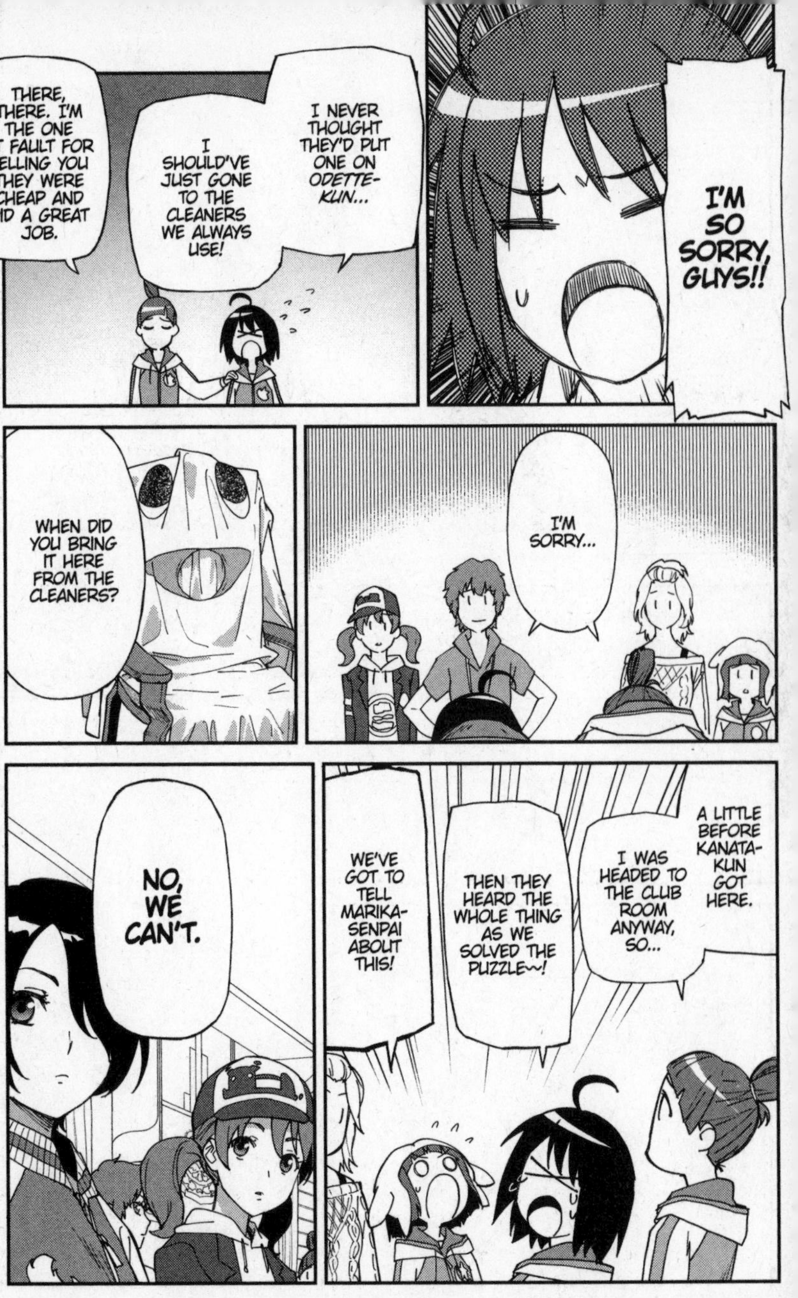
I'M SO SORRY, GUYS!!
I NEVER THOUGHT THEY'D PUT ONE ON ODETTE-KUN...
I SHOULD'VE JUST GONE TO THE CLEANERS WE ALWAYS USE!
THERE, THERE. I'M THE ONE AT FAULT FOR TELLING YOU THEY WERE CHEAP AND DID A GREAT JOB.
I'M SORRY...
WHEN DID YOU BRING IT HERE FROM THE CLEANERS?
A LITTLE BEFORE KANATA-KUN GOT HERE.
I WAS HEADED TO THE CLUB ROOM ANYWAY, SO...
THEN THEY HEARD THE WHOLE THING AS WE SOLVED THE PUZZLE~!
WE'VE GOT TO TELL MARIKA-SENPAI ABOUT THIS!
NO, WE CAN'T.

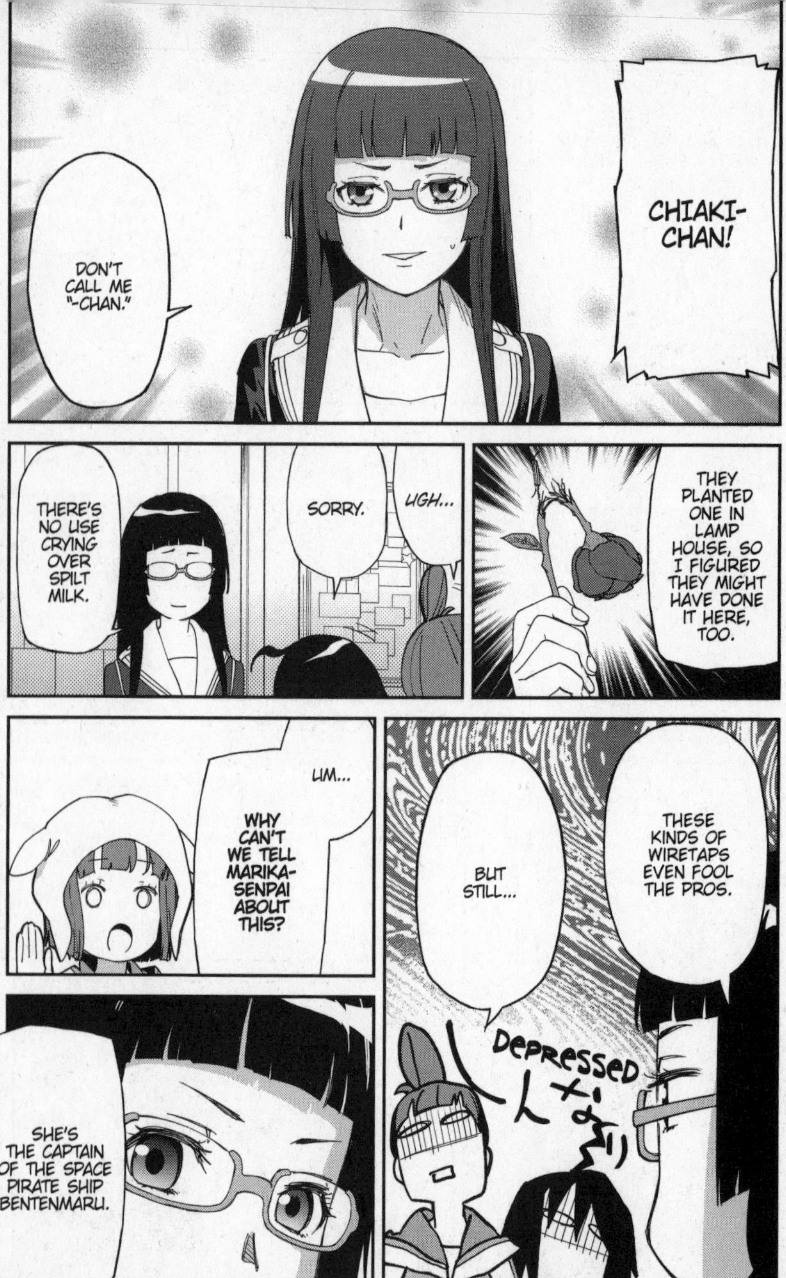
CHIAKI-CHAN!
DON'T CALL ME "-CHAN."
THEY PLANTED ONE IN LAMP HOUSE, SO I FIGURED THEY MIGHT HAVE DONE IT HERE, TOO.
UGH...
SORRY.
THERE'S NO USE CRYING OVER SPILT MILK.
THESE KINDS OF WIRETAPS EVEN FOOL THE PROS.
BUT STILL...
Depressed
UM...
WHY CAN'T WE TELL MARIKA-SENPAI ABOUT THIS?
SHE'S THE CAPTAIN OF THE SPACE PIRATE SHIP BENTENMARU.

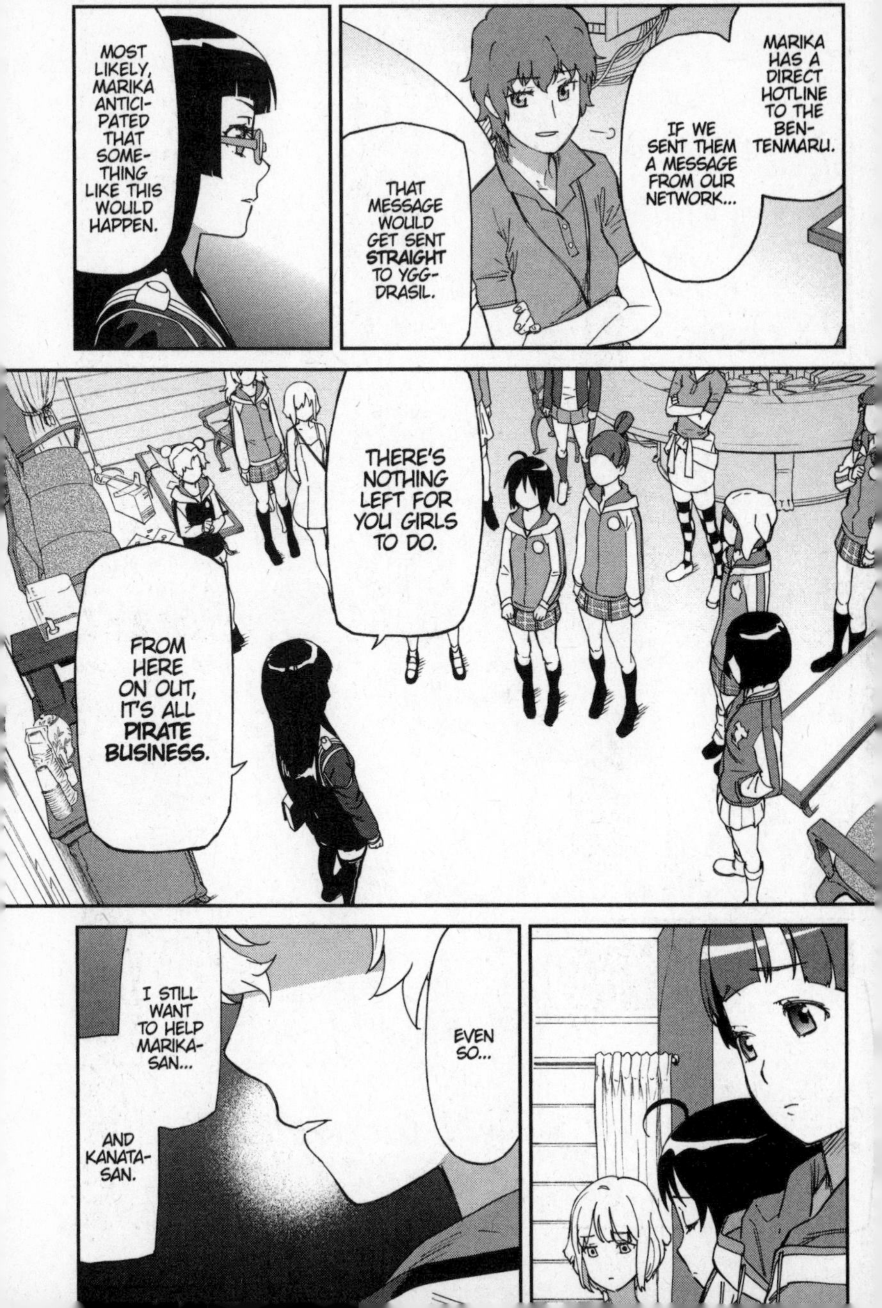
MARIKA HAS A DIRECT HOTLINE TO THE BEN-TENMARU.
IF WE SENT THEM A MESSAGE FROM OUR NETWORK...
THAT MESSAGE WOULD GET SENT STRAIGHT TO YGG-DRASIL.
MOST LIKELY, MARIKA ANTICI-PATED THAT SOME-THING LIKE THIS WOULD HAPPEN.
THERE'S NOTHING LEFT FOR YOU GIRLS TO DO.
FROM HERE ON OUT, IT'S ALL PIRATE BUSINESS.
EVEN SO...
I STILL WANT TO HELP MARIKA-SAN...
AND KANATA-SAN.

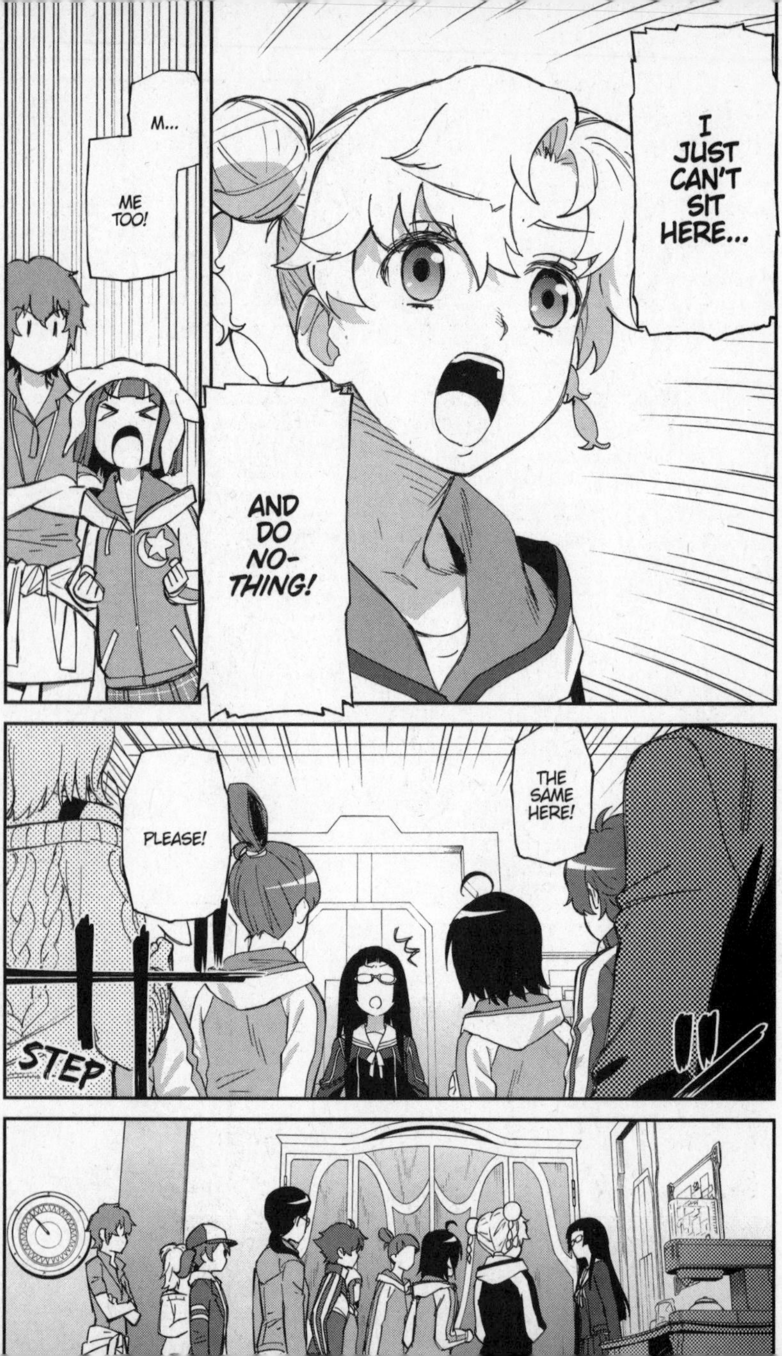
I JUST CAN'T SIT HERE...
AND DO NO-THING!
M...
ME TOO!
THE SAME HERE!
PLEASE!
STEP

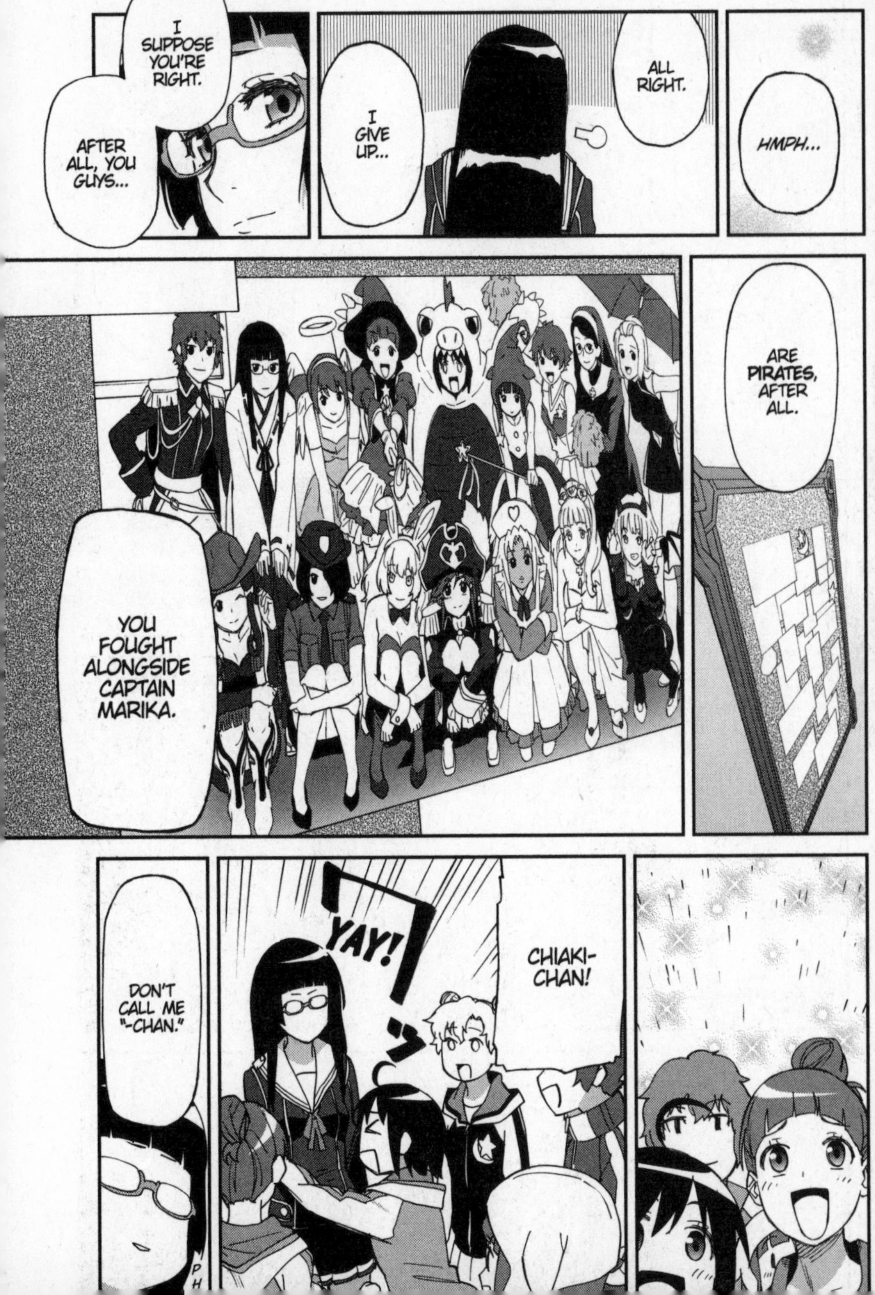
HMPH...
ALL RIGHT.
I GIVE UP...
I SUPPOSE YOU'RE RIGHT.
AFTER ALL, YOU GUYS...
ARE PIRATES, AFTER ALL.
YOU FOUGHT ALONGSIDE CAPTAIN MARIKA.
CHIAKI-CHAN!
YAY!
DON'T CALL ME "-CHAN."

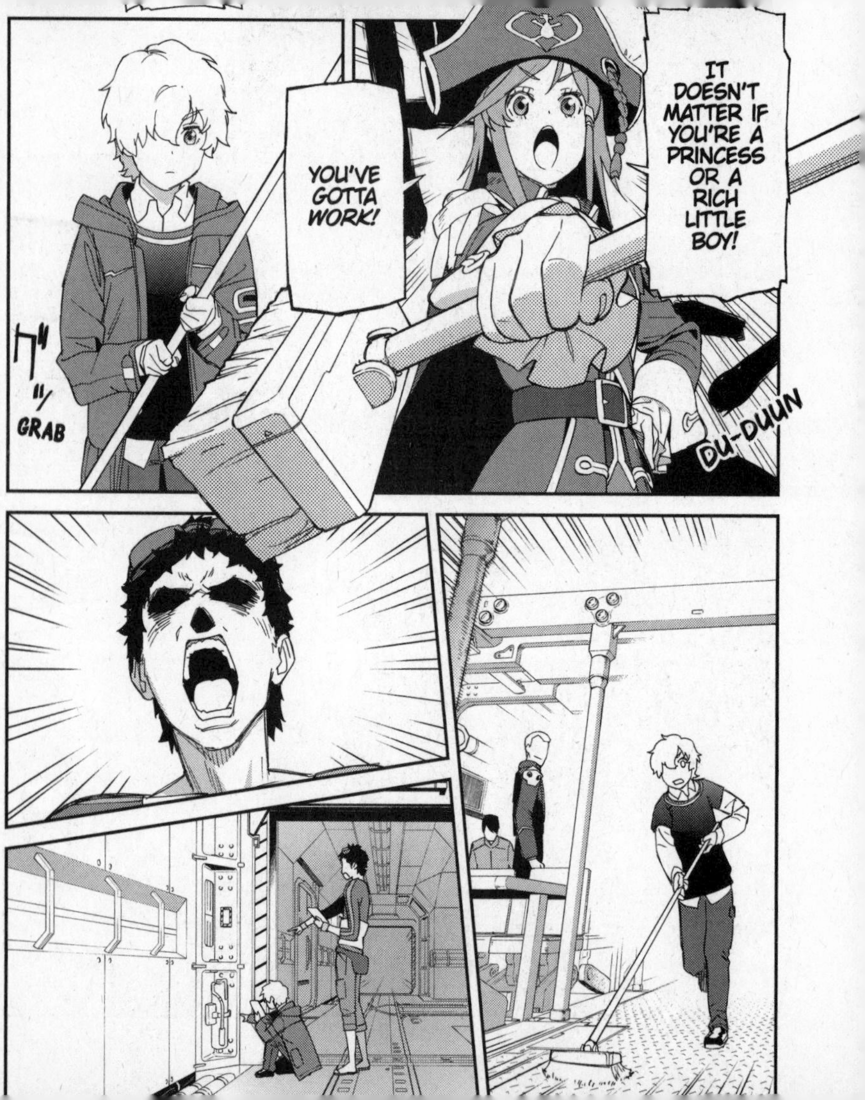
IT DOESN'T MATTER IF YOU'RE A PRINCESS OR A RICH LITTLE BOY!
YOU'VE GOTTA WORK!
DU-DUUN
GRAB

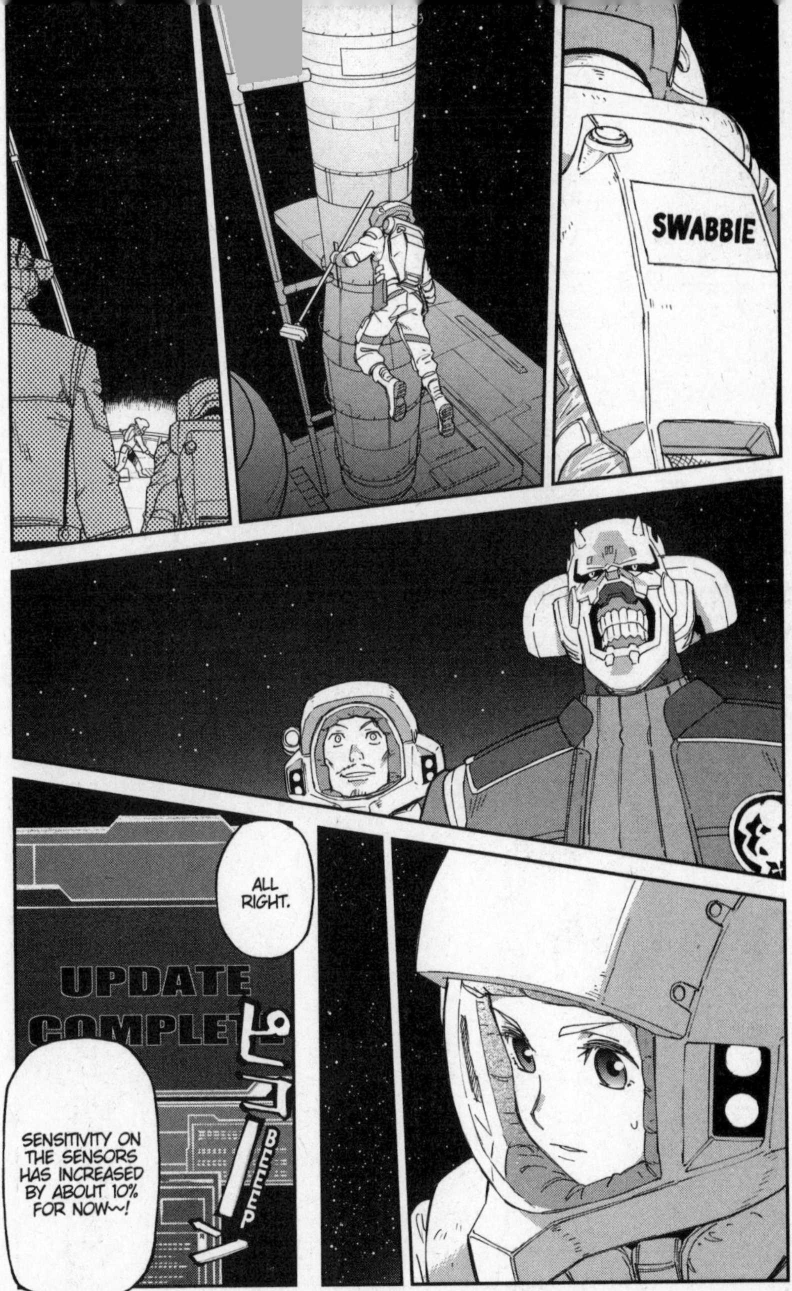
SWABBIE
ALL RIGHT.
UPDATE
COMPLET
BEEEP
SENSITIVITY ON THE SENSORS HAS INCREASED BY ABOUT 10% FOR NOW~~!

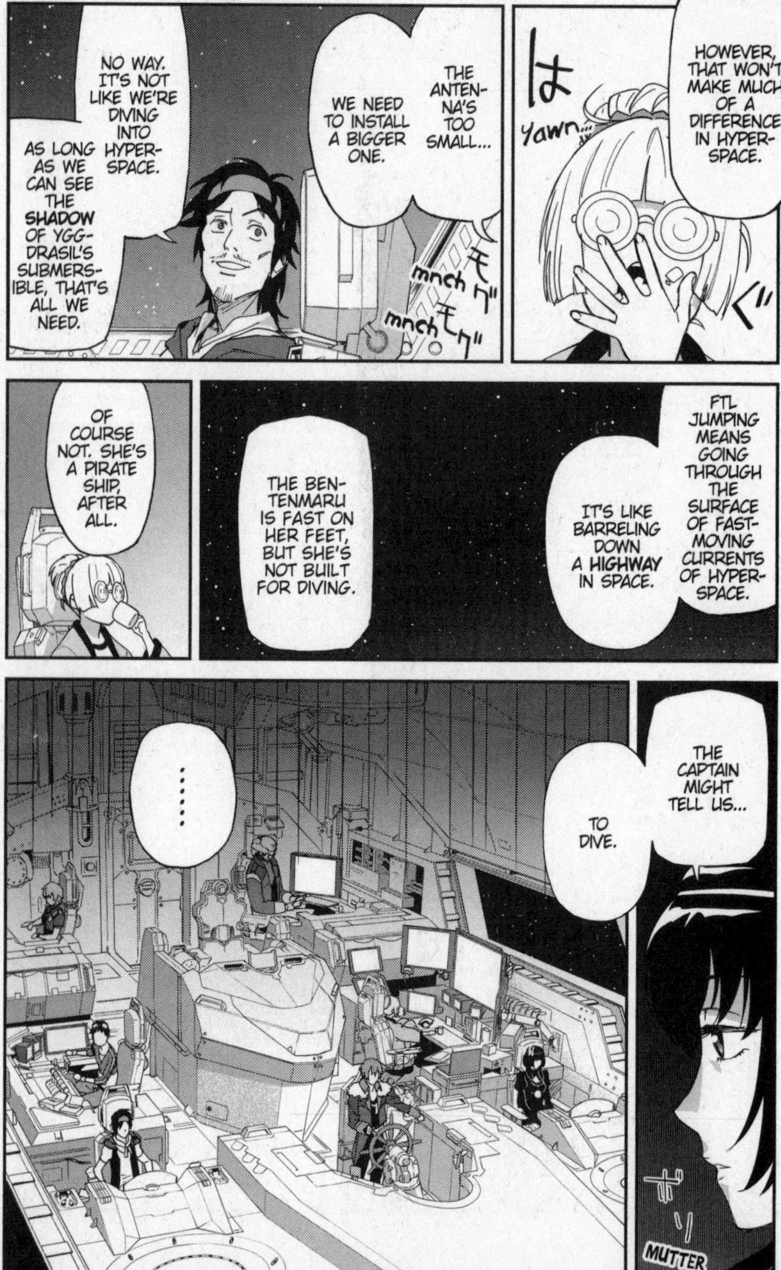
HOWEVER, THAT WON'T MAKE MUCH OF A DIFFERENCE IN HYPER-SPACE.
は
Yawn...
ぐ
THE ANTEN-NA'S TOO SMALL...
WE NEED TO INSTALL A BIGGER ONE.
モグ mnch
モグ mnch
NO WAY. IT'S NOT LIKE WE'RE DIVING INTO HYPER-SPACE.
AS LONG AS WE CAN SEE THE SHADOW OF YGG-DRASIL'S SUBMERS-IBLE, THAT'S ALL WE NEED.
FTL JUMPING MEANS GOING THROUGH THE SURFACE OF FAST-MOVING CURRENTS OF HYPER-SPACE.
IT'S LIKE BARRELING DOWN A HIGHWAY IN SPACE.
THE BEN-TENMARU IS FAST ON HER FEET, BUT SHE'S NOT BUILT FOR DIVING.
OF COURSE NOT. SHE'S A PIRATE SHIP, AFTER ALL.
THE CAPTAIN MIGHT TELL US...
TO DIVE.
ボソ
MUTTER
......

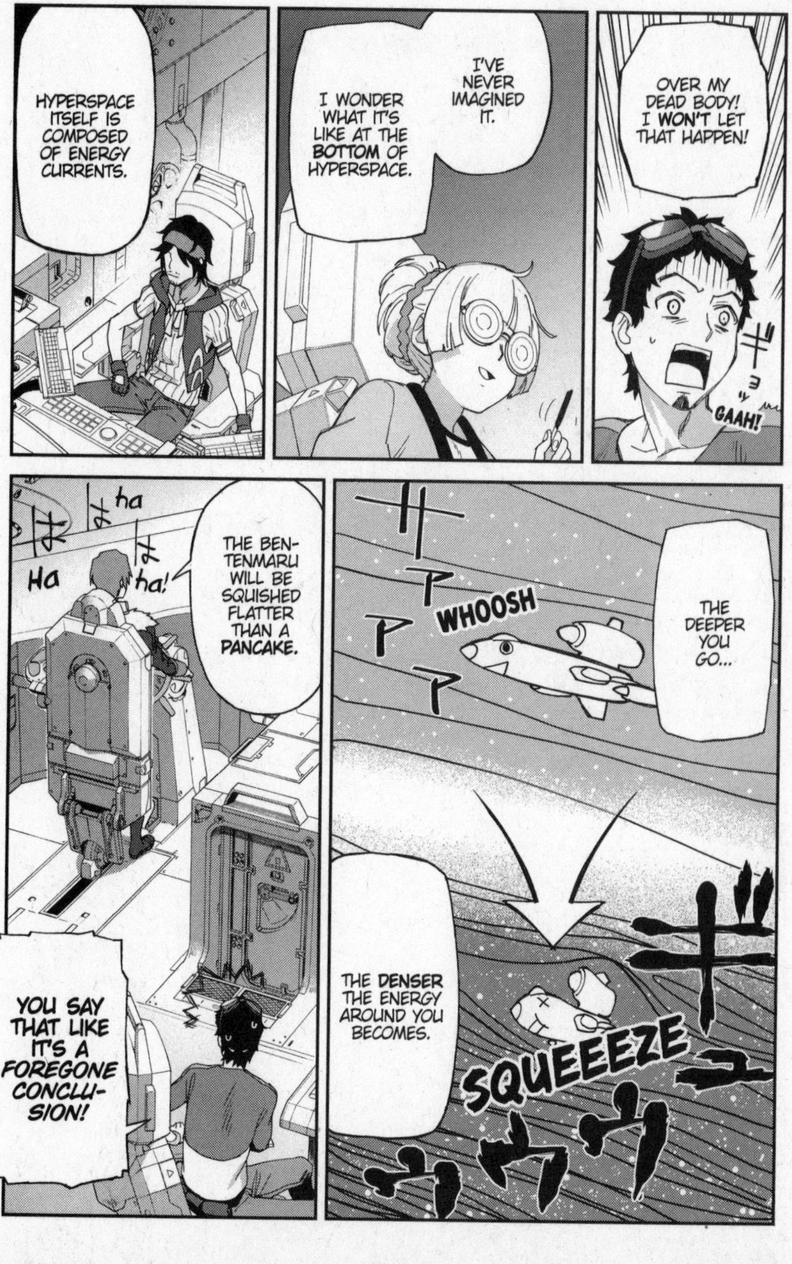
OVER MY DEAD BODY! I WON'T LET THAT HAPPEN!
GAAH!
I'VE NEVER IMAGINED IT.
I WONDER WHAT IT'S LIKE AT THE BOTTOM OF HYPERSPACE.
HYPERSPACE ITSELF IS COMPOSED OF ENERGY CURRENTS.
THE DEEPER YOU GO...
WHOOSH
THE DENSER THE ENERGY AROUND YOU BECOMES.
SQUEEEZE
ha
Ha
ha!
THE BEN-TENMARU WILL BE SQUISHED FLATTER THAN A PANCAKE.
YOU SAY THAT LIKE IT'S A FOREGONE CONCLUSION!

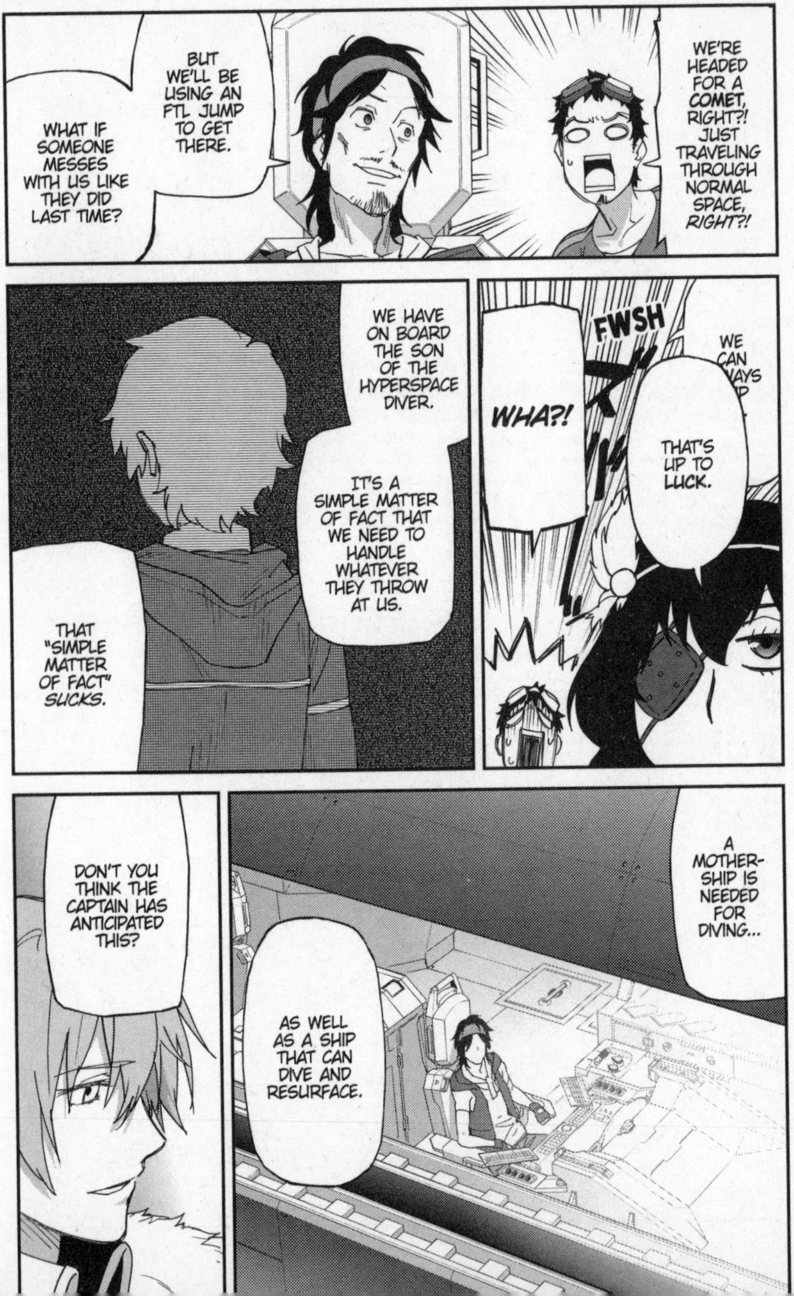
WE'RE HEADED FOR A COMET, RIGHT?! JUST TRAVELING THROUGH NORMAL SPACE, RIGHT?!
BUT WE'LL BE USING AN FTL JUMP TO GET THERE.
WHAT IF SOMEONE MESSES WITH US LIKE THEY DID LAST TIME?
WE CAN
FWSH
THAT'S UP TO LUCK.
WHA?!
WE HAVE ON BOARD THE SON OF THE HYPERSPACE DIVER.
IT'S A SIMPLE MATTER OF FACT THAT WE NEED TO HANDLE WHATEVER THEY THROW AT US.
THAT "SIMPLE MATTER OF FACT" SUCKS.
A MOTHER-SHIP IS NEEDED FOR DIVING...
AS WELL AS A SHIP THAT CAN DIVE AND RESURFACE.
DON'T YOU THINK THE CAPTAIN HAS ANTICIPATED THIS?

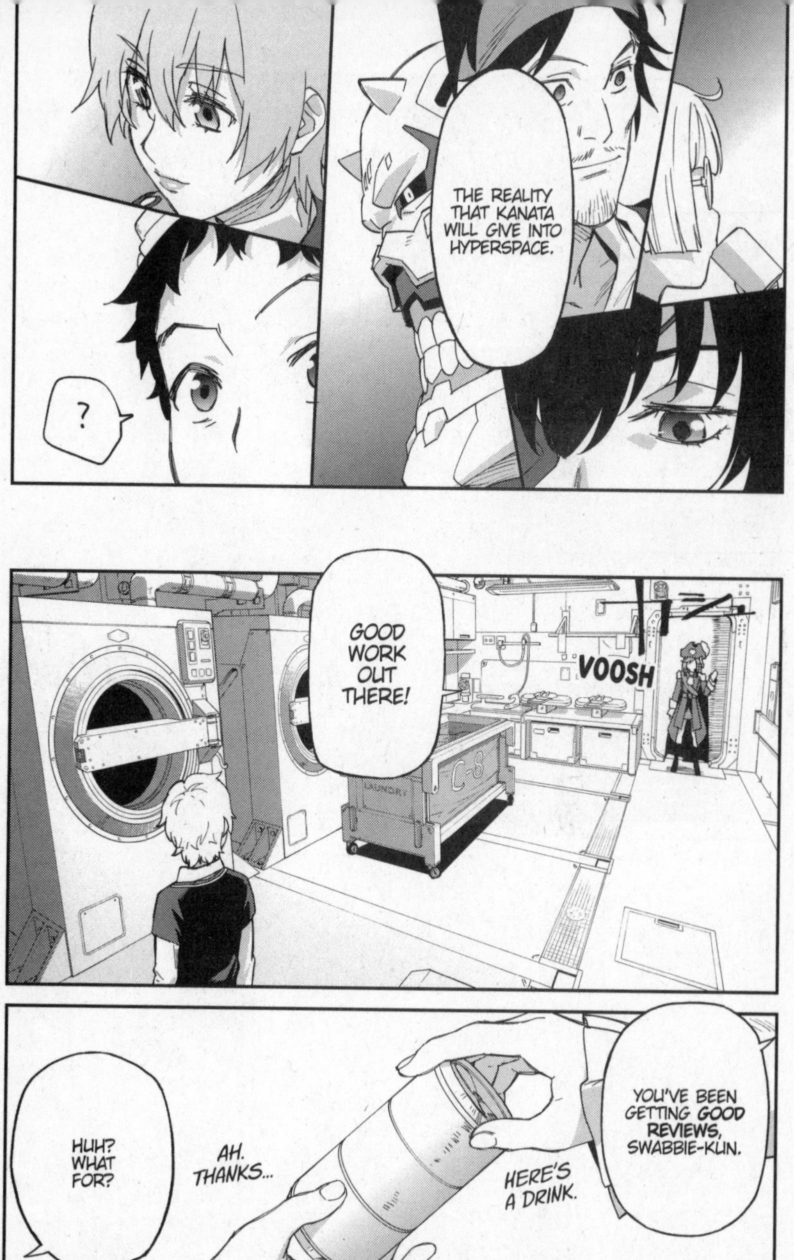
THE REALITY THAT KANATA WILL GIVE INTO HYPERSPACE.
?
VOOSH
GOOD WORK OUT THERE!
YOU'VE BEEN GETTING GOOD REVIEWS, SWABBIE-KUN.
HERE'S A DRINK.
AH. THANKS...
HUH? WHAT FOR?

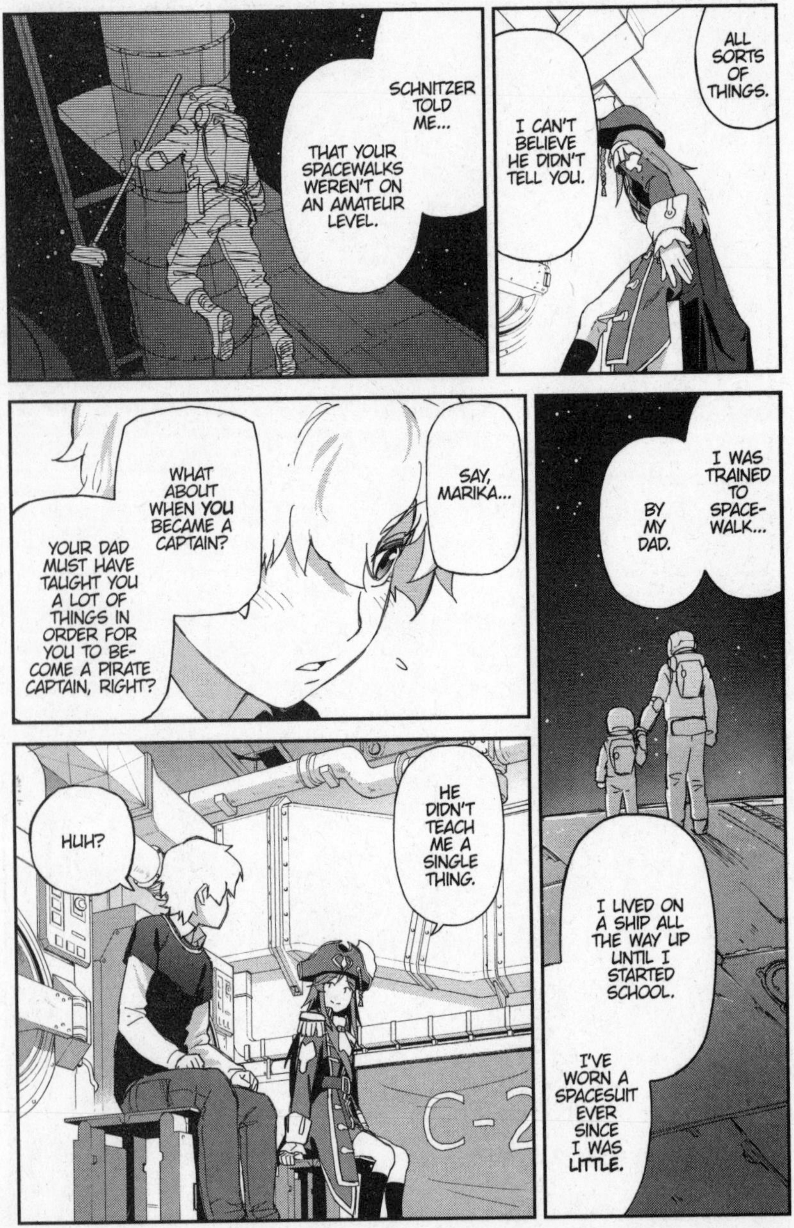
ALL SORTS OF THINGS.
I CAN'T BELIEVE HE DIDN'T TELL YOU.
SCHNITZER TOLD ME...
THAT YOUR SPACEWALKS WEREN'T ON AN AMATEUR LEVEL.
I WAS TRAINED TO SPACE-WALK...
BY MY DAD.
I LIVED ON A SHIP ALL THE WAY UP UNTIL I STARTED SCHOOL.
I'VE WORN A SPACESUIT EVER SINCE I WAS LITTLE.
SAY, MARIKA...
WHAT ABOUT WHEN YOU BECAME A CAPTAIN?
YOUR DAD MUST HAVE TAUGHT YOU A LOT OF THINGS IN ORDER FOR YOU TO BE-COME A PIRATE CAPTAIN, RIGHT?
HE DIDN'T TEACH ME A SINGLE THING.
HUH?

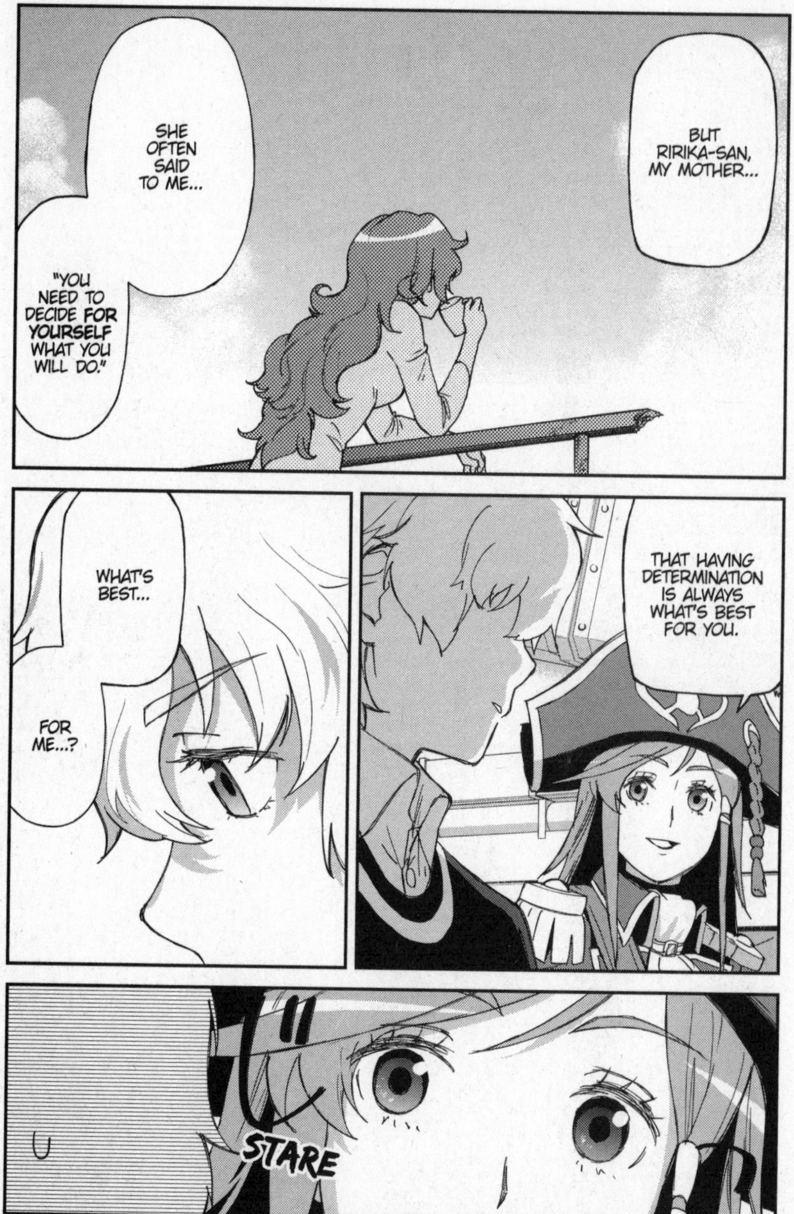
BUT RIRIKA-SAN, MY MOTHER...
SHE OFTEN SAID TO ME...
"YOU NEED TO DECIDE FOR YOURSELF WHAT YOU WILL DO."
THAT HAVING DETERMINATION IS ALWAYS WHAT'S BEST FOR YOU.
WHAT'S BEST...
FOR ME...?
STARE

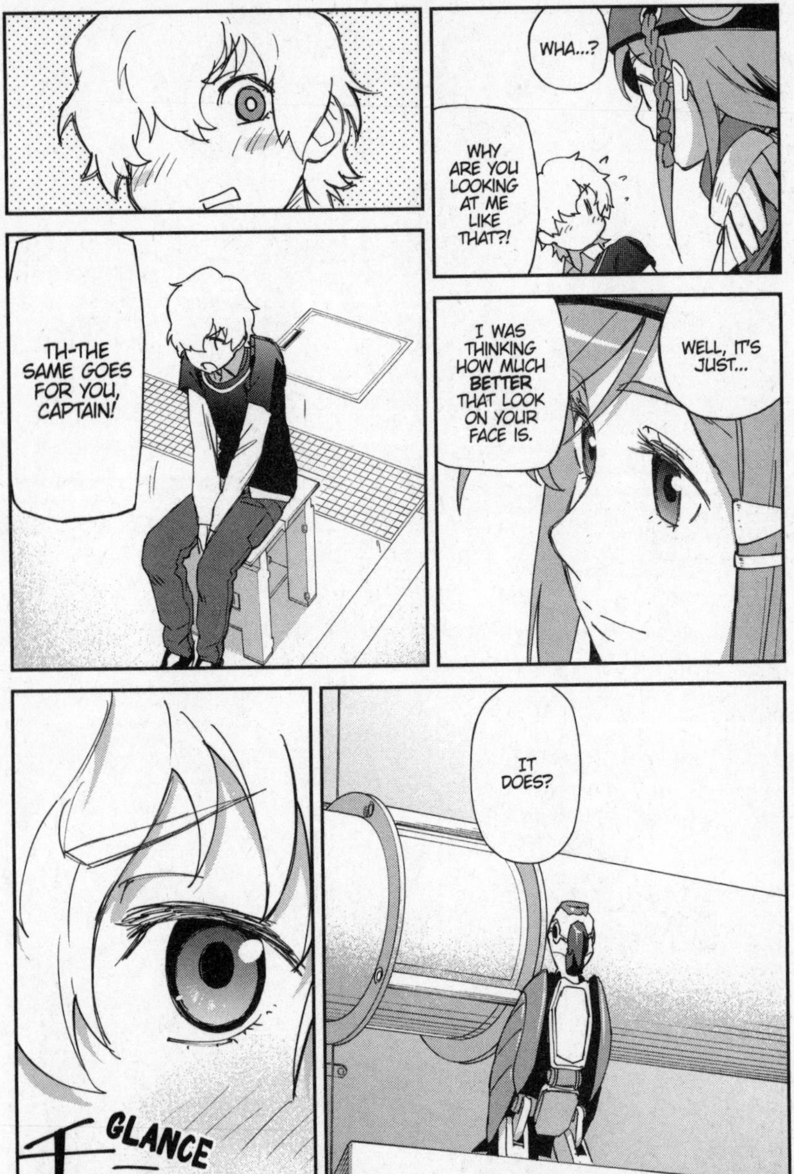
WHA...?
WHY ARE YOU LOOKING AT ME LIKE THAT?!
TH-THE SAME GOES FOR YOU, CAPTAIN!
WELL, IT'S JUST...
I WAS THINKING HOW MUCH BETTER THAT LOOK ON YOUR FACE IS.
IT DOES?
チラ
GLANCE

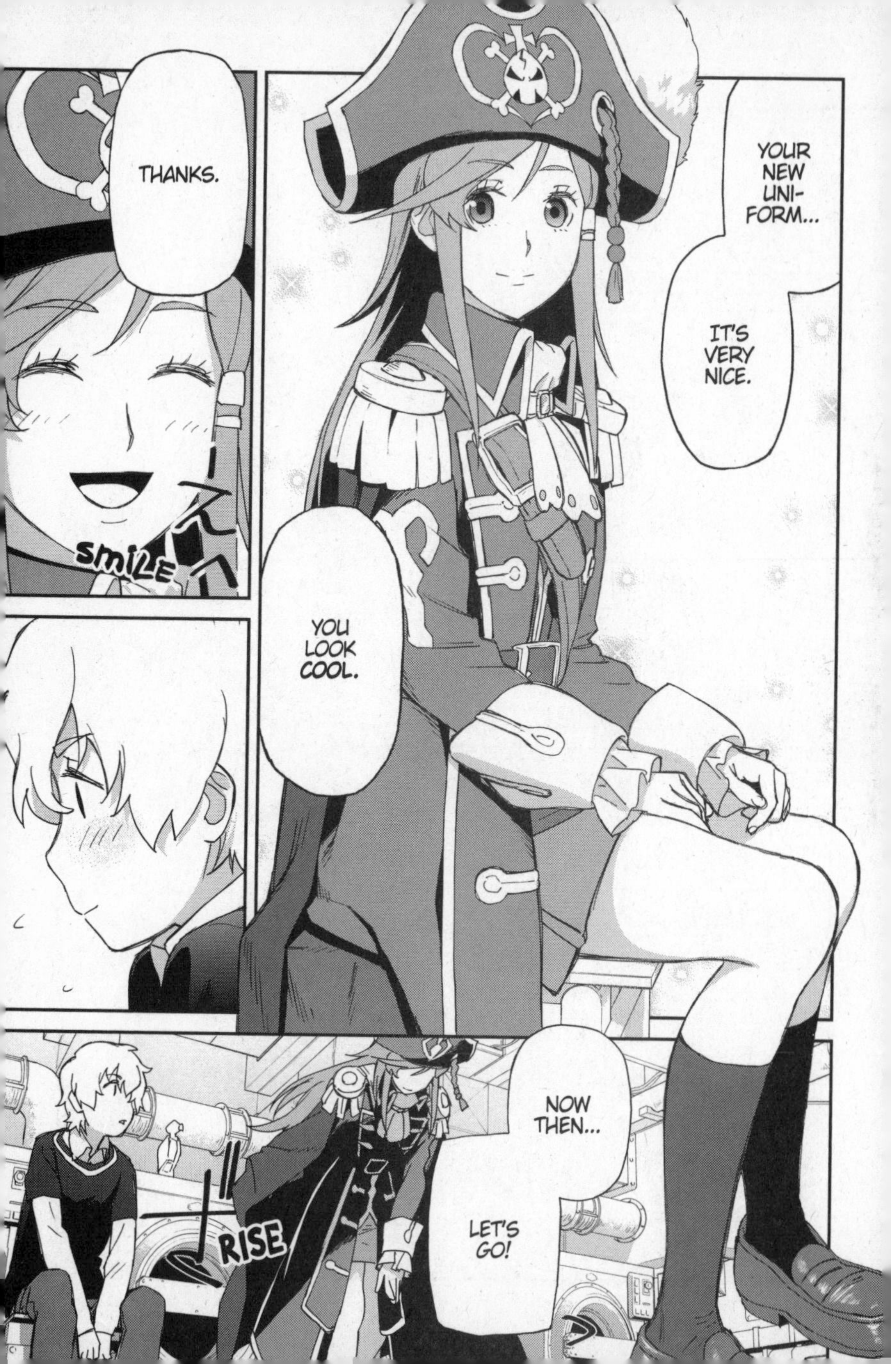
YOUR NEW UNI-FORM...
IT'S VERY NICE.
THANKS.
SMILE
YOU LOOK COOL.
NOW THEN...
LET'S GO!
RISE

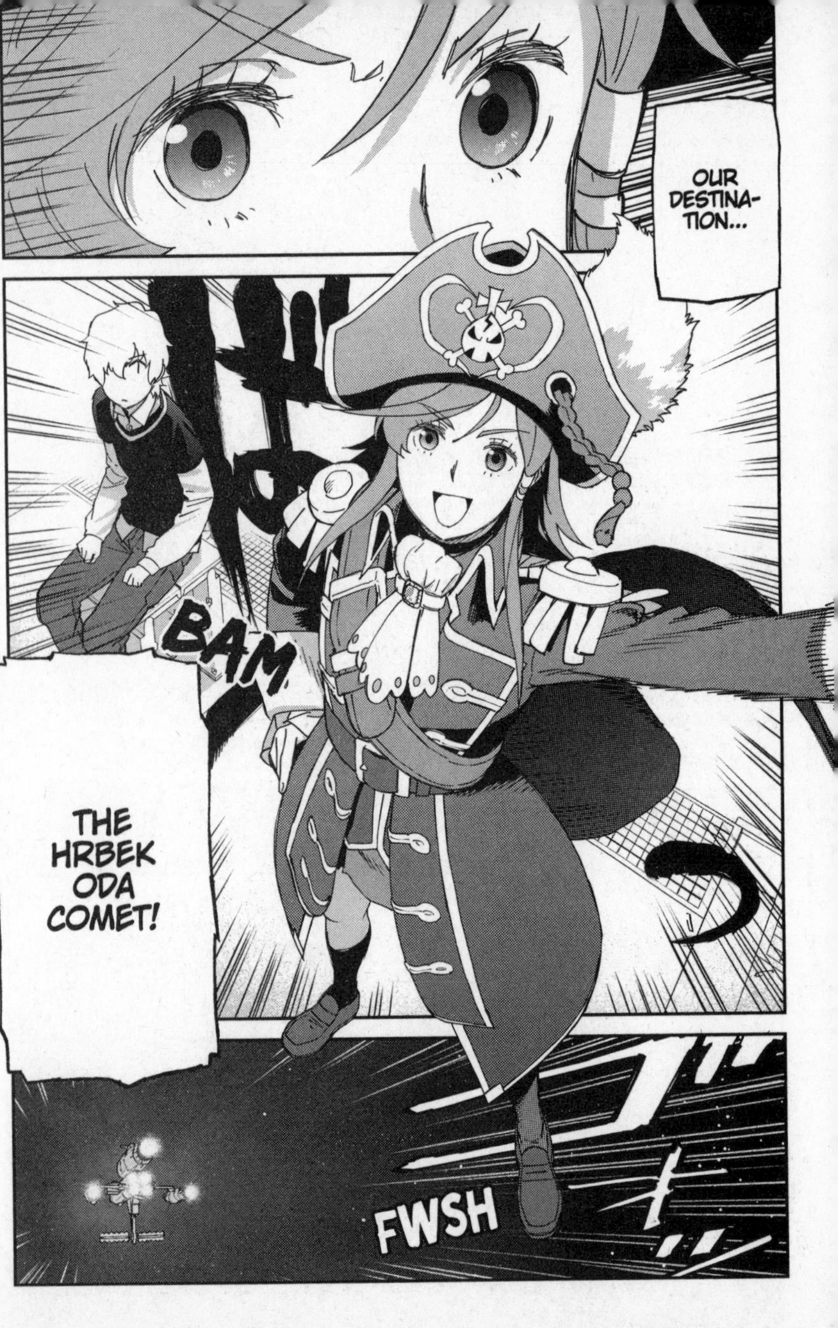
OUR DESTINATION...
BAM
THE HRBEK ODA COMET!
FWSH

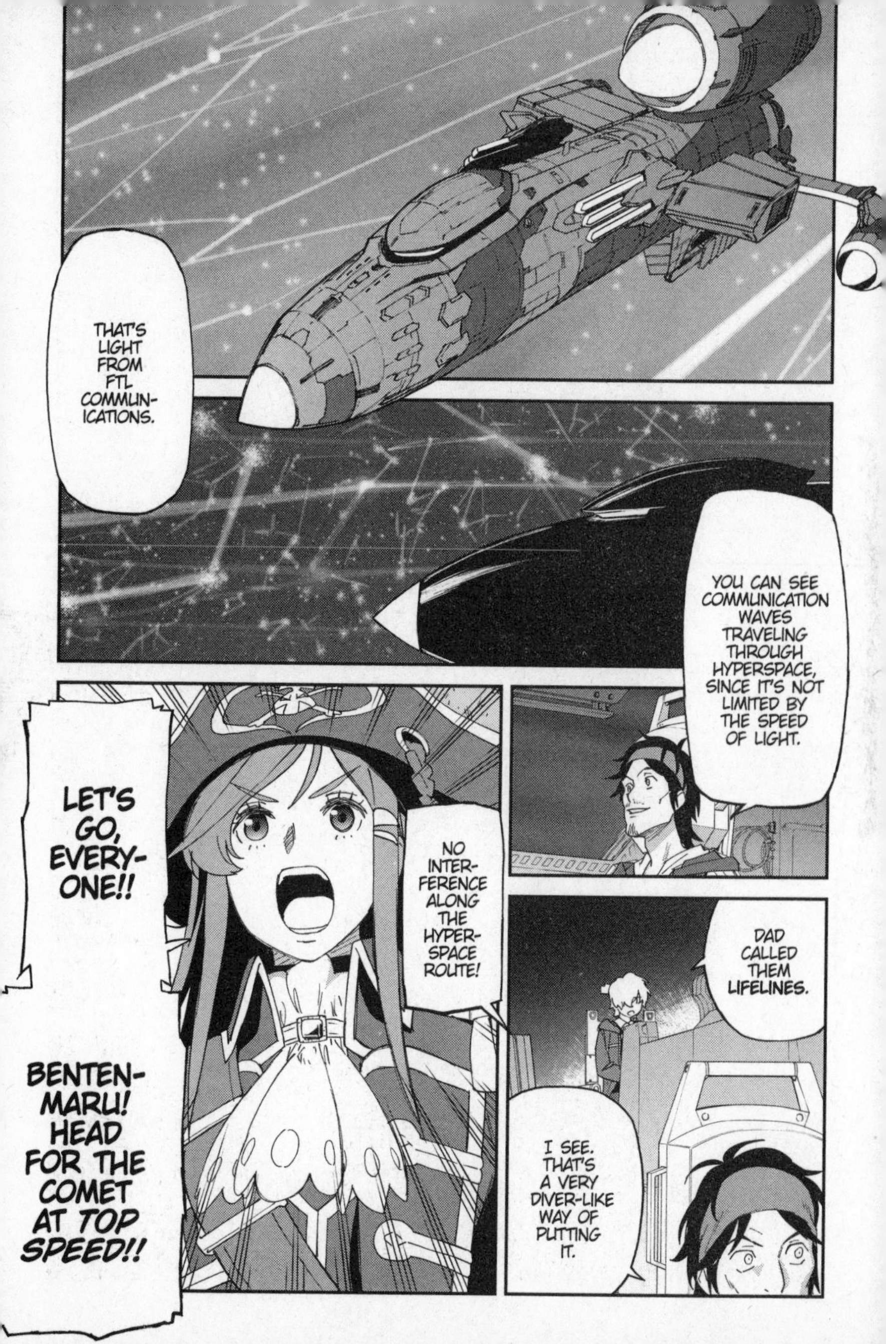
THAT'S LIGHT FROM FTL COMMUNICATIONS.
YOU CAN SEE COMMUNICATION WAVES TRAVELING THROUGH HYPERSPACE, SINCE IT'S NOT LIMITED BY THE SPEED OF LIGHT.
DAD CALLED THEM LIFELINES.
I SEE. THAT'S A VERY DIVER-LIKE WAY OF PUTTING IT.
NO INTERFERENCE ALONG THE HYPERSPACE ROUTE!
LET'S GO, EVERYONE!!
BENTEN-MARU! HEAD FOR THE COMET AT *TOP SPEED*!!

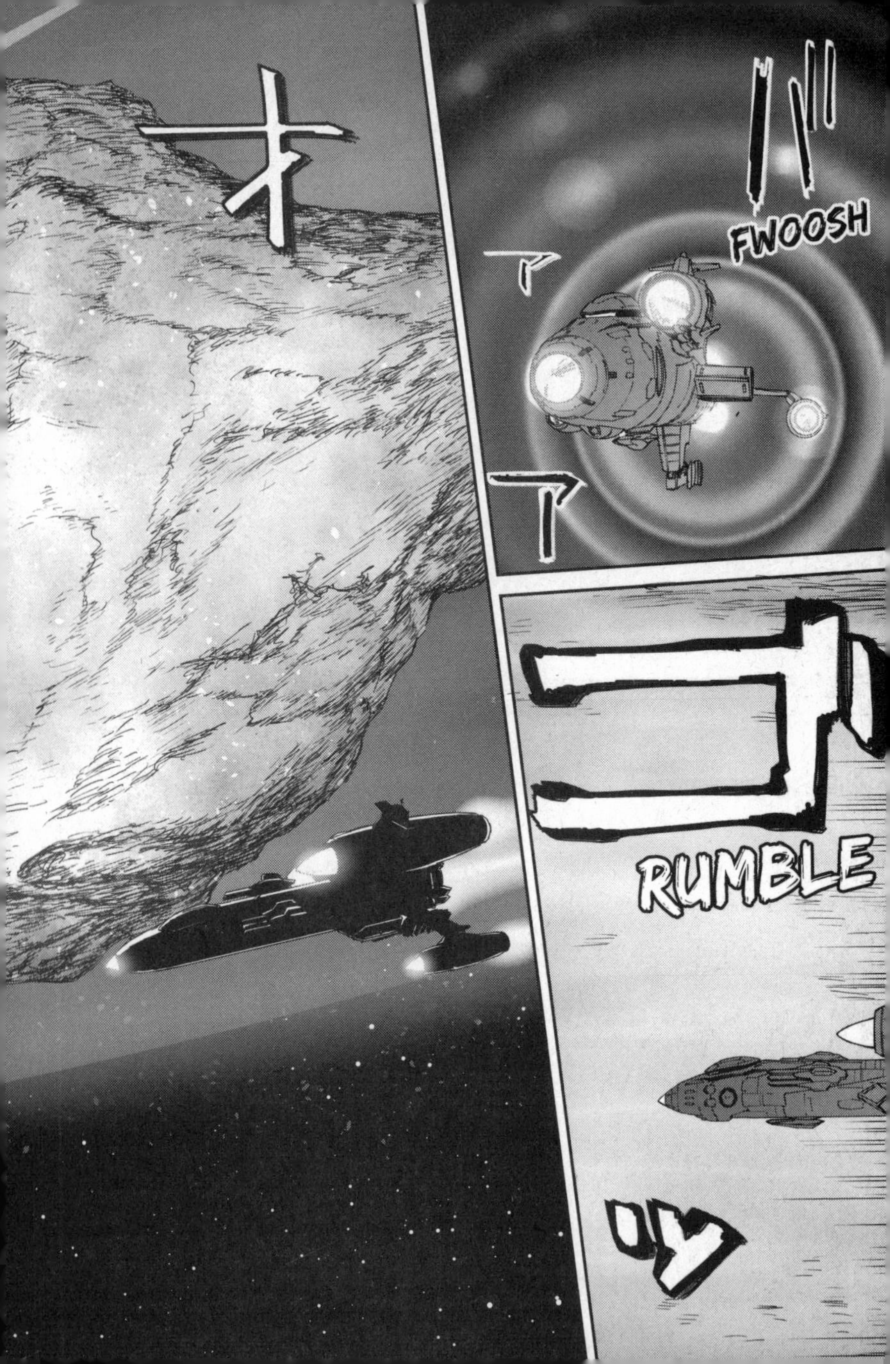
バ
ア
ア
FWOOSH
ゴ
ッ
RUMBLE
オ

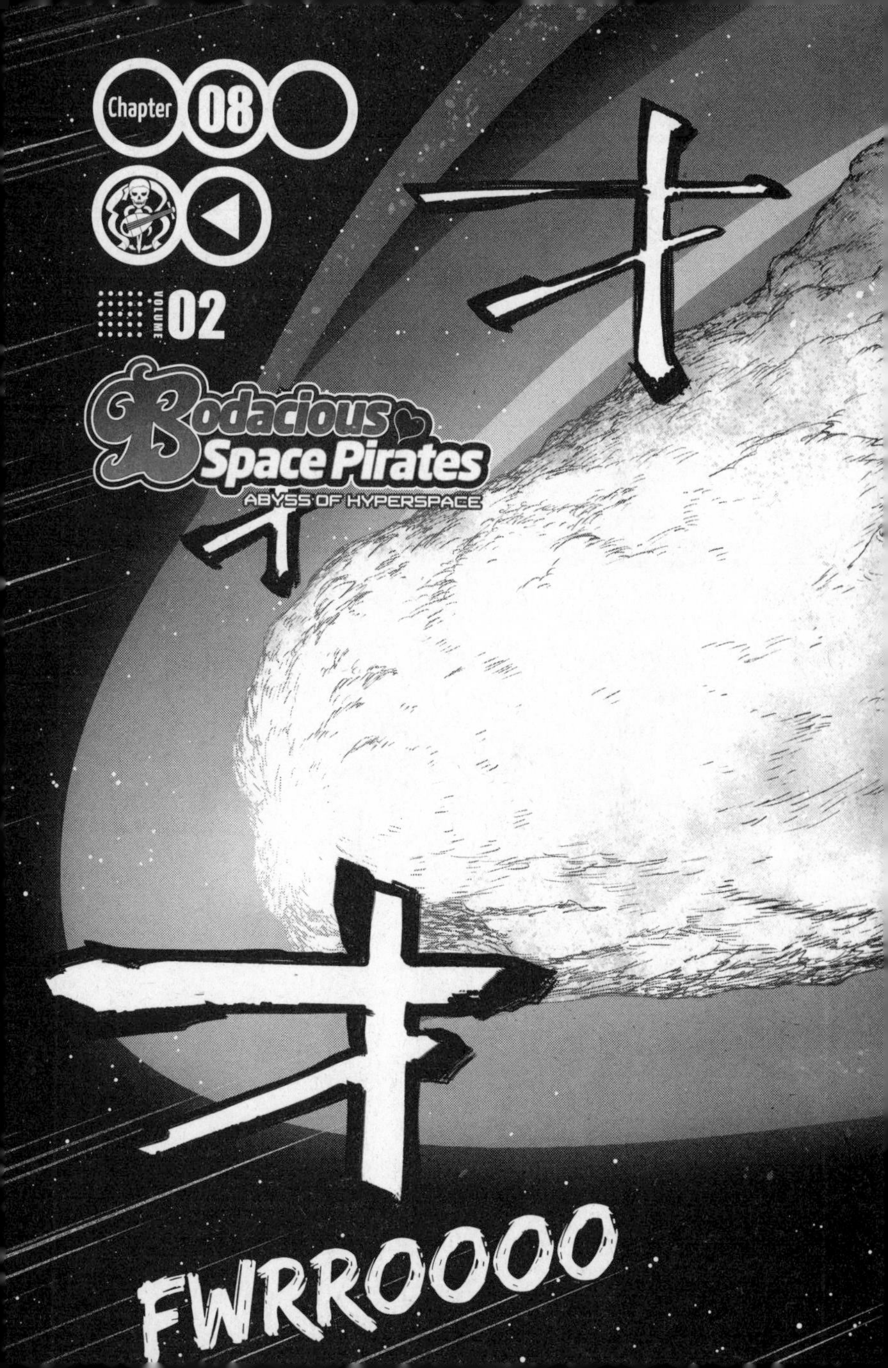
Chapter 08
VOLUME 02
Bodacious Space Pirates
ABYSS OF HYPERSPACE
FWRROOOO

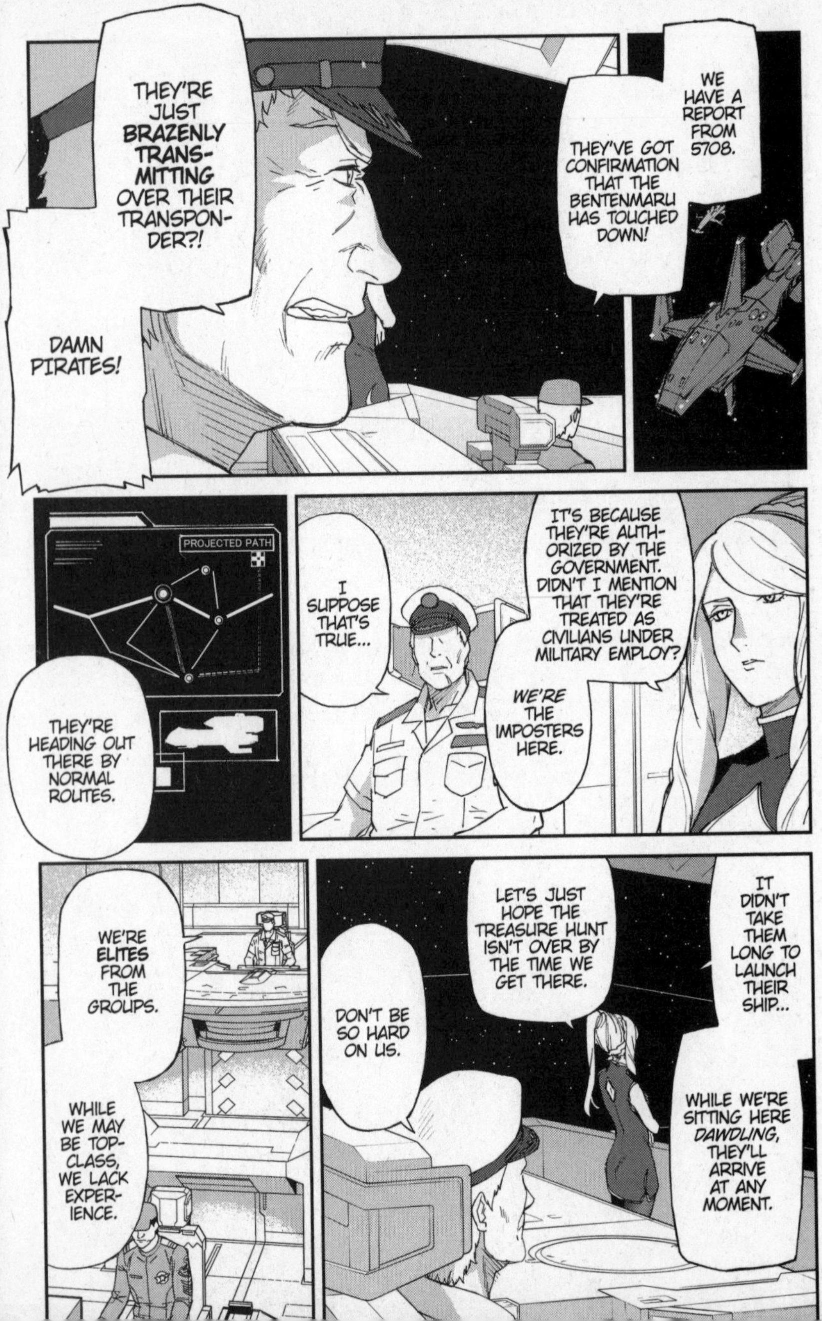
WE HAVE A REPORT FROM 5708.
THEY'VE GOT CONFIRMATION THAT THE BENTENMARU HAS TOUCHED DOWN!
THEY'RE JUST BRAZENLY TRANS-MITTING OVER THEIR TRANSPON-DER?!
DAMN PIRATES!
IT'S BECAUSE THEY'RE AUTH-ORIZED BY THE GOVERNMENT. DIDN'T I MENTION THAT THEY'RE TREATED AS CIVILIANS UNDER MILITARY EMPLOY?
I SUPPOSE THAT'S TRUE...
WE'RE THE IMPOSTERS HERE.
PROJECTED PATH
THEY'RE HEADING OUT THERE BY NORMAL ROUTES.
IT DIDN'T TAKE THEM LONG TO LAUNCH THEIR SHIP...
LET'S JUST HOPE THE TREASURE HUNT ISN'T OVER BY THE TIME WE GET THERE.
WHILE WE'RE SITTING HERE DAWDLING, THEY'LL ARRIVE AT ANY MOMENT.
DON'T BE SO HARD ON US.
WE'RE ELITES FROM THE GROUPS.
WHILE WE MAY BE TOP-CLASS, WE LACK EXPERI-ENCE.

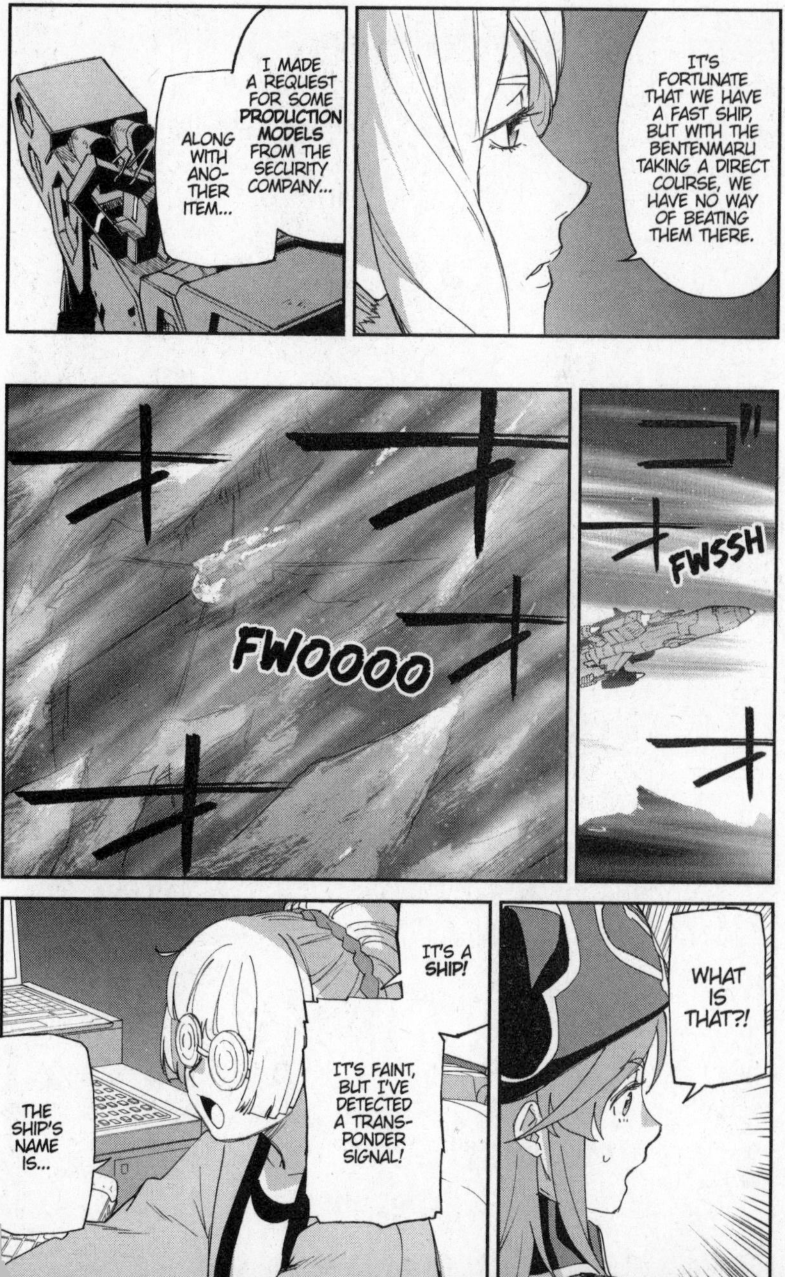
IT'S FORTUNATE THAT WE HAVE A FAST SHIP, BUT WITH THE BENTENMARU TAKING A DIRECT COURSE, WE HAVE NO WAY OF BEATING THEM THERE.
I MADE A REQUEST FOR SOME PRODUCTION MODELS FROM THE SECURITY COMPANY...
ALONG WITH ANO-THER ITEM...
FWSSH
FWOOOO
WHAT IS THAT?!
IT'S A SHIP!
IT'S FAINT, BUT I'VE DETECTED A TRANS-PONDER SIGNAL!
THE SHIP'S NAME IS...

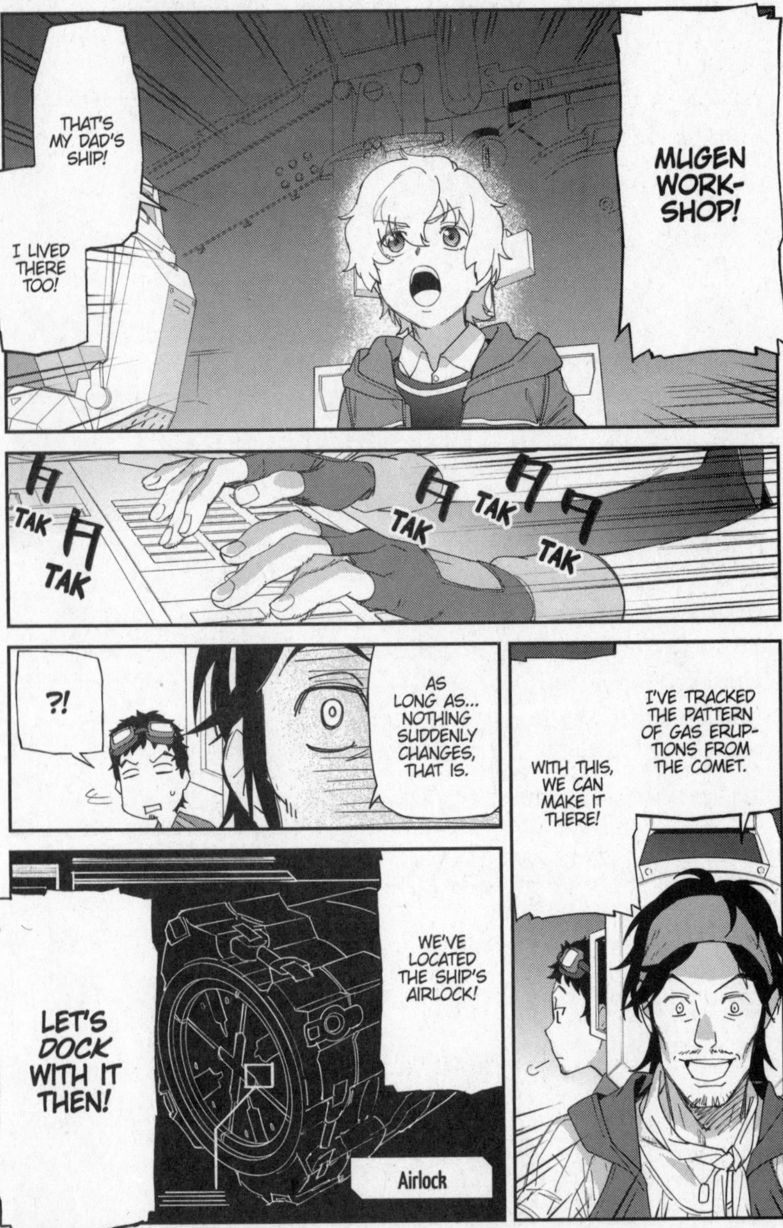
MUGEN WORK-SHOP!
THAT'S MY DAD'S SHIP!
I LIVED THERE TOO!
TAK
TAK
TAK
TAK
TAK
I'VE TRACKED THE PATTERN OF GAS ERUP-TIONS FROM THE COMET.
WITH THIS, WE CAN MAKE IT THERE!
AS LONG AS... NOTHING SUDDENLY CHANGES, THAT IS.
?!
WE'VE LOCATED THE SHIP'S AIRLOCK!
Airlock
LET'S DOCK WITH IT THEN!

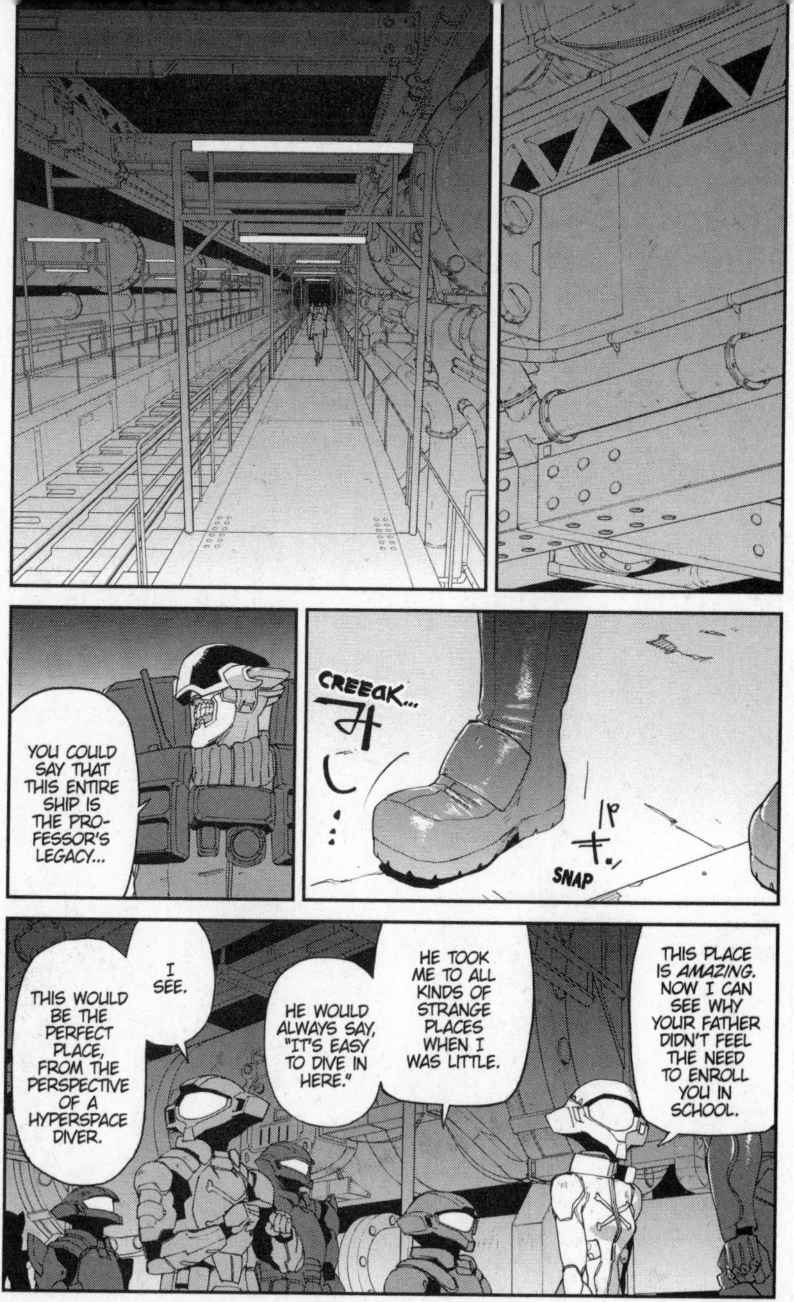
CREEAK...
みし…
パキッ
SNAP
YOU COULD SAY THAT THIS ENTIRE SHIP IS THE PRO-FESSOR'S LEGACY...
THIS PLACE IS *AMAZING*. NOW I CAN SEE WHY YOUR FATHER DIDN'T FEEL THE NEED TO ENROLL YOU IN SCHOOL.
HE TOOK ME TO ALL KINDS OF STRANGE PLACES WHEN I WAS LITTLE.
HE WOULD ALWAYS SAY, "IT'S EASY TO DIVE IN HERE."
I SEE.
THIS WOULD BE THE PERFECT PLACE, FROM THE PERSPECTIVE OF A HYPERSPACE DIVER.

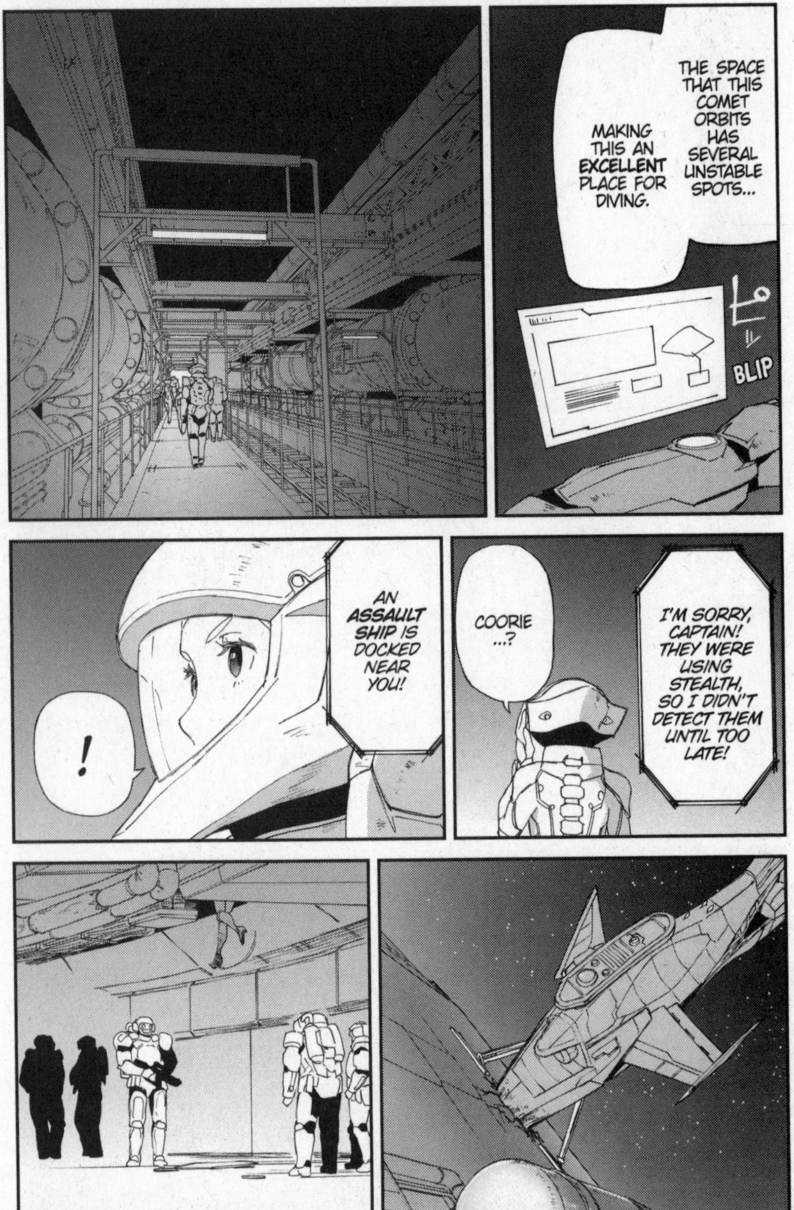
THE SPACE THAT THIS COMET ORBITS HAS SEVERAL UNSTABLE SPOTS...
MAKING THIS AN EXCELLENT PLACE FOR DIVING.
ピッ
BLIP
I'M SORRY, CAPTAIN! THEY WERE USING STEALTH, SO I DIDN'T DETECT THEM UNTIL TOO LATE!
COORIE ...?
AN ASSAULT SHIP IS DOCKED NEAR YOU!
!

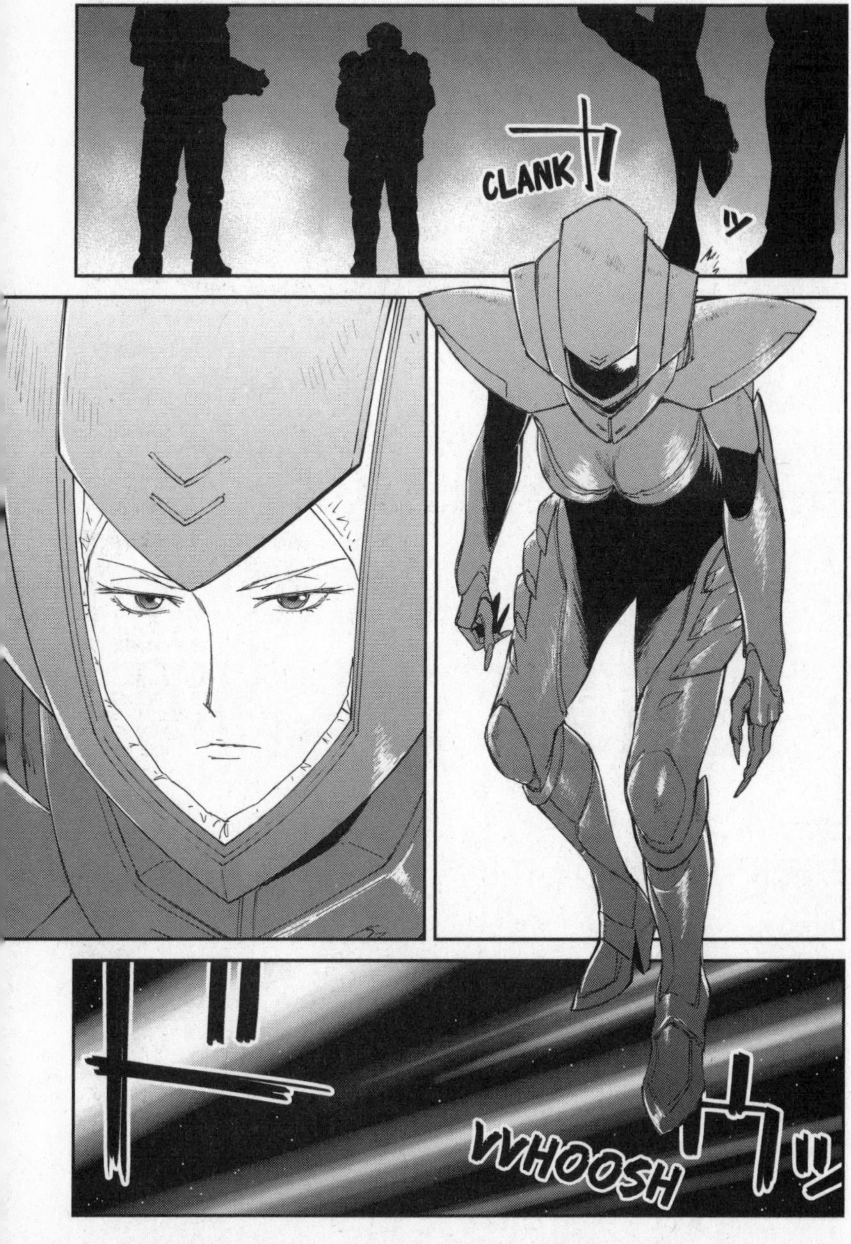
CLANK
VVHOOSH

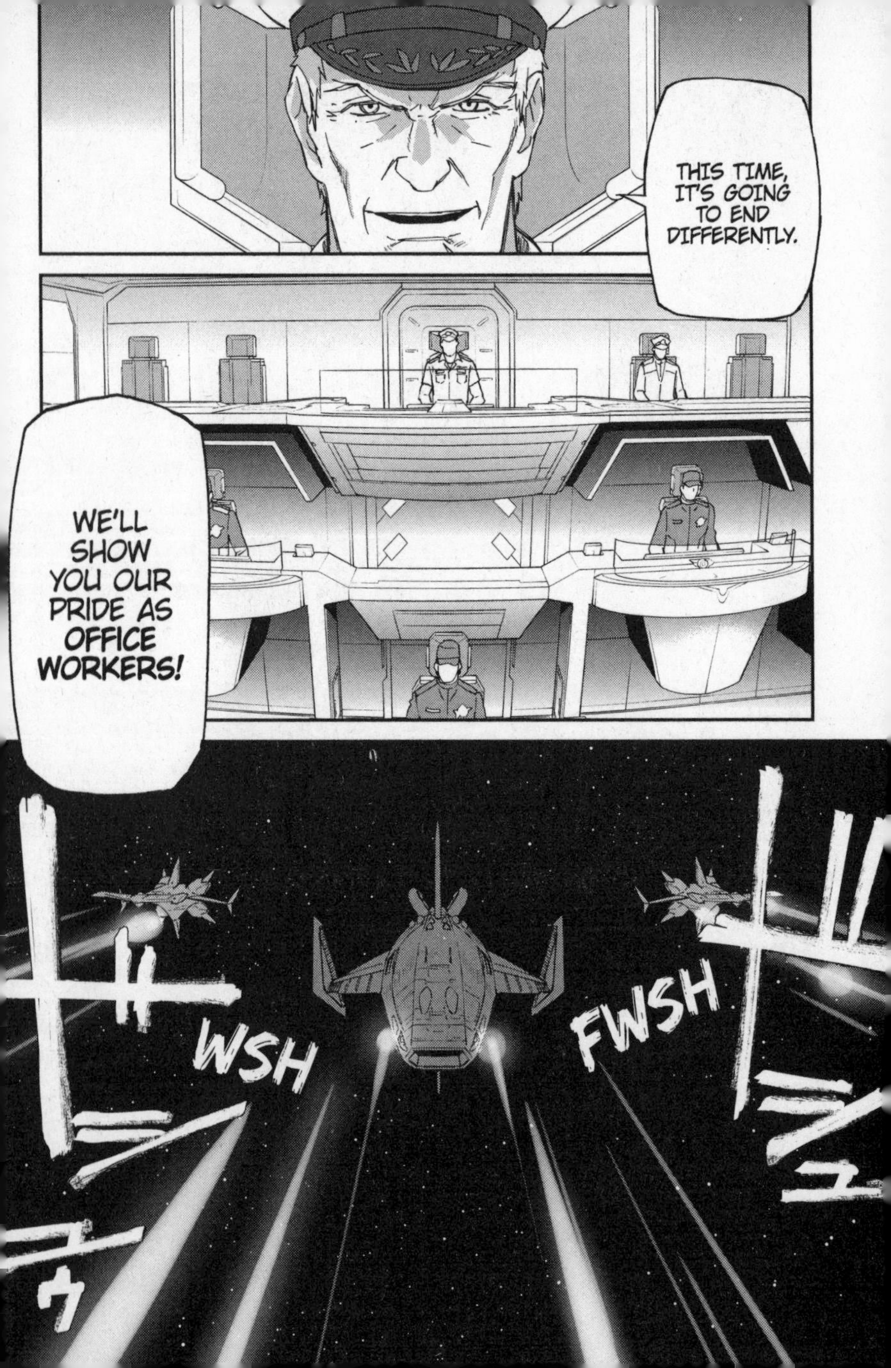
THIS TIME, IT'S GOING TO END DIFFERENTLY.
WE'LL SHOW YOU OUR PRIDE AS OFFICE WORKERS!
FWSH
WSH

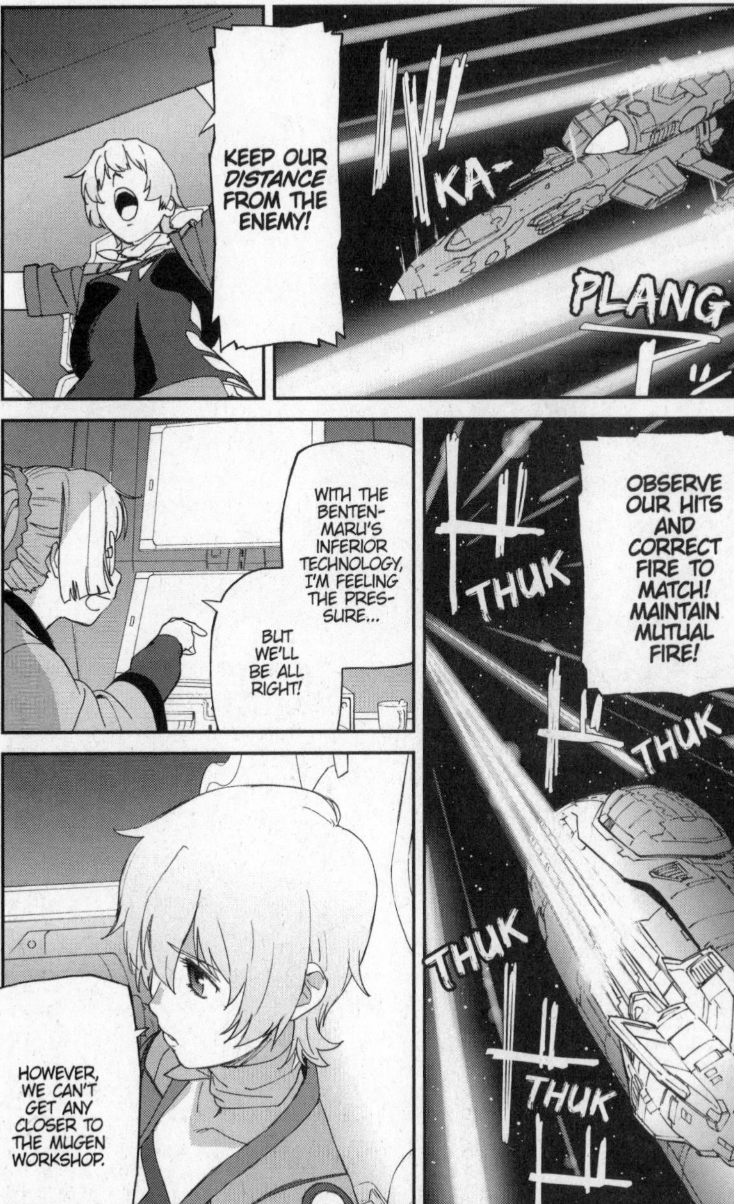
KA-
PLANG
アッ
KEEP OUR DISTANCE FROM THE ENEMY!
OBSERVE OUR HITS AND CORRECT FIRE TO MATCH! MAINTAIN MUTUAL FIRE!
THUK
THUK
THUK
THUK
WITH THE BENTEN-MARU'S INFERIOR TECHNOLOGY, I'M FEELING THE PRES-SURE...
BUT WE'LL BE ALL RIGHT!
HOWEVER, WE CAN'T GET ANY CLOSER TO THE MUGEN WORKSHOP.

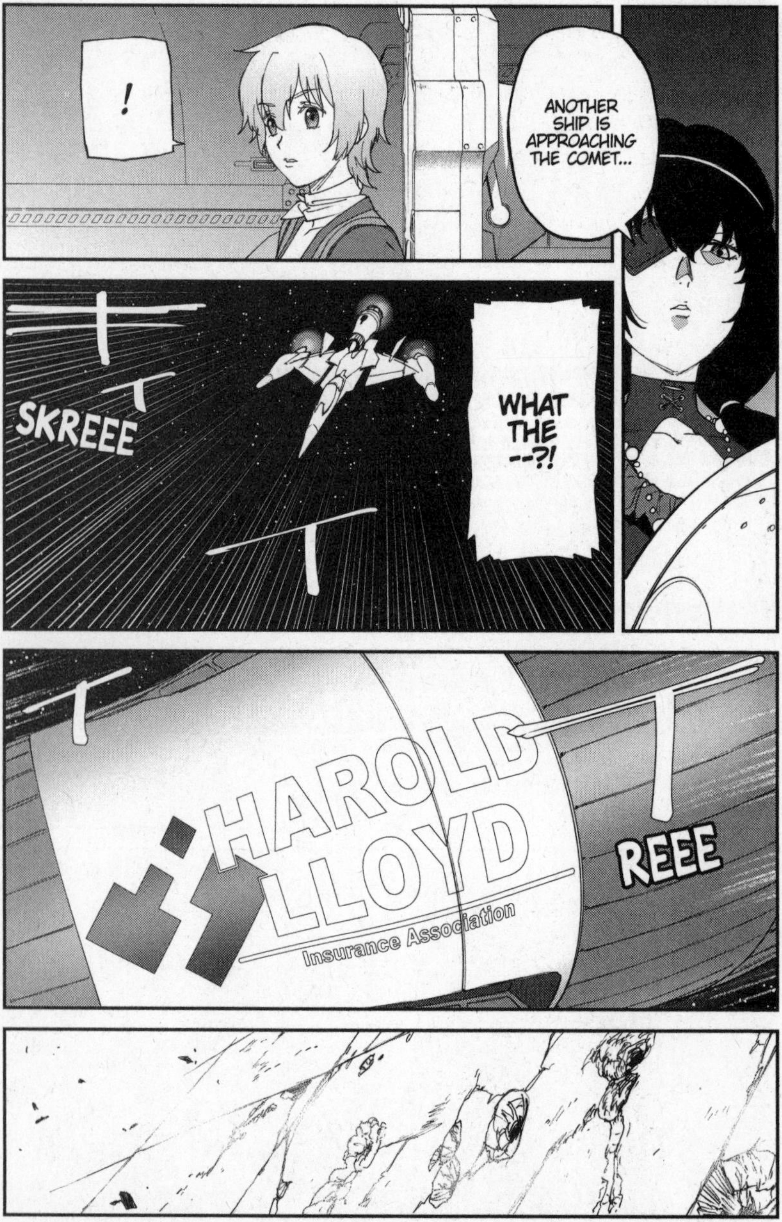
ANOTHER SHIP IS APPROACHING THE COMET...
!
WHAT THE --?!
SKREEE
REEE
HAROLD LLOYD
Insurance Association

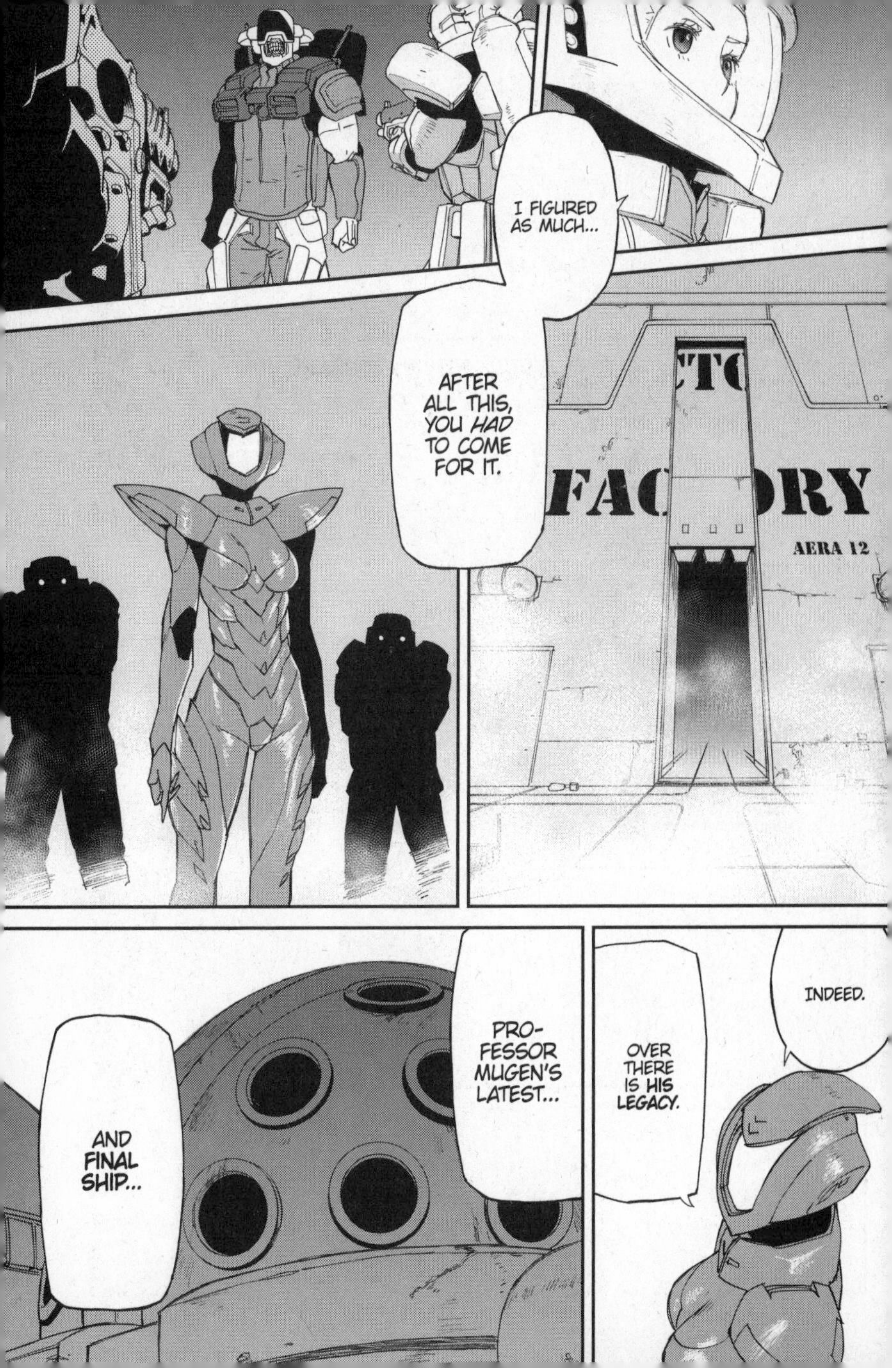
I FIGURED AS MUCH...
AFTER ALL THIS, YOU HAD TO COME FOR IT.
AERA 12
INDEED.
OVER THERE IS HIS LEGACY.
PRO-FESSOR MUGEN'S LATEST...
AND FINAL SHIP...

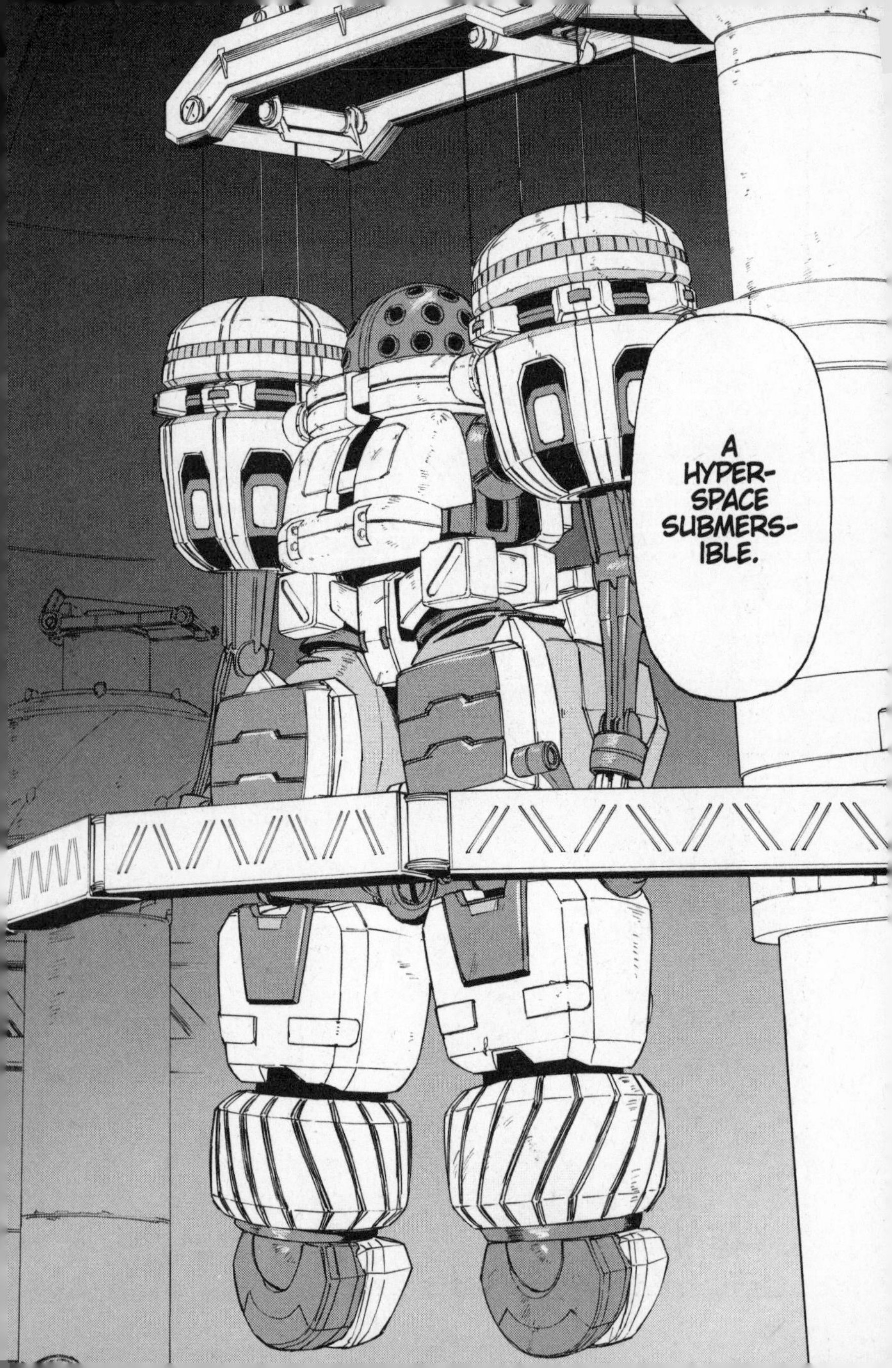
A HYPER-SPACE SUBMERS-IBLE.

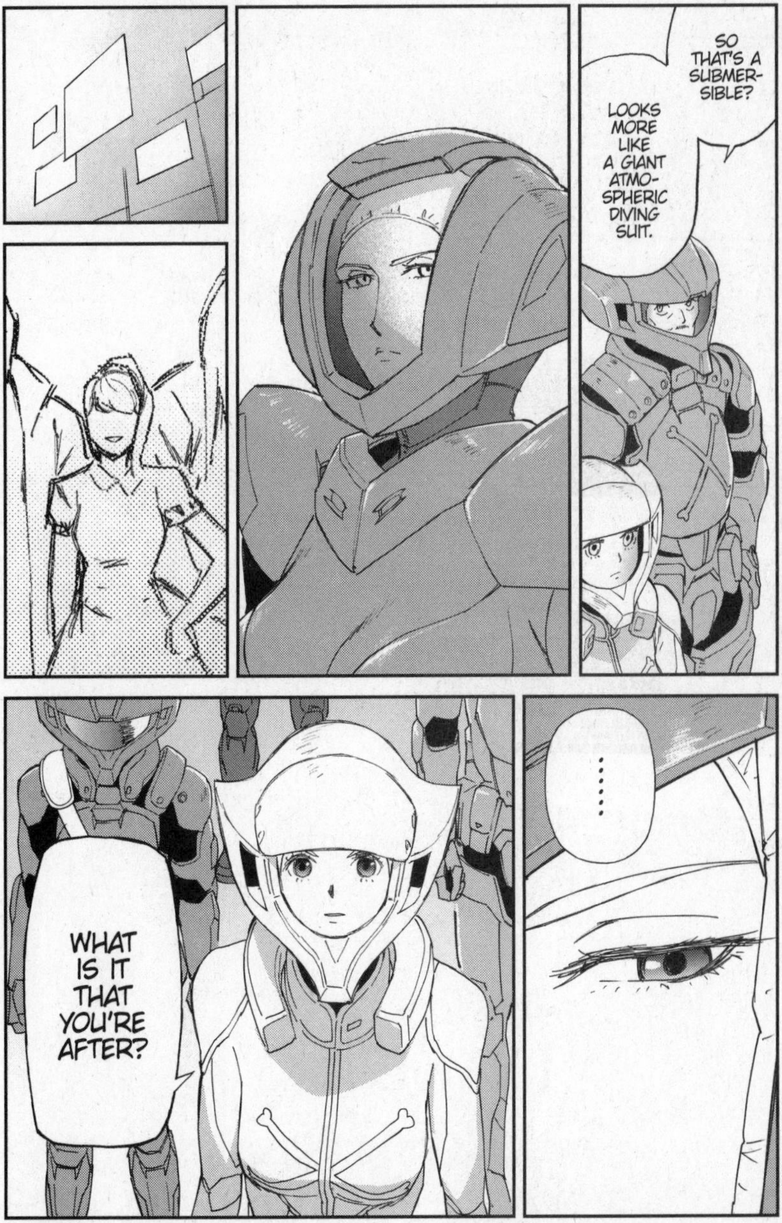
SO THAT'S A SUBMERSIBLE?
LOOKS MORE LIKE A GIANT ATMOSPHERIC DIVING SUIT.
......
WHAT IS IT THAT YOU'RE AFTER?

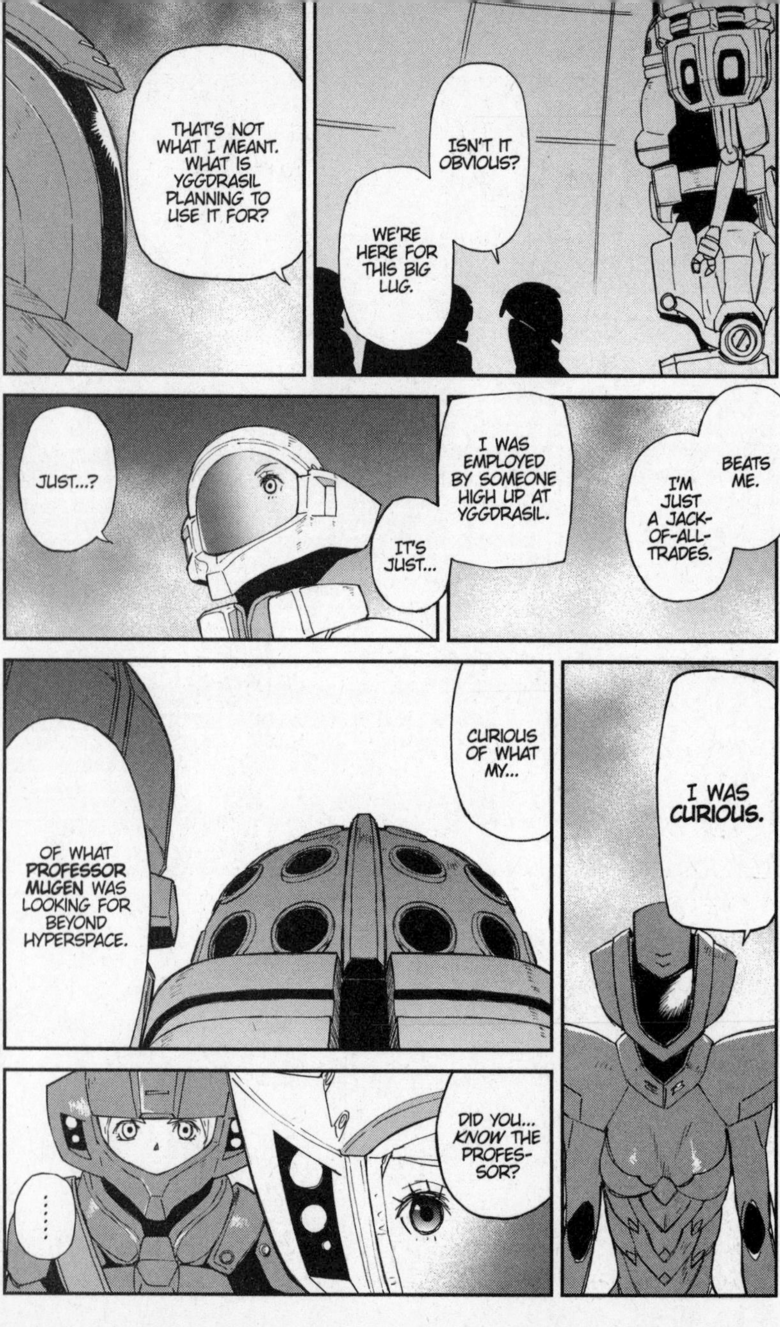
ISN'T IT OBVIOUS?
WE'RE HERE FOR THIS BIG LUG.
THAT'S NOT WHAT I MEANT. WHAT IS YGGDRASIL PLANNING TO USE IT FOR?
BEATS ME.
I'M JUST A JACK-OF-ALL-TRADES.
I WAS EMPLOYED BY SOMEONE HIGH UP AT YGGDRASIL.
IT'S JUST...
JUST...?
I WAS **CURIOUS.**
CURIOUS OF WHAT MY...
OF WHAT **PROFESSOR MUGEN** WAS LOOKING FOR BEYOND HYPERSPACE.
DID YOU... *KNOW* THE PROFES-SOR?
......

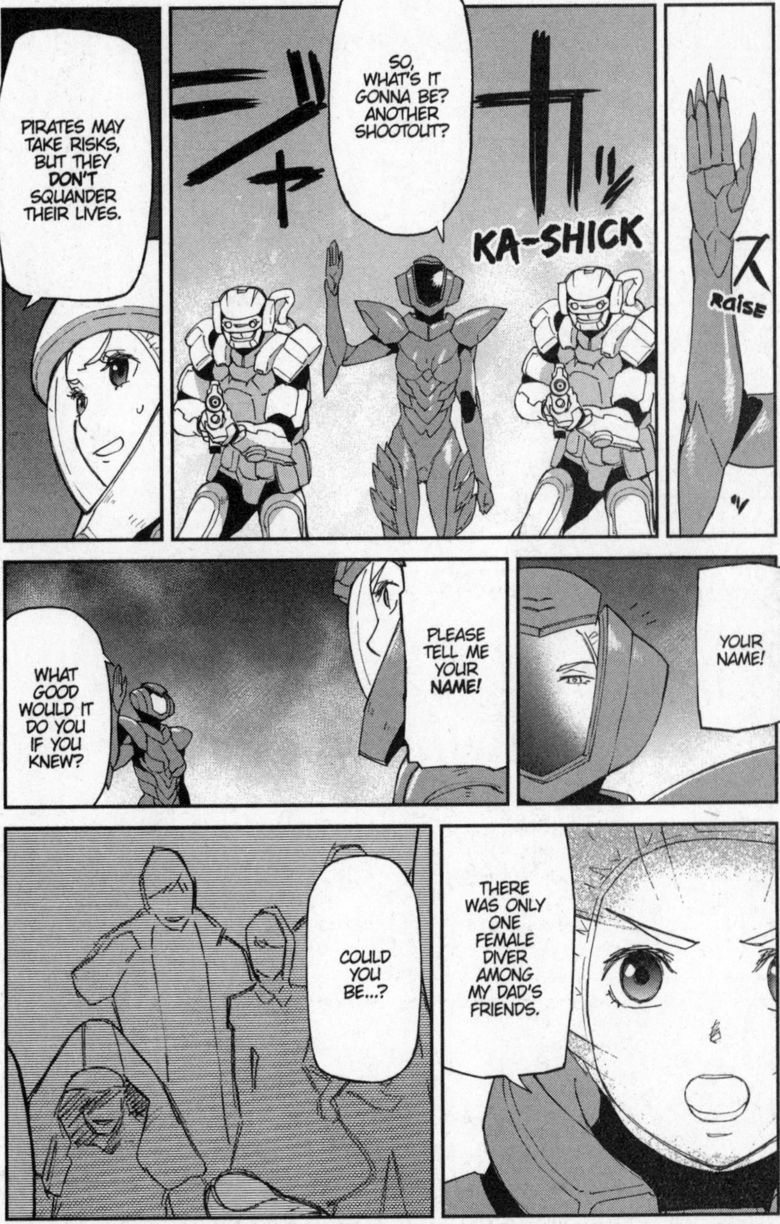

ス
RAISE
SO, WHAT'S IT GONNA BE? ANOTHER SHOOTOUT?
ジャキッ
KA-SHICK
PIRATES MAY TAKE RISKS, BUT THEY DON'T SQUANDER THEIR LIVES.
YOUR NAME!
PLEASE TELL ME YOUR NAME!
WHAT GOOD WOULD IT DO YOU IF YOU KNEW?
THERE WAS ONLY ONE FEMALE DIVER AMONG MY DAD'S FRIENDS.
COULD YOU BE...?

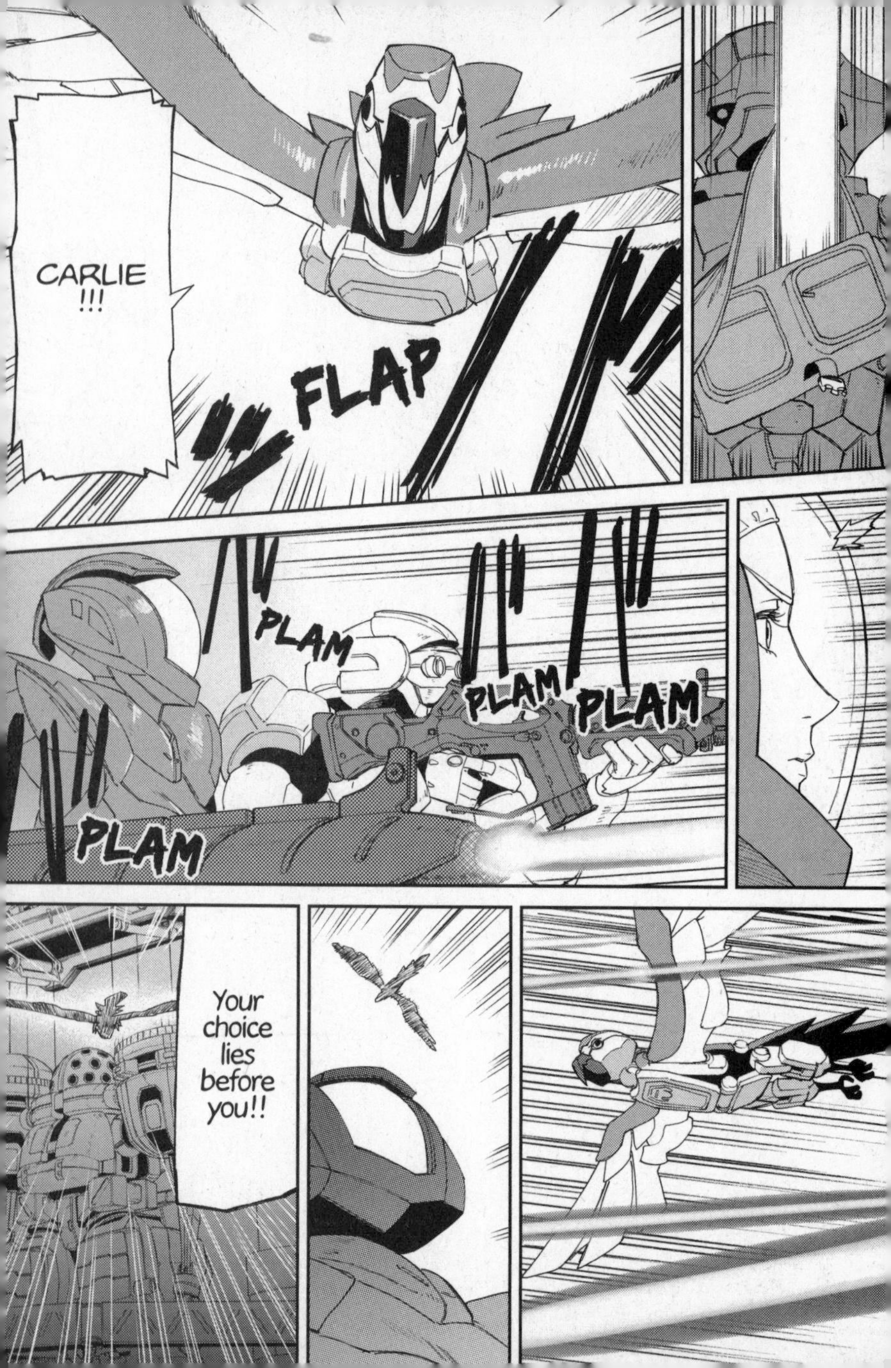
CARLIE!!!
FLAP
PLAM
PLAM
PLAM
PLAM
Your choice lies before you!!

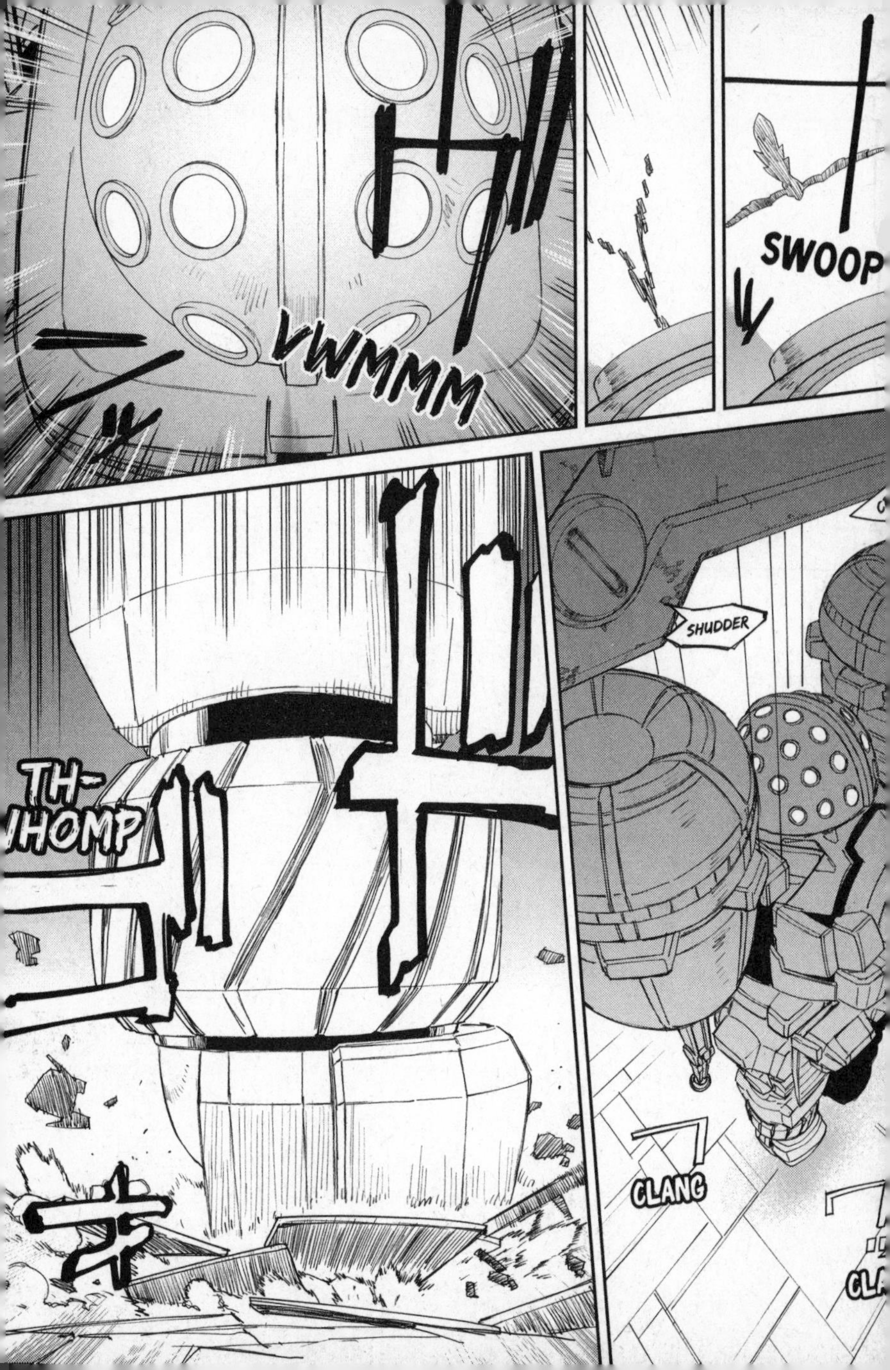
SWOOP
VWMMM
SHUDDER
CLANG
TH-

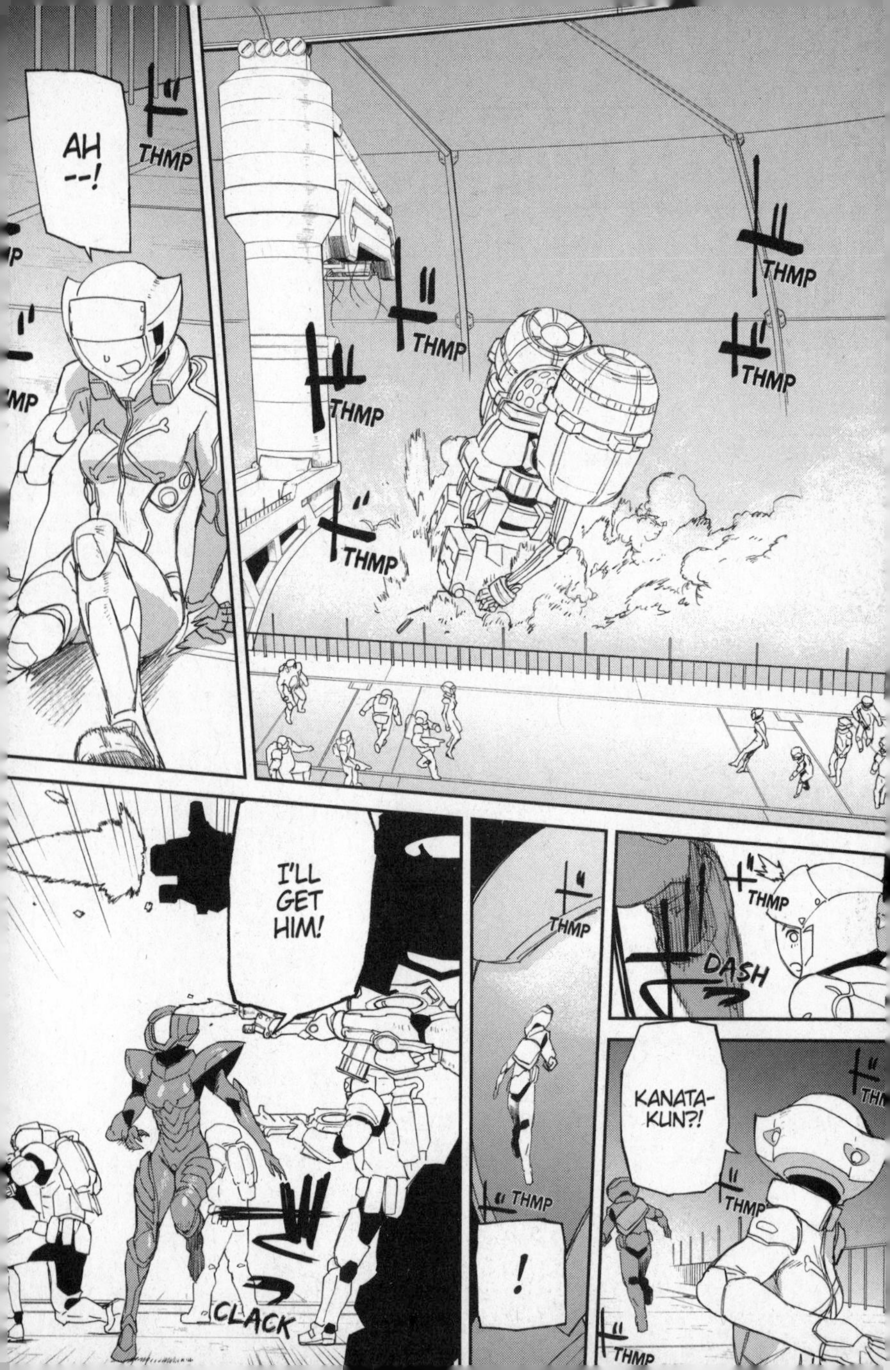
THMP
THMP
THMP
THMP
THMP
THMP
AH --!
THMP
THMP
DASH
THMP
KANATA-KUN?!
THMP
THMP
THMP
THMP
!
I'LL GET HIM!
CLACK

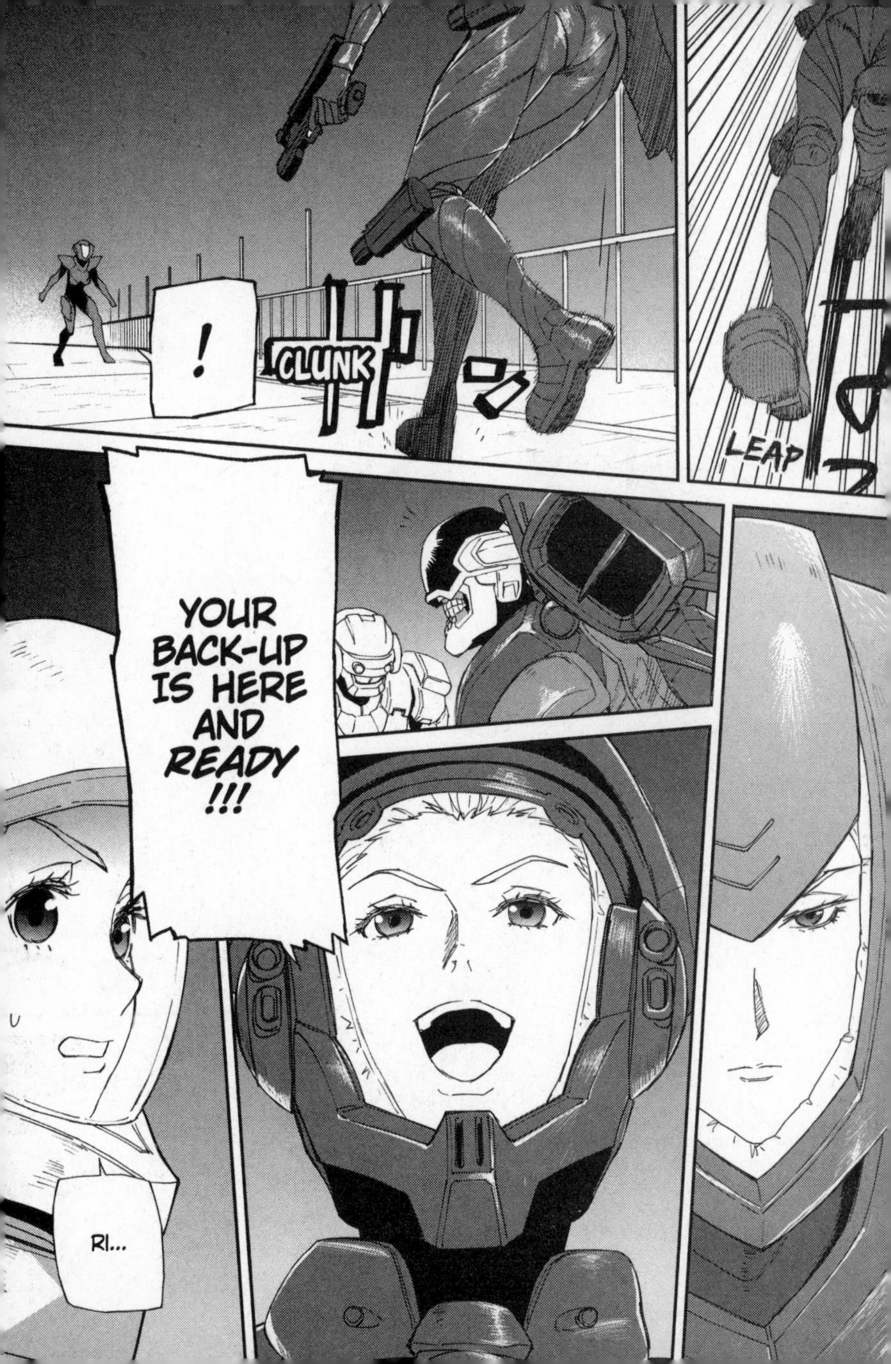
LEAP
!
CLUNK
YOUR BACK-UP IS HERE AND READY!!!
RI...

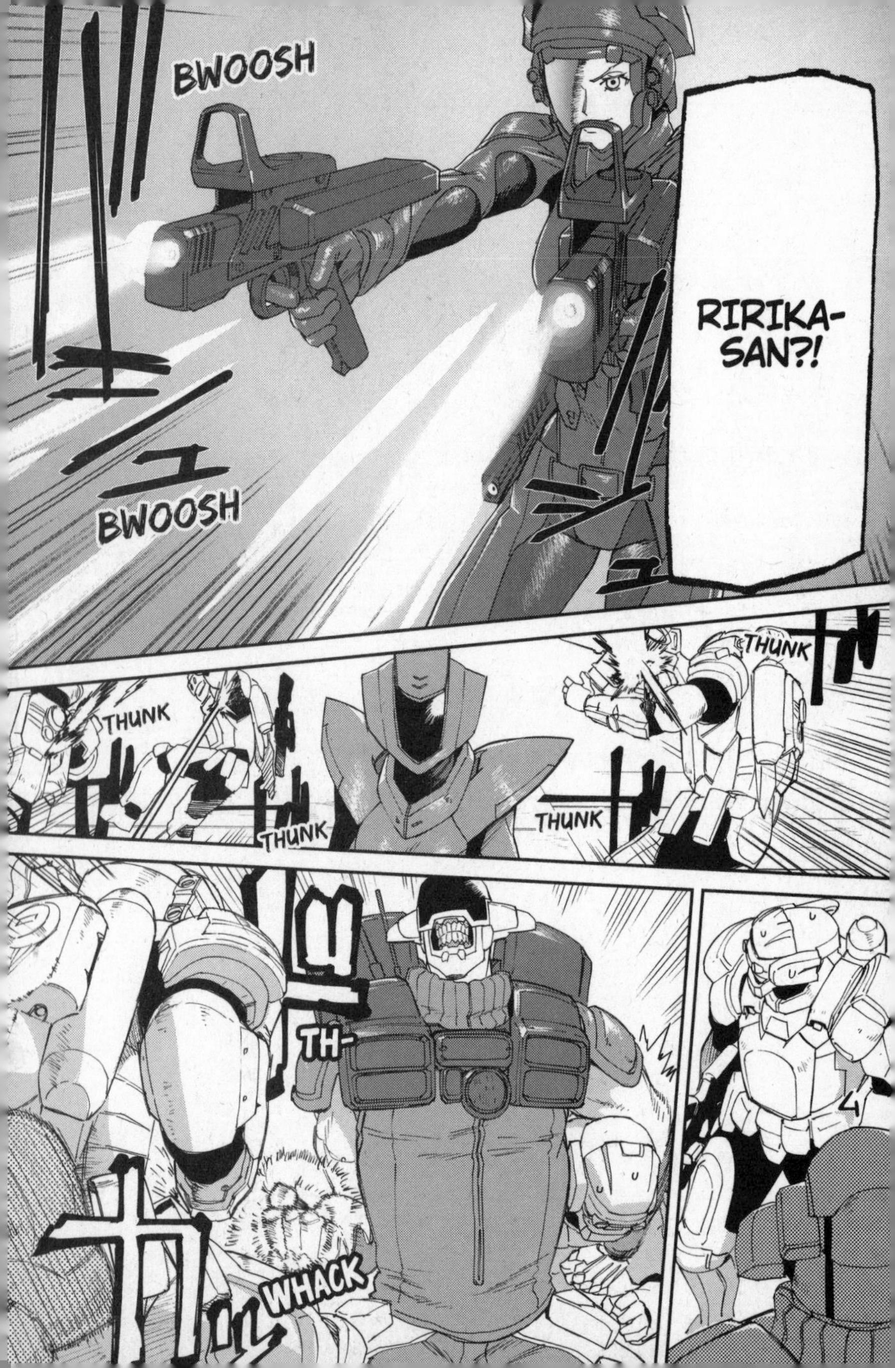
RIRIKA-SAN?!
BWOOSH
BWOOSH
THUNK
THUNK
THUNK
THUNK
TH-
WHACK

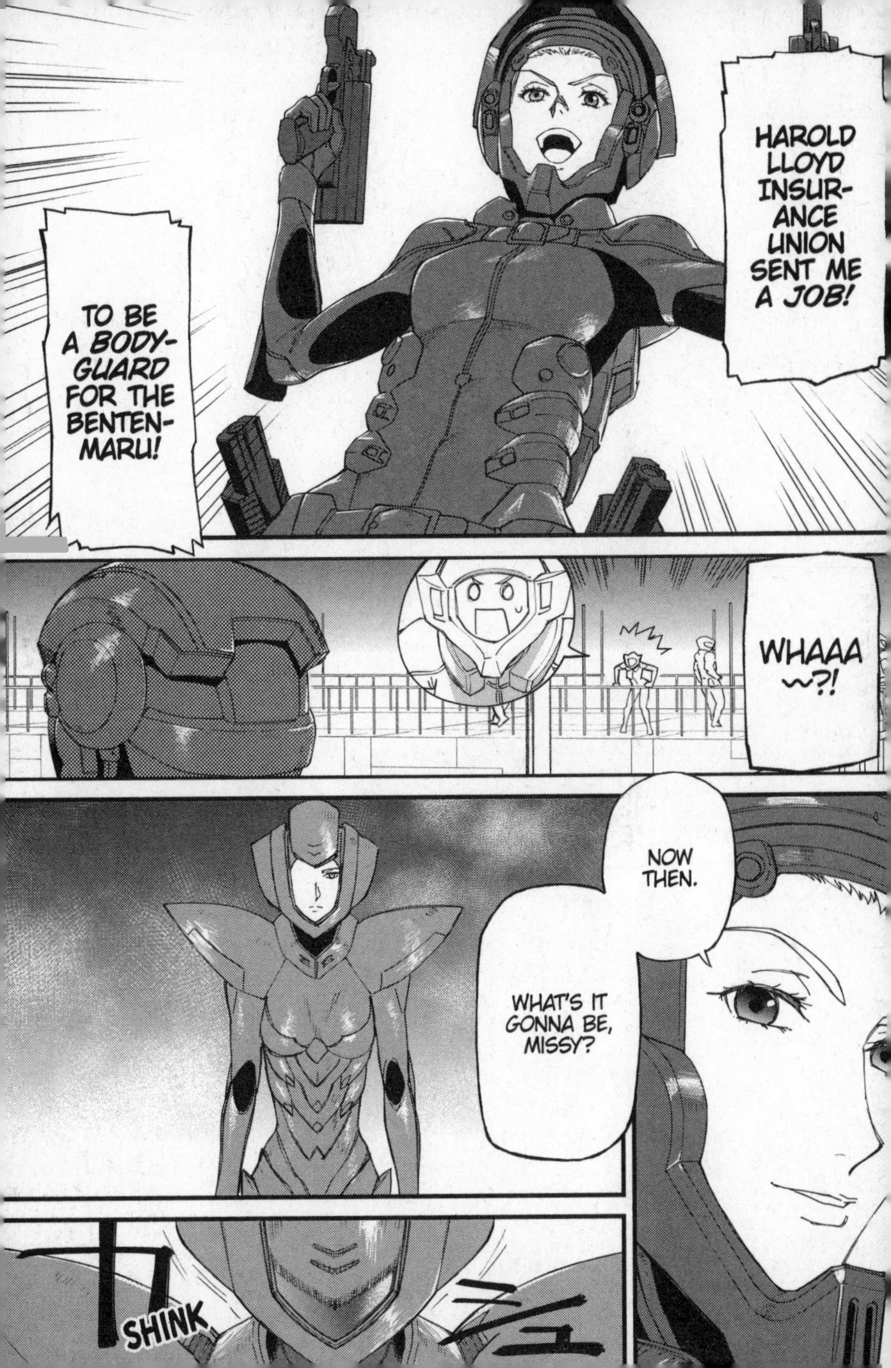
HAROLD LLOYD INSURANCE UNION SENT ME A *JOB*!
TO BE A *BODYGUARD* FOR THE BENTEN-MARU!
WHAAA ~?!
NOW THEN.
WHAT'S IT GONNA BE, MISSY?
SHINK

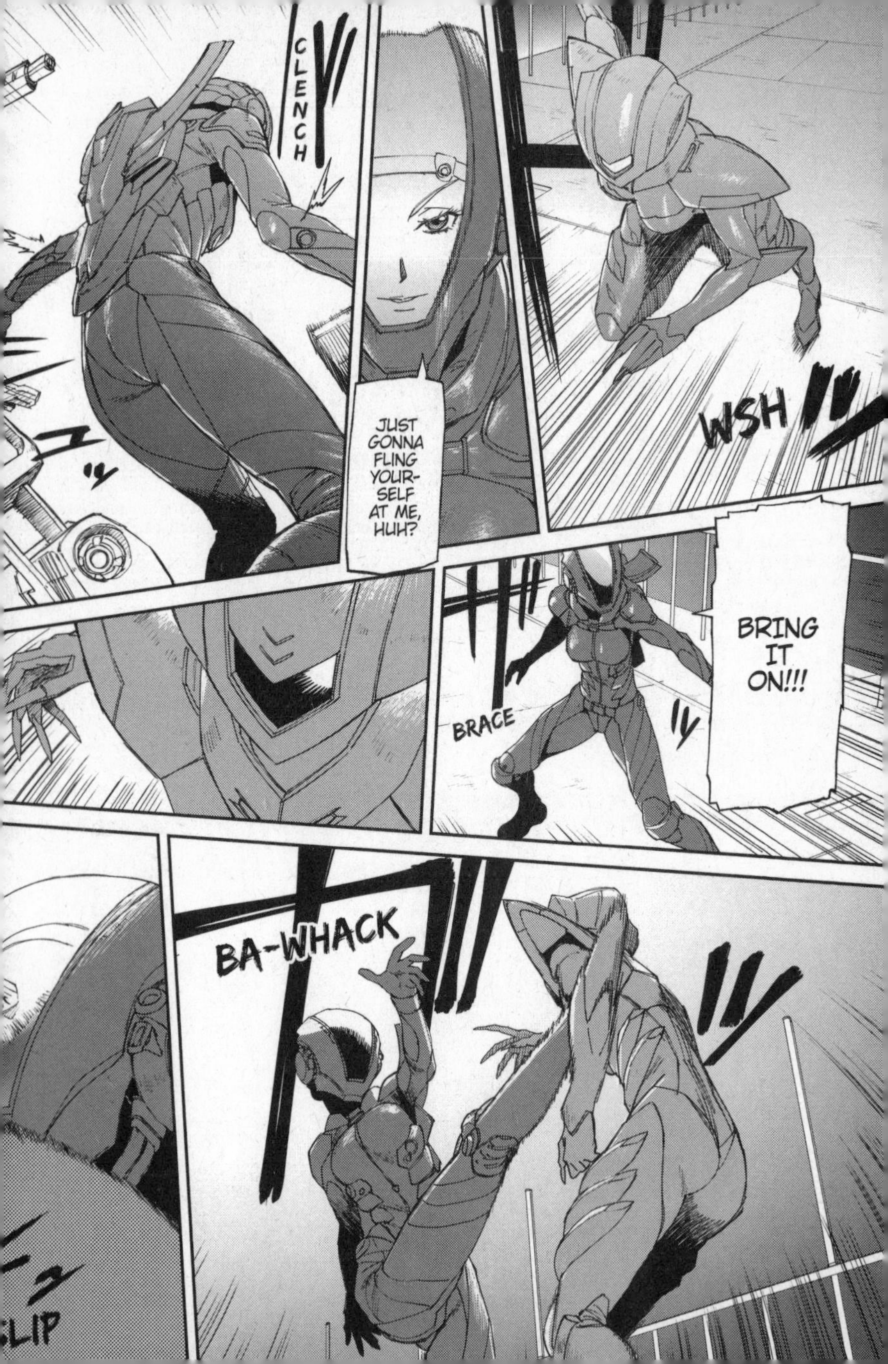

WSH
JUST GONNA FLING YOUR-SELF AT ME, HUH?
CLENCH
BRING IT ON!!!
BRACE
BA-WHACK
LIP

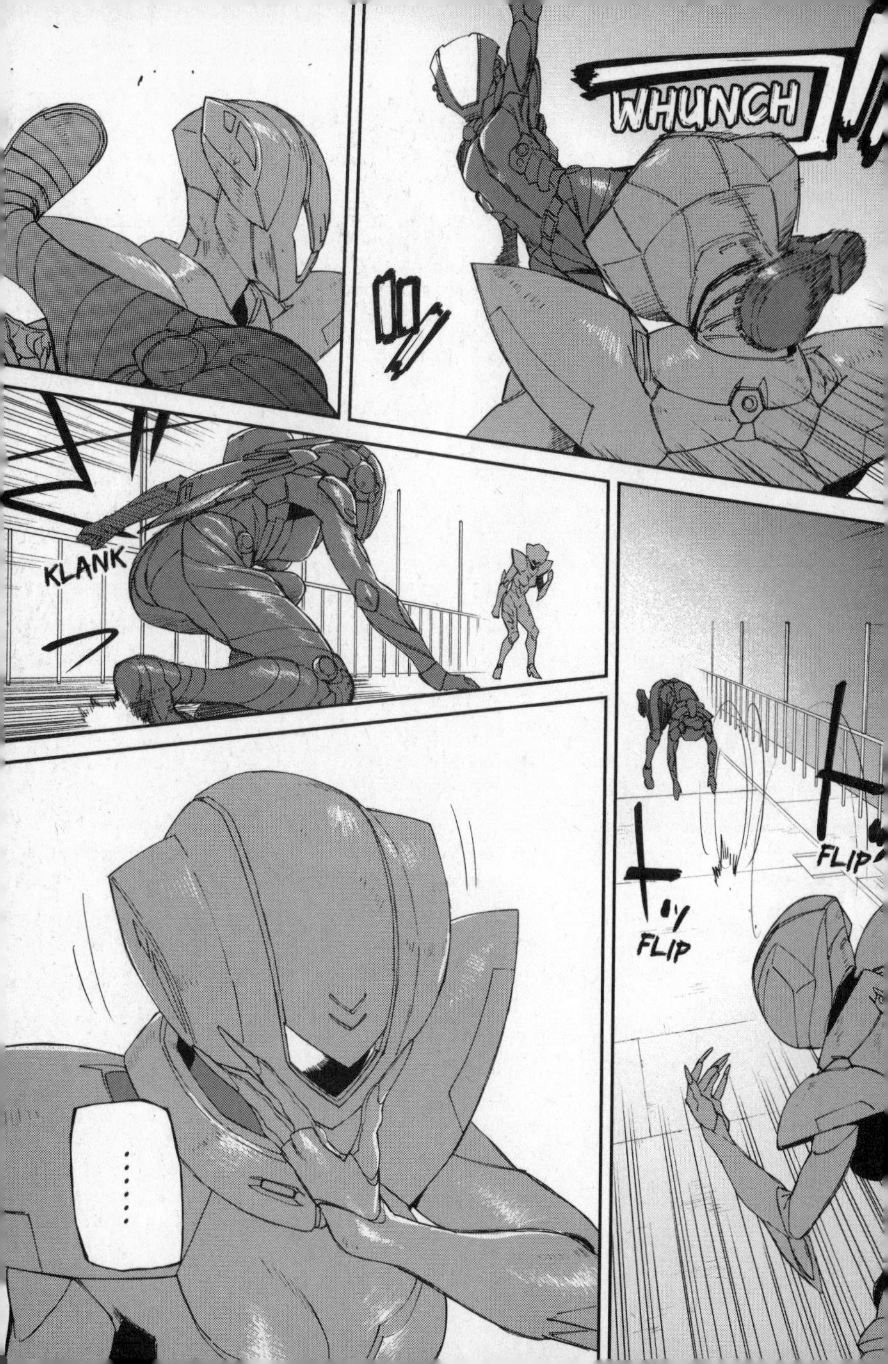
WHUNCH
FLIP
FLIP
KLANK
......

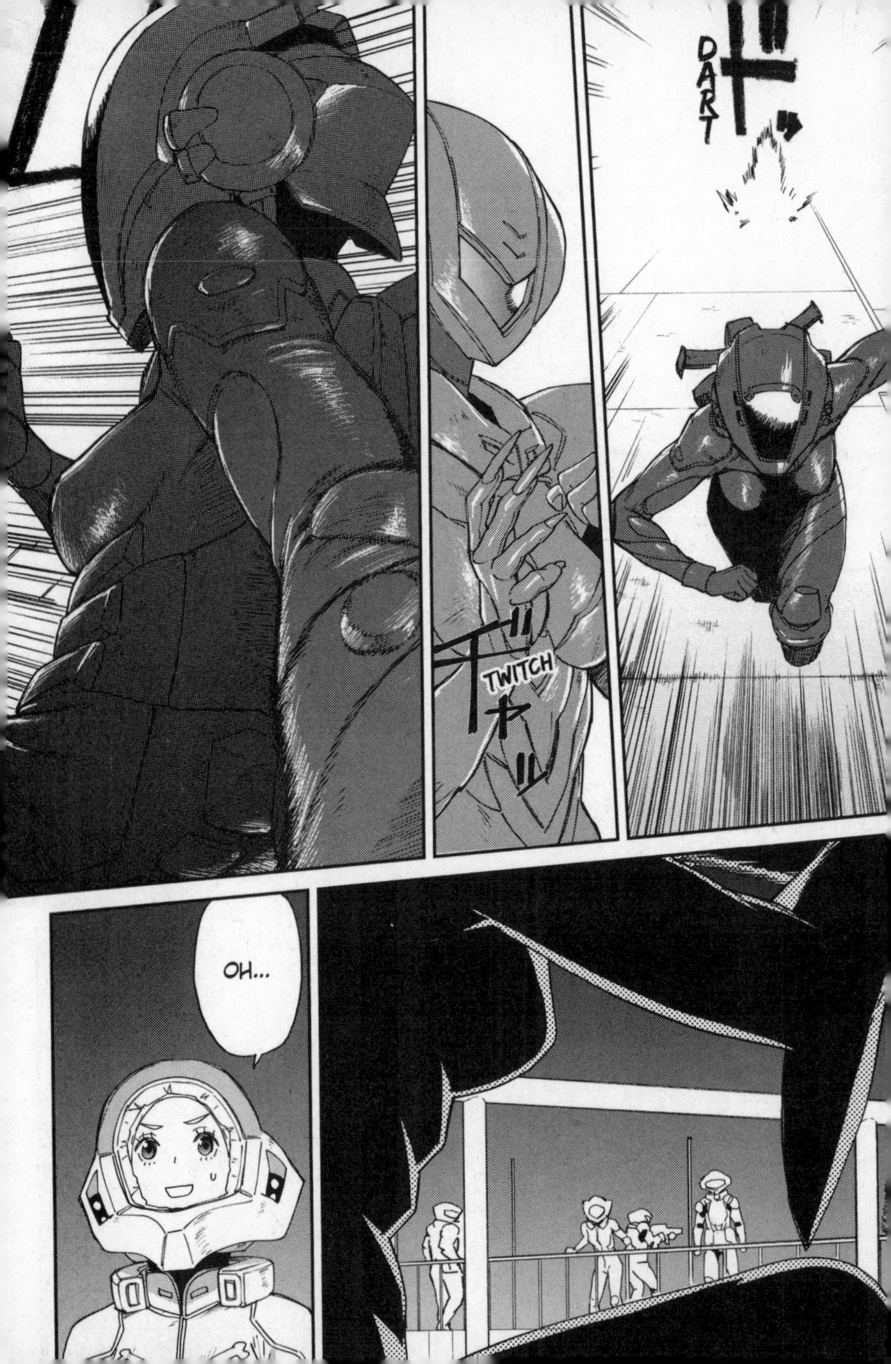
DART
TWITCH
OH...

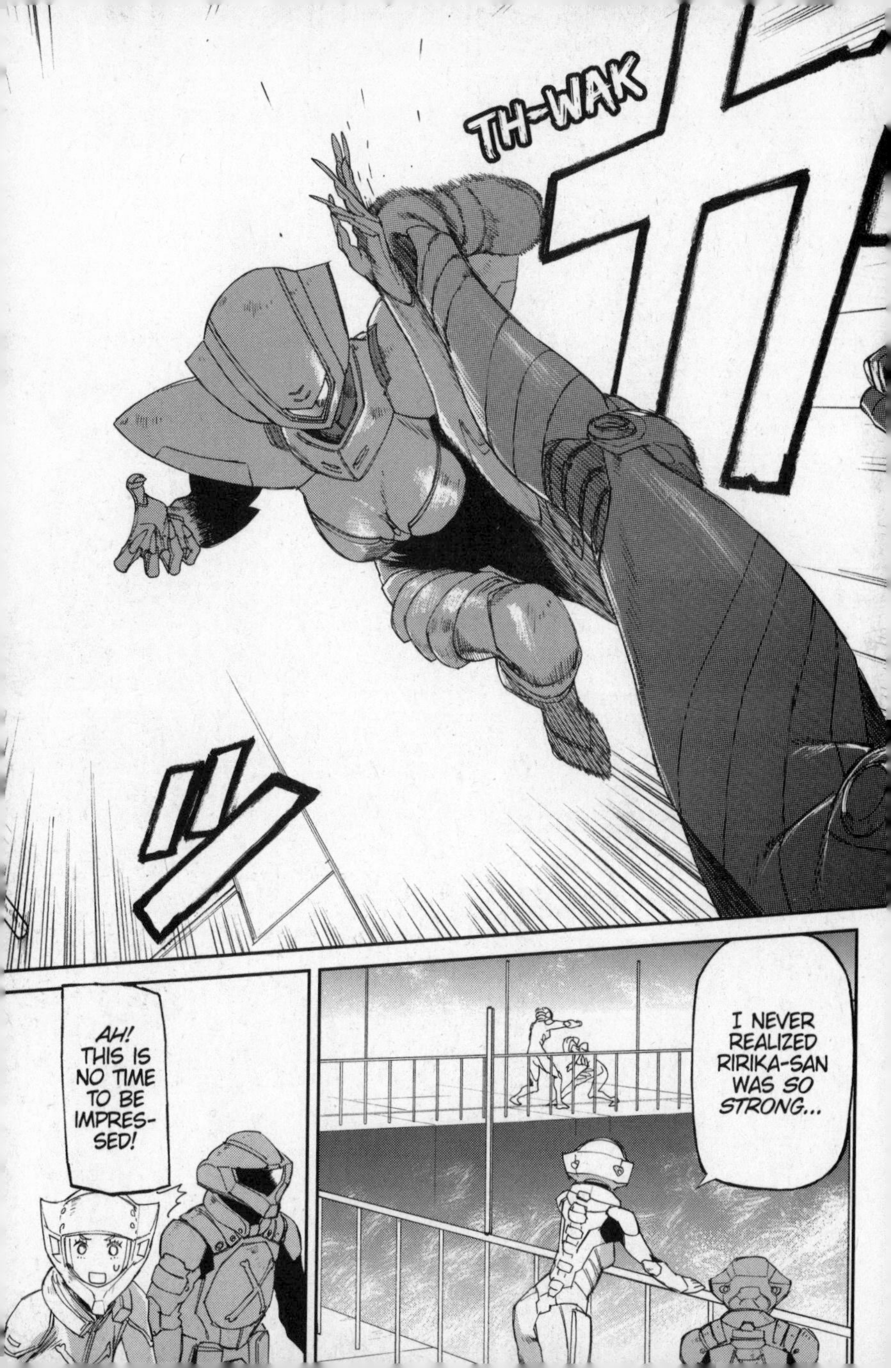
TH-WAK
I NEVER REALIZED RIRIKA-SAN WAS SO STRONG...
AH! THIS IS NO TIME TO BE IMPRES-SED!

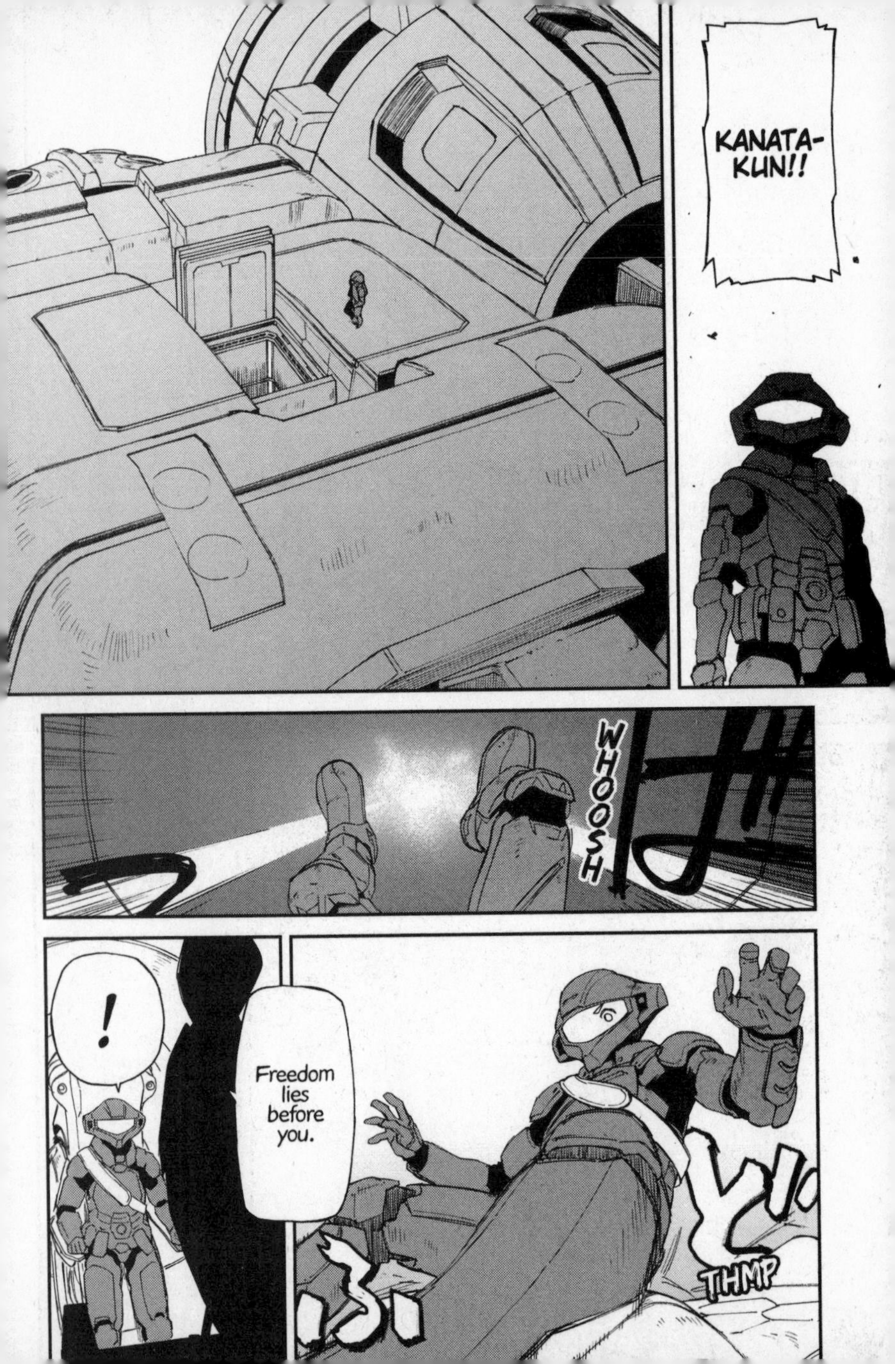
KANATA-KUN!!
WHOOOSH
Freedom lies before you.
THMP
!

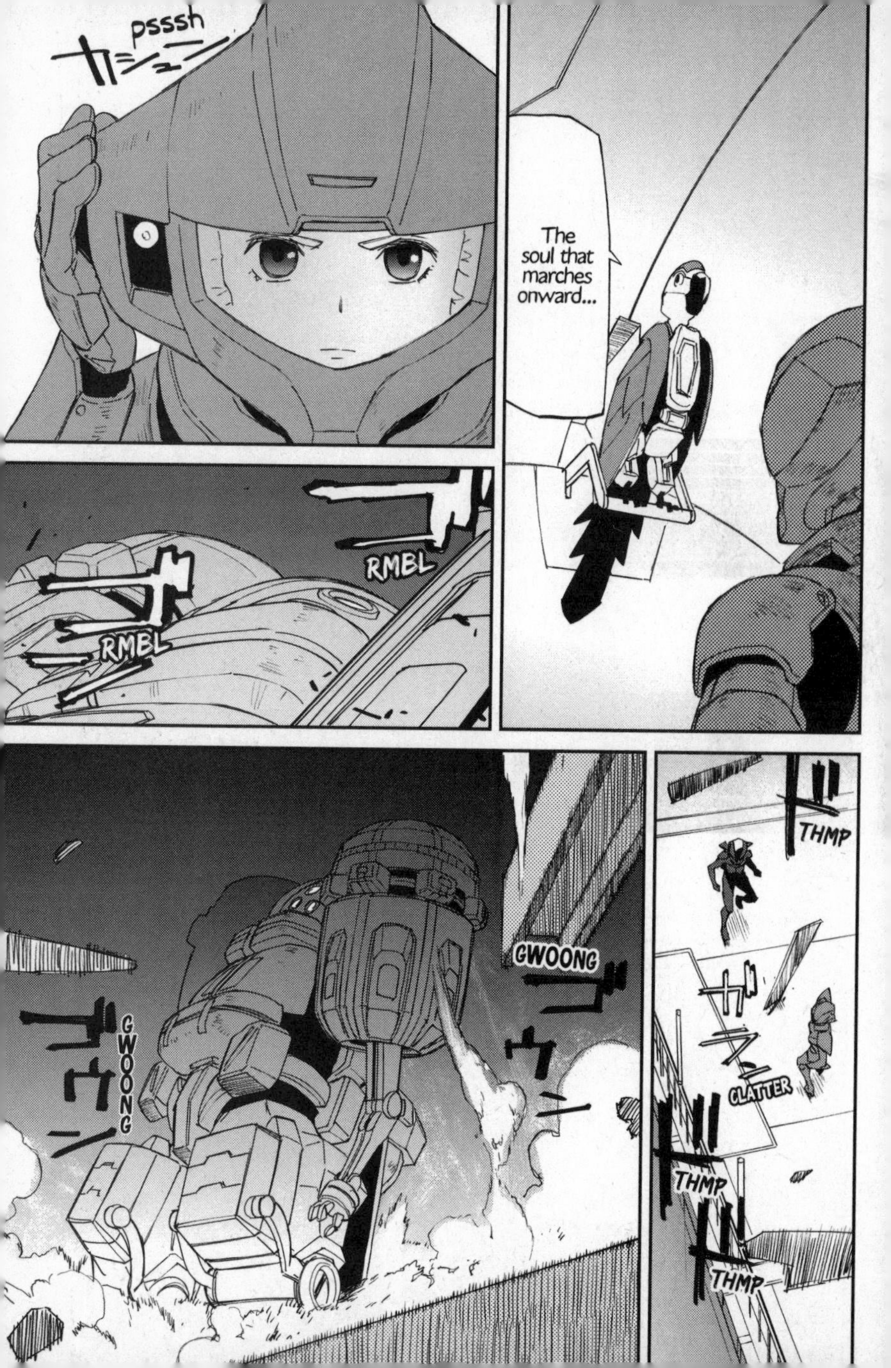
The soul that marches onward...
psssh
RMBL
RMBL
THMP
CLATTER
THMP
THMP
GWOONG
GWOONG

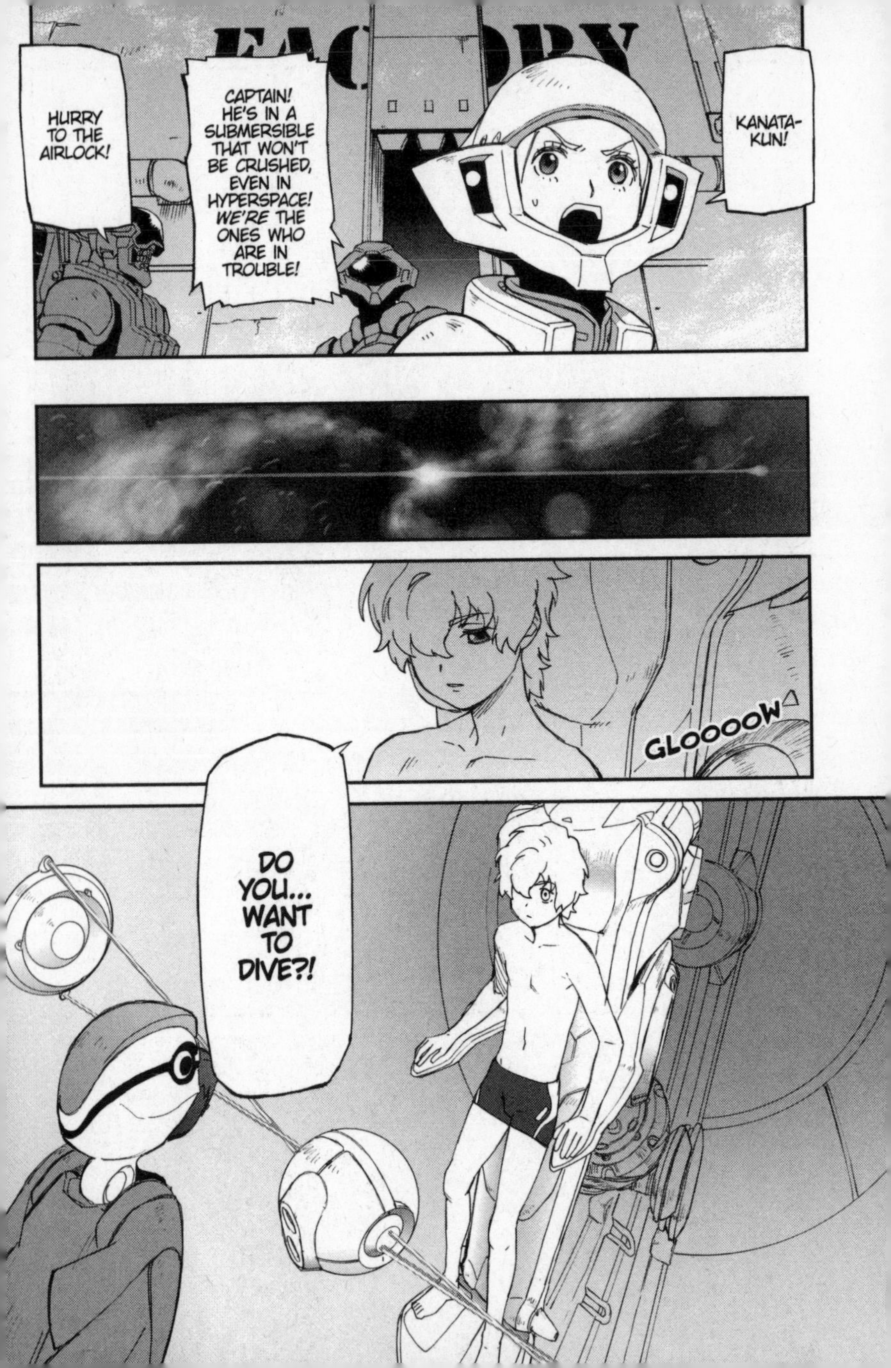
KANATA-KUN!
CAPTAIN! HE'S IN A SUBMERSIBLE THAT WON'T BE CRUSHED, EVEN IN HYPERSPACE! WE'RE THE ONES WHO ARE IN TROUBLE!
HURRY TO THE AIRLOCK!
GLOOOOW
DO YOU... WANT TO DIVE?!

blip
START UP
whrrl
TK
TK
TK
TK
TK
TK
TK
TK
TK
TK
TK

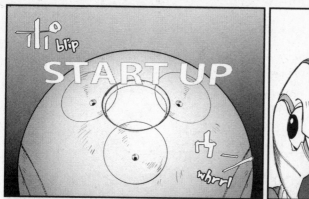

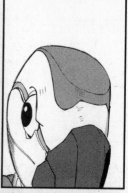

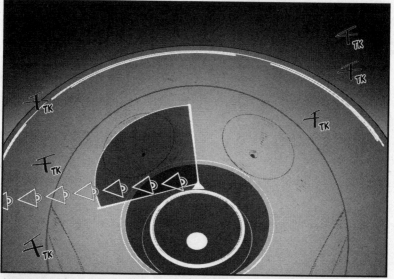

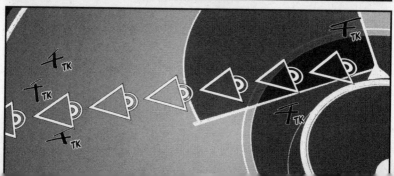

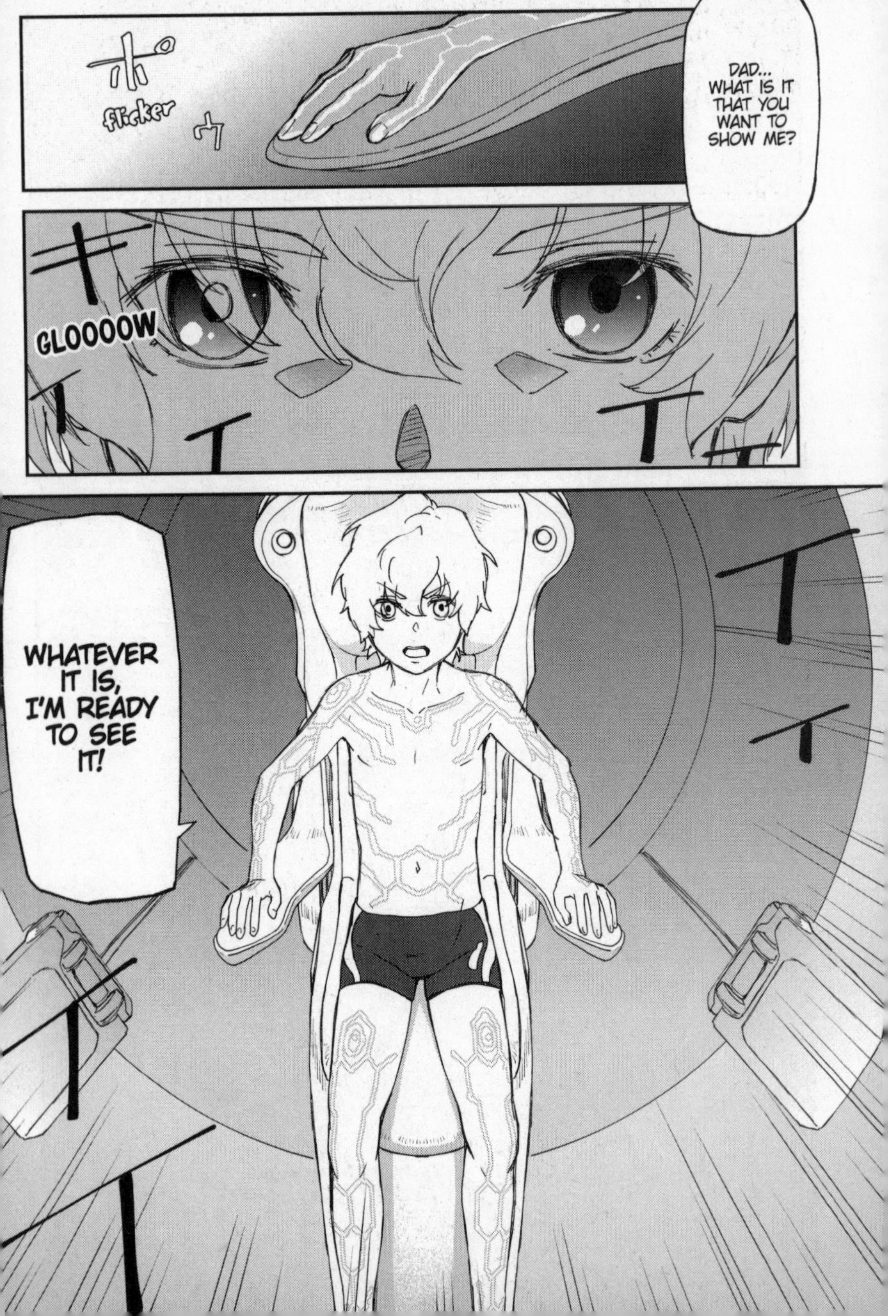
DAD... WHAT IS IT THAT YOU WANT TO SHOW ME?
flicker
GLOOOOW
WHATEVER IT IS, I'M READY TO SEE IT!

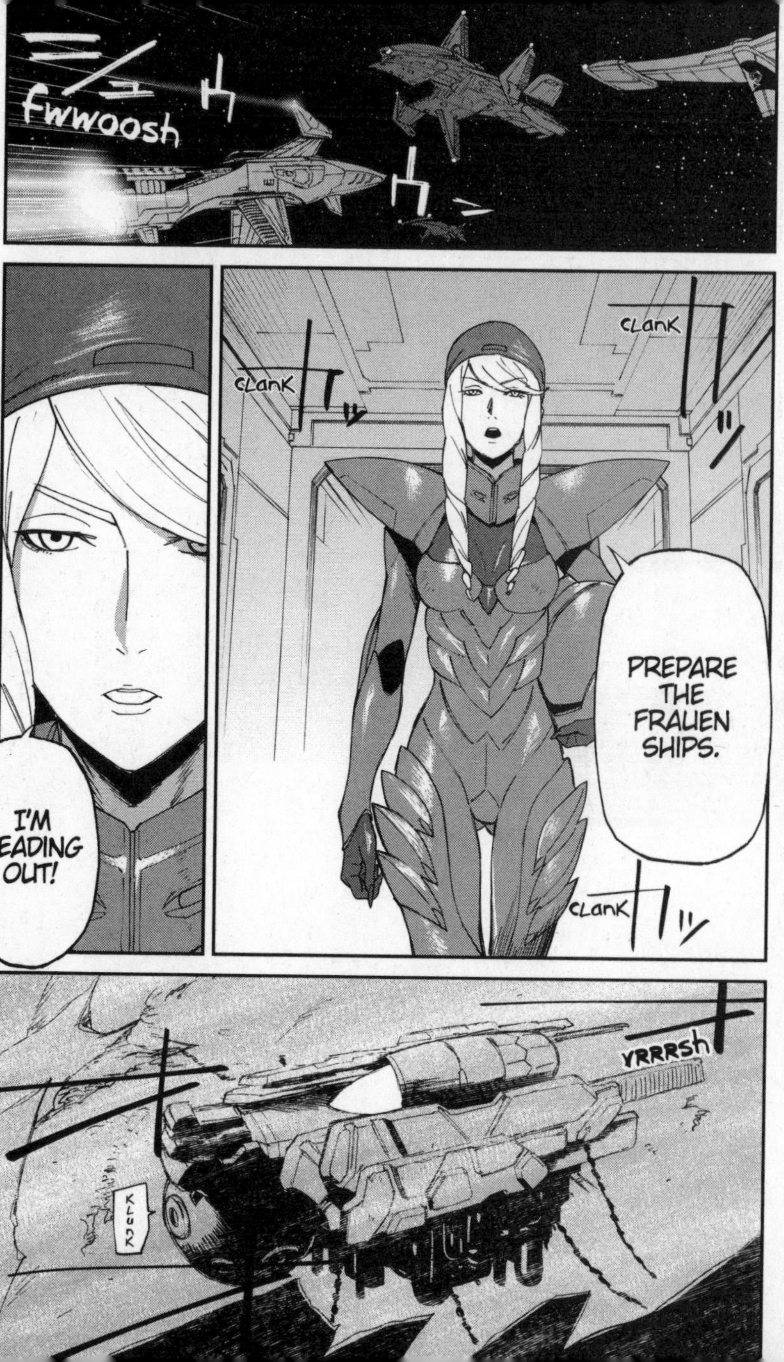
fwwoosh
CLANK
CLANK
PREPARE THE FRAUEN SHIPS.
CLANK
I'M HEADING OUT!
YRRRSH
KLUNK

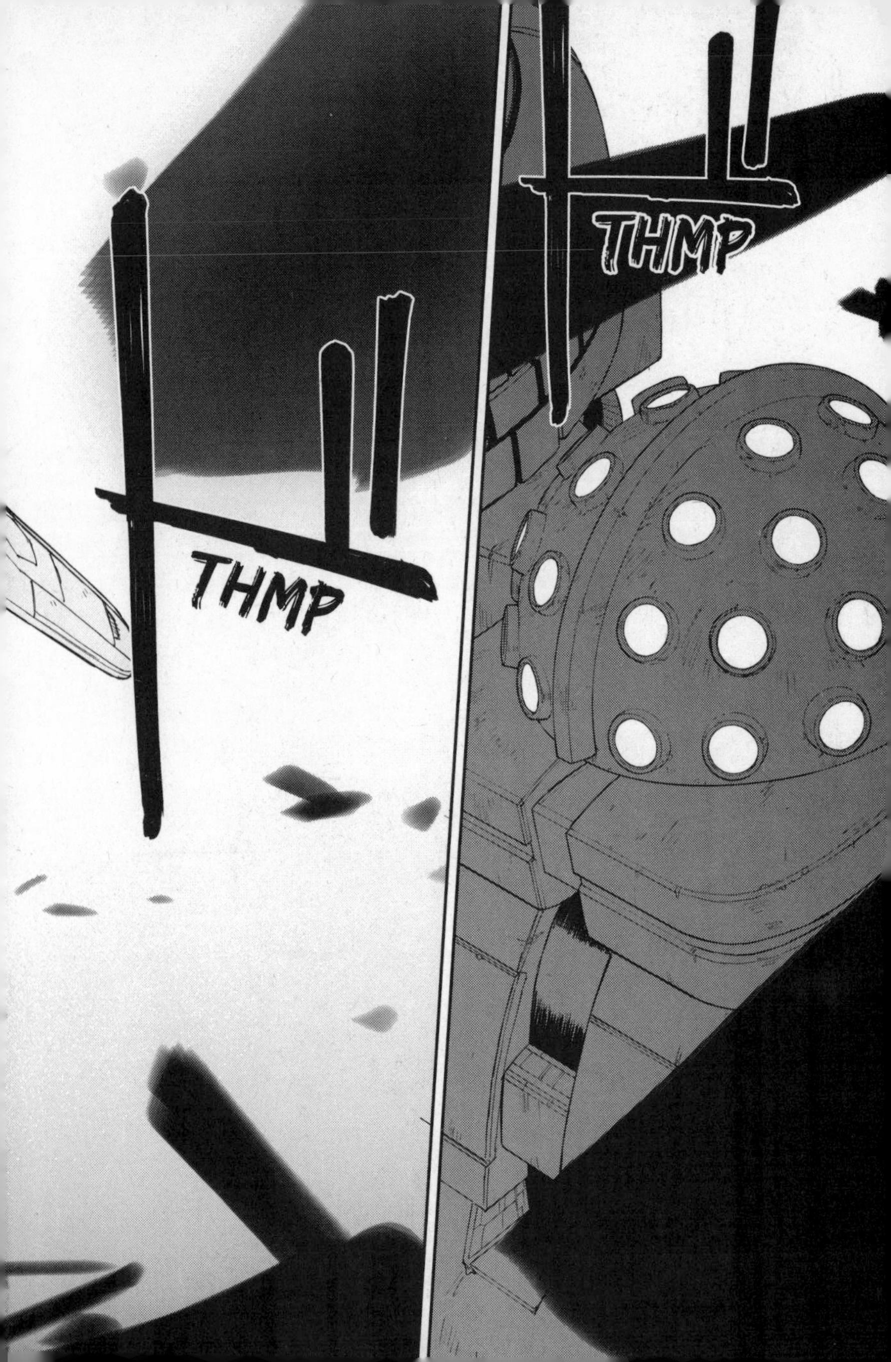
THMP
THMP

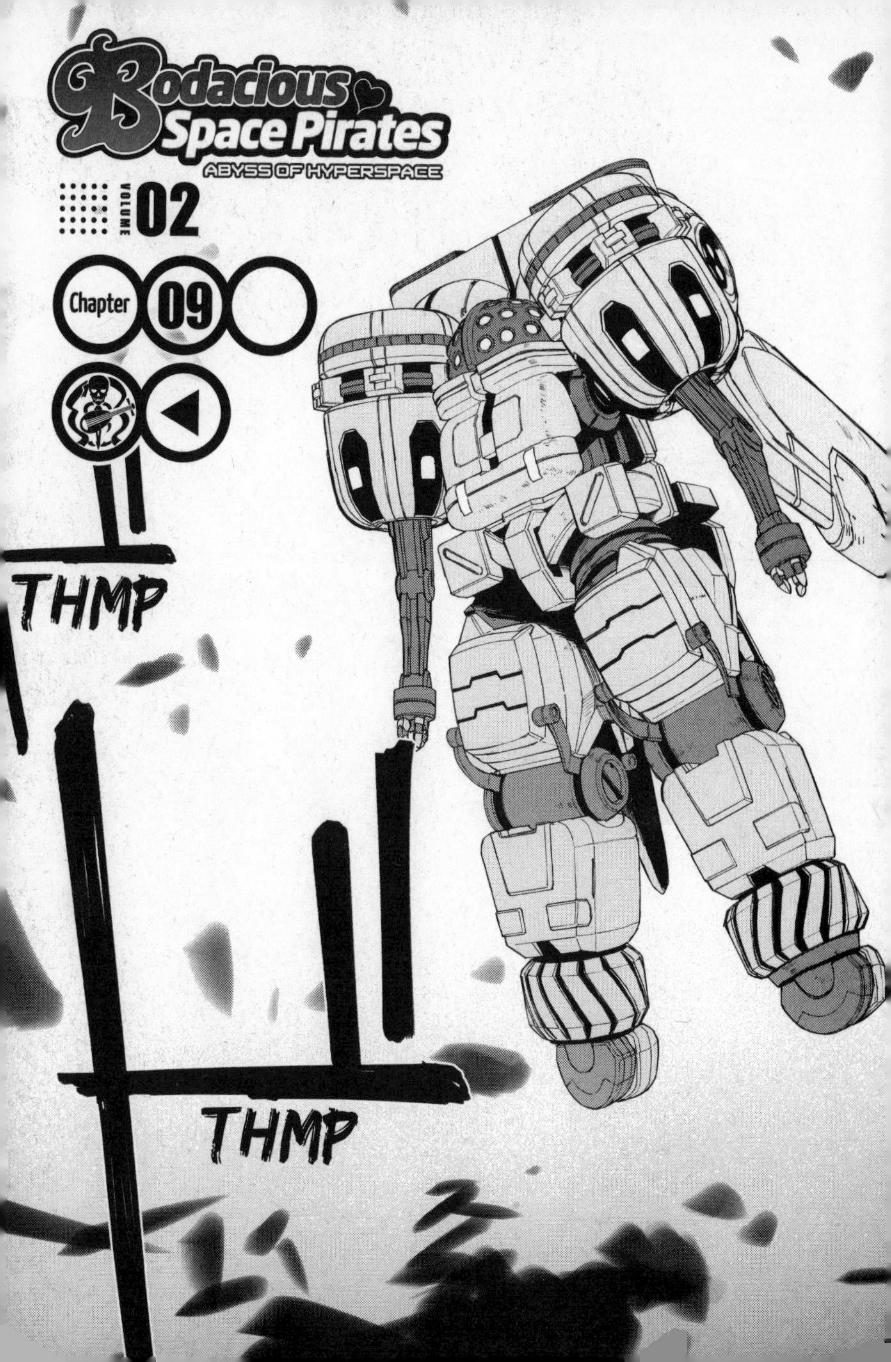
Bodacious Space Pirates
ABYSS OF HYPERSPACE
VOLUME 02
Chapter 09
THMP
THMP

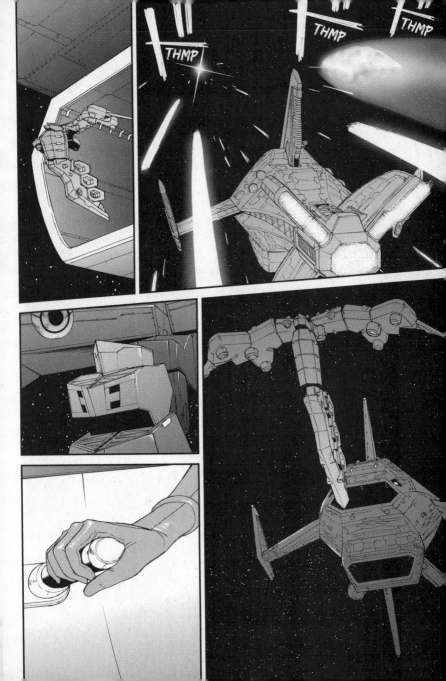

THMP

THMP

THMP

FRAUEN PLATOON...

WE WILL BE PURSUING PROFESSOR MUGEN'S SUBMERSIBLE.

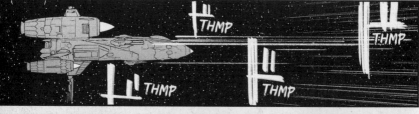

THMP THMP THMP THMP THMP

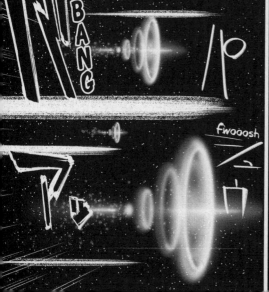

BANG

Fwooosh

SKREEE

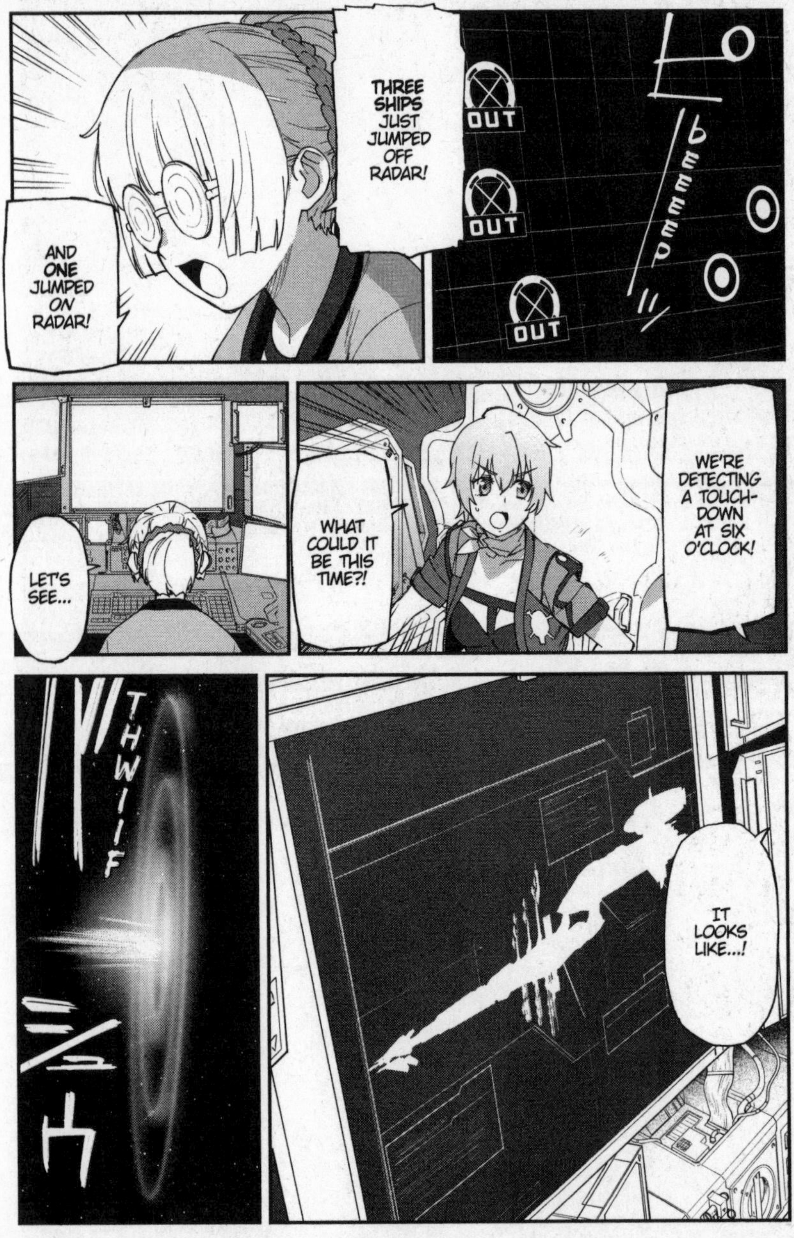
BEEEEEP
OUT
OUT
OUT
THREE SHIPS JUST JUMPED OFF RADAR!
AND ONE JUMPED ON RADAR!
WE'RE DETECTING A TOUCH-DOWN AT SIX O'CLOCK!
WHAT COULD IT BE THIS TIME?!
LET'S SEE...
IT LOOKS LIKE...!
THWIIIF

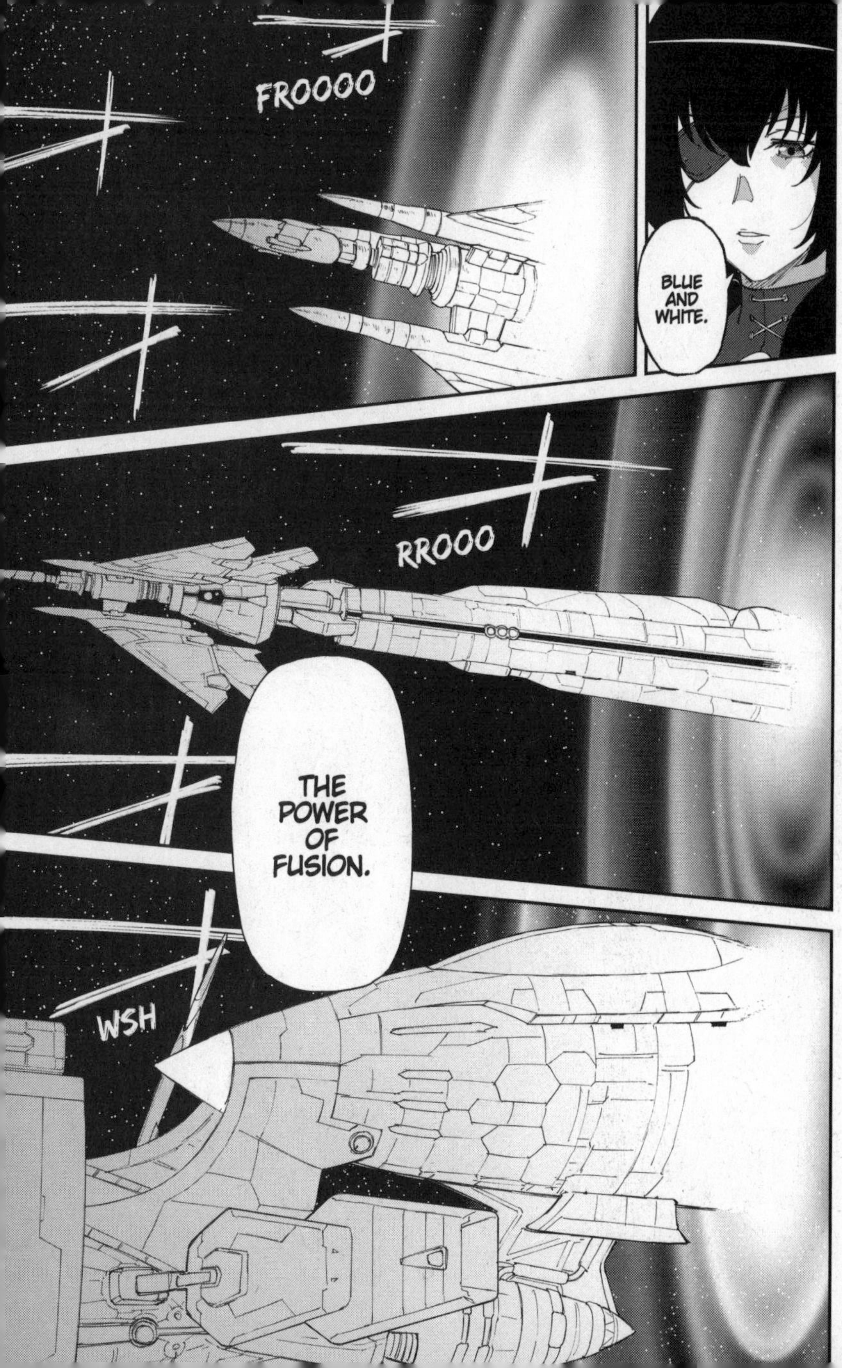
BLUE AND WHITE.
FROOOO
RROOO
THE POWER OF FUSION.
WSH

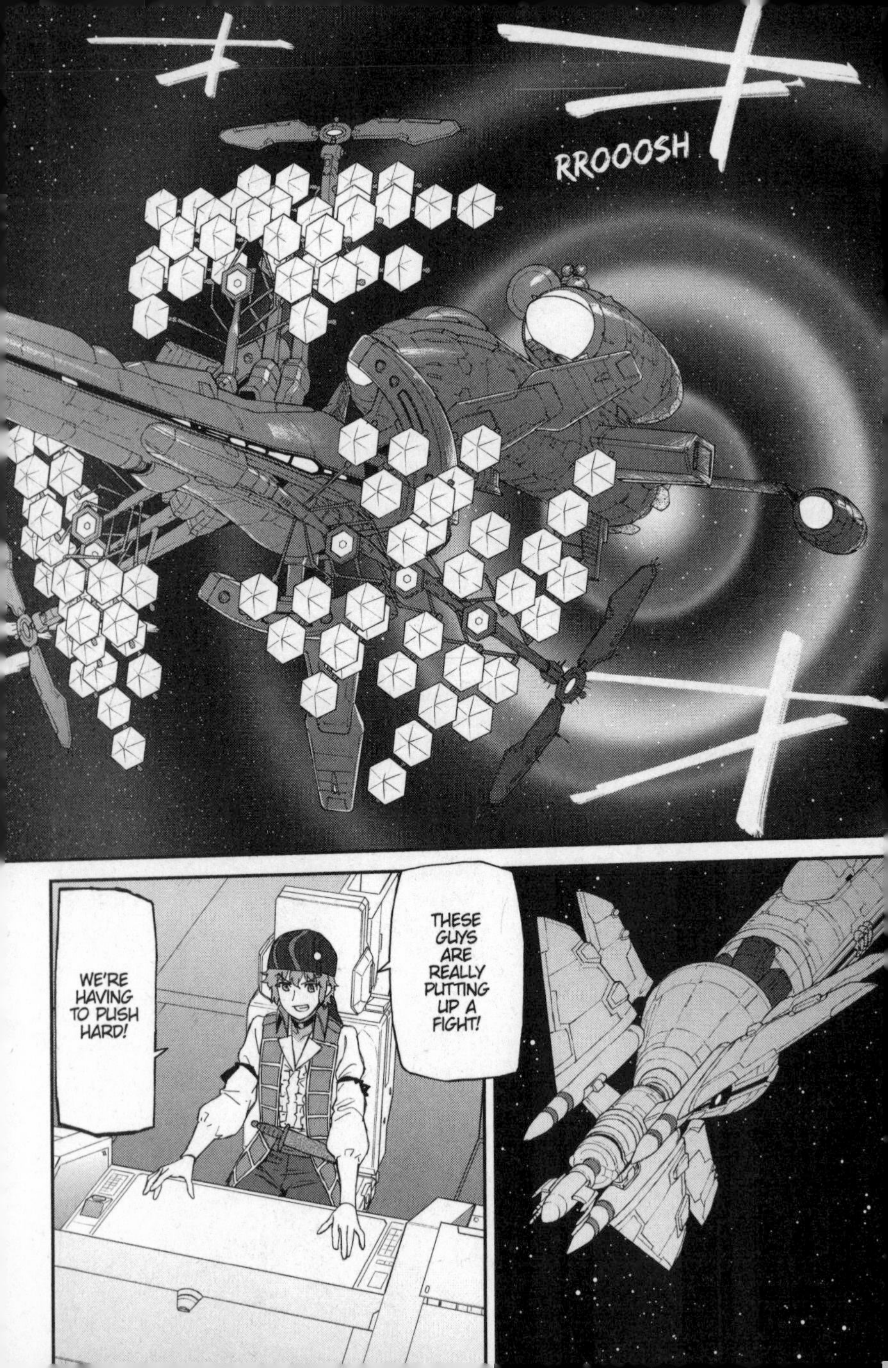
RROOOSH
THESE GUYS ARE REALLY PUTTING UP A FIGHT!
WE'RE HAVING TO PUSH HARD!

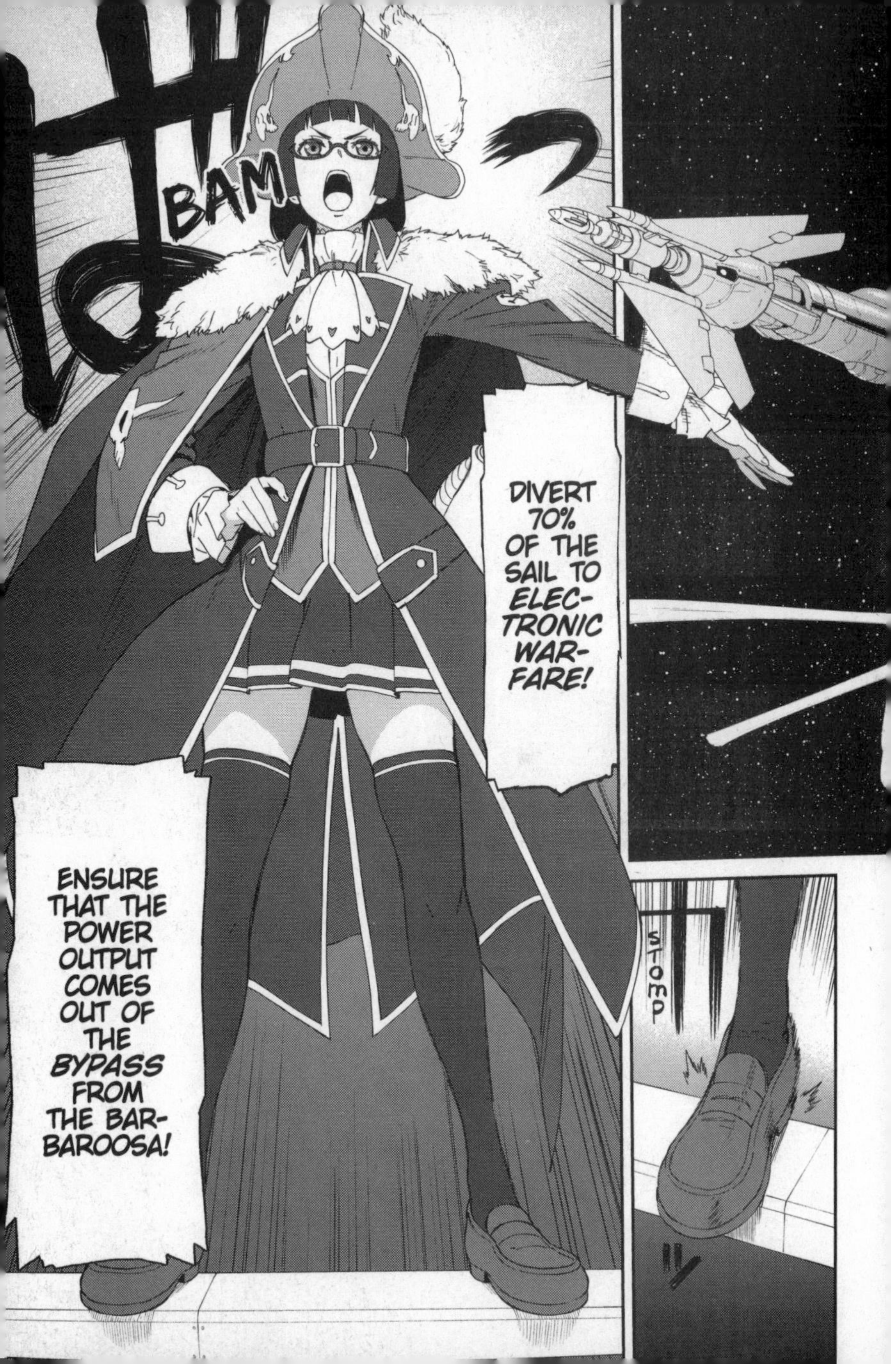
STOMP
BAM
DIVERT 70% OF THE SAIL TO *ELECTRONIC WARFARE!*
ENSURE THAT THE POWER OUTPUT COMES OUT OF THE *BYPASS* FROM THE BARBAROOSA!

OUTPUT IS STABLE! IT'S HOLDING!

nod

ROGER!!!

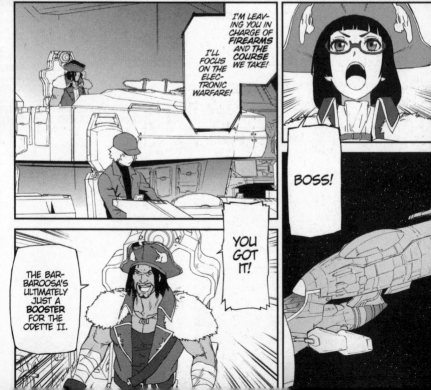

I'M LEAVING YOU IN CHARGE OF FIREARMS AND THE COURSE WE TAKE!

I'LL FOCUS ON THE ELECTRONIC WARFARE!

BOSS!

THE BARBAROOSA'S ULTIMATELY JUST A BOOSTER FOR THE ODETTE II.

YOU GOT IT!

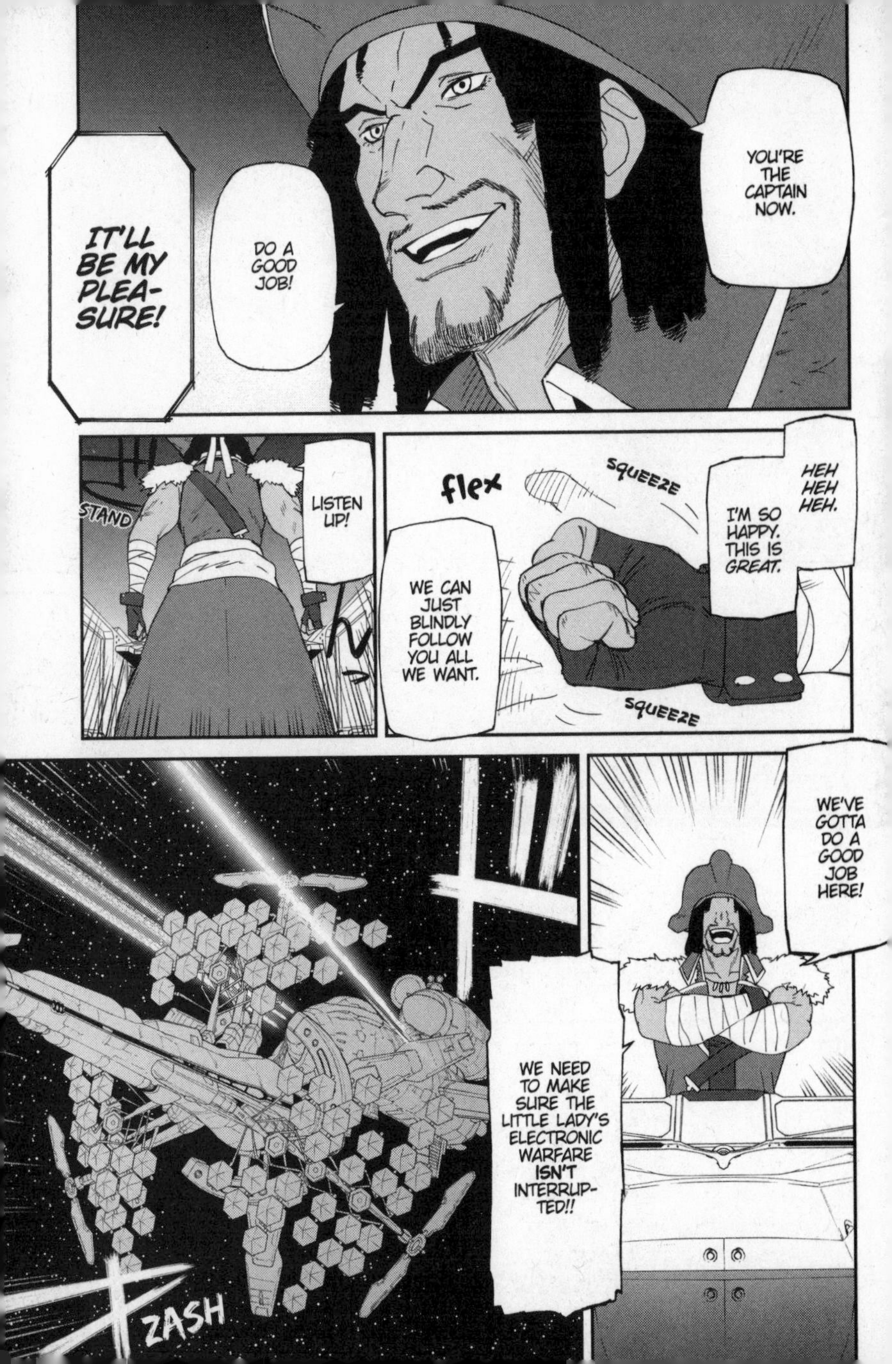
YOU'RE THE CAPTAIN NOW.
DO A GOOD JOB!
IT'LL BE MY PLEASURE!
HEH HEH HEH.
I'M SO HAPPY. THIS IS GREAT.
SQUEEZE
flex
WE CAN JUST BLINDLY FOLLOW YOU ALL WE WANT.
SQUEEZE
LISTEN UP!
STAND
WE'VE GOTTA DO A GOOD JOB HERE!
WE NEED TO MAKE SURE THE LITTLE LADY'S ELECTRONIC WARFARE ISN'T INTERRUPTED!!
ZASH

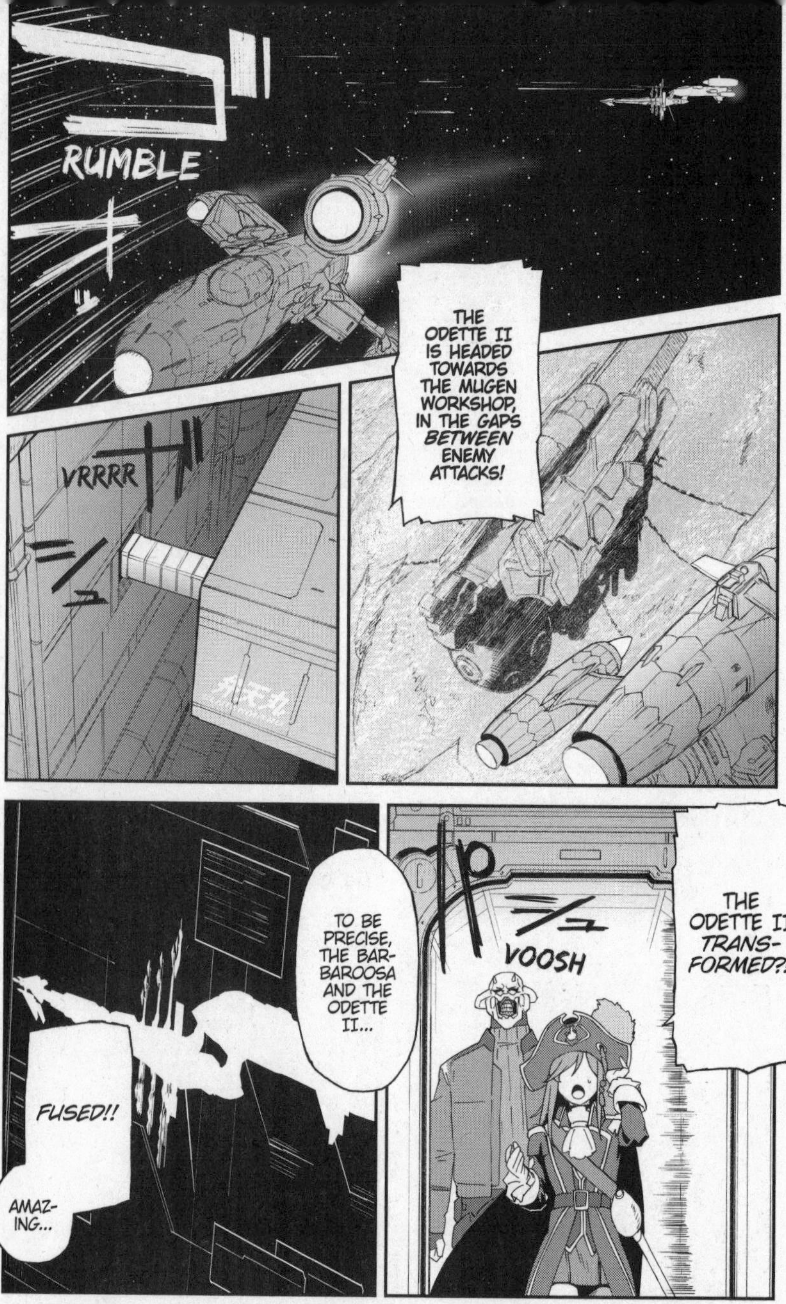
RUMBLE
THE ODETTE II IS HEADED TOWARDS THE MUGEN WORKSHOP, IN THE GAPS *BETWEEN* ENEMY ATTACKS!
VRRRR
THE ODETTE II *TRANSFORMED?!*
TO BE PRECISE, THE BARBAROOSA AND THE ODETTE II...
VOOSH
FUSED!!
AMAZING...

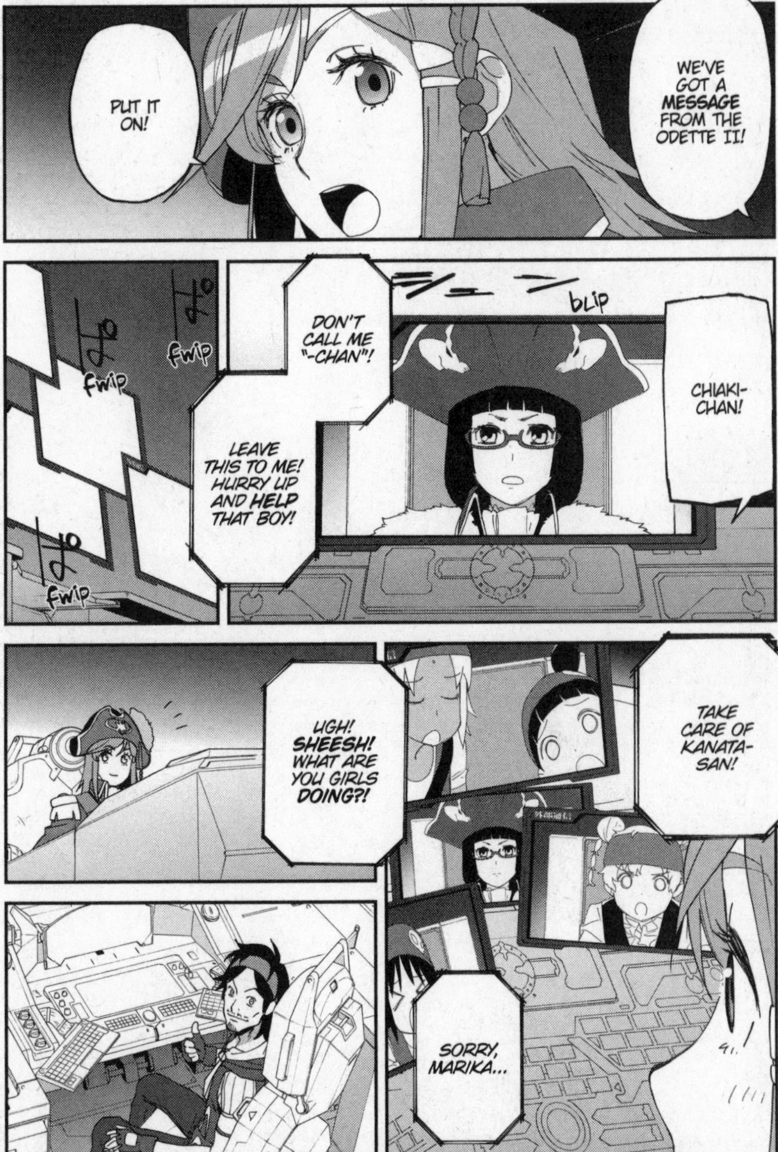

WE'VE GOT A MESSAGE FROM THE ODETTE II!
PUT IT ON!
blip
CHIAKI-CHAN!
DON'T CALL ME "-CHAN"!
LEAVE THIS TO ME! HURRY UP AND HELP THAT BOY!
fwip
fwip
fwip
TAKE CARE OF KANATA-SAN!
SORRY, MARIKA...
UGH! SHEESH! WHAT ARE YOU GIRLS DOING?!

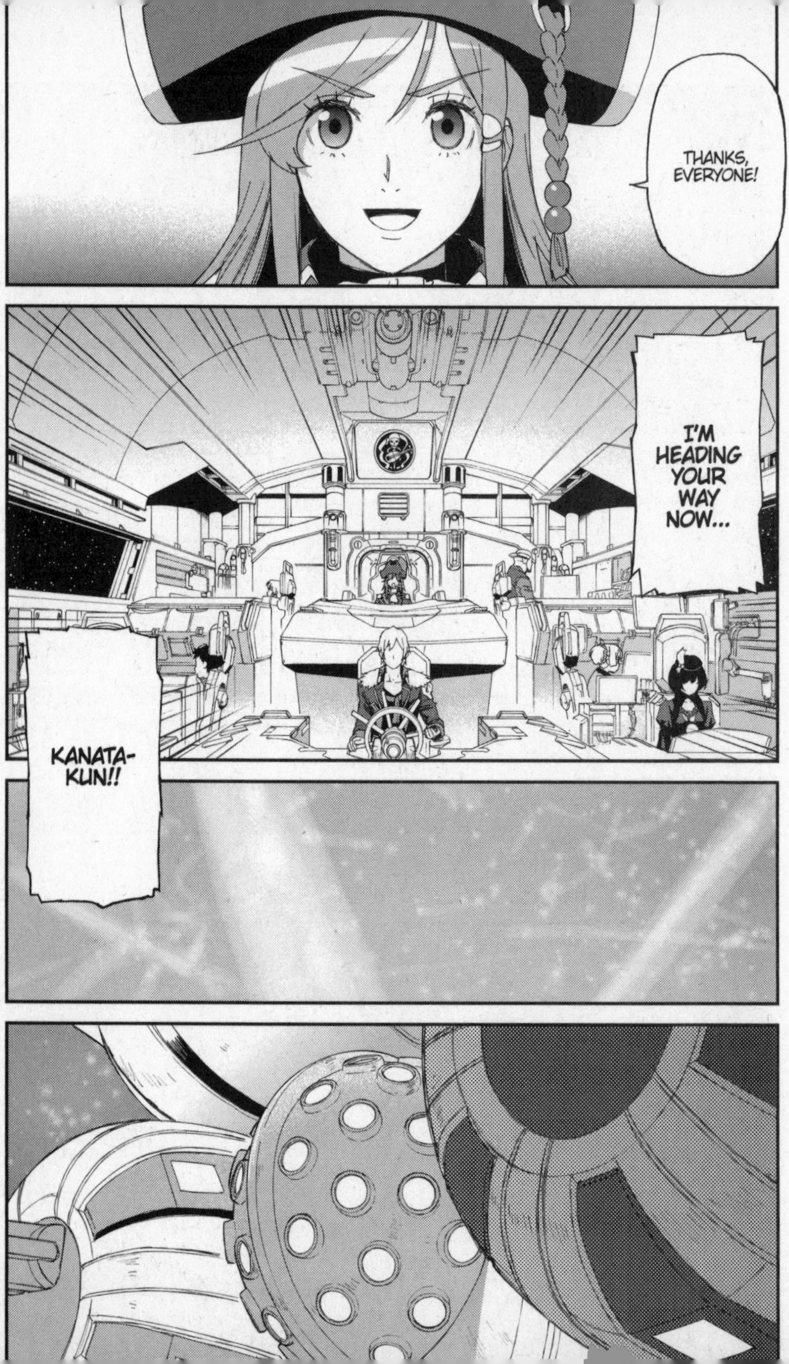
THANKS, EVERYONE!
I'M HEADING YOUR WAY NOW...
KANATA-KUN!!

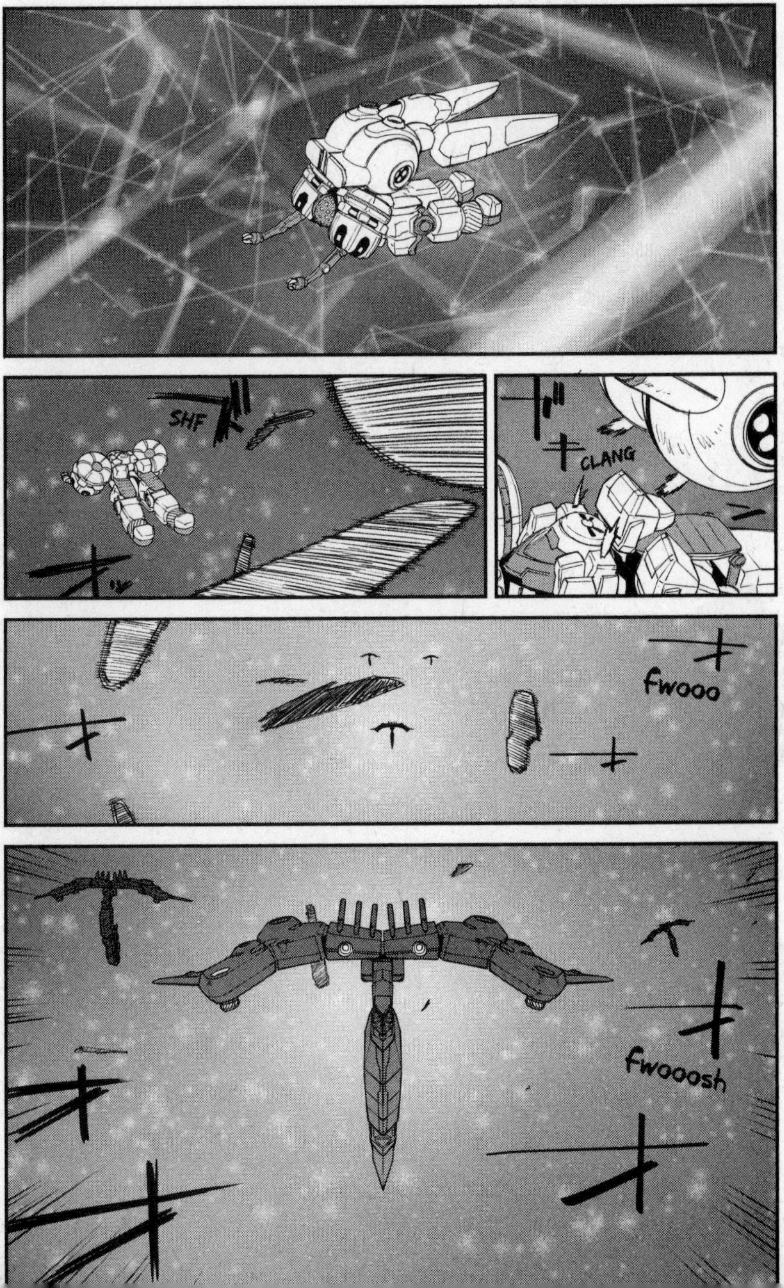
CLANG
SHF
fwooo
fwooosh

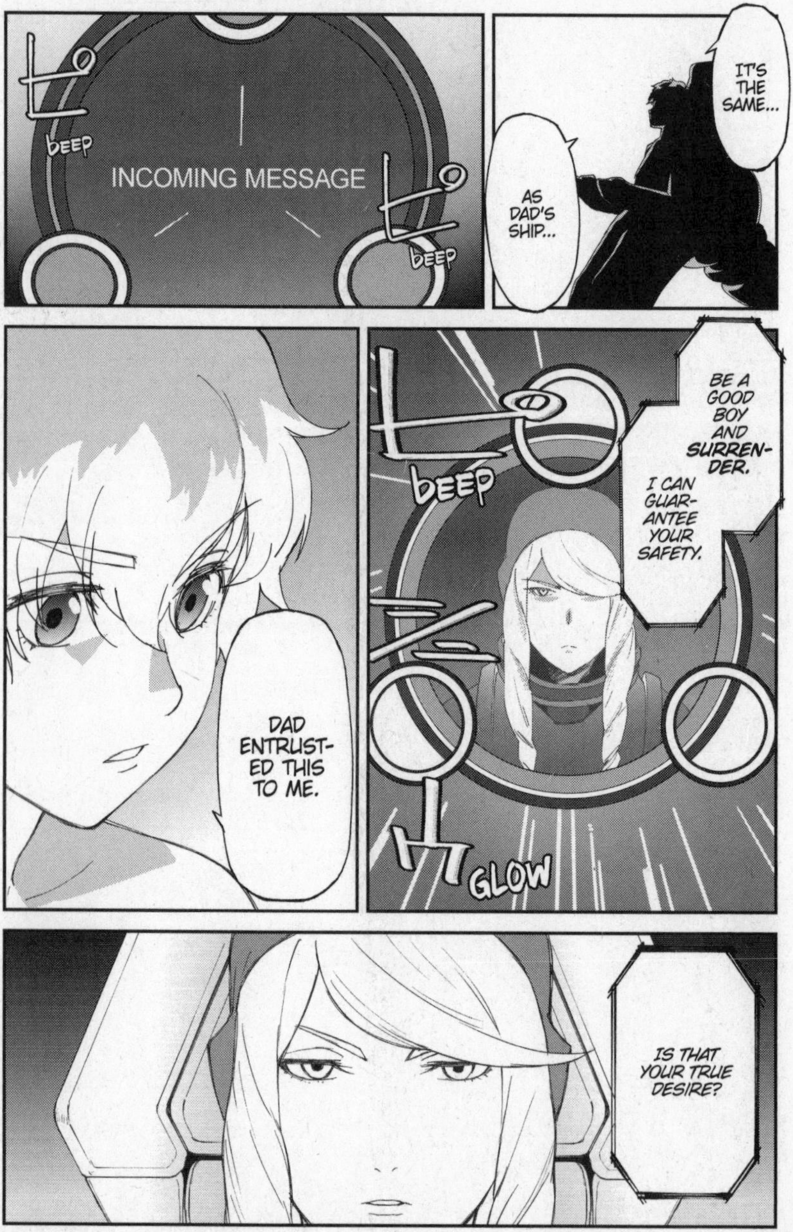
IT'S THE SAME...
AS DAD'S SHIP...
beep
INCOMING MESSAGE
beep
BE A GOOD BOY AND SURREN-DER.
I CAN GUAR-ANTEE YOUR SAFETY.
beep
GLOW
DAD ENTRUST-ED THIS TO ME.
IS THAT YOUR TRUE DESIRE?

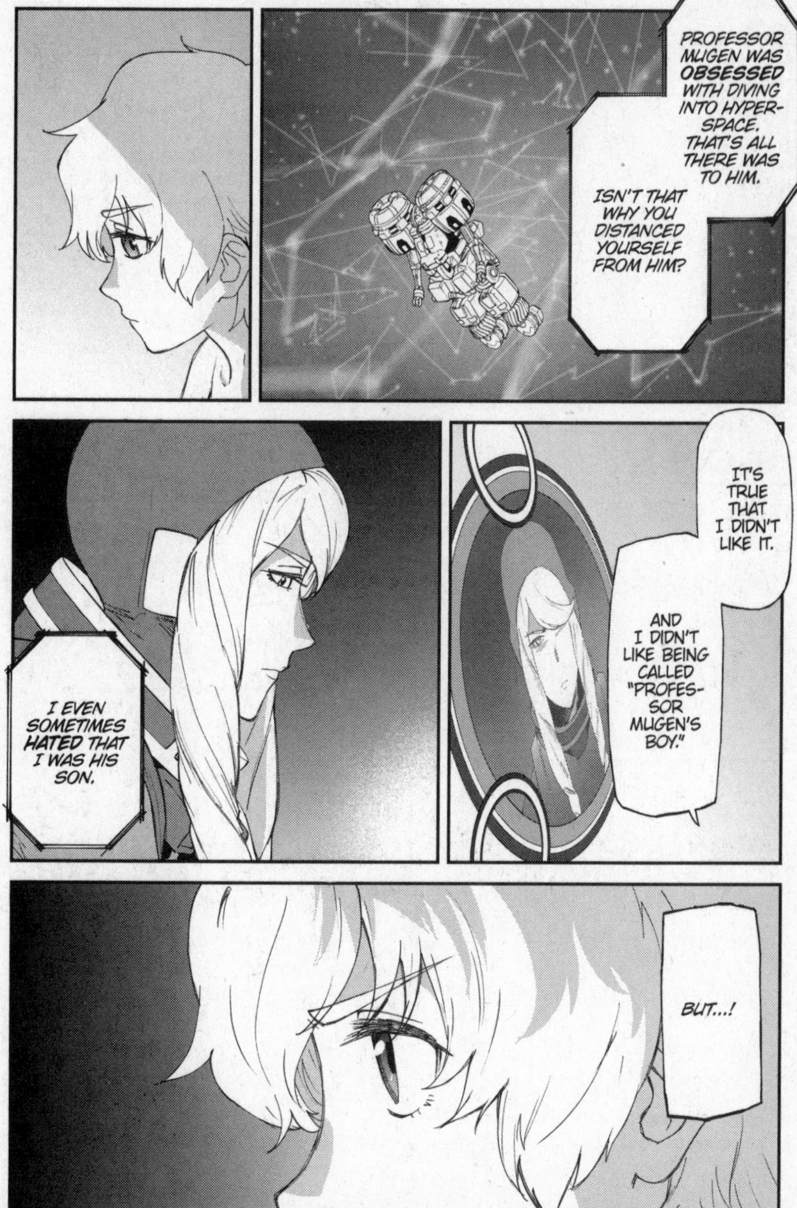
PROFESSOR MUGEN WAS **OBSESSED** WITH DIVING INTO HYPER-SPACE. THAT'S ALL THERE WAS TO HIM.
ISN'T THAT WHY YOU DISTANCED YOURSELF FROM HIM?
IT'S TRUE THAT I DIDN'T LIKE IT.
AND I DIDN'T LIKE BEING CALLED "PROFES-SOR MUGEN'S BOY."
I EVEN SOMETIMES **HATED** THAT I WAS HIS SON.
BUT...!

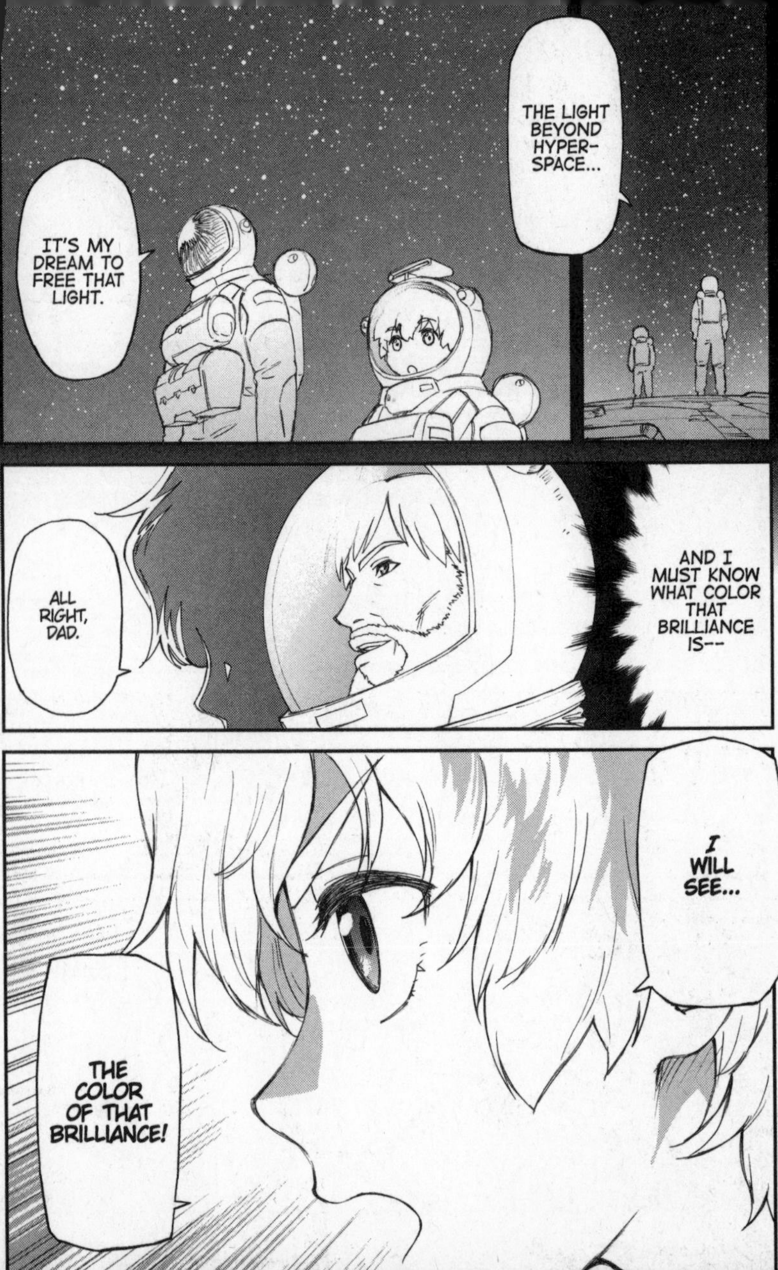
THE LIGHT BEYOND HYPER-SPACE...
IT'S MY DREAM TO FREE THAT LIGHT.
AND I MUST KNOW WHAT COLOR THAT BRILLIANCE IS--
ALL RIGHT, DAD.
I WILL SEE...
THE COLOR OF THAT BRILLIANCE!

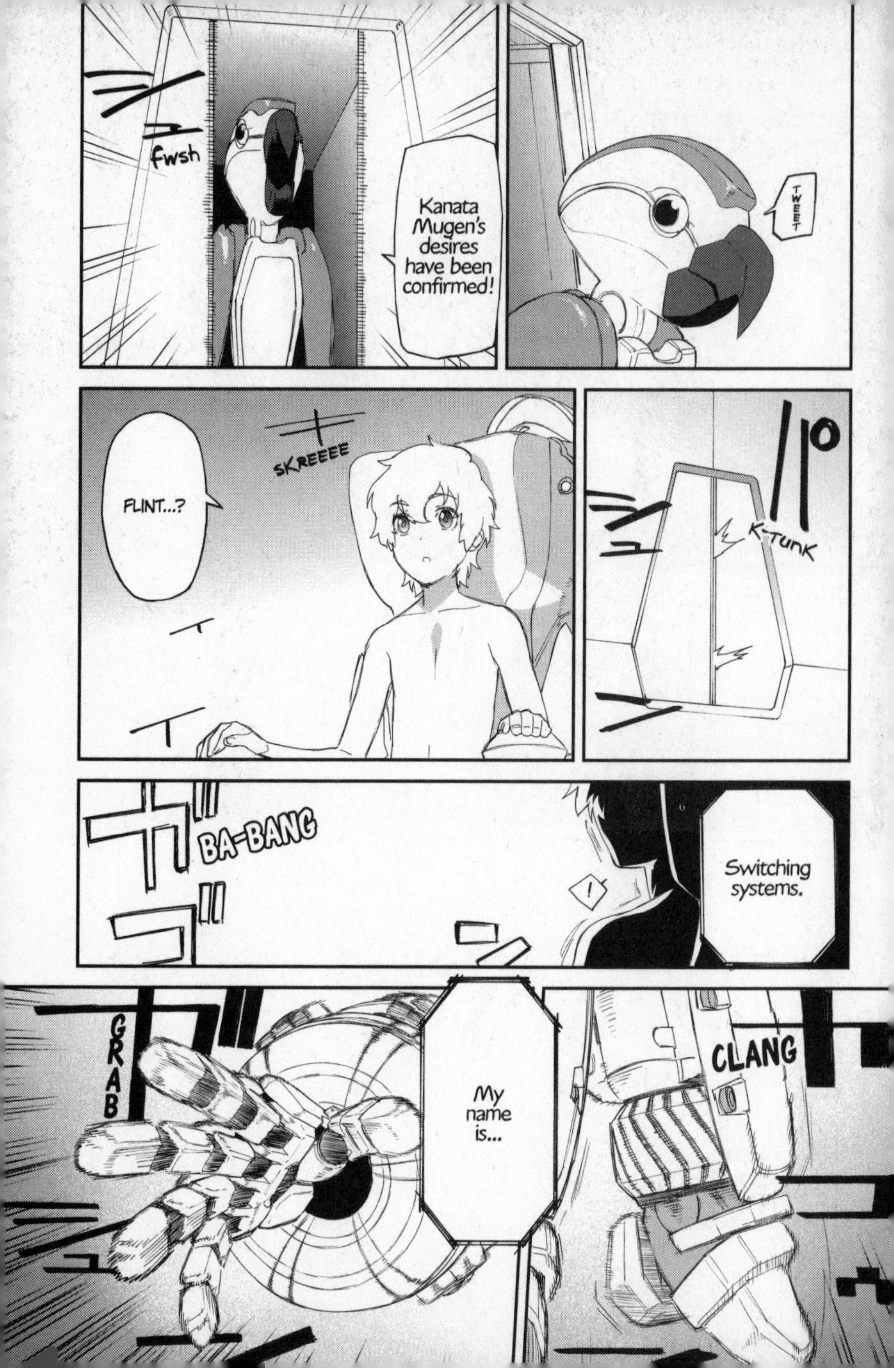
TWEET
fwsh
Kanata Mugen's desires have been confirmed!
K-TUNK
SKREEEE
FLINT...?
Switching systems.
!
BA-BANG
CLANG
My name is...
GRAB

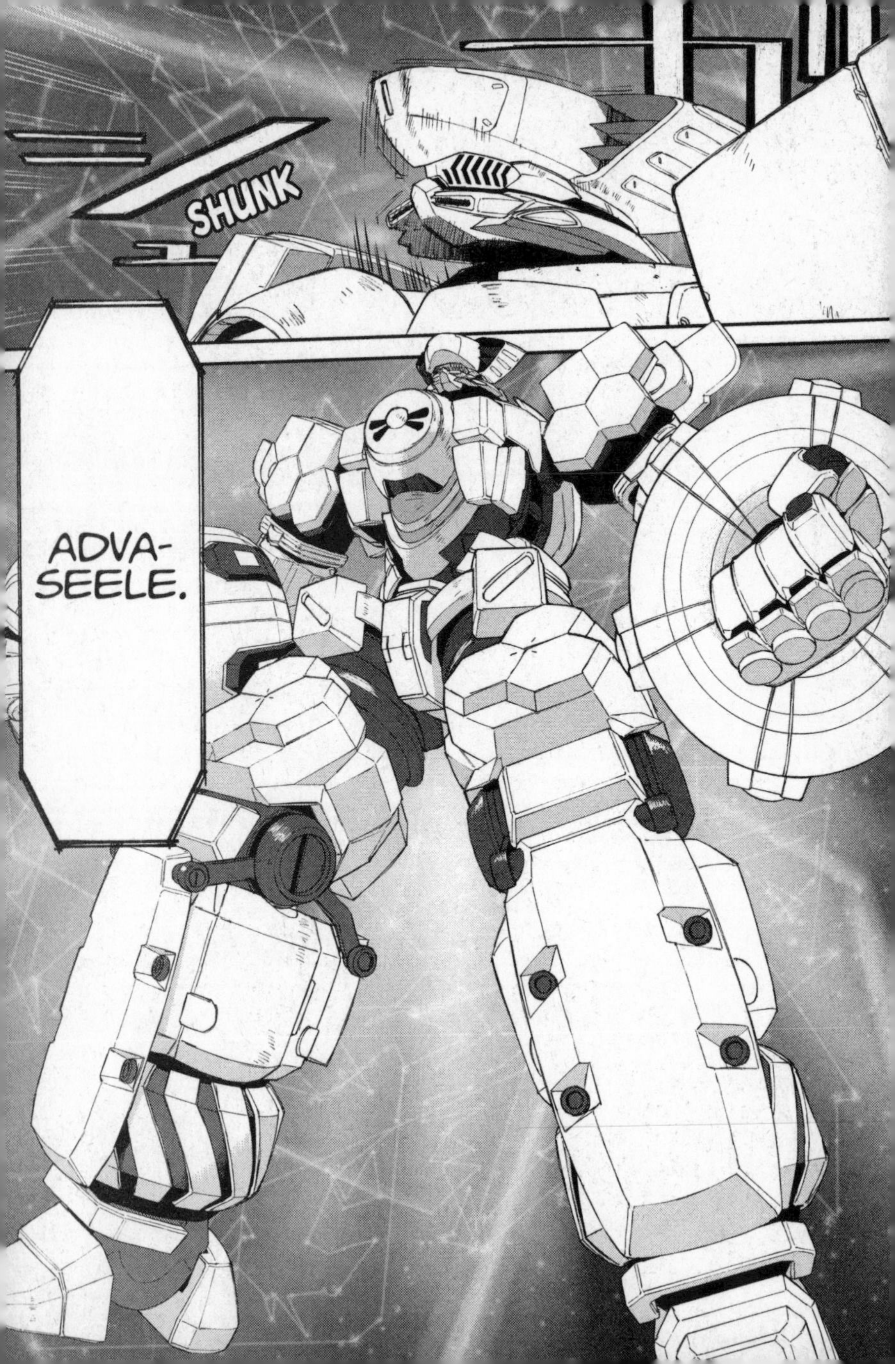
SHUNK
ADVA-SEELE.

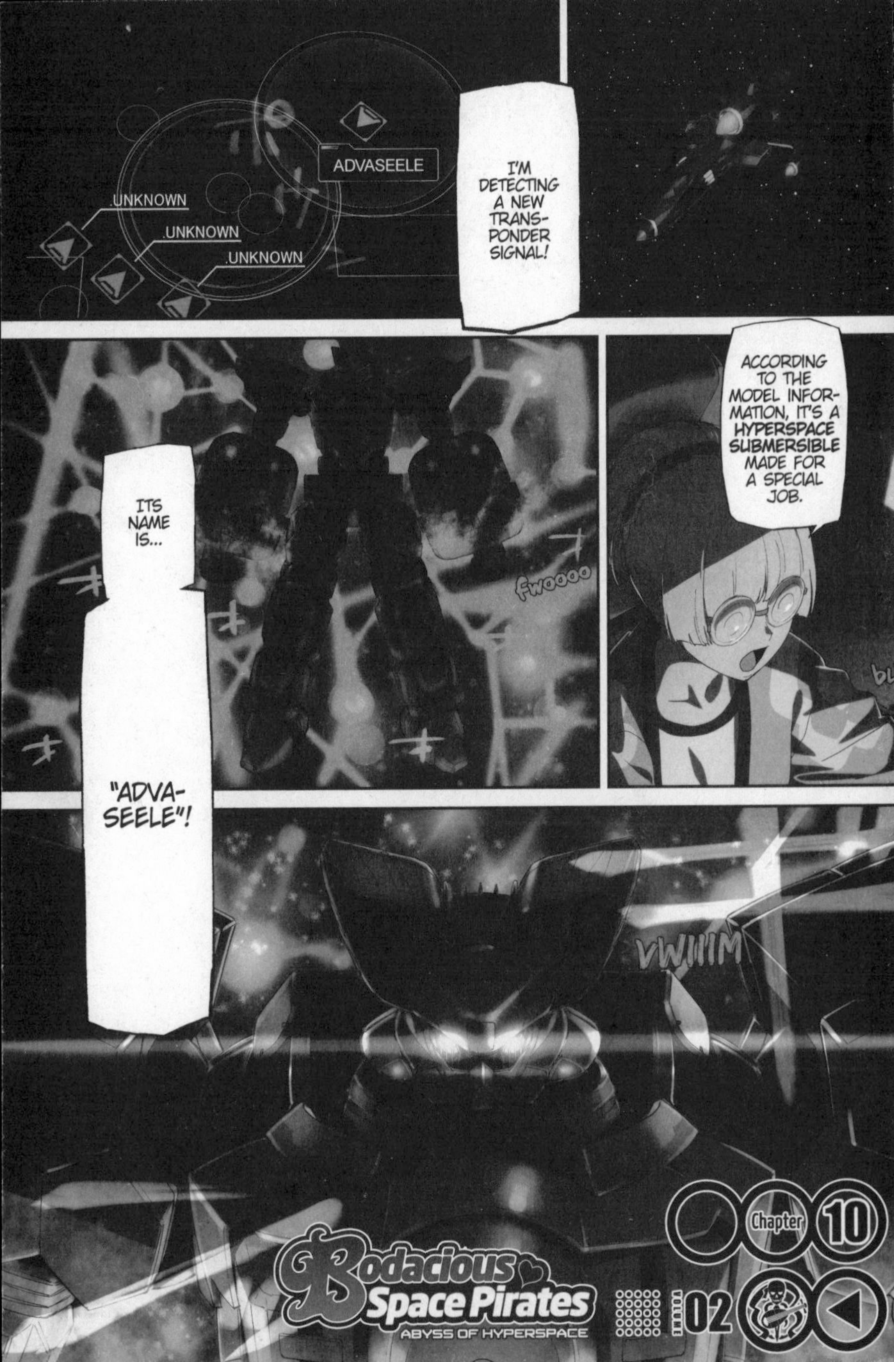
I'M DETECTING A NEW TRANS-PONDER SIGNAL!
ADVASEELE
.UNKNOWN
.UNKNOWN
.UNKNOWN
ACCORDING TO THE MODEL INFOR-MATION, IT'S A **HYPERSPACE SUBMERSIBLE** MADE FOR A SPECIAL JOB.
ITS NAME IS...
fwoooo
"ADVA-SEELE"!
VWIIIM
Bodacious Space Pirates
ABYSS OF HYPERSPACE
Chapter 10
VOLUME 02

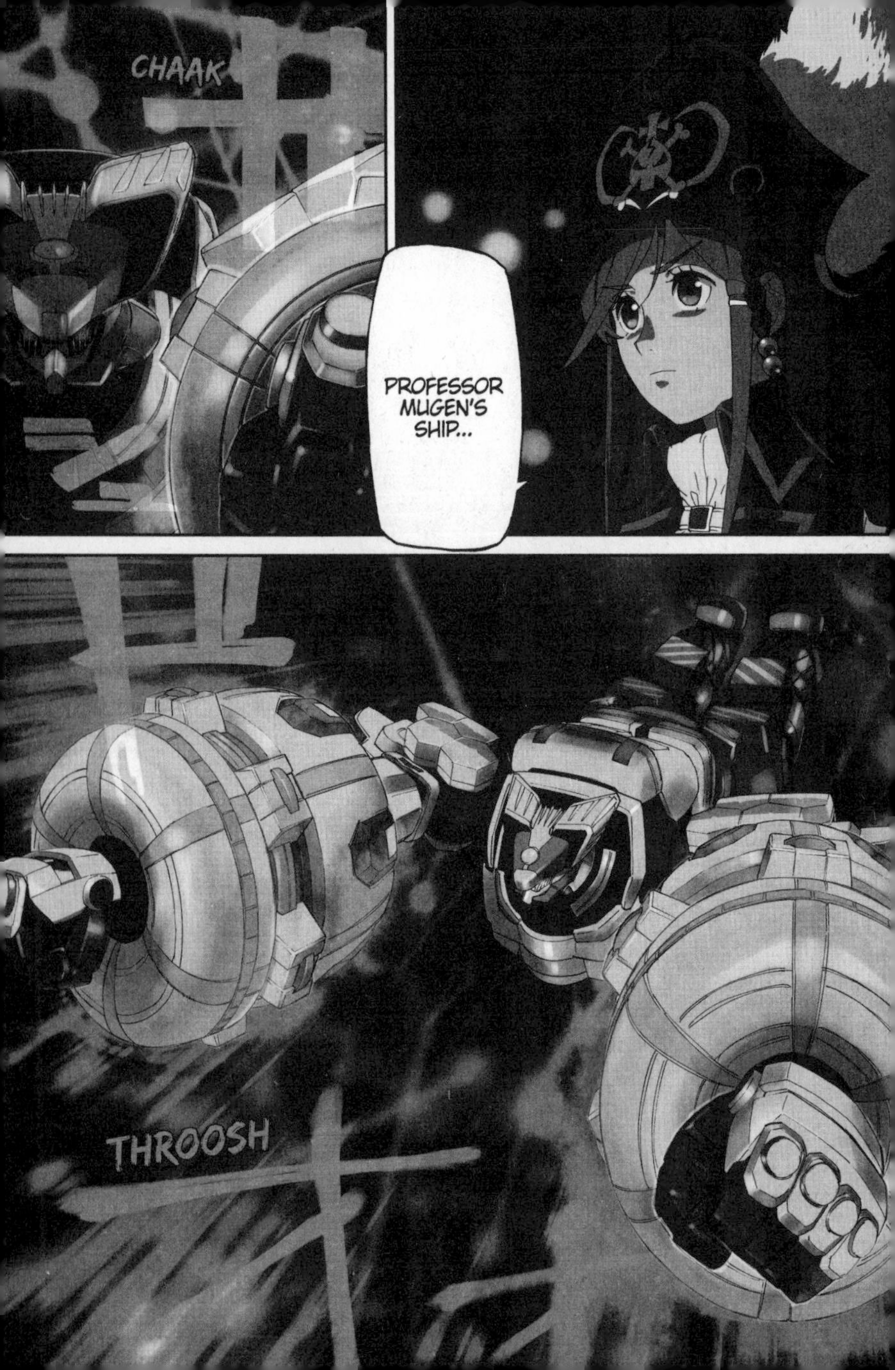
PROFESSOR MUGEN'S SHIP...
CHAAK
THROOSH

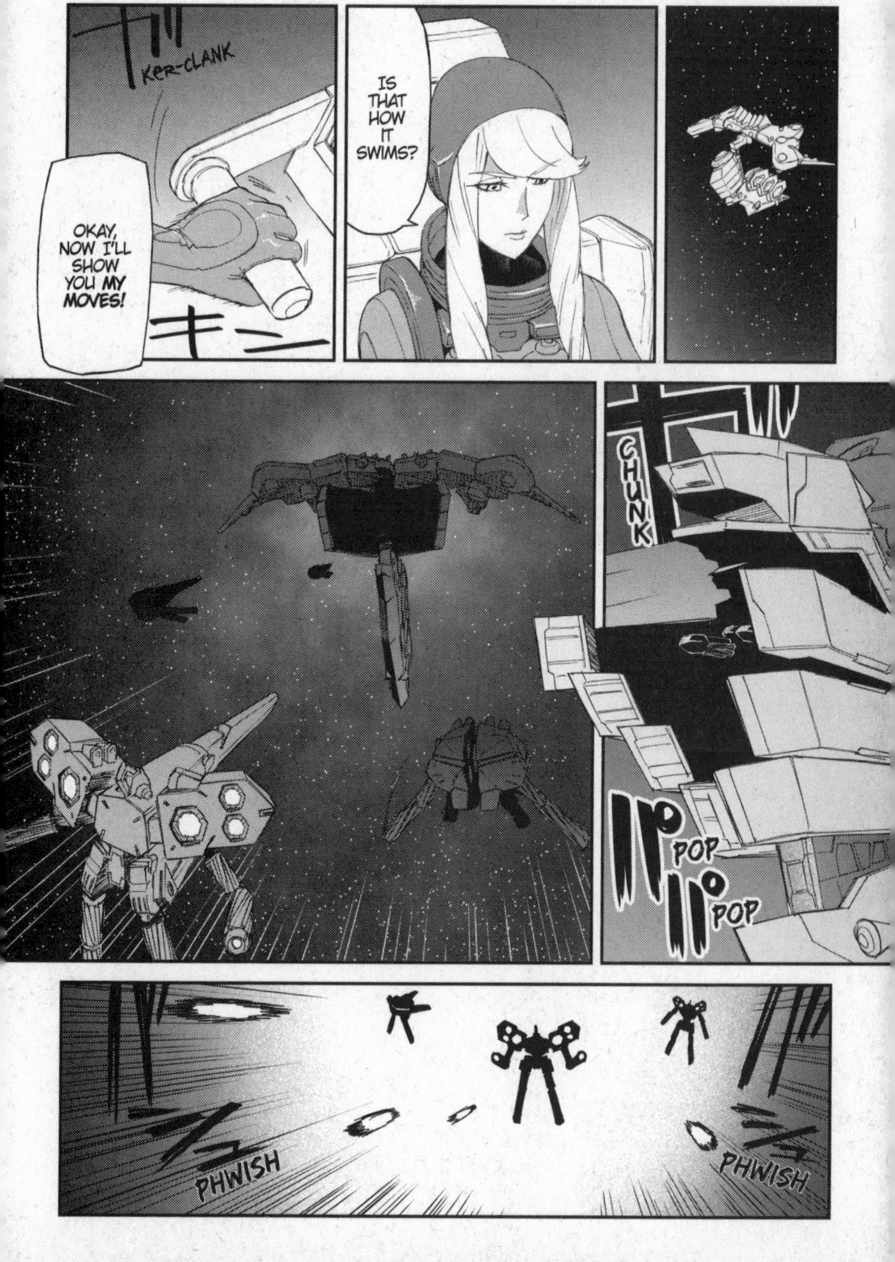
IS THAT HOW IT SWIMS?
Ker-CLANK
OKAY, NOW I'LL SHOW YOU MY MOVES!
CHUNK
POP
POP
PHWISH
PHWISH

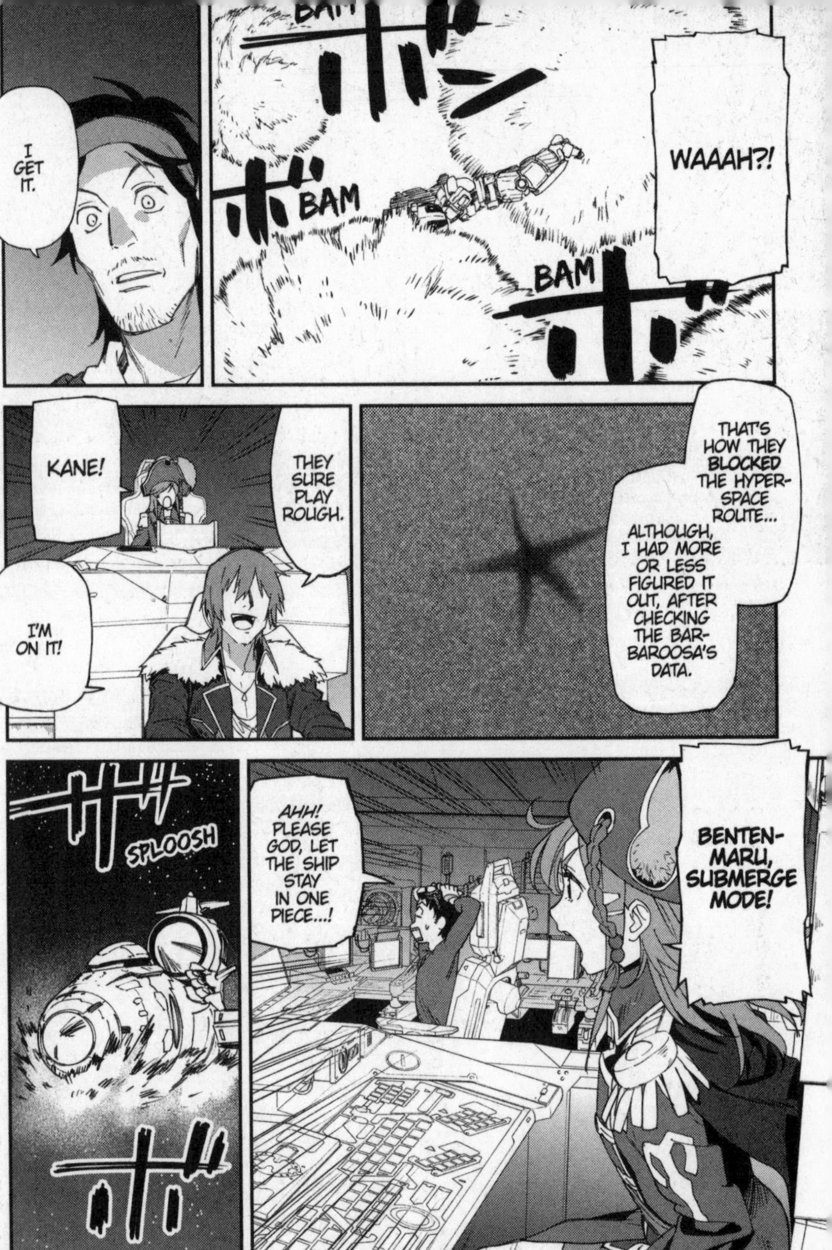
WAAAH?!
BAM
BAM
BAM
I GET IT.
THAT'S HOW THEY BLOCKED THE HYPER-SPACE ROUTE...
ALTHOUGH, I HAD MORE OR LESS FIGURED IT OUT, AFTER CHECKING THE BAR-BAROOSA'S DATA.
THEY SURE PLAY ROUGH.
KANE!
I'M ON IT!
BENTEN-MARU, SUBMERGE MODE!
AHH! PLEASE GOD, LET THE SHIP STAY IN ONE PIECE...!
SPLOOSH

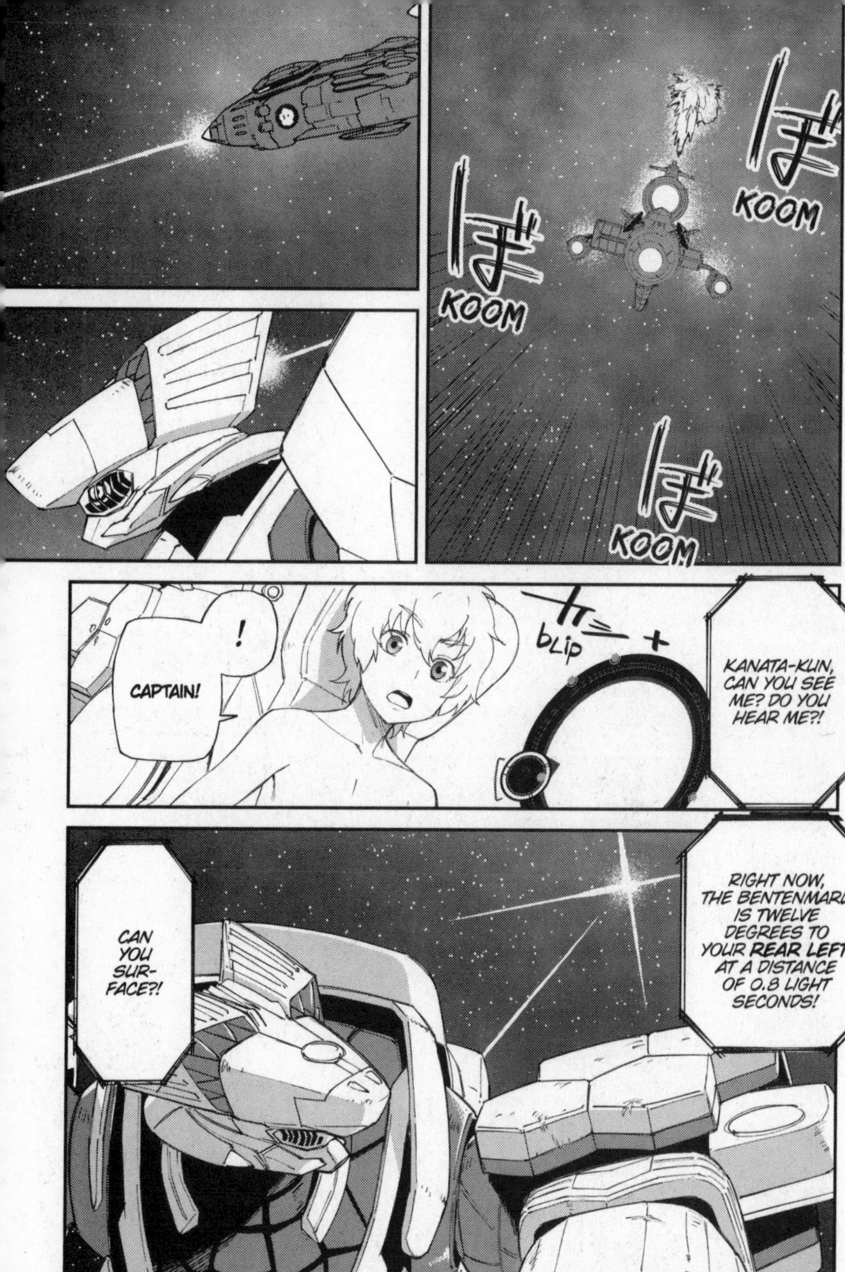

ば
KOOM
ば
KOOM
ば
KOOM
KANATA-KUN, CAN YOU SEE ME? DO YOU HEAR ME?!
blip
!
CAPTAIN!
RIGHT NOW, THE BENTENMARU IS TWELVE DEGREES TO YOUR **REAR LEFT,** AT A DISTANCE OF 0.8 LIGHT SECONDS!
CAN YOU SUR-FACE?!

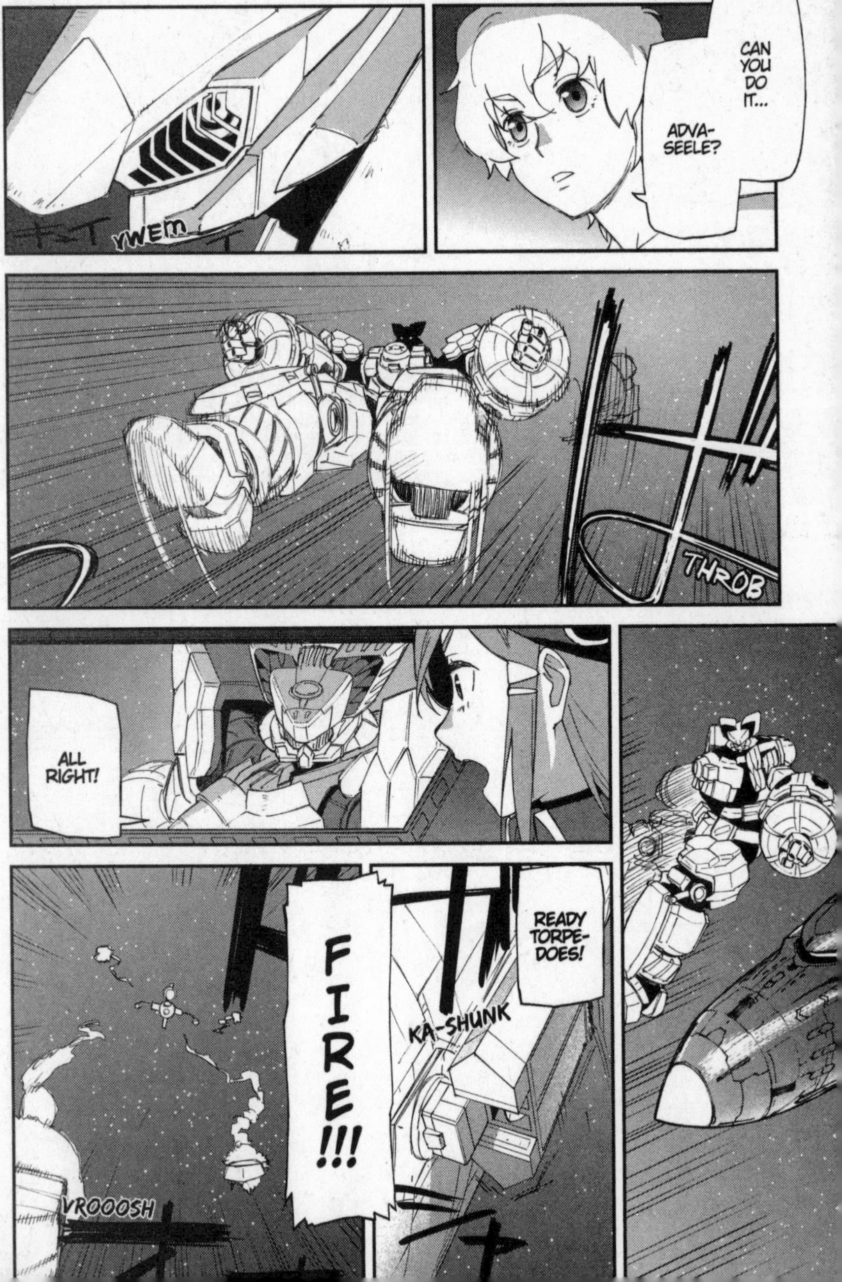
CAN YOU DO IT...
ADVA-SEELE?
YWEM
THROB
ALL RIGHT!
READY TORPE-DOES!
KA-SHUNK
FIRE!!!
VROOOSH

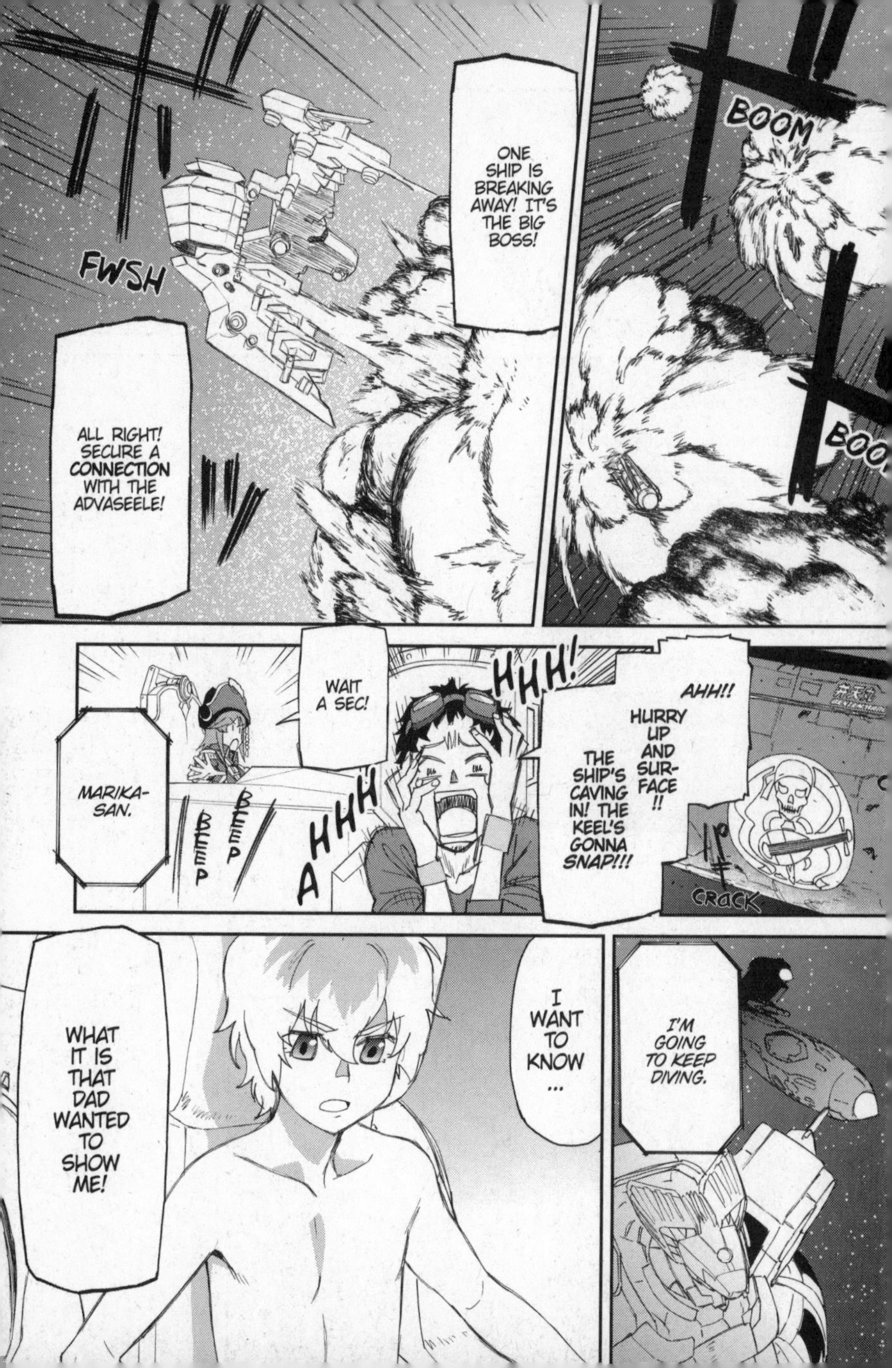
BOOM
BOO
ONE SHIP IS BREAKING AWAY! IT'S THE BIG BOSS!
FWSH
ALL RIGHT! SECURE A CONNECTION WITH THE ADVASEELE!
AHH!!
HURRY UP AND SURFACE!!
THE SHIP'S CAVING IN! THE KEEL'S GONNA SNAP!!!
CRACK
HHH!
WAIT A SEC!
AHHH
BEEP
BEEP
MARIKA-SAN.
I'M GOING TO KEEP DIVING.
I WANT TO KNOW...
WHAT IT IS THAT DAD WANTED TO SHOW ME!

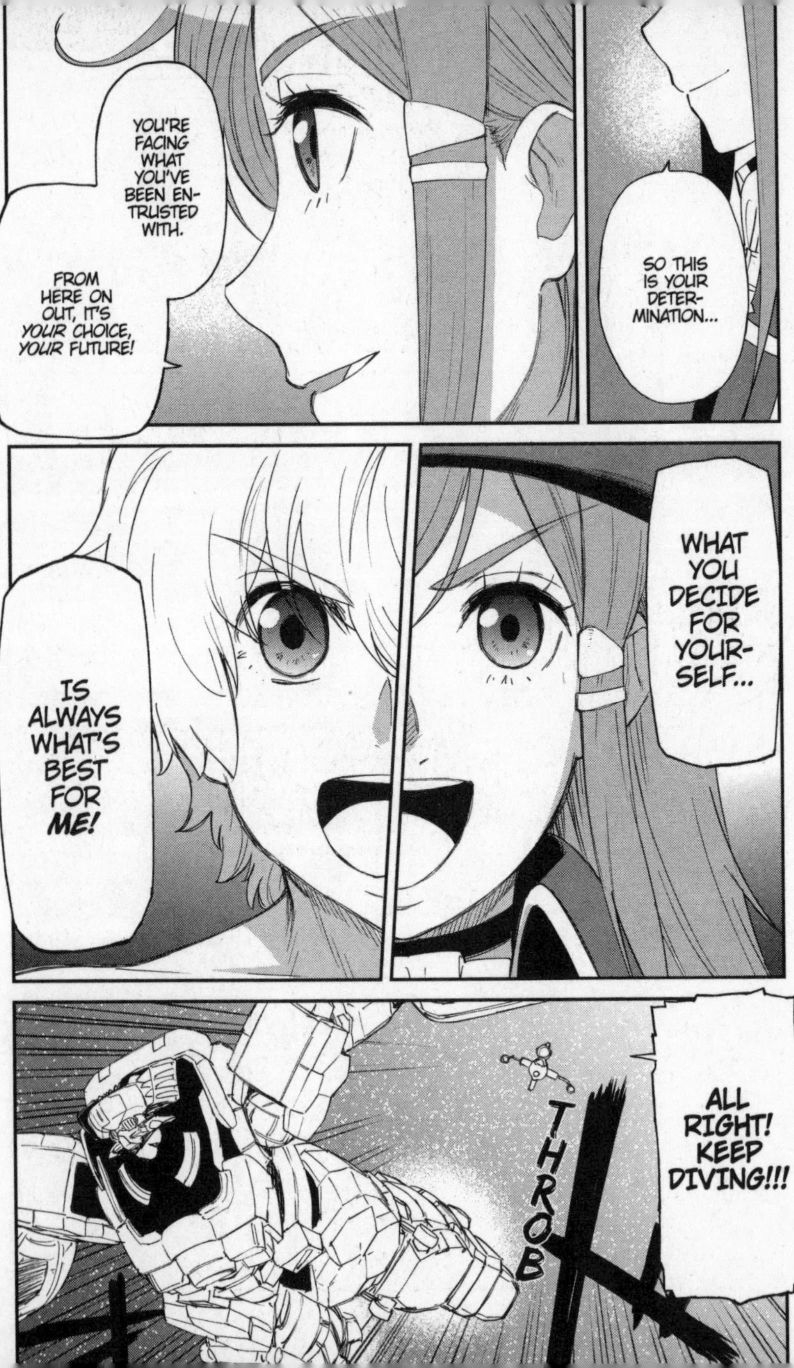
SO THIS IS YOUR DETER-MINATION...
YOU'RE FACING WHAT YOU'VE BEEN EN-TRUSTED WITH.
FROM HERE ON OUT, IT'S *YOUR* CHOICE, *YOUR* FUTURE!
WHAT YOU DECIDE FOR YOUR-SELF...
IS ALWAYS WHAT'S BEST FOR ***ME!***
ALL RIGHT! KEEP DIVING!!!
THROB

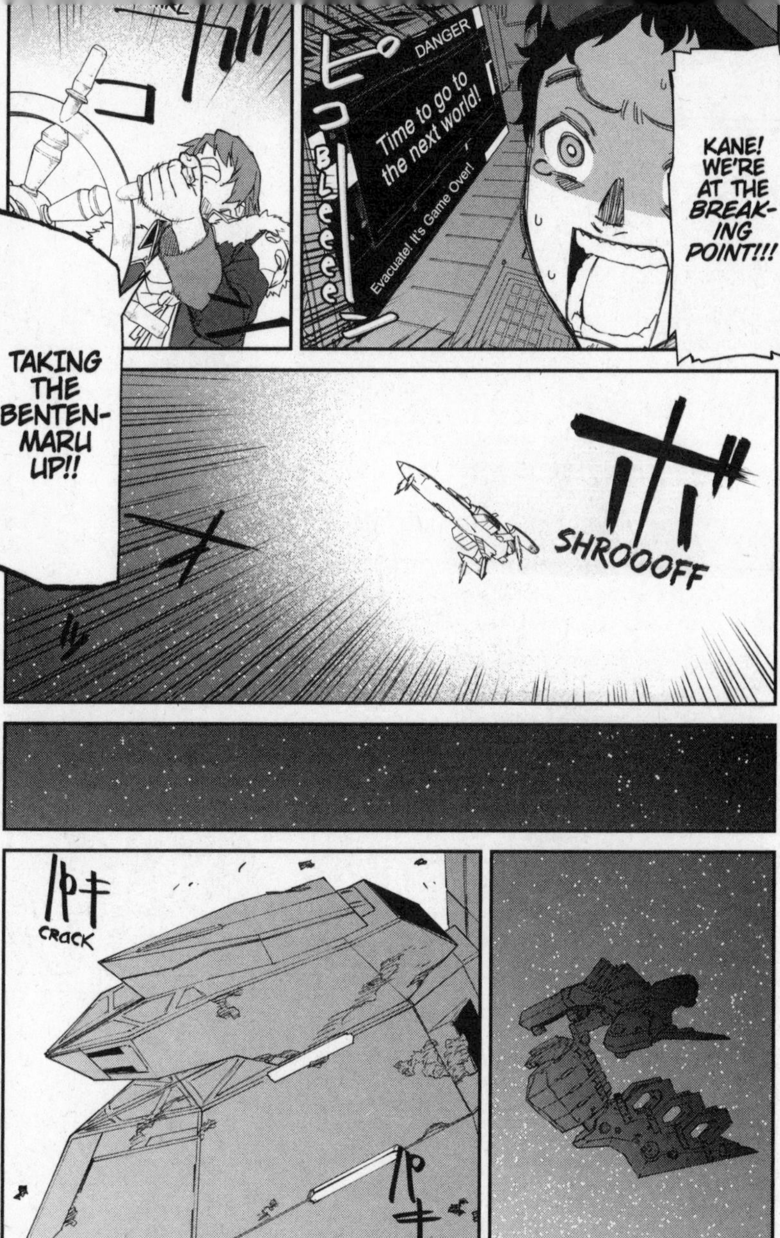
KANE! WE'RE AT THE BREAKING POINT!!!
DANGER
Time to go to the next world!
Evacuate! It's Game Over!
BLeeee
TAKING THE BENTEN-MARU UP!!
SHROOOFF
CRACK
CRACK

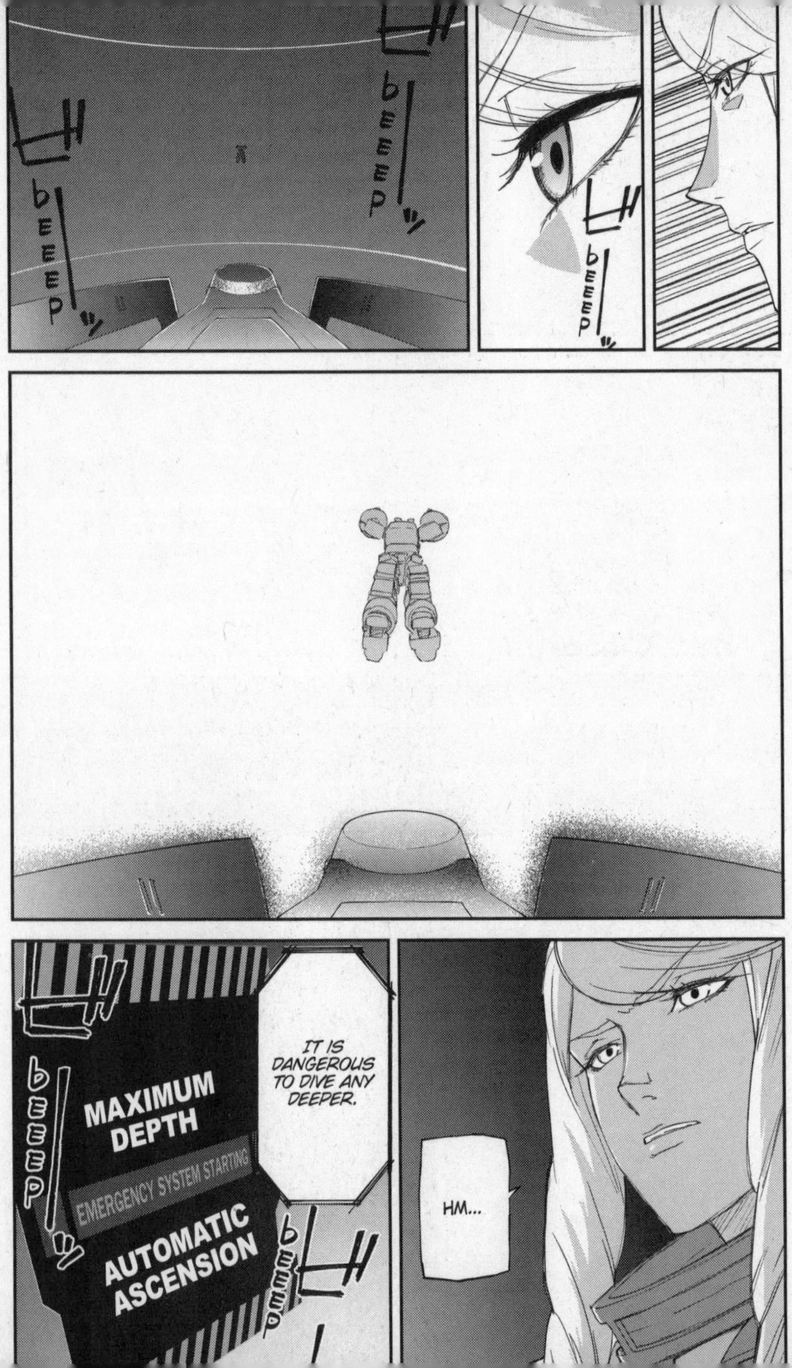
beeep
beeep
beeep
HM...
IT IS DANGEROUS TO DIVE ANY DEEPER.
MAXIMUM DEPTH
EMERGENCY SYSTEM STARTING
AUTOMATIC ASCENSION
beeep
beeep

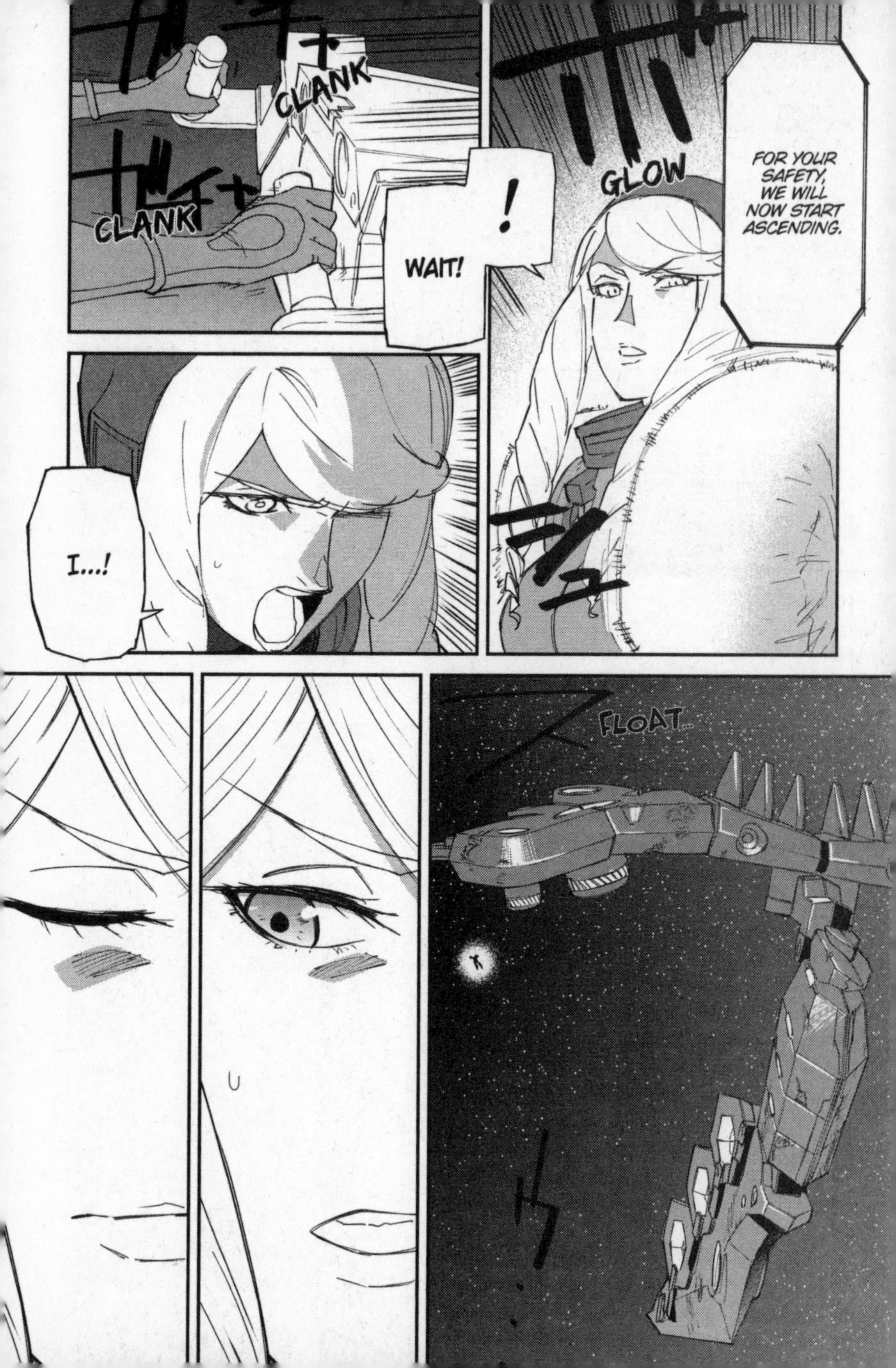
FOR YOUR SAFETY, WE WILL NOW START ASCENDING.
GLOW
CLANK
CLANK
!
WAIT!
I...!
FLOAT...

IN THE END, YOU'RE JUST LIKE HIM...

YOU LEFT ME.

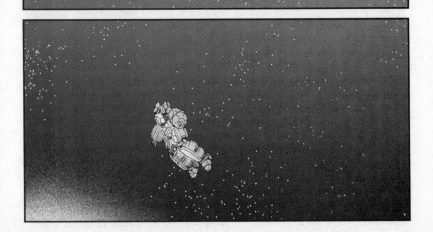

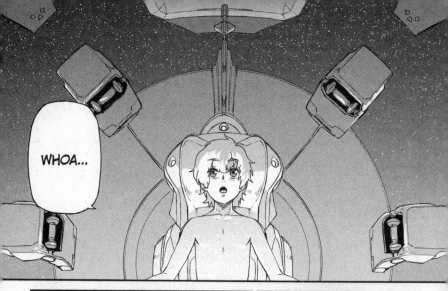

WHOA...
HM? WE'RE RECEIVING **DATA** FROM KANATA-KUN!
FROM THE ADVASEELE...? CAN WE RESPOND?
NO CAN DO. IT'S A ONE-WAY, DATA-ONLY STREAM. WE CAN'T CONVERSE WITH HIM.
HYAKUME! **ANALYSIS**, PLEASE!
I'M ON IT!
THERE'S A LAYER OF HYPERSPACE TURBULENCE...
WOW... MASSES OF HIGH ENERGY ARE FLYING RIGHT PAST ONE ANOTHER INDISCRIMINATELY, DUE TO THE CURRENTS OF SEVERAL ROUTES.
IT'S A DOMAIN FIT ONLY FOR DEEP HYPERSPACE DIVERS.

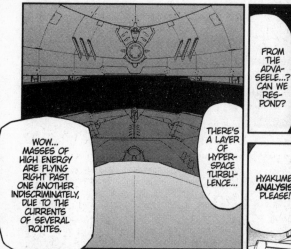

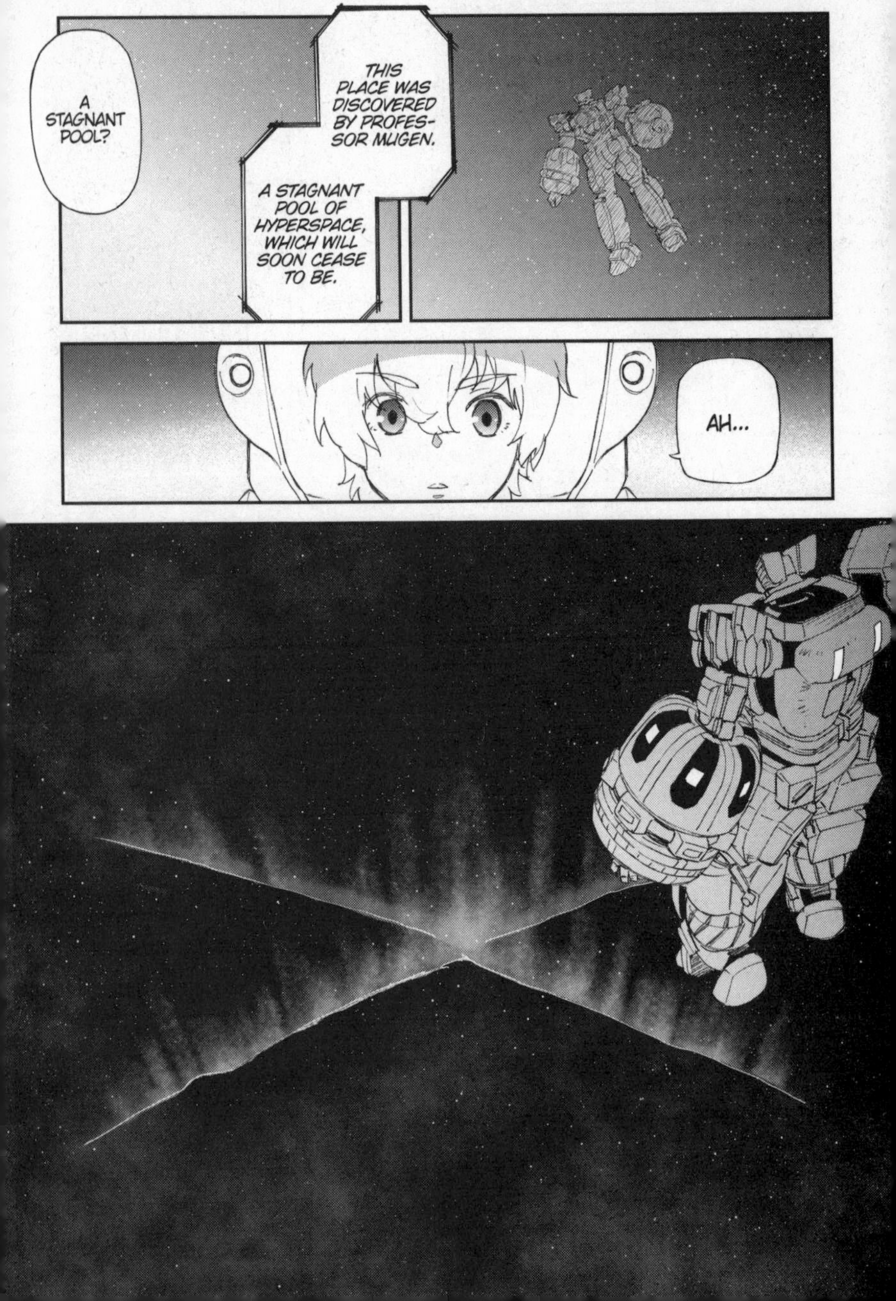
THIS PLACE WAS DISCOVERED BY PROFES-SOR MUGEN.
A STAGNANT POOL?
A STAGNANT POOL OF HYPERSPACE, WHICH WILL SOON CEASE TO BE.
AH...

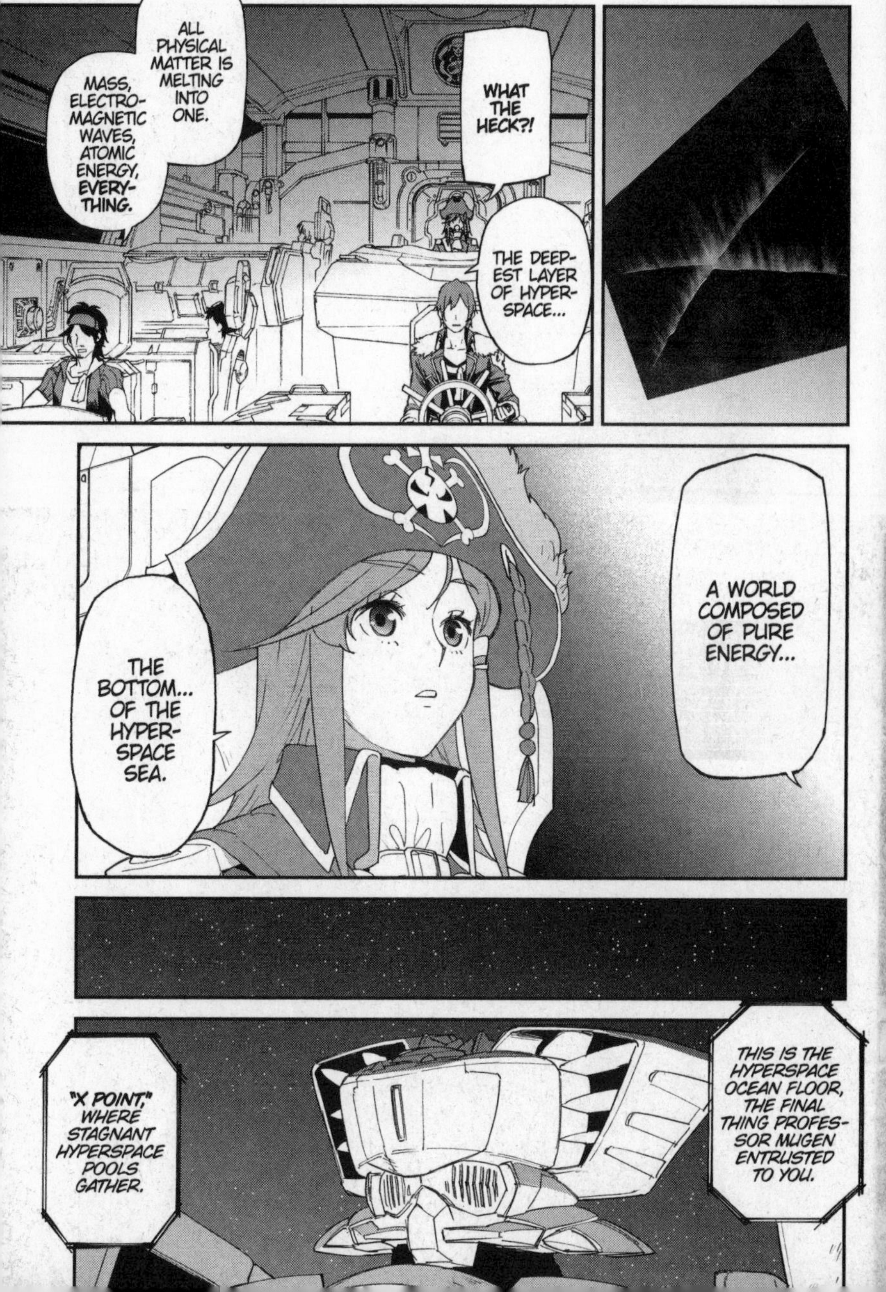
WHAT THE HECK?!
THE DEEPEST LAYER OF HYPERSPACE...
ALL PHYSICAL MATTER IS MELTING INTO ONE.
MASS, ELECTROMAGNETIC WAVES, ATOMIC ENERGY, EVERYTHING.
A WORLD COMPOSED OF PURE ENERGY...
THE BOTTOM... OF THE HYPERSPACE SEA.
THIS IS THE HYPERSPACE OCEAN FLOOR, THE FINAL THING PROFESSOR MUGEN ENTRUSTED TO YOU.
"X POINT," WHERE STAGNANT HYPERSPACE POOLS GATHER.

THE PROFESSOR SAW A NEW PATH HERE.

A NEW PATH...?

K-CLUNK

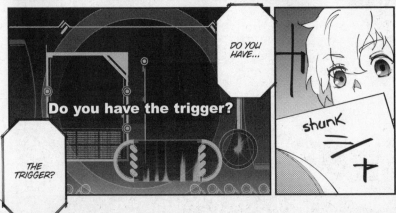

DO YOU HAVE...

Do you have the trigger?

THE TRIGGER?

shunk

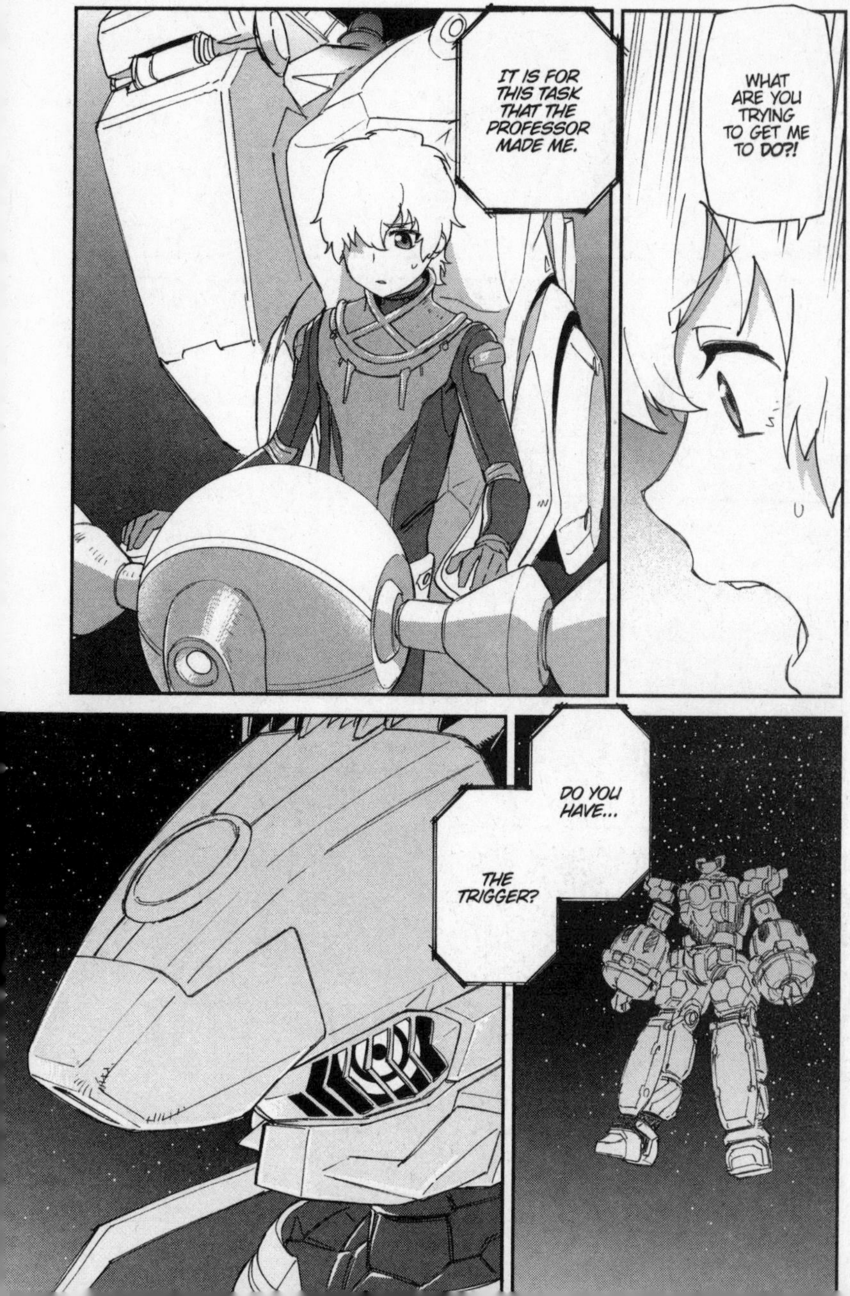
WHAT ARE YOU TRYING TO GET ME TO DO?!
IT IS FOR THIS TASK THAT THE PROFESSOR MADE ME.
DO YOU HAVE...
THE TRIGGER?

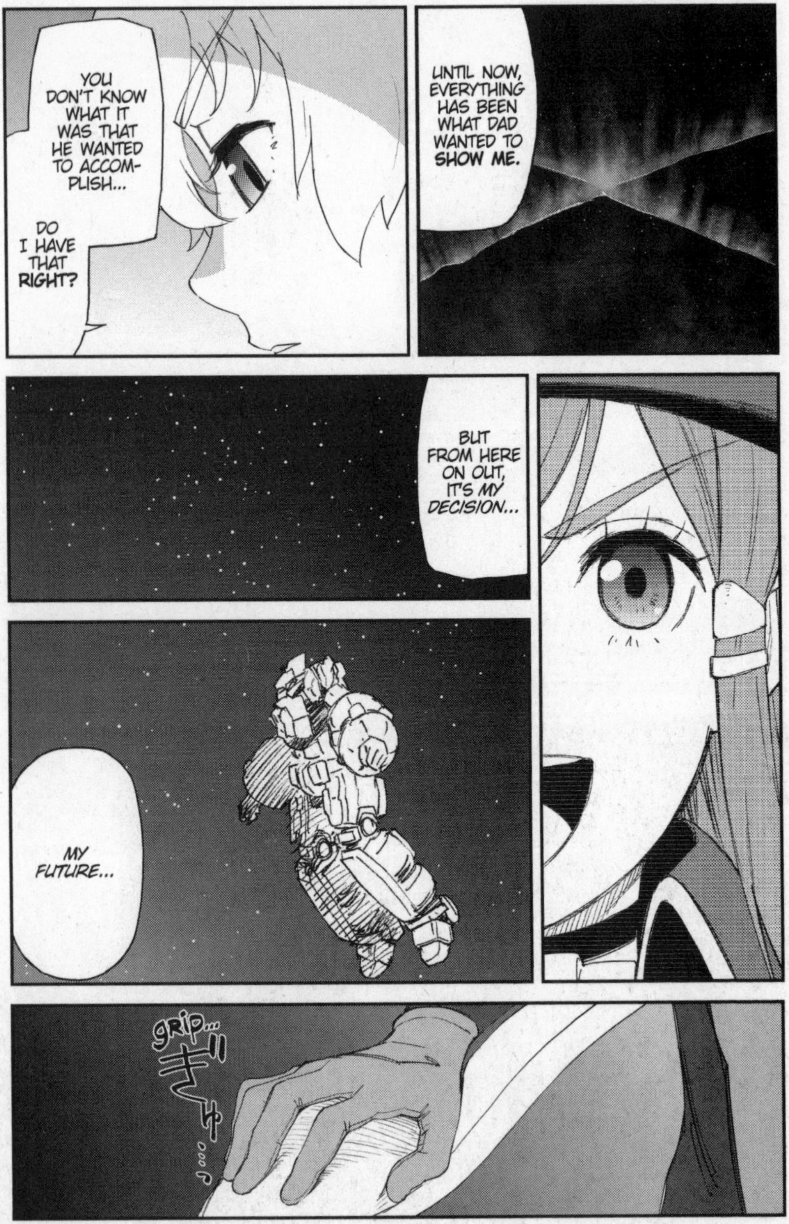
UNTIL NOW, EVERYTHING HAS BEEN WHAT DAD WANTED TO SHOW ME.
YOU DON'T KNOW WHAT IT WAS THAT HE WANTED TO ACCOMPLISH...
DO I HAVE THAT RIGHT?
BUT FROM HERE ON OUT, IT'S MY DECISION...
MY FUTURE...
grip...
ぎゅ…

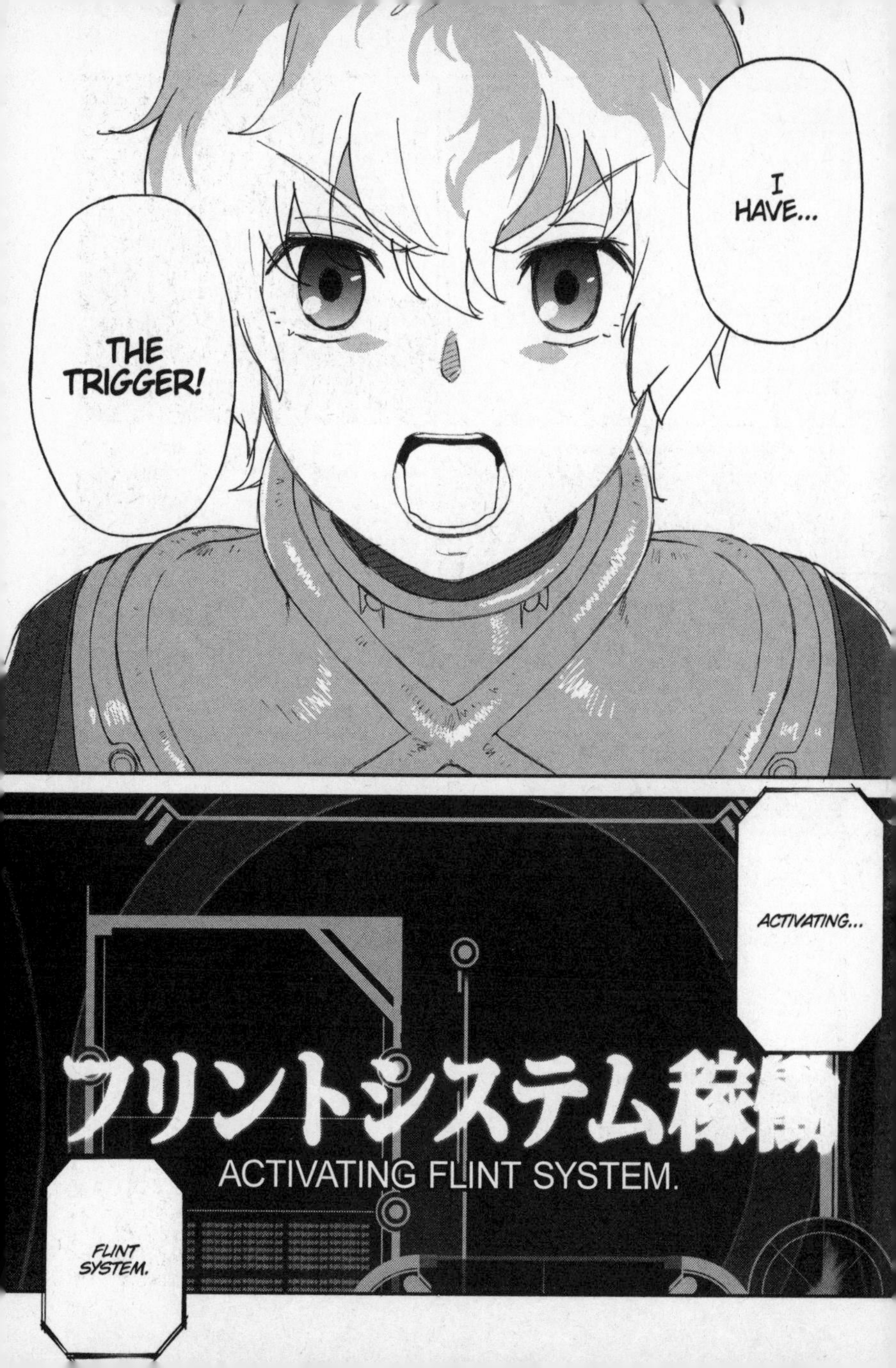
I HAVE...
THE TRIGGER!
ACTIVATING...
フリントシステム稼働
ACTIVATING FLINT SYSTEM.
FLINT SYSTEM.

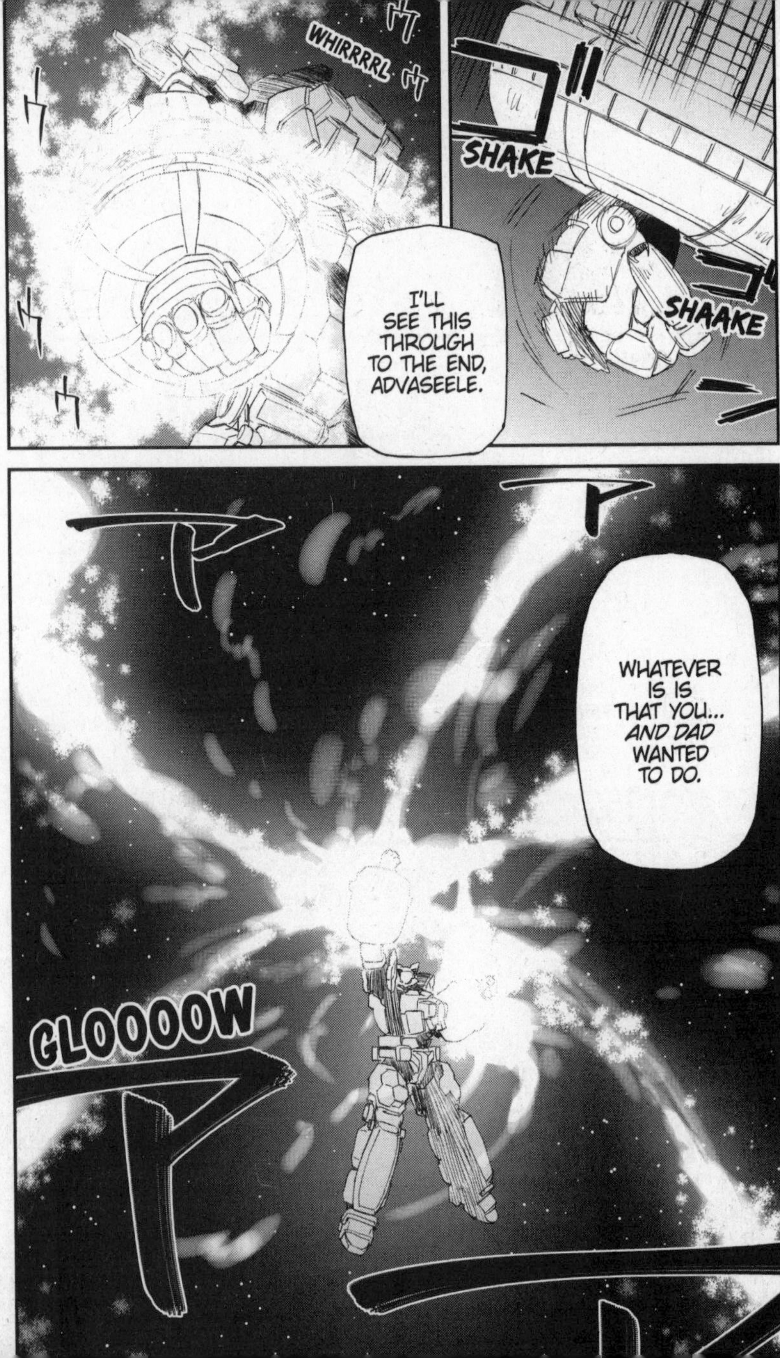
SHAKE
SHAAKE
I'LL SEE THIS THROUGH TO THE END, ADVASEELE.
WHIRRRRL
WHATEVER IS IS THAT YOU... *AND DAD* WANTED TO DO.
GLOOOOW

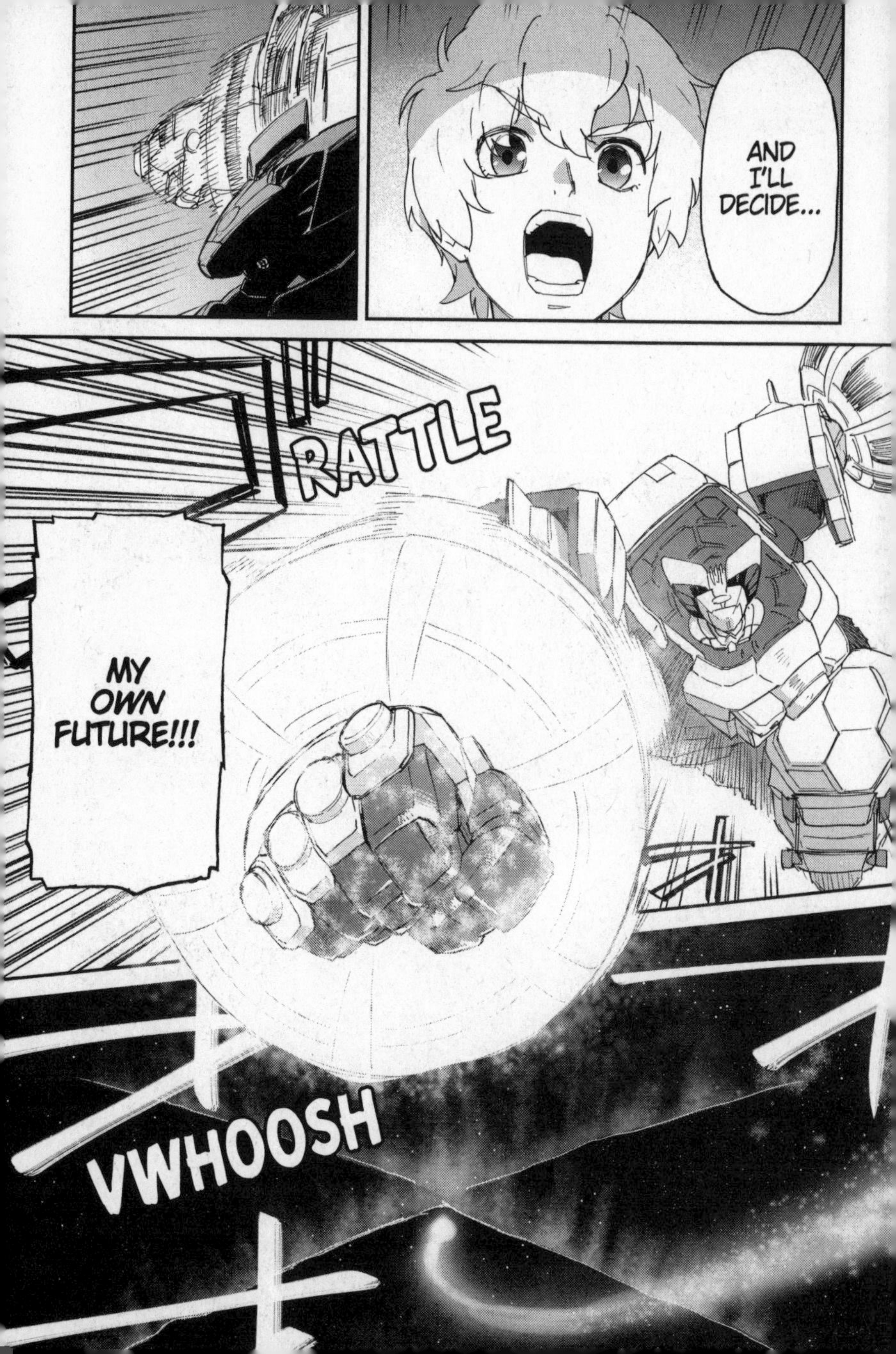
AND I'LL DECIDE...
RATTLE
MY OWN FUTURE!!!
VWHOOSH

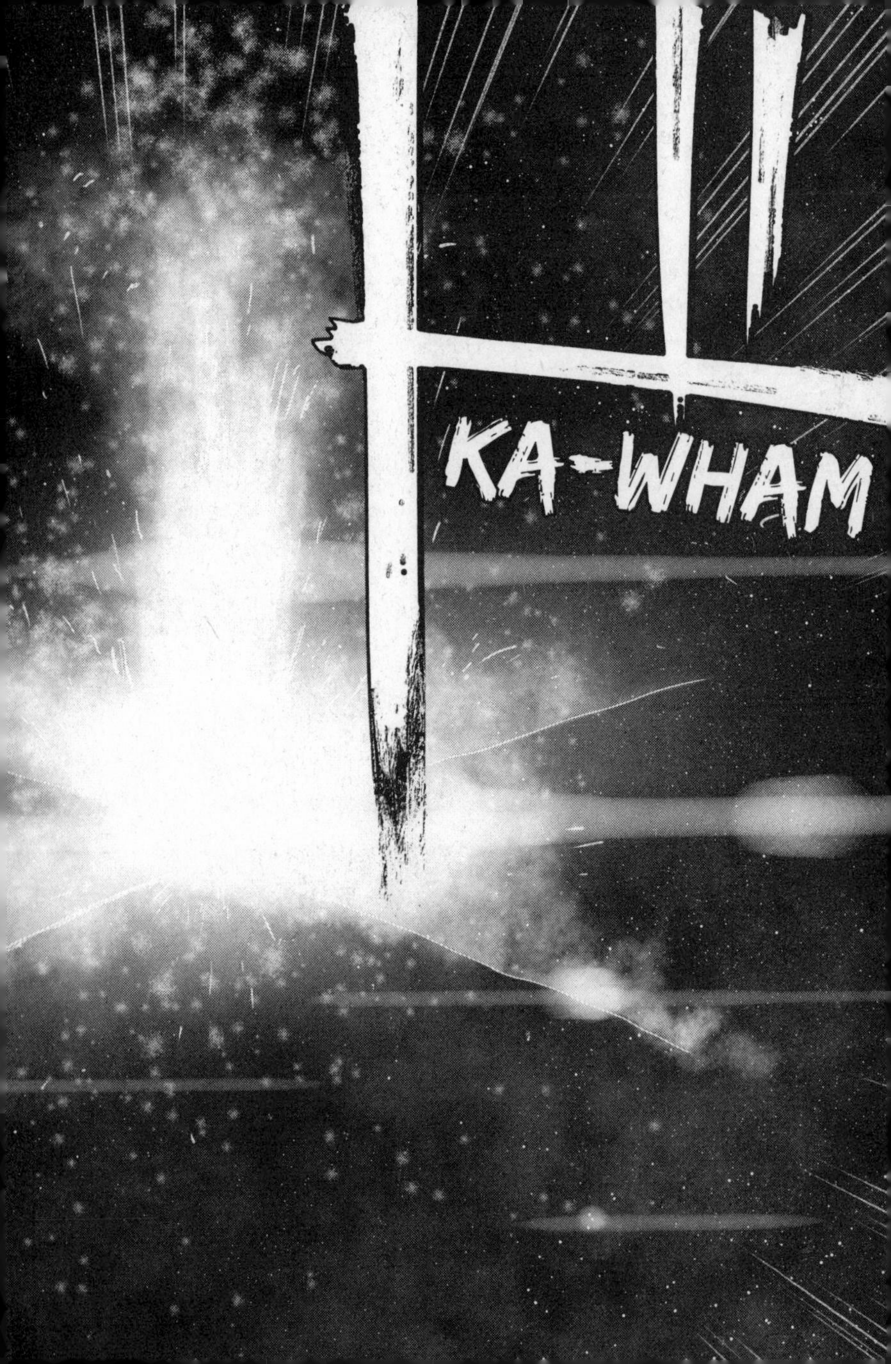
KA-WHAM

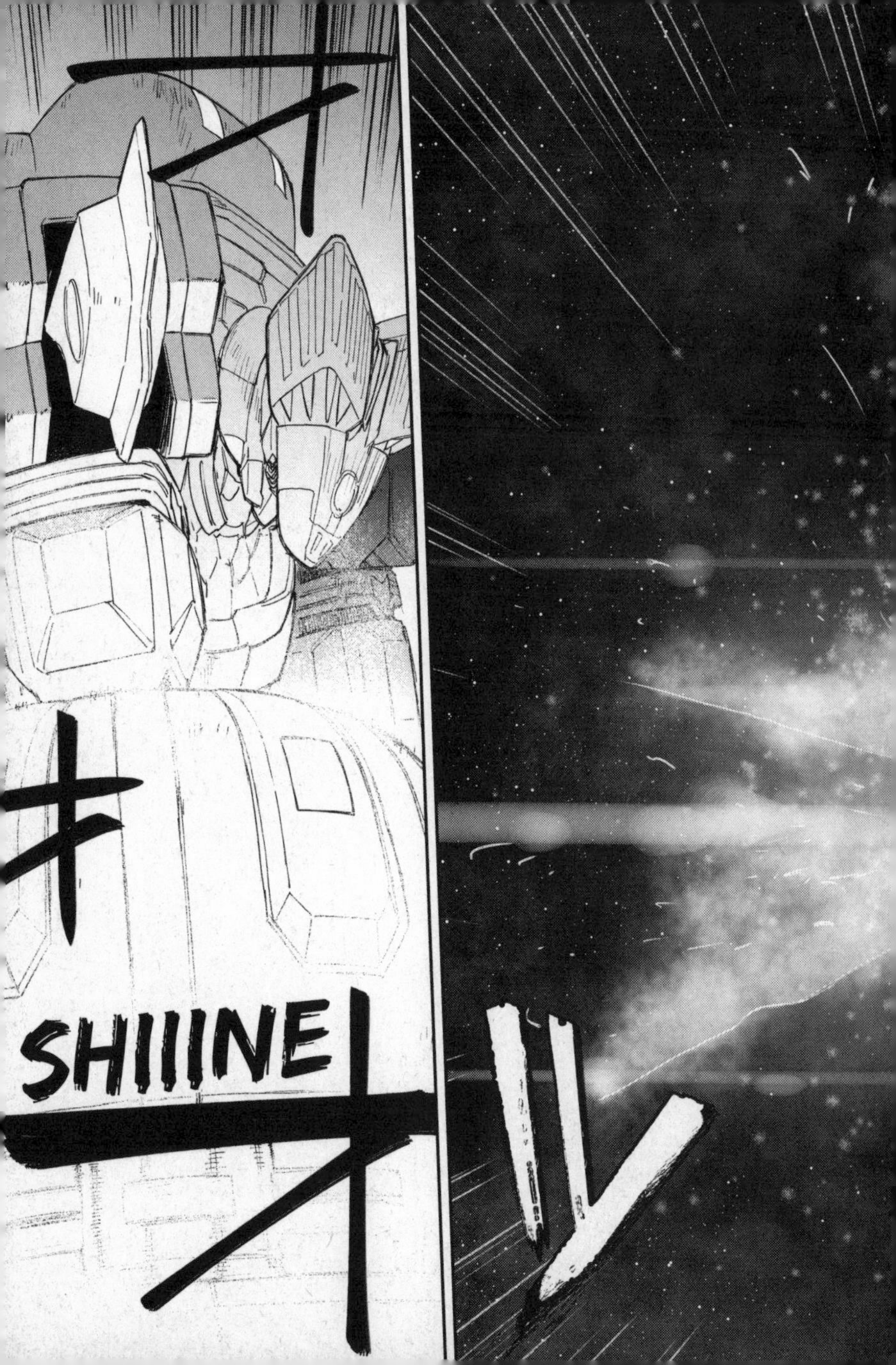
SHIIINE

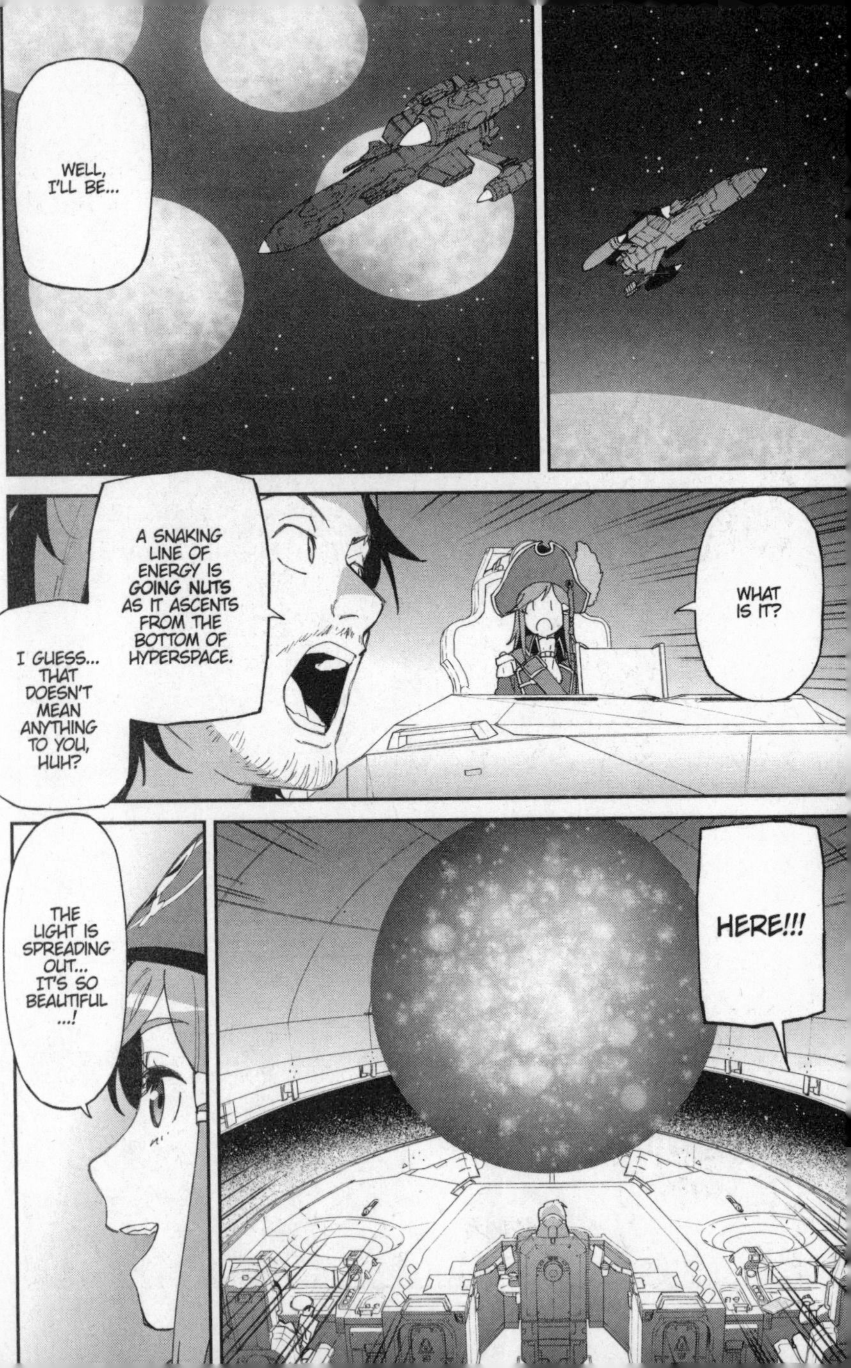
WELL, I'LL BE...
WHAT IS IT?
A SNAKING LINE OF ENERGY IS GOING NUTS AS IT ASCENTS FROM THE BOTTOM OF HYPERSPACE.
I GUESS... THAT DOESN'T MEAN ANYTHING TO YOU, HUH?
HERE!!!
THE LIGHT IS SPREADING OUT... IT'S SO BEAUTIFUL ...!

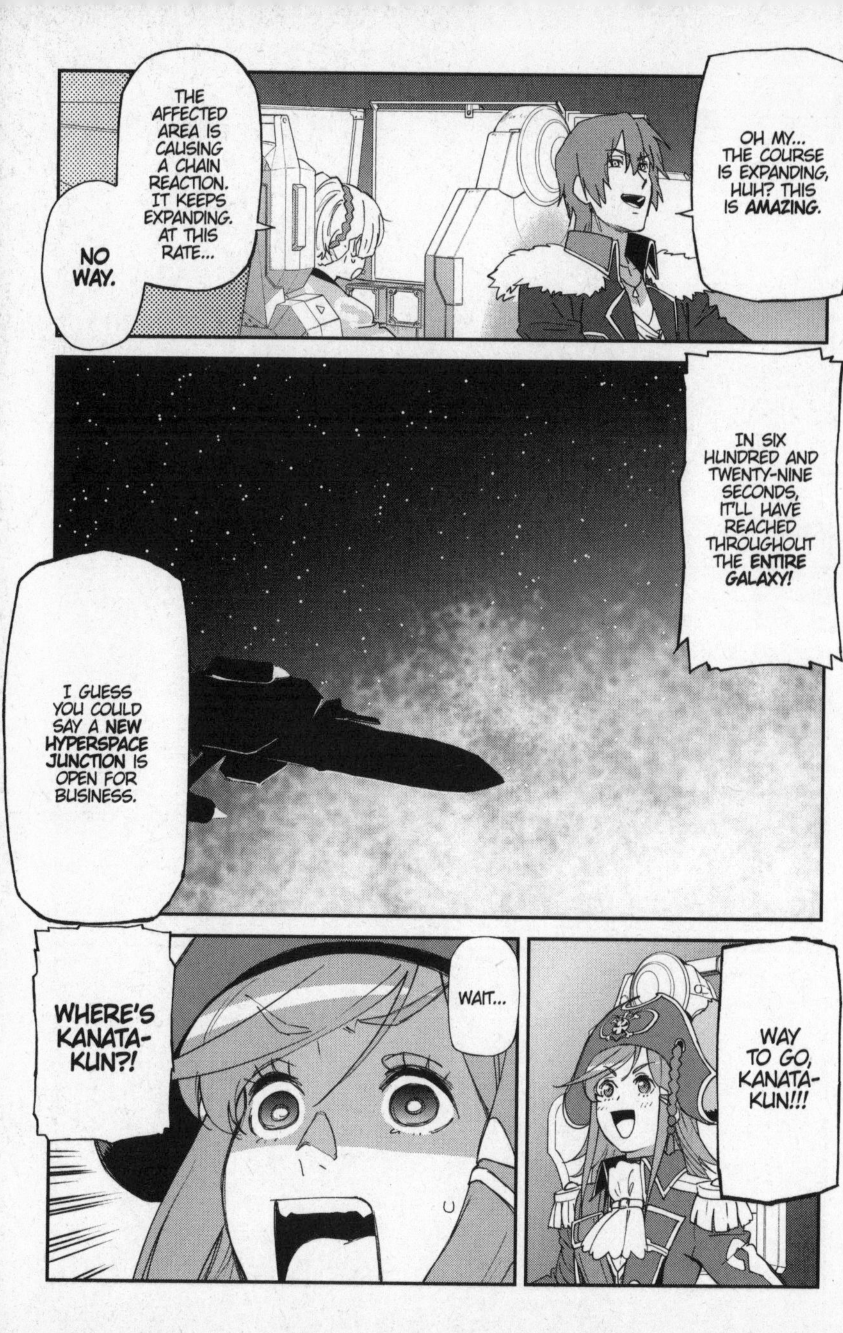
OH MY... THE COURSE IS EXPANDING, HUH? THIS IS AMAZING.
THE AFFECTED AREA IS CAUSING A CHAIN REACTION. IT KEEPS EXPANDING. AT THIS RATE...
NO WAY.
IN SIX HUNDRED AND TWENTY-NINE SECONDS, IT'LL HAVE REACHED THROUGHOUT THE ENTIRE GALAXY!
I GUESS YOU COULD SAY A NEW HYPERSPACE JUNCTION IS OPEN FOR BUSINESS.
WAY TO GO, KANATA-KUN!!!
WAIT...
WHERE'S KANATA-KUN?!

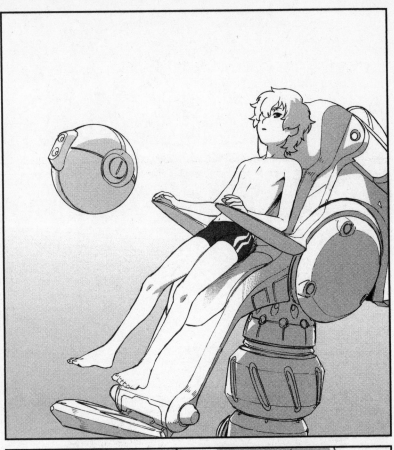

HYPER-
SPACE
SURE IS...

STRANGE.

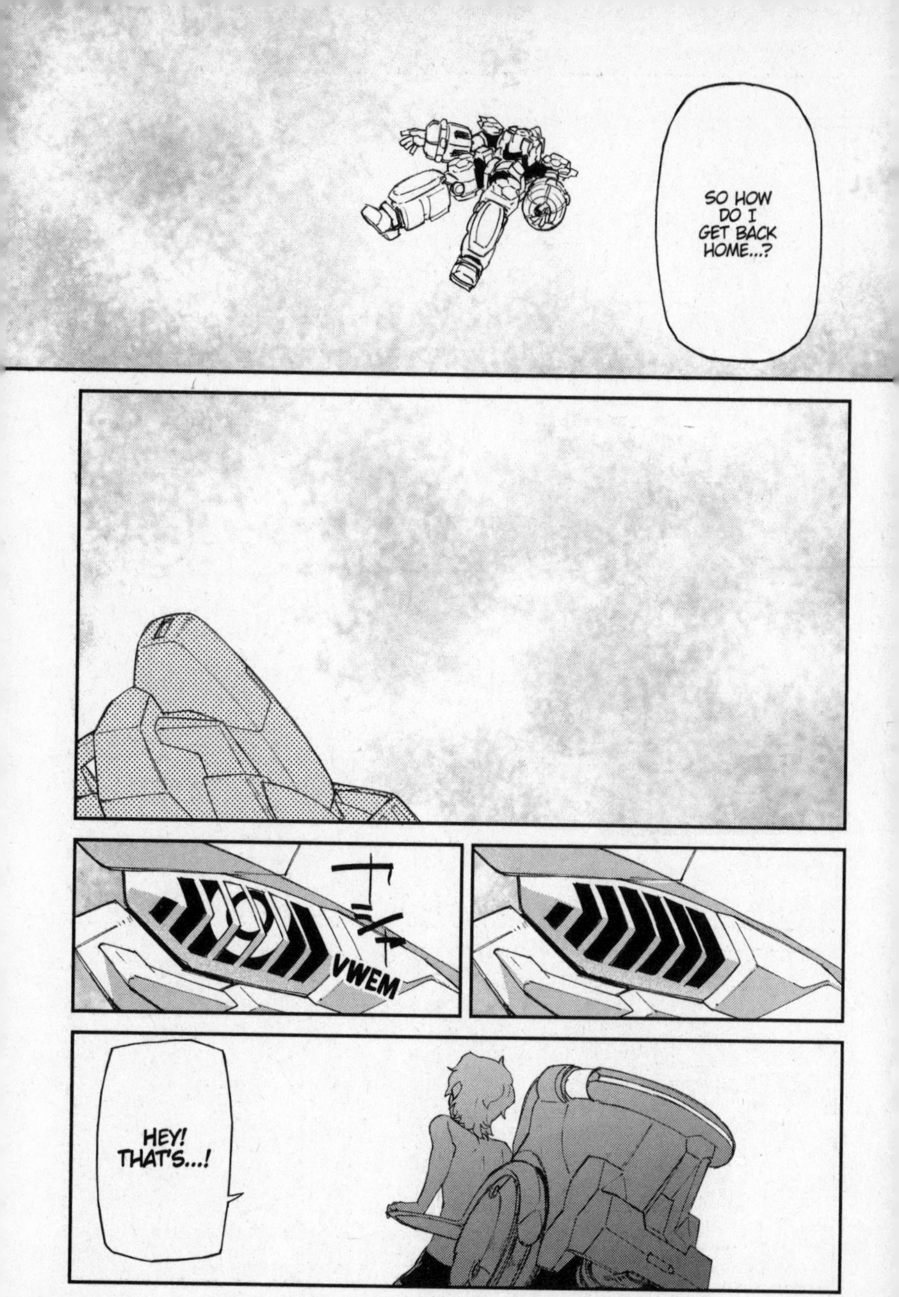
SO HOW DO I GET BACK HOME...?
VWEM
HEY! THAT'S...!

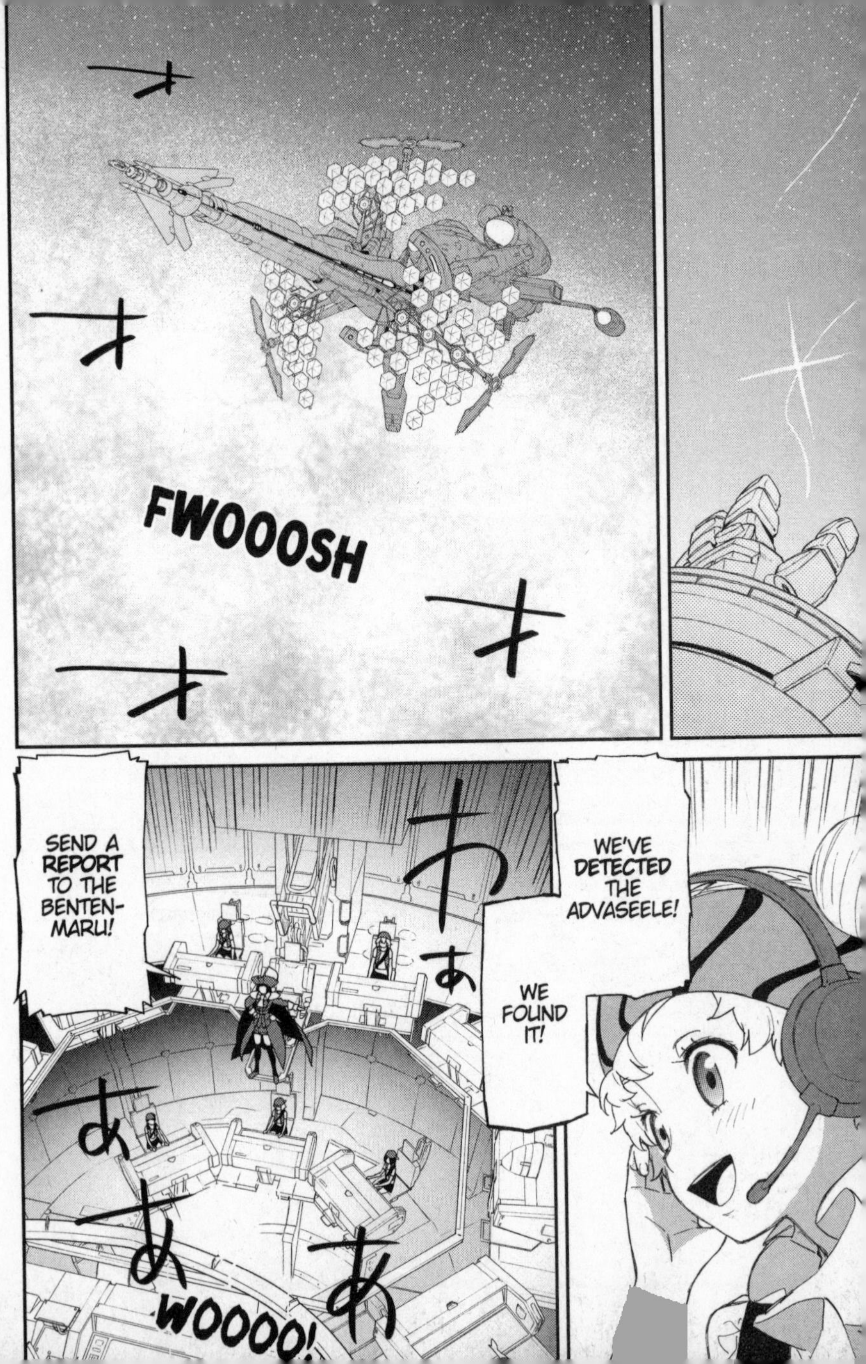
オオオオ
FWOOOSH
WE'VE DETECTED THE ADVASEELE!
WE FOUND IT!
SEND A REPORT TO THE BENTEN-MARU!
わあああああ
WOOOO!

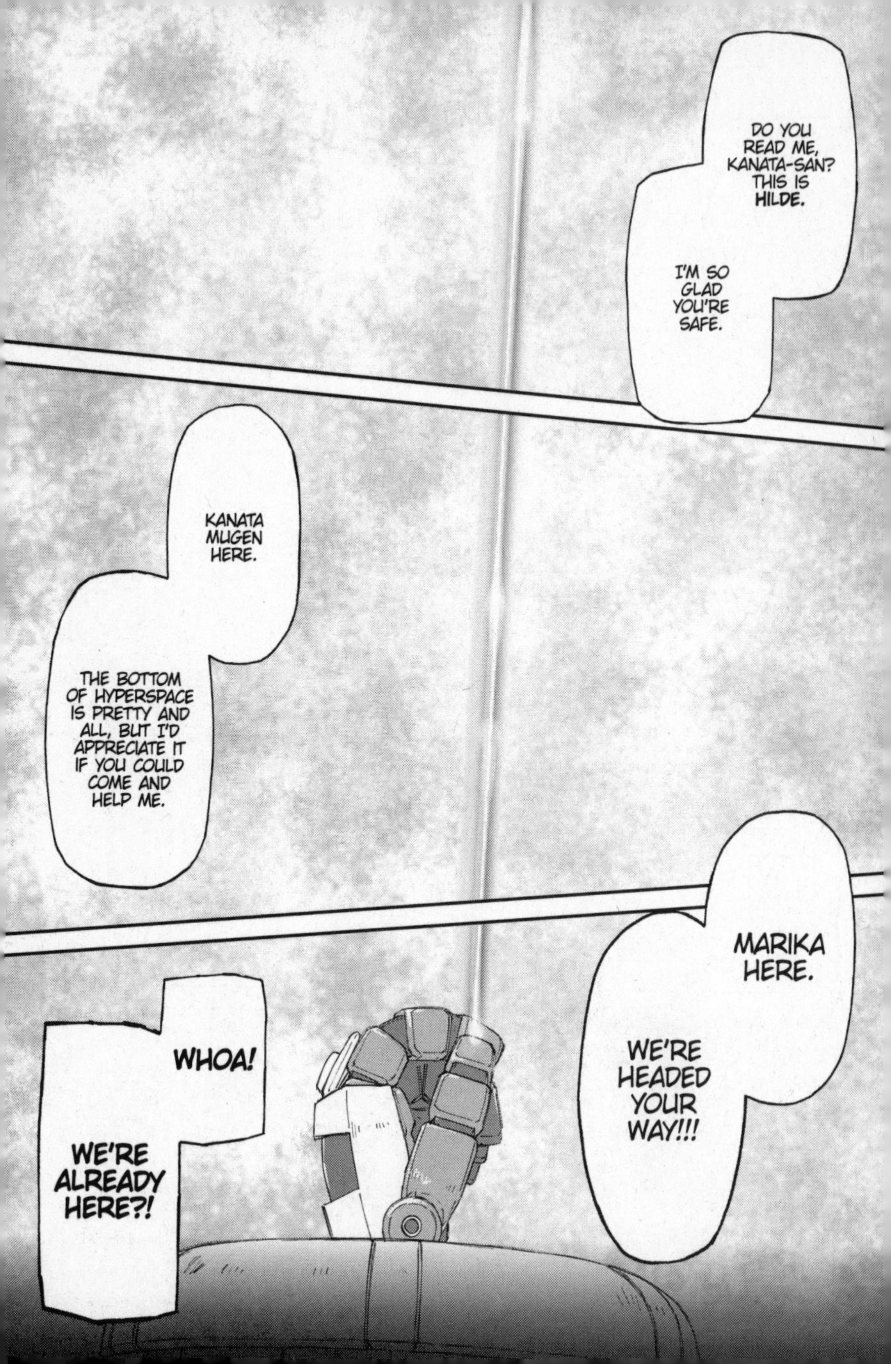
DO YOU READ ME, KANATA-SAN? THIS IS HILDE.
I'M SO GLAD YOU'RE SAFE.
KANATA MUGEN HERE.
THE BOTTOM OF HYPERSPACE IS PRETTY AND ALL, BUT I'D APPRECIATE IT IF YOU COULD COME AND HELP ME.
MARIKA HERE.
WE'RE HEADED YOUR WAY!!!
WHOA!
WE'RE ALREADY HERE?!

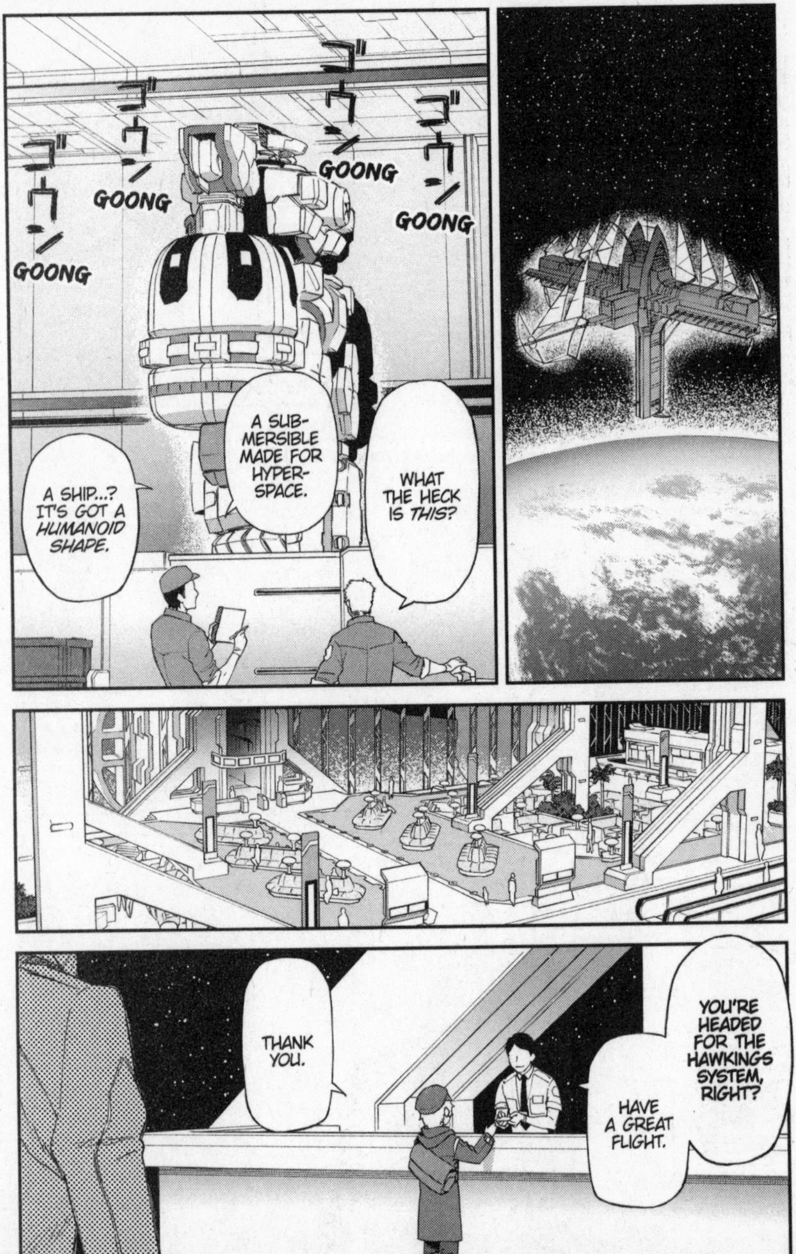
GOONG
GOONG
GOONG
GOONG
WHAT THE HECK IS *THIS*?
A SUB-MERSIBLE MADE FOR HYPER-SPACE.
A SHIP...? IT'S GOT A *HUMANOID SHAPE*.
YOU'RE HEADED FOR THE HAWKINGS SYSTEM, RIGHT?
HAVE A GREAT FLIGHT.
THANK YOU.

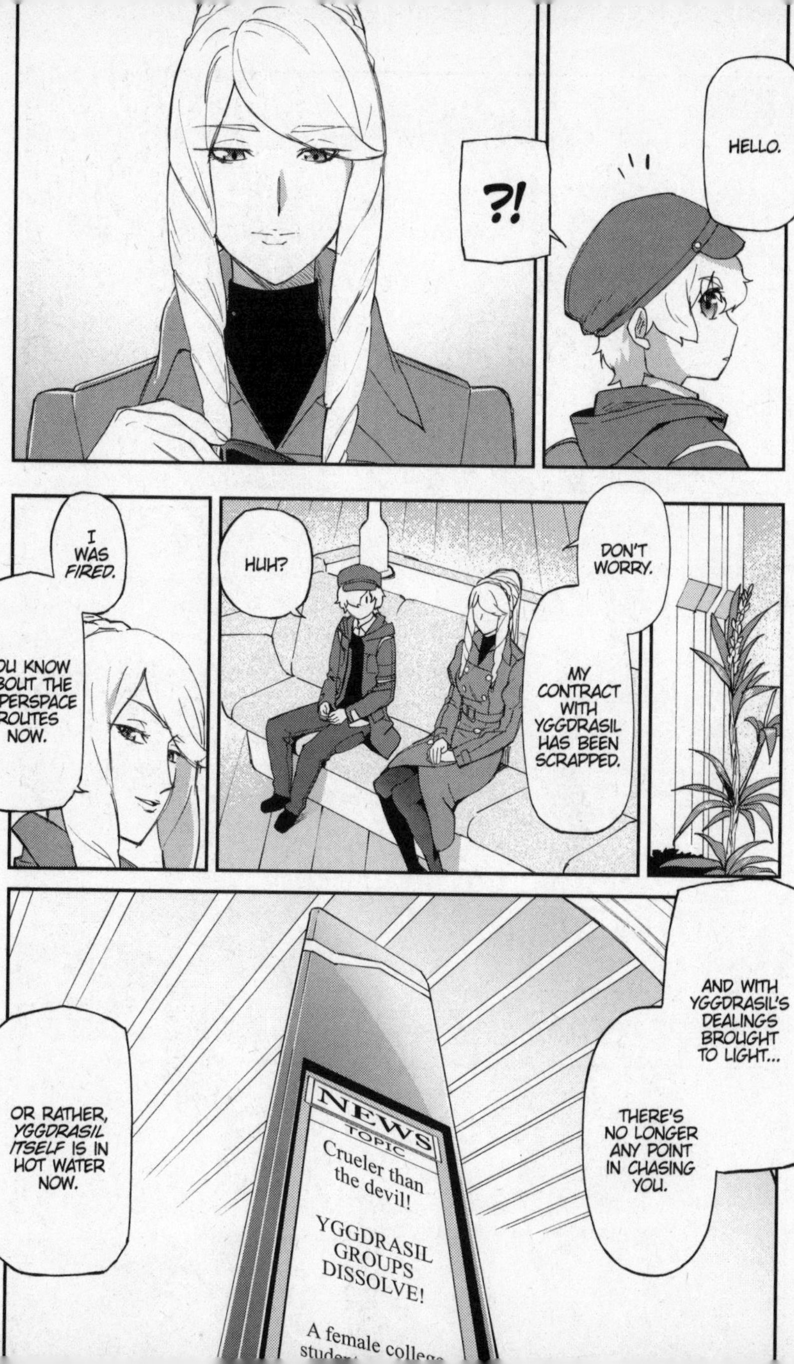
HELLO.
?!
DON'T WORRY.
MY CONTRACT WITH YGGDRASIL HAS BEEN SCRAPPED.
HUH?
I WAS *FIRED.*
YOU KNOW ABOUT THE HYPERSPACE ROUTES NOW.
AND WITH YGGDRASIL'S DEALINGS BROUGHT TO LIGHT...
THERE'S NO LONGER ANY POINT IN CHASING YOU.
OR RATHER, *YGGDRASIL ITSELF* IS IN HOT WATER NOW.
NEWS
TOPIC
Crueler than the devil!
YGGDRASIL GROUPS DISSOLVE!

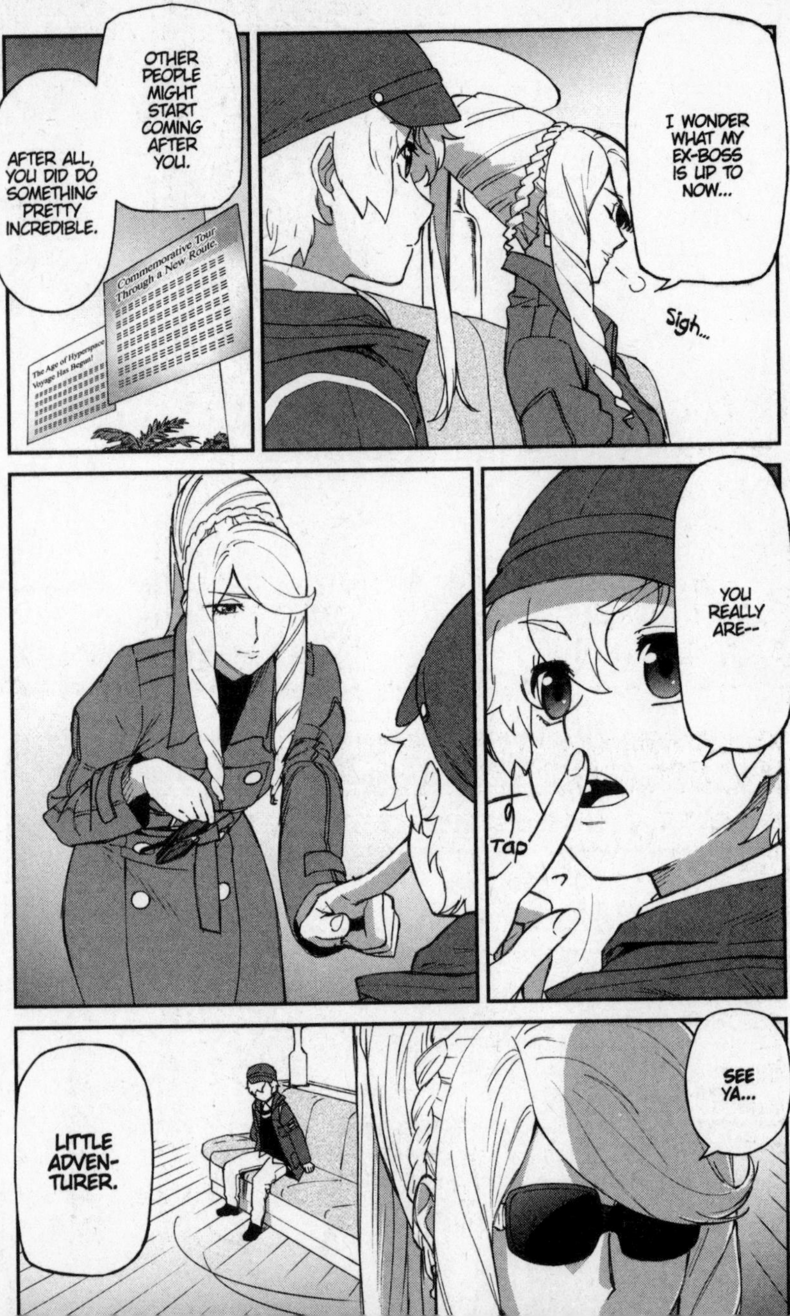
I WONDER WHAT MY EX-BOSS IS UP TO NOW...
Sigh...
OTHER PEOPLE MIGHT START COMING AFTER YOU.
AFTER ALL, YOU DID DO SOMETHING PRETTY INCREDIBLE.
Commemorative Tour Through a New Route.
The Age of Hyperspace Voyage Has Begun!
YOU REALLY ARE--
Tap
SEE YA...
LITTLE ADVEN-TURER.

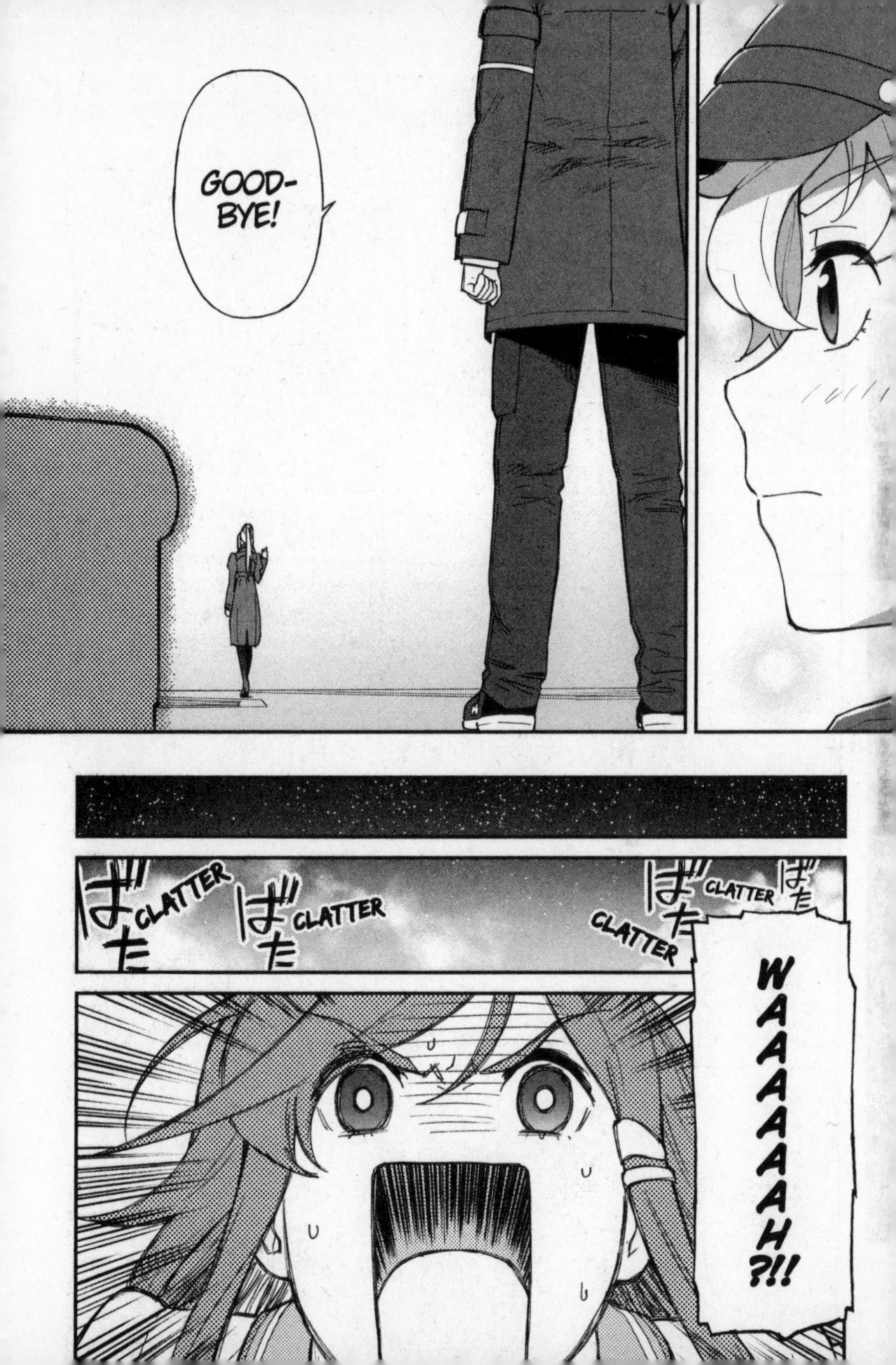
GOOD-BYE!
ばた
CLATTER
ばた
CLATTER
ばた
CLATTER
ばた
CLATTER
WAAAAAAH?!!

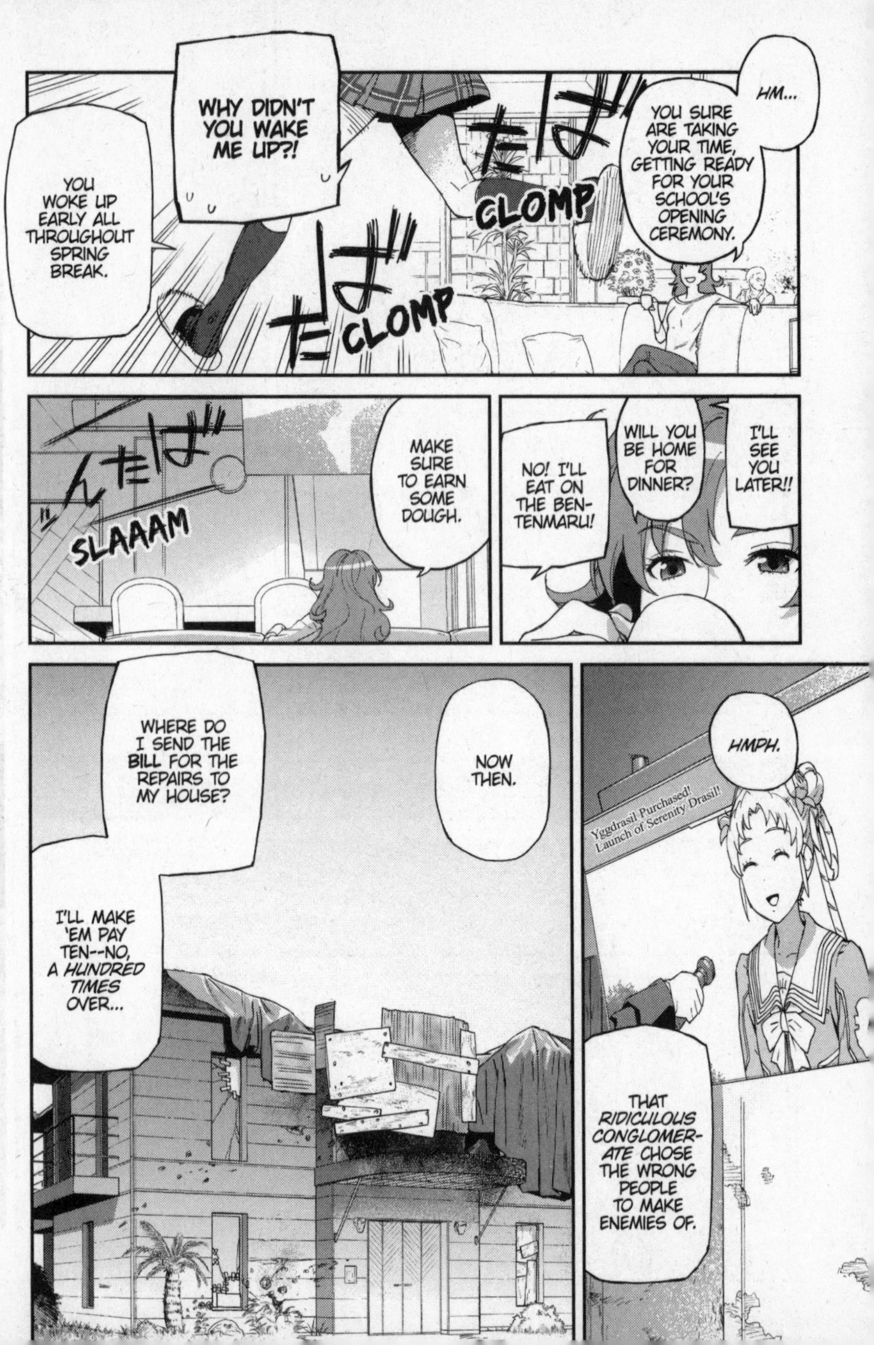
HM...
YOU SURE ARE TAKING YOUR TIME, GETTING READY FOR YOUR SCHOOL'S OPENING CEREMONY.
CLOMP
WHY DIDN'T YOU WAKE ME UP?!
YOU WOKE UP EARLY ALL THROUGHOUT SPRING BREAK.
CLOMP
I'LL SEE YOU LATER!!
WILL YOU BE HOME FOR DINNER?
NO! I'LL EAT ON THE BEN-TENMARU!
MAKE SURE TO EARN SOME DOUGH.
SLAAAM
HMPH.
Yggdrasil Purchased! Launch of Serenity Drasil!
THAT RIDICULOUS CONGLOMERATE CHOSE THE WRONG PEOPLE TO MAKE ENEMIES OF.
NOW THEN.
WHERE DO I SEND THE BILL FOR THE REPAIRS TO MY HOUSE?
I'LL MAKE 'EM PAY TEN--NO, A HUNDRED TIMES OVER...

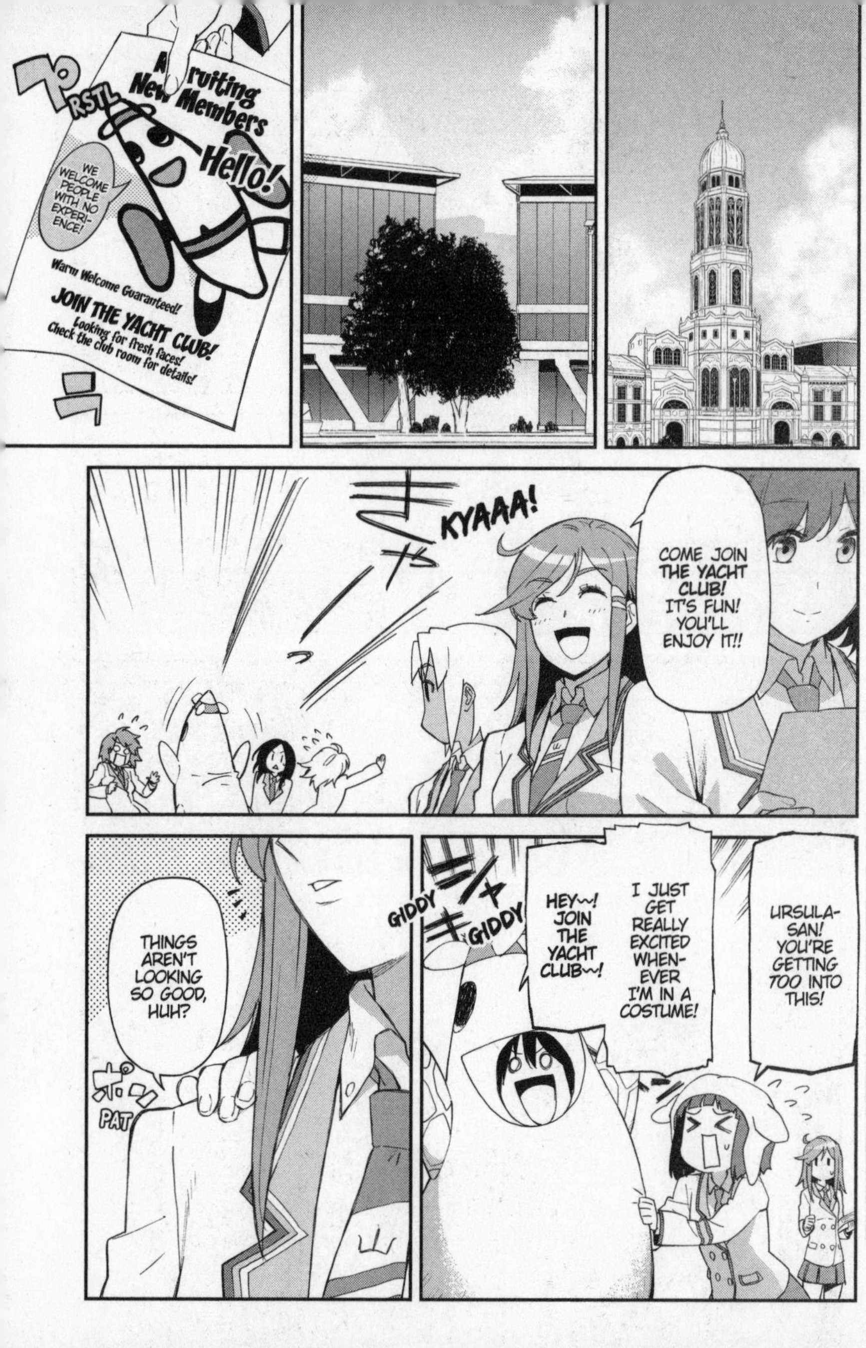
RSTL
ruiting
New Members
Hello!
WE WELCOME PEOPLE WITH NO EXPERIENCE!
Warm Welcome Guaranteed!
JOIN THE YACHT CLUB!
Looking for fresh faces!
Check the club room for details!
COME JOIN THE YACHT CLUB! IT'S FUN! YOU'LL ENJOY IT!!
KYAAA!
URSULA-SAN! YOU'RE GETTING TOO INTO THIS!
I JUST GET REALLY EXCITED WHENEVER I'M IN A COSTUME!
HEY~! JOIN THE YACHT CLUB~!
GIDDY
GIDDY
THINGS AREN'T LOOKING SO GOOD, HUH?
PAT

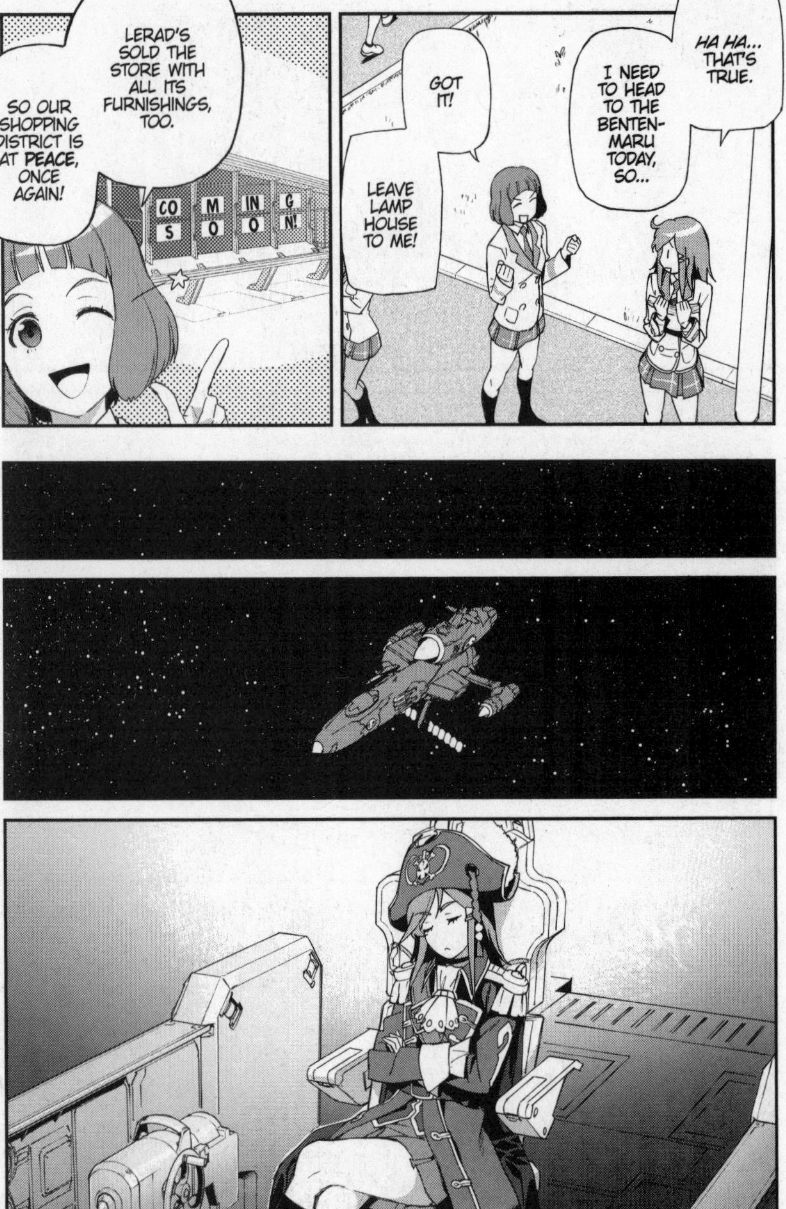
HA HA... THAT'S TRUE.
I NEED TO HEAD TO THE BENTEN-MARU TODAY, SO...
GOT IT!
LEAVE LAMP HOUSE TO ME!
LERAD'S SOLD THE STORE WITH ALL ITS FURNISHINGS, TOO.
SO OUR SHOPPING DISTRICT IS AT PEACE, ONCE AGAIN!
COMING SOON!

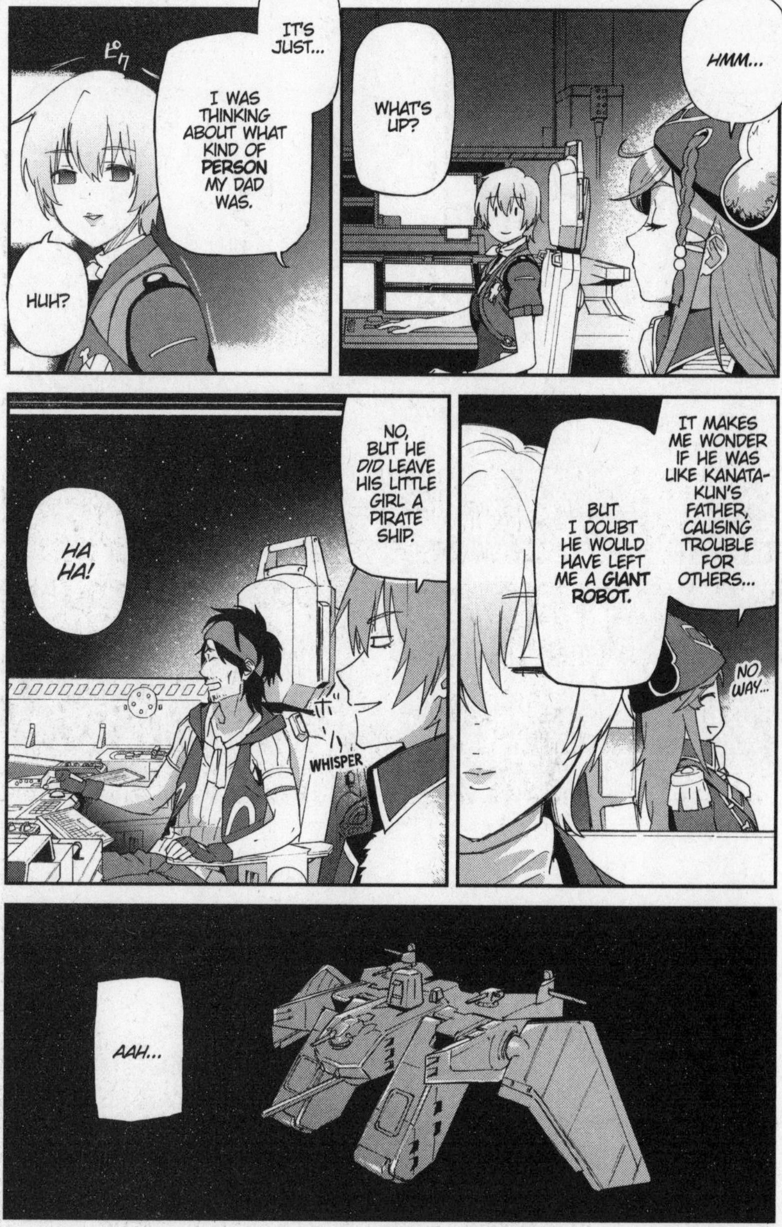
HMM...
WHAT'S UP?
IT'S JUST...
I WAS THINKING ABOUT WHAT KIND OF PERSON MY DAD WAS.
HUH?
IT MAKES ME WONDER IF HE WAS LIKE KANATA-KUN'S FATHER, CAUSING TROUBLE FOR OTHERS...
BUT I DOUBT HE WOULD HAVE LEFT ME A GIANT ROBOT.
NO WAY...
NO, BUT HE DID LEAVE HIS LITTLE GIRL A PIRATE SHIP.
HA HA!
WHISPER
AAH...

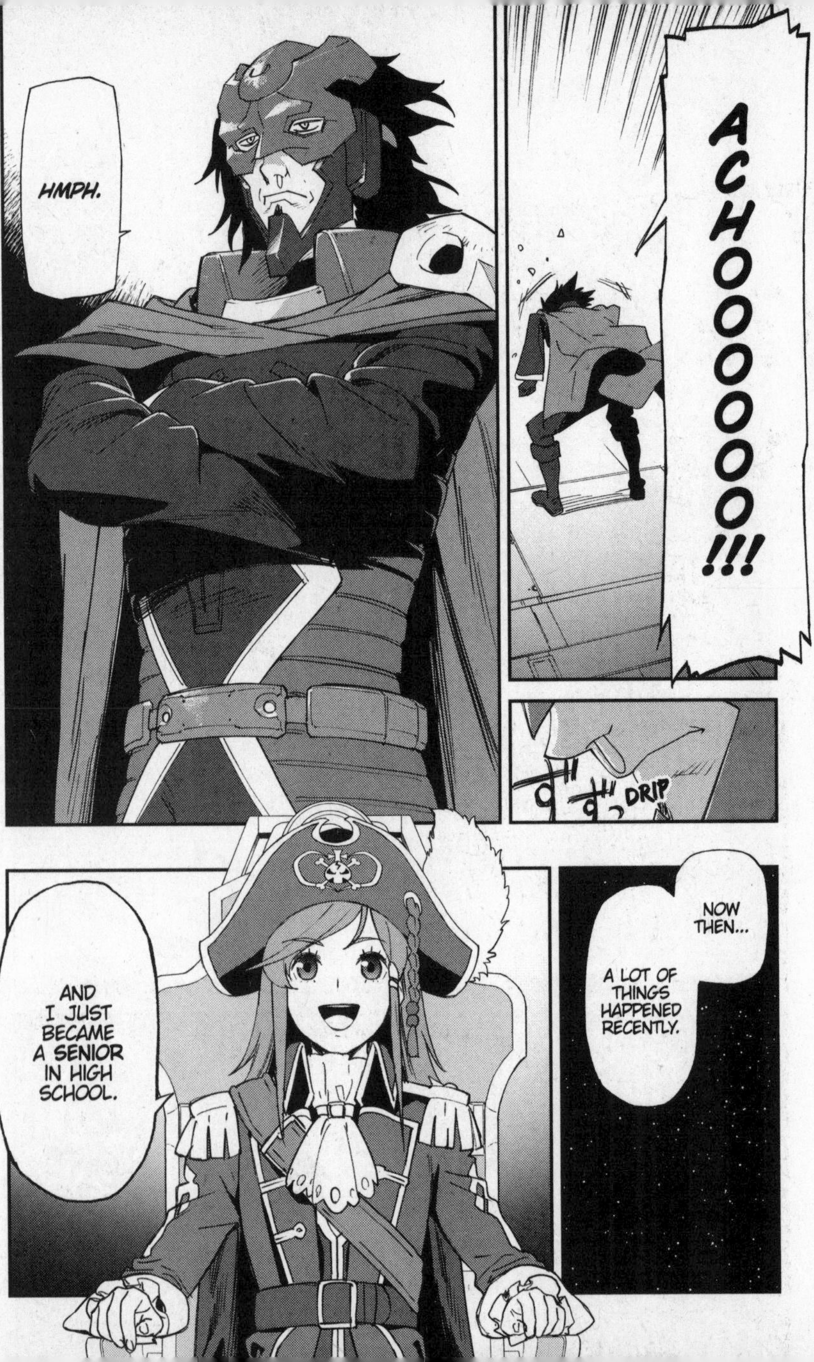
ACHOOOOOOOO!!!
DRIP
HMPH.
NOW THEN...
A LOT OF THINGS HAPPENED RECENTLY.
AND I JUST BECAME A SENIOR IN HIGH SCHOOL.

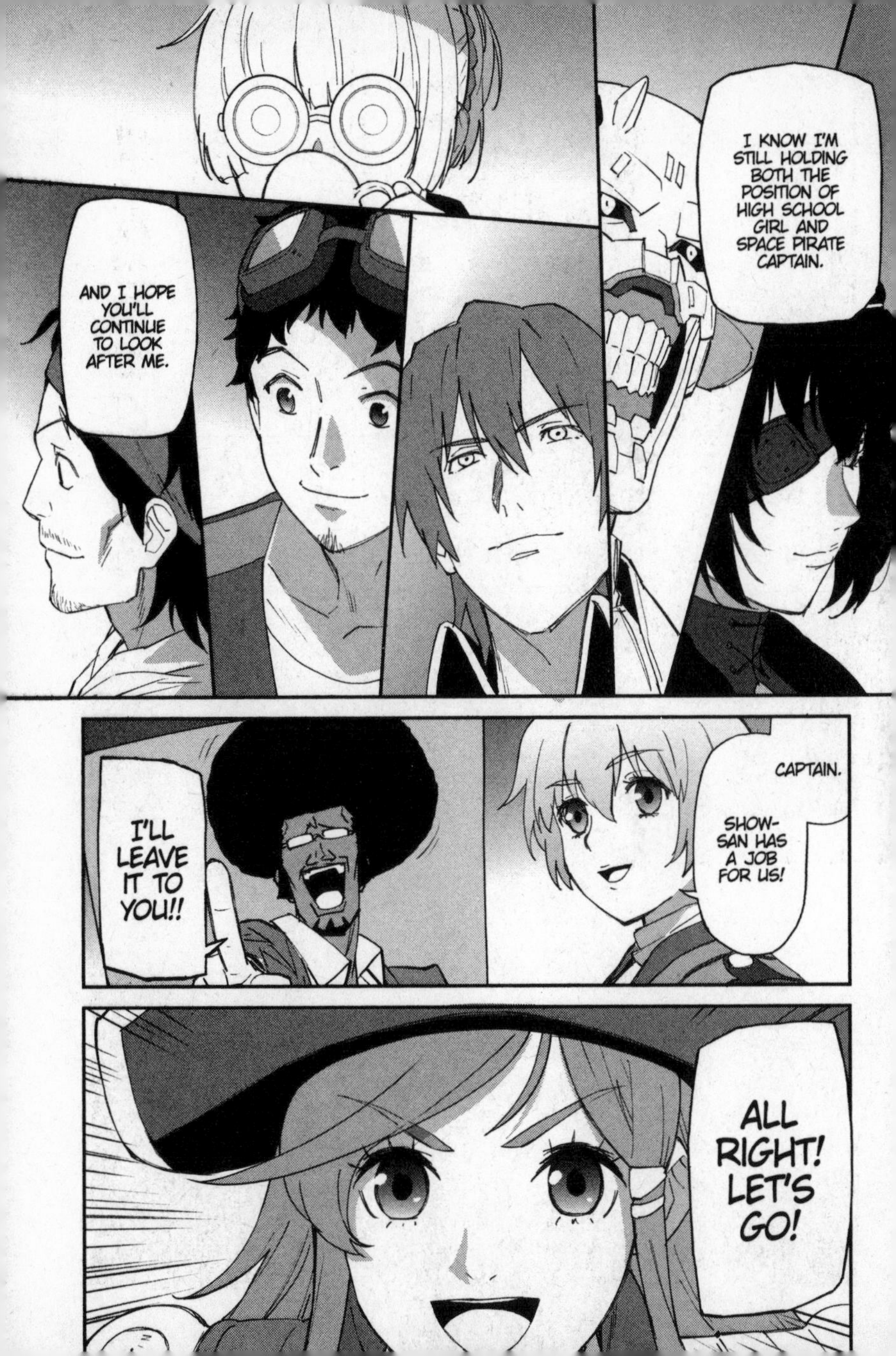
I KNOW I'M STILL HOLDING BOTH THE POSITION OF HIGH SCHOOL GIRL AND SPACE PIRATE CAPTAIN.
AND I HOPE YOU'LL CONTINUE TO LOOK AFTER ME.
CAPTAIN.
SHOW-SAN HAS A JOB FOR US!
I'LL LEAVE IT TO YOU!!
ALL RIGHT! LET'S GO!

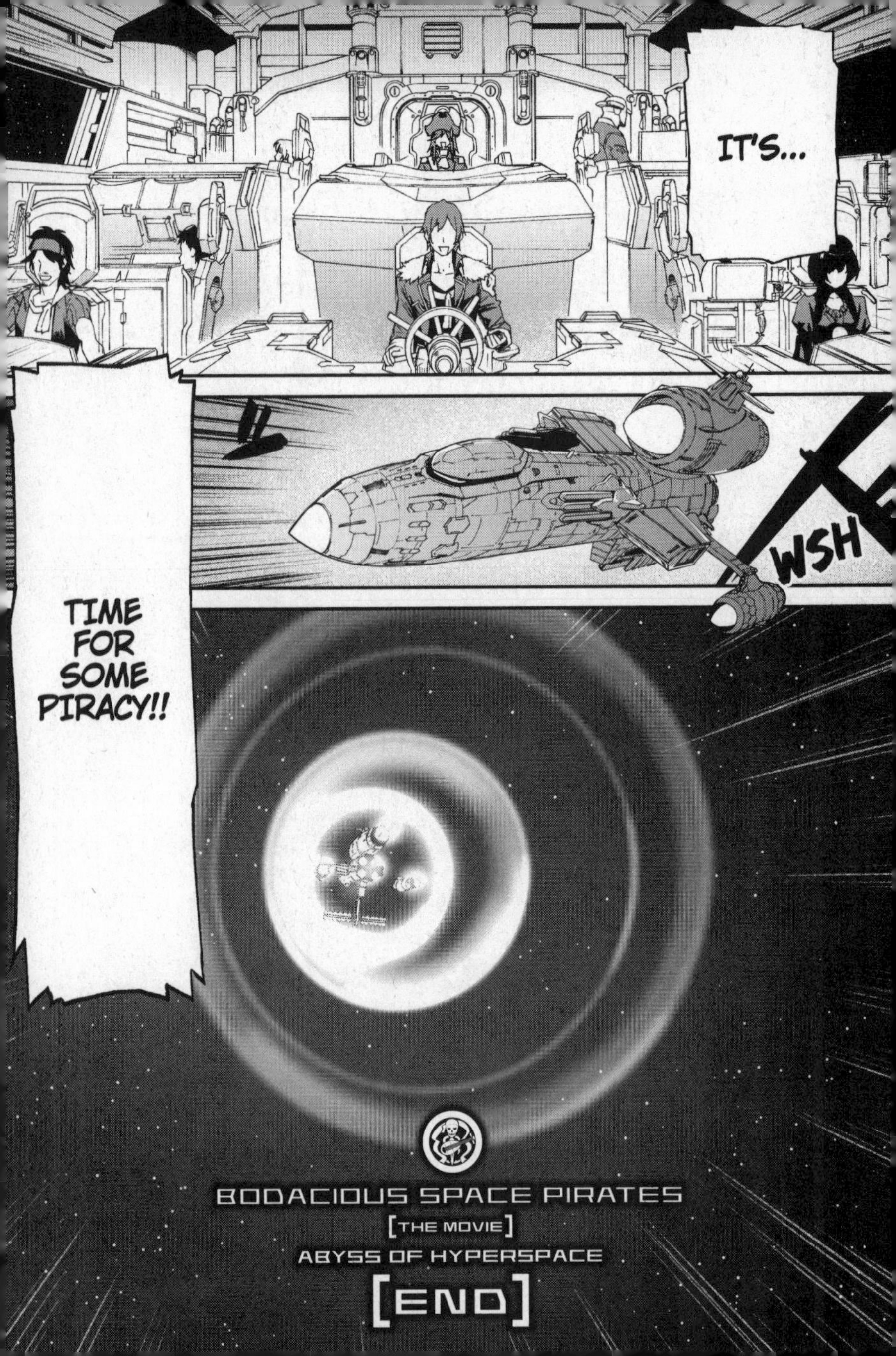
IT'S...
WSH
TIME FOR SOME PIRACY!!
BODACIOUS SPACE PIRATES
[THE MOVIE]
ABYSS OF HYPERSPACE
[END]

BODACIOUS
SPACE
PIRATES
[THE MOVIE]
ABYSS OF HYPERSPACE

モーレツ★宇宙海賊

ABYSS OF HYPERSPACE ——亜空の深淵——

VOLUME 02

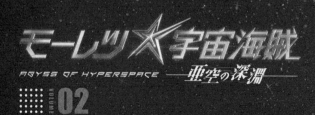

BODACIOUS
SPACE
PIRATES
[THE MOVIE]

ABYSS OF HYPERSPACE

Writer's Afterword

Time to celebrate! *Bodacious Space Pirates The Movie* is finished!

I decided to party by myself.

I was somehow able to finish the story in two volumes. This ends Marika and Kanata's story! Just kidding, it seems like there's a little more. You'll just have to get the first edition of the Blu-Ray. (Shameless plug!)

But to be honest, I was thinking one more volume would have been nice, but that would have caused some problems (mostly for the people around me), so I managed to wrap it up. It was particularly rough on my assistant, who I made draw backgrounds.

When I showed him the backgrounds for the anime, he seemed to die (spiritually), but thanks to ~~forsaking~~ entrusting it to my assistant, we were able to finish it. Aren't my assistants amazing? *Ha ha ha!* Ah, but I did draw the entire first chapter of Volume 1 all by myself, so it's not like I *couldn't* have done the whole thing by myself. (Idle boasting!)

But really, I caused a lot of trouble for a lot of people. To show that I've learned my lesson, next time, I'll... Next time, I'll... I'm not sure there will be a next time for Chibimaru. *Wah!*

Ah, it seems like my handwriting has gotten really small and hard to read...

Chibimaru

SEVEN SEAS ENTERTAINMENT PRESENTS

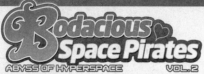

Bodacious Space Pirates

ABYSS OF HYPERSPACE VOL. 2

art: CHIBIMARU / script: TATSUO SATO / plot: BODACIOUS SPACE PIRATES MOVIE PRODUCTION COMMITTEE / original concept: YUICHI SASAMOTO / character design: AKIMAN

TRANSLATION
Ryan Peterson

ADAPTATION
Janet Houck

LETTERING AND LAYOUT
Alexandra Gunawan

COVER DESIGN
Nicky Lim

PROOFREADER
Danielle King

ASSISTANT EDITOR
Lissa Pattillo

MANAGING EDITOR
Adam Arnold

PUBLISHER
Jason DeAngelis

Edited by MEDIA FACTORY.
First published in Japan in 2014 by KADOKAWA CORPORATION, Tokyo.
English translation rights reserved by Seven Seas Entertainment, LLC.
under the license from KADOKAWA CORPORATION, Tokyo.

ISBN: 978-1-626922-10-5
Printed in Canada
First Printing: November 2015
10 9 8 7 6 5 4 3 2 1

FOLLOW US ONLINE: ***www.gomanga.com***

READING DIRECTIONS

The manga prelude and epilogue sections that bookend this light novel read from right to left, Japanese style. If this is your first time reading manga, you start reading from the top right panel on each page and take it from there. If you get lost, just follow the numbered diagram here. Enjoy!!

1
2
3
4
5
6
7
8
9

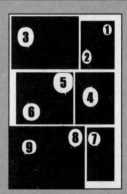